TARGETS

The radio is drowned out by a series of explosions within one hundred feet of our besieged ambush. The NVA have switched targets. They finally have the right bean field.

The volume and size of the concussions that rattle the earth increase substantially. My body and mind are consumed by the continuous thundering roar. Brilliant flashes of light strike through my closed eyelids. Squeezing the handgrip of the machine gun with my right hand to keep my arm from shaking, I pull the gun closer to me while checking the ammo belt with my left hand. There is no point in hiding much longer. This is it.

The beautiful, terrifying scream of a jet pulling out of a dive reaches through the mass of noise to lift my spirit in exhilaration. I realize that the latest bombardments are the explosions of rockets fired from Phantoms, as one after another they streak overhead, firing their load of terror into the trees. What will happen in a minute or two when the last rocket is fired?

The jets are gone as suddenly as they arrived. Silence crashes upon us. Nothing comes to fill the void. Tension mounts in the stillness as hundreds of men lie on their bellies, waiting. Waiting for whatever will happen to them next.

Thank God everything that flies is ours.

ONE SOLDIER

JOHN SHOOK

BANTAM BOOKS

TORONTO • NEW YORK • LONDON • SYDNEY • AUCKLAND

ONE SOLDIER

A Bantam Book / August 1986

Illustrations by Tom and Greg Beecham.

Maps by Alan McKnight.

All rights reserved.
Copyright © 1986 by John H. Shook
Cover art copyright © 1986 by Bantam Books, Inc.
This book may not be reproduced in whole or in part, by
mimeograph or any other means, without permission.
For information address: Bantam Books, Inc.

ISBN 0-553-26051-0

Published simultaneously in the United States and Canada

Bantam Books are published by Bantam Books, Inc. Its trademark,
consisting of the words "Bantam Books" and the portrayal of a
rooster, is Registered in U.S. Patent and Trademark Office and in
other countries. Marca Registrada. Bantam Books, Inc., 666 Fifth
Avenue, New York, New York 10103.

PRINTED IN THE UNITED STATES OF AMERICA

O   0 9 8 7 6 5 4 3 2 1

DEDICATION

To the 2.8 million U.S. troops who served in Vietnam, especially those 153,300 who were wounded in that service. To the memory of the 1.75 million people who died during that conflict.

And to Kristen, for her support and eternal optimism.

AUTHOR'S NOTE

All of the events described in this book are as true and accurate as my memory, old letters, and research will allow. Except for the occasional reference to people of historical significance, all the names of the people who appear in these pages have been changed to preserve their privacy. The dialogue is, of course, my own invention.

CONTENTS

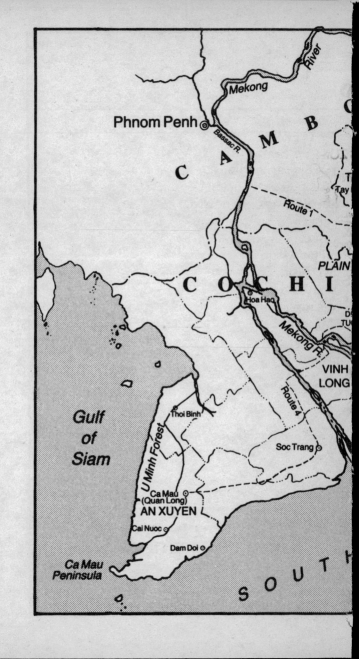

PRELIMINARY CONFUSION

A handful of hippies cling together in uneasy protest on the sidewalk in front of the Portland, Oregon, induction center. Despite their lack of numerical strength and the tentative nature of their actions, the small island of protesters manage to infuse the windy fall day with a palpable tension. Their success in drawing attention to themselves is evident by the rigorous manner in which they are ignored. No one pauses to read the clutter of small print on the placards. No one stops to argue philosophy or to question morals. A void is carefully maintained around the colorful band of dissenters, as if the space would effectively quarantine any unhealthy spread of this flagrant display of disloyalty to home and to country.

Pulling my light jacket closer around me, I cross the street to join the steady flow of young men funneling into the government building. As I reach the door a beaded girl takes three defiant steps in my direction.

"Stop the draft," she demands in a high, tense voice. "Get the U.S. out of Vietnam."

Well-timed sentiments if ever I heard them. If those goals could be achieved sometime in the next few minutes, I would be particularly pleased. However, I am afraid she is addressing the wrong person. I do not know the location of the lever that shuts down the military machine, or even if it should be pulled. Isn't there a need for an armed force to protect our country from the hungry, the greedy, and the mad?

1

Not wishing to get into trouble here on the Army's very doorstep, I retreat into the building to confront long forms and longer lines. A group of us is sent upstairs, where we are instructed to form a circle and strip. The acrid smell of nervous sweat fills the room as our group of reluctant future soldiers has its private parts peered into and probed. My mind strays to the demonstrators.

I have listened to the sounds of protest many times, and what I heard was rhetoric, slogans, and mob emotion. How can people hold such adamant views in the face of so much confusion? Is all this dissension merely a fad, or do these protesters see clearly where I do not? Wherever the truth, as soon as this physical is over I will be granted the privilege of watching the mysteries of Vietnam unravel from the safe vantage of the casual civilian observer. After all those years of struggling to gauge the distance of fly balls, long passes, and basketball hoops, my one-eyed vision is finally going to be of some advantage. Although I can see vague images out of my left eye if I close the right one, the vision is poor enough to qualify me as legally blind in one eye.

After giving a representative sample of each of our vital fluids into the care of a host of grumpy men, we are finally led to the eye examination machine. My right eye tests out at 20/20, as expected. When I relate the unidentifiable blur of patterns appearing before my left eye to the man behind the machine, his only response is to speed up the scenes flashing before me.

When he finishes marking my chart he says, "Okay, fine. Move to the next table."

Automatically I get up and take a step before it dawns on me that his comment was not as it should have been. Quickly moving back in front of the machine to block the next man in line, I inquire, "What do you mean, 'Okay, fine'? Are you telling me I passed the eye test?"

Without taking his attention off the pile of papers before him, the private answers, "Of course you passed. Now move along, people are waiting."

I am frozen in place by the implications of the bored man's words. I'm going to be drafted? Holy shit! This can't be happening. I can't let it happen.

Aware that I am still blocking the front of his machine, the private finally glances up to fix me with a dour gaze.

"What is your problem? Do I have to call the sergeant over here to motivate you?"

His threat loosens my tongue. "Call whoever you want. I'm not moving until you mark my chart correctly."

He studies me for a moment before relenting with a shrug. "Okay, have it your way. But I'm telling you it won't make a damn bit of difference."

But it does make a difference. At the end of the regular physical I am sent several blocks uptown to a private optometrist. On the way back from the doctor's office I open the manila envelope containing his report. With a rush of relief I find the report to be totally accurate: right eye, 20/20; left eye, 20/600. Thus bolstered by clear evidence of what the local draft board assured me would disqualify me from military duty, I turn in the doctor's report at the induction center and catch the bus back to Eugene, confident that I will soon be singing the I'm-not-good-enough-to-be-a-soldier jubilation blues.

Tilting back in the dining room chair with a copy of *The Sun Also Rises* propped against the table, I stretch my lunch hour to the limit. A change outside the window causes me to glance up in time to catch a maverick ray of sunlight slice through the gray drab noon. For a moment the interminable sogginess is transformed into a sparkling freshness before the fault in the perfect gray covering is mended and the errant ray returned to California.

My roommate bangs through the front door with a case of beer in his arms. "Ah, good, you're home. Our government has sent you a letter. When I found it in the box, I headed straight for the store to get the makings for a toast to your freedom or the first of many drunks."

The envelope lies unopened before me. This, I know, is one of the big moments of my life. Maybe if I never open the letter I will never get drafted, never get sent to Vietnam, never be shipped home in a box. Ridiculous. Assuring myself of my unacceptability, I rip open the envelope. Reading the salutation causes a rude sound to escape my throat and my hand to cast the letter into the still air of the living room.

"What's going on? What did it say?" Ned probes for answers while I drain a beer.

"It said, 'Greetings from the President of the United States.'"

"Uh-oh. What else did it say?"

"That's it. That's all I read."

"Well, shit. Read the rest of it—the suspense is killing me."

"As far as I know, there's only one kind of letter that starts off the way that one does."

"You don't know that for sure. It's just possible that it's not what you think it is."

"There is little doubt that it is what I think it is, but if you're so curious, *you* read it."

"I'm not going to read it."

"Then have a beer and we'll just let it air awhile."

Viewing the offending message from afar we discuss the possibilities and ramifications through two more bottles of beer. Ned is right, of course. This is not the kind of thing you can just leave lying in the middle of the living room floor. I must either accept my fate or start running, but first I need to verify the bad news. On hands and knees, I consult the form letter that speaks of my future.

"Sure as hell, I've been drafted. 'Report to the San Jose, California, induction center, November twenty-seventh, 1967.' That's only two weeks from now. They don't believe in giving you a lot of time to sort out your life, do they? What about my job? They want a minimum of two weeks' notice. And what about Julie? It has taken me a lifetime of diligent hustling to get a girl that fine to fall in love with me. I know damn well she isn't going to wait two years for my glorious return. Man, this here's a major depression."

"So, what are you going to do?"

"What *can* I do? I either do what they want or become the proverbial man without a country. Being an illegal alien is not what I had in mind for the rest of my life."

By 4:00 P.M. a plan comes through the beery haze. I will quit my job and head for sunny Mexico.

As I stroll into the office three secretaries swivel their heads from typewriters to clock, in silent admonishment of my late return. With a slight list to starboard and a beer-fume wake, I plow into the boss's office.

"Hi ya, Jim," I open, a huge grin unaccountably spreading across my face.

"What's up?" he asks in his usual friendly, easy manner.

"I've been drafted."

"Drafted?"

"Yeah, sure as hell, drafted."

"I thought you were 4-F."

"So did I. Buggers must've changed the rules. Anyway, I've come to tell you that I'm quitting."

"Yes, of course. This is to be your two-week notice then, I take it?"

"I'm afraid not. I'll be in the Army in two weeks."

"Oh, I see. Well how much notice do you want to give then? A week and a half? A week?"

"No, sir. I had something more like a half hour in mind."

He stares at me in silence as I grow increasingly uncomfortable. This is a good man standing before me who knows that I am drunk, but if he doesn't say something soon he is going to be staring at empty space because I have got to get out of here.

"Okay, John. I'll see if I can get your pay to you before you leave."

"Oh? Yeah, that would be great. Thanks." He really is a nice guy.

Mexico. Ah, yes. I will walk the white sand beaches, bodysurf the ocean waves, bask in the sunshine, ease my mind with *cerveza,* and dream of brown-skinned maidens. It would be nice if I could talk someone into going with me. I wonder where my old college roommate, Mike Parsons, is these days? I haven't seen him since graduation, almost a year ago.

Three phone calls to mutual friends produce the news that Mike is still in Corvallis working as a milkman while he waits for his Air Force enlistment date to come up. I dial the number I have been given, and Mike's voice comes over the line. I explain about being drafted, about quitting my job an hour ago, about going to Mexico in the morning. He mulls the idea over for a few minutes before deciding that he deserves to have some fun before he becomes the property of the Air Force.

With that settled, I drive the one-hundred miles to Portland to hold, love, and say good-bye to Julie. This is the hard part. I hate hurting this girl who has been so good to me. The intensity of her heartbreak is more than I can endure. She does not understand why I am going to Mexico instead of spending my last two weeks with her. Frankly, neither do I. Feeling the warmth of her body against mine, knowing her need and her pain, I am almost convinced to stay. But it won't do. Things are closing in. I have to move.

Beyond the window of the run-down San Diego hotel a torrent of water falls into the street. This is the second full day of heavy rain. The storm sewers are backing up.

A head cold presses against my eyes and brain.

My car is in a local garage having a piston replaced.

Mike is quiet and withdrawn.

The nurse jabs the needle into my left shoulder. Late last night on the outskirts of Tucson, Arizona, I stepped on a rusty nail while walking from the edge of the highway into the desert to sleep for the night. The nail went in flush with the sole of my shoe. I could not pull it out or take off my shoe. I had to hop back to the car on one foot to pull the nail out with a pair of pliers. I woke this morning with the rising of the sun, my foot throbbing in time with the beating of my heart.

Things had not gone well in Mexico. It rained the entire week. It rained more during that week than it usually does in an entire year. The streets were flooded. There was a greater weight of flies in the bakeries than doughnuts. We did not have enough money. We missed our women. We did not get drunk or meet anyone or have any fun. We did not seem to know how to have any fun.

The nurse picks up the empty vial to record the use of the drug in her log. "Oh," she says, dropping the vial into the covered garbage pail. "That's the wrong one."

She rummages in the refrigerator until I hear an a-ha of satisfaction. "Here it is. Tetanus."

"What did you give me?" I ask.

"Pardon me?"

"What was in the syringe you gave me?"

"Oh, nothing important."

"Nonetheless, I would like to know what it was."

"Oh, very well," she says, looking piqued, "if you must know." She reluctantly dips a thumb and an index finger in the waste pail to retrieve the discarded vial. Holding it up to the light she says, "I told you so. It's nothing important. Just some flu vaccine."

Perfect. A final touch of misery. I always get the flu from flu vaccine.

Broke, and out of time, we head for California where the Army awaits its 190 pounds of flesh.

BASIC TRAINING

My career in the U.S. Army starts in a long line, as all service careers should. After all, it is a time-honored tradition. From the age of early man, it has been the lot of those who serve to wait for those who rule to finish their tea and get on with the business of deciding what to do with that mob of low life outside in the rain.

After nineteen hours on a cramped bus, fifty California lads in short-sleeved shirts are lined up on the asphalt in the rain. It is 11:00 P.M. The temperature is 38 degrees.

A half hour passes. Then another. Fort Lewis's latest recruits stand shivering in the cold, their arms crossed tightly against their chests, teeth chattering in the darkness. Time slows until each second is felt, absorbed, and endured. Another half hour grates by.

As I watch the rain slant through the pool of illumination cast by the single yard light, visions of a detention camp somewhere in Europe play across my mind. I do not think I am going to like it here.

Finally, someone decides we are sufficiently rinsed to be allowed entrance to the Quonset hut to drip-dry. From 12:30 A.M. until 3:00 A.M. our soggy minds are subjected to a battery of tests designed to help the Army determine how we can best serve our country. The Army has no need of microbiologists, physicists, or chemical engineers. Its manpower needs, and our resulting military careers, fall into only two categories. If it takes you more than fifteen minutes to write your

8

name and address, you are a cook. Everyone else is an
infantryman.

With the testing over and the hour late, we abandon the
puddles under our chairs to be herded into an ice-cold barracks. The U.S. Army, always mindful of the health of its
troops, has decreed that every window in the barracks be
open nine inches at the top and bottom to allow for adequate
ventilation. Since there are windows aplenty in an army
barracks, this thoughtful policy ensures that the temperature
inside and out remains consistent.

The rain has stopped, but the temperature continues to
drop until the piles of soaked clothing lying on the floor
freeze. Curled into a ball in an attempt to warm my body
enough to stop shaking, I almost convince myself I can go to
sleep to the choir of twenty-four coughing, groaning, snoring
men when 5:00 A.M. and a drill sergeant burst upon the scene.
Our leader is more an embodiment of noise than of form. He
yells and berates and lectures. We cower and scurry and
shiver.

Outside in ice-encrusted puddles, we wait for and then
watch the sun come up, wondering if its pale gray heat will
reach us before we freeze in our wet summer clothes.

The sergeant stands on the raised platform delivering his
standard lecture on company and battalion parade formations.
An assistant holds the three-foot by four-foot diagrams firmly
on their stand to prevent them from being carried away by
the wind. The sergeant increases the volume of his delivery
to counter the growing storm, and stabs his pointer through
the snow to fix his chart with meaning.

His audience is not interested. This has nothing to do
with staying alive. We will muddle through the formations
when the time comes. What the sergeant's audience does
care about is the snow. The snow that is now two inches thick
on our shoulders, arms, and legs.

Back in our barracks there are neatly folded piles of
woolen shirts and pants, long woolen underwear, liners for
our cotton field jackets, overshoes, and lined overcoats. I
appreciate the fact that our cotton shirts, pants, and unlined
jackets have been the standard winter uniform here for many
years, and I take appropriate comfort in knowing that our
counterparts in California, Texas, and Georgia are wearing
exactly the same winter unform. I can even understand what

an awesome undertaking it is for the general in charge of this fort to change the rules of dress merely to accommodate a winter that is thirty percent colder than average, but with my chilly bum parked here on the frozen ground I hope the icy fingers of the devil cause a malfunction in the heater of the man's limousine.

I peek from under the lip of my helmet toward the platform. The sergeant, his diagrams, and even his voice have disappeared, swallowed by the storm. The assembled troops are covered with a white blanket of increasing thickness, their constant shivering undetectable through the heavy flakes. With their helmets tilted into the wind, and their necks hunched into the collars of their jackets, the men are as still as a picture of a Valley Forge winter.

I can only assume that we remain in this formation because the good sergeant is still somewhere above us, faithfully delivering his lecture, unwilling to repeat this performance merely because the task was left unfinished.

Two weeks have passed and still the snow persists. The Army has taken away all my hair and replaced it with a steel pot. These helmets allow the 17-degree morning air free access to our scalps, and I have been wondering if we are in danger of having our brains freeze—I have seen plenty of evidence to verify this concern.

We are now well practiced at standing in formation for hours to watch the sun come up. However, some of us are still having trouble with the more complicated maneuvers. Fred, who is being recycled through basic for previous failures, can be counted upon to fuck up everything he does. It is not that Fred is mud stupid the way he pretends, it is just that Fred does not want to be here. Doing everything wrong is his way of trying to get released.

Whenever the platoon does a right face, Fred does a left face. When the platoon does a right shoulder arms, Fred can be counted on to do any of a wide variety of movements, but never with the ordered results. When the company marches off in formation, one man will always be seen marching off at a tangent in his own parade.

We have done hundreds of push-ups and sit-ups and squat thrusts because of Fred's program for personal freedom. The Army feels punishing the rest of us for Fred's misbehavior will make Fred want to be one of us. It is not working.

Fred is not alone in his defiance. We also have a hip black named Bobby who has been sleeping in for an extra three hours every morning for a week now. Considering that we are disciplined for the flicker of an eye or the incorrect alignment of a thumb while at attention, it is a mystery to us how Bobby can get away with such a flagrant breach of the rules.

This morning Fred decided that if one man can stay snuggled in the warmth of his bed instead of freezing in the snow, then why not two? As a result, four sergeants are now huddled together to discuss the two men's absence from our formation. Since I am the leader of Fred's squad, I am summoned to accompany the sergeants as they head for the barracks. I follow in their wake with a mixture of dread for the misery to be inflicted and curiosity over the mystery of Bobby's charmed disobedience.

The first sergeant to reach Fred's bunk gives it a vicious kick. "Get up, you worthless maggot."

Without waiting for a response, another sergeant grabs the mattress and rolls Fred onto the floor.

"Getting a little extra beauty sleep, are you, sweet pea? An ugly little rat like you needs all the beauty sleep he can get, doesn't he, sweet pea?"

Fred lies tangled in his blankets with his pale limbs sticking out at odd angles, looking extremely vulnerable.

"I asked you a question, maggot."

"It isn't talking to us again today, is it, maggot?"

Two of the sergeants give one edge of the blankets a hefty yank, sending Fred's passive form sprawling into the feet of the two remaining NCOs.

"Get off my boots, you slimy piece of wormy shit!" screams one of the sergeants. "Jesus, it touched me. That fairy actually touched me. Fairy, I'm going to break your bones for that."

"Wait a minute. Let's make him sweat a little first."

"Why waste our time on this garbage? Let's just kill him and get it over with."

"No killing. The captain will have our asses if we kill a man before breakfast. Let's sweat him now and then kill him after breakfast."

"On your stomach, puke. Let's start with twenty push-ups."

While Fred does his push-ups, I glance across the bay and down four bunks. Bobby is stretched out flat on his mattress, lying perfectly still, waiting.

"Get off your belly, stockade bait," a sergeant yells at Fred who has collapsed after six push-ups.

Faking a mighty effort, Fred raises his chest two inches off the floor before collapsing with a sigh. Fred is like that. He puts out just enough effort so they can't claim he is defying their orders. So far his plan for improving his lot in life is not working too well, but he obviously feels that if he keeps to his program long enough the Army will eventually give him an unadaptable or undesirable discharge.

"Okay, dung heap. You want to rest, let's go outside."

While two sergeants escort Fred from the barracks, the remaining sergeants approach Bobby's bunk. I linger at the far end of the bay to watch what happens.

The bunk and its occupant crash to the floor. Bobby rolls over once and springs to his feet, flashing anger.

"You've got two minutes to get dressed and haul your butt out into formation," yells a sergeant as he heads down the stairs.

Is that it? Is that all they are going to do for a week's worth of defiance?

Back outside, I find Fred doing a rocking exercise on his belly in the snow. White limbs and white underwear rocking and shaking with the cold of the white morning snow.

My drill sergeant orders me to low crawl around the company area. I expected as much. It is my punishment for allowing one of my men to miss formation, a psychological ploy to bring maximum peer pressure to focus on Fred, to force him into the mold of a soldier. But Fred has already invested too much suffering into his program to yield without breaking. I would rather low crawl than deal with Fred.

Last night the barracks sounded like a pneumonia ward. When my third and last illegally obtained cough drop shot from my mouth during one of my fits of coughing, I decided the time had come for me to join the larger half of the company reporting daily to sick call.

But this morning, when a call came for blood donors, I decided to volunteer, figuring that when my sickly blood was rejected I could sneak to the infirmary for a bottle of cough syrup. Perhaps some sweet embodiment of motherhood will melt at the sight of my misery and tuck me into a warm bed with orders to stay put until I am well and the earth has thawed.

Snugly stashed in a warm room with a thermometer sticking from my mouth like the handle of a lollipop, I watch the blood drain from the bodies lying in a row on the three tables before me. An almost cute Red Cross girl plucks the thermometer from my lips and flashes me the first smile I have seen in weeks.

"One hundred and one," she reads. "I'm sorry, we won't be able to accept your blood until your temperature goes down."

One hundred and one? How can I feel so rotten and only have a temperature of 101 degrees? The infirmary won't even look at me unless my temperature is at least 103 degrees. Neither a heart attack nor cancer will get you so much as an aspirin and an orderly unless you possess proof of a super-heated 103-degree body, which is a tough accomplishment when you live in a freezer.

So far, only nine of our men have been admitted to the hospital. One of the men that has not made it is the leader of our fourth squad. Every night he coughs up half a helmetful of bloody expectorate, but his temperature never exceeds 102 degrees so he is not entitled to medical attention.

By midmorning, 120 temperatures have been taken, five men have been relieved of some of their blood, and the company is reunited and on the march. We march across fields, down roads, and through a building where two rows of men shoot jets of fluid into our arms with high-pressure squirt guns. We are advised not to flinch, as this action causes a slice rather than a puncture.

By nightfall the alien microbes introduced into our already weakened bodies begin to make their presence felt. Our future good health, if we should live so long, is now insured against smallpox, cholera, typhoid, tetanus, typhus, polio, influenza, and, of course, the plague.

For entertainment a group of us walk from bunk to bunk, trying to guess who is showing symptoms of which disease.

"Look at this dude. Red with purple blotches. A plague case if ever I've seen one."

"When have you ever seen a plague case, you dumb shit?"

"Looks like a case of too much coughing to me."

"I'm telling you, that's the plague."

"Now over here we have a desperate case. I think this is one we can all agree upon." We stand over Fred as the pronouncement is made. "A severe case of lockjaw caused by a tetanus infection inflicted upon him by his local draft board. May he soon be delivered to his final resting place."

"Amen."

Our English auto mechanic scoots by, heading for the latrine, his body bent around his clutched midsection.

"A-ha, the cholera clutch and scoot."

"Yes, yes. Cholera, pure and simple."

"Probably the plague."

Next we come across our husky Basque alien buried under six blankets and soaked in sweat, shivering in violent rhythm to his chattering teeth.

"Hmm. This is our most serious case yet."

"Yeah. I'll bet his temperature is over one hundred and three."

"Looks like malaria to me," offers one of the guys already gathered around the bed. "First he's freezing, then he's boiling."

"Yep, the classic symptoms of malaria all right. There is just one thing wrong with your prognosis. We didn't get a malaria shot."

"Yeah, right. It's probably the plague."

"Could be influenza."

"I'll give you two to one on typhoid fever."

"I've got five that says you're wrong."

"You're on."

"Hey. How we gonna find out who wins?"

"Good question."

I expected basic training to be a combination of football training camp and Boy Scouts for big kids. It is not like that. It is more like reform school for old, retarded juvenile delinquents. Here the pursuit of excellence is exchanged for a tentative grasp on the lowest order of competence. Everything is geared to the slowest and the dullest. Ninety percent of the men spend ninety percent of their time and energy waiting, hoping, praying, that on this, the ninety-ninth try, everyone will remember which is his left foot.

They talk a lot about unit pride, but where is the pride when the best you can hope for is occasional mediocrity. We are training to manage the minimum and to stay out of trouble.

I am tinkering with my gear, putting it in neat rows, splashing a little Brasso on this and that, and generally getting ready for this evening's inspection when a shout comes from the far end of the bay. Everyone scrambles to attention. The drill sergeant's boots squeak across our highly polished vinyl floor.

"Shook," yells the voice above the squeak, "you've got five minutes to get cleaned up. We're going before the captain. Be downstairs knocking on my door at 1925."

I must be in big trouble. I wonder what I have done that is important enough to get the captain involved? Well, there is no sense speculating about it. It could be one of a hundred different things.

The crunch of our boots on the snow is the only sound disturbing the darkness of the company compound until the sergeant speaks in a quiet, conversational voice I have never heard before.

"I know you haven't had much of a chance to study for this, but if the captain chooses you for soldier of the month I'll see to it that you get the free time you need before the fortwide competition tomorrow night."

"Uh . . . excuse me, Sergeant, are you sure you have the right guy?"

"What?"

"I mean, I . . . I don't know what you are talking about."

He stops and turns to face me. "Soldier of the month. You know, like soldier of the week? The man who has scored the highest in all phases of training. That's you, right?"

"It is? That's news to . . . I mean, I don't know, Sergeant."

"You got the maximum score on the physical training test, didn't you?"

"Yes, Sergeant."

"And the other tests? Didn't your platoon guide tell you about the soldier of the week award last week? Didn't he tell you to be ready for tonight's selection?"

"This is the first I have heard about it, Sergeant."

"So you haven't been studying? You're not prepared for this at all?"

"No, Sergeant."

He stares at me, then off into the night. "Well, it's too late to do anything about it now. Come on, the captain is waiting for us."

Inside the orderly room the sergeant quickly leafs through the pamphlets on the first sergeant's desk. Laying a copy of *The Uniform Code of Military Justice* before me, he says, "Just stay cool and try not to embarrass me."

I try to concentrate on the dry verbiage but the room is too warm, and my nose is running, and I'm nervous, and I haven't been paying attention during the lectures, and what the hell do I care about being soldier of the week, or month—or whatever, anyway?

Well, I guess I should try.

Over the past few weeks, I have come to appreciate how fortunate our platoon has been to draw the drill sergeant we have. Sure, he yells at us and puts us through all manner of unpleasant, tedious routines, but he does not keep us up all night scrubbing the floor with our toothbrushes and he is not petty, cruel, or malicious. He has been through a tour in Vietnam that seems to have taken the gung ho out of him. When given the chance, he seeks the sanctity of his private room to the right of the barrack's front door. At night, if you listen closely, you can hear his little portable TV playing, and sometimes there is the faint whiff of marijuana.

The door to the captain's office opens to emit a studious looking private with a bad complexion. Someone from the hollow of the office calls my name.

I come to attention in front of the captain's desk. All the drill sergeants are here, standing or leaning against the walls in a semicircle behind me. The first lieutenant half sits on the window ledge to my left front. The questions begin. My tongue is suffering from partial paralysis. The room is claustrophobic. There is a restriction in the flow of blood to my brain. To avoid the quagmire of confusion summoned by infinite possibilites, I give the first answer entering my head that seems to relate to the topic.

At last the captain settles back in his chair to ask, "Now then, Private Shook, what is your opinion of the basic training you have received so far?"

My opinion? He's actually asking for my opinion? That's

the one thing I was sure would *never* happen. There's nothing in my index of ready things to say that goes with this question, nothing but the truth, and that won't do at all.

"Just give us your honest opinion. You have nothing to fear. There will be no reprisals of any kind."

"I . . . ah . . . sir, I don't know what to tell you."

"I don't know what you're going to tell me either, but you had better tell me something."

"Yes, sir." There is no way I can conjure polite platitudes fast enough to be believed. "Well, sir, I am getting in worse shape with each passing day. What I have learned in five weeks here I could have learned in two days. There is great emphasis placed on harassment and almost none on excellence. The lectures put everyone to sleep. The troops are incredibly unhealthy and morale is nonexistent." It all poured from my mouth, with no thought of caution or tact.

The room is silent. At attention, I have no opportunity to look at the faces of the men around me.

"That will be all, Private. You are dismissed."

I thankfully shuffle out into the night, glad for once for the purity of the cold Washington air. I don't think I will need to worry about being picked for soldier of the month.

Drill Corporal Gausser is a pompous ass. He comes to us straight from drill corporal school, chock-full of enthusiasm for the job of making other people miserable. Drill Corporal Gausser's greatest pleasure is sticking the brim of his Smokey-the-Bear hat in a man's face and unleashing a venomous rage. Getting yelled at is bad enough, but getting yelled at from a distance of two inches with such soul-shattering hate is quite something else. It is a rare man who can absorb one of the corporal's verbal lashings without experiencing a nearly overwhelming desire to strike back.

Gausser is solidly built and slightly less than six feet tall. His training technique consists of a single theme that is carried out with fanatic vigor. He is not so much interested in how we march, how we handle our rifles, or how accomplished we are at hand-to-hand combat as he is in our absolute acceptance of his authority. He constantly baits us, tempting us to revolt. Can he insult a man's heritage, debase his person, bring him to the edge of fury with spittle-flecked screams from two inches, grind his face in the mud, and then challenge him to a fight—and still have that man refuse? The refusals to fight are coming with more and more reluctance, but so far the men are held in check by their fear of what the Army will do to them if they strike a superior, and of course, Gausser only challenges the smallest men in the platoon.

Gausser infuriates me. He fills me with hate. I both long for an excuse to bring him down and dread that he may provide one. If he screams in my face with enough fury, my rifle butt will smash into his chin with all the power I can muster. I have gone through the short butt stroke a thousand times in my mind—his jaw pulverized, my face behind bars.

Hitting Gausser would mean disaster for me. I know this, and I know just as clearly that if challenged I will respond.

Is my obsessive desire to shatter another man an indication that the Army's training is taking effect? Is the combination of displaced individuality, loss of freedom, constant debasement coupled with constant encouragement toward violence and mindless obedience enough to change the basic personality of a man? Is it possible that, despite all its ineptitude, the Army is succeeding in making a soldier out of me? Or is it merely that I have never previously met a man so malicious, a man so deserving of violent alteration?

I think I am actually beginning to like marching down the road singing these corny old military songs. Walking, even running, is preferable to standing immobile. And I like to sing, especially when the drill sergeant leads the song. It cuts down considerably on the yelling.

Our leader has been in a good mood ever since he received his promotion to staff sergeant. Since life here dips and crests on his humor, our lot is looking up. Even that cretin Gausser has not been harassing us much lately. He has been away every morning attending some kind of class. When he returns to us in the afternoon he is seldom given the opportunity to have us to himself the way he likes.

The weather is also becoming cheerier. Finally, in the latter part of January, the temperature has returned to normal. The pristine whiteness of the landscape is transforming into a lovely expanse of 40-degree mud. Rain, exceedingly common in these parts, has been acknowledged and provided for by the Army. We are allowed the use of our rubber overshoes and raincoats. My feet are warm for the first time since I arrived. Strange that we are permitted to wear more clothing now that the temperature has risen 25 degrees.

The sign coming up on my right reads "Division of Chemical, Biological and Radiological Warfare." It doesn't sound friendly, but it could be interesting.

Following a lecture on our country's nuclear, chemical, and biological warfare capabilities, we are treated to a sampling of their practical application. In a dirt-floored hut we experience the eye-burning, nose-running, coughing effects of tear gas. With the release of more gas we practice digging our masks out of their pouches, putting them on, and clearing them of bad air with the bad air in our lungs—an art requiring persistence and faith.

After a bit of airing we are herded into a second hut. They tell us that the gas to be released in this hut is a stronger brew called CS gas. After a practice run we are expected to take out our masks and clear them in a room already full of gas. Not everyone is successful. Three or four men burst out the door, gagging.

From our affected comrades we learn about the effect of CS gas on the human body. Half a normal breath of the gas makes all your mucous membranes weep, your eyes burn, your stomach contract. You also experience a panicky sensation of not being able to breathe. One normal breath adds dizziness and vomiting to the symptoms. Two breaths of the gas results in unconsciousness, followed by violent nausea upon awakening.

For our final experience we are instructed to crawl under a heavy wire net suspended eighteen inches above the ground. We are warned that if anyone puts his mask on before the gas is released, the exercise will be repeated.

Smoke grenades are set off on line with my feet to disguise the release of the gas. Taking a big breath of air, I hold it until the need for another breath approaches, then I take a cautious sniff. If the air is clear, I quickly exhale and take another big breath. The fourth time I repeat the procedure there is no mistaking the noxious odor. My stomach heaves. I swallow hard and loosen my mask from its pouch. Blowing every ounce of air in my lungs into the mask to expel the gaseous air now occupying that space, I pause, dreading the need to inhale. No longer able to put it off, I take a tentative breath.

Gas!

My stomach sends its contents into my throat and mouth. I swallow. And then again. And again.

Pandemonium breaks out in front of me. Men in utter panic break through the wire net—a feat not normally even attempted—and fight their way blindly through the circle of sergeants and junior officers to run stumbling and falling into the woods. Some pass out on the way; others sprawl on their hands and knees, vomiting.

I take a gulp of air and immediately blow it out hard into the mask. After swallowing my lunch four more times, I attempt another breath. The air is now slightly less than nauseating. It's going to be all right.

I crawl out the far side of the net to find that half the platoon is still in the woods. The other half mills around, yelling through their masks or bent over at the waist spitting and recovering. Our drill sergeant is furious—at the panic, at the lack of response to his commands, at the slowness of our return to formation. He orders us back under the net.

The men receive the order with yells of defiance. Other sergeants and officers are drawn to the sounds of anger. The sergeants threaten. The men stand firm. They are not going back under the net. There is gas and revolution in the air.

Ten minutes later we lie under the net, waiting for our second dose of gas. We are here because of a captain's intervention. Never have I witnessed such presence of command, such confidence of power, such believable threats.

This time I have managed to position myself well away from the rear of the pack where the gas is released. When I hear the wave of frantic movement approach up the field of fifty men, I whip on my mask without waiting to smell the gas. My first intake through the mask is a marvel of fresh air.

I am in the midst of congratulating myself when a boot steps on the back of my head, quickly followed by a blow to the face that dislodges my mask. Repositioning and clearing the mask involves the same stomach-wrenching, vomit-swallowing, sinus-draining procedure as before, but after a few minutes the situation is under control.

The results of our second trip beneath the net is little better than the first. Thankfully, time and the sour mood of the men discourages any thought of a third effort. The platoon double-times from the area in disgrace.

*   *   *

After a series of inspections that spanned the better part of a day and a half, we have finally been released. With our duffel bags near at hand, we mill about self-consciously in our new dress-green uniforms and bald heads. From a military point of view we are polished up and squared away. To a civilian eye we must look like something just emerged from a 1940's prison.

Well, we learned to take orders all right, and we learned to march, but I do not see anybody in the mood to strut. No, there is no pride here that I can detect. These people just want to get on with it. The next stop may not be better, but at least it will be different. Few friends have been made, and there are no foolish promises of reunion to be heard.

Alone or in small groups, the men shoulder their bags and head for the buses. Basic training is over at last.

ADVANCED INFANTRY TRAINING

The second phase of my training began with another time-honored tradition—peeling potatoes. I have had my butt parked on this overturned bucket, deskinning spuds with hands water-swollen to a puckered wrinkle for three solid days. This is a job usually reserved for those who have committed some minor infraction, but my only fault was arriving at Fort Ord, California, at an awkward time. The leadership potential course I was scheduled to take began a week and a half before I got here, while the men who will make up my advanced infantry training class have not yet arrived. After some initial confusion about what to do with me, they stuck me in this potato bin.

Before leaving Fort Lewis, I was offered the choice of going to drill corporal school or officer candidate school. After having the distinct displeasure of knowing Drill Corporal Gausser, I had no desire to visit the place where he was made. However, unless the most recent escalation of the Vietnam War had resulted in a relaxation in the rules of eligibility for OCS, my bad eye would prevent me from being eligible. After two hours of inquiry, a lieutenant and I learned that the physical requirements for OCS had indeed been downgraded. One good eye was now all that was needed to be a leader of men, yet two good eyes were still required for combat duty. I heralded their wisdom and signed on the dotted line.

Dropping another bald spud into the pot, I glanced at

the automatic potato peeler standing at my side. It is reportedly in need of repair, but I suspect it is merely in need of a good plugging in.

Back in the days of the Great Depression my father had joined the Army as a way of sustaining himself. After serving for four years as a private, he went to college, married, and started a family. When World War II came along he was disappointed when his application for admittance to the officer training programs was denied because of his dependence on glasses.

Even though I do not share his faith in our current leaders, perhaps his unfulfilled desire had something to do with my volunteering for OCS, or perhaps I felt if I had to serve I might as well do so as an officer. In any case, I had volunteered, and my decision hung over me uneasily. From the little I have learned about Army life, it seems to be a profession of regimented minds frozen decades back in time when the standard methods of operation first jelled. And while I do feel an obligation to help protect America's freedoms, I wonder if the present Vietnam situation has anything to do with that obligation. Perhaps, as the dissenters claim, this war is moving our country further from the path of justice and freedom. I do not know. All I know is how much I hate being a slave to the whims of other men.

I've peeled enough damn potatoes to feed a battalion. I've had enough of this shit. No one's been around to check on me for hours, and it's almost quitting time, anyway. Leaving at the rear of the mess hall, I stroll off looking for the nearest haven for the bewildered and the bored.

The large beer hall I find has only a smattering of customers. Men in baggy green talk quietly to their companions, or sit alone staring into their private thoughts. Discarding the idea of having my first drink in the Army in cheery fellowship, I sit at an empty table and begin to think through the possibilities of escape.

Getting off the base is easy enough. All I have to do is climb over the barbed wire at the top of the fence and jump to freedom on the other side. From there I can catch one of the regular buses that pass the fort and be on my way to anywhere—as long as anywhere doesn't cost too much money. I only have three hundred dollars. Maybe I could go to my father's house for awhile. No I couldn't. That patriot would probably turn me in. Well, finding a place to live under an assumed name is not the problem. How to make money without using my Social Security number would seem to be the major hurdle. I could work with the other illegals in the fields. The trouble with this idea is that a six-foot three-inch white boy would tend to stand out in a field of short, brown Mexicans. Maybe I should go to Canada, or sell drugs. Christ! This whole idea is depressing.

Being assigned to Ford Ord was a lucky draw. It is sunny and warm, with a moderate ocean breeze blowing gently across the rolling hills and sand dunes. Whatever winter there was seems to be gone. We spend most of our time attending classes on land navigation, rocket launchers, mortars, mines, communications, and first aid. It is a vast improvement over being yelled at all day.

Nonetheless, the mainstay of Army life is still boredom. It seems strange. Now that things have improved, I think constantly of escape. Yet despite the hours I have devoted to the subject, a satisfactory plan—or sufficient courage—has so far failed to develop.

Today, however, my yearning for long-term freedom is overshadowed by more immediate desires. Julie has come to California. Contrary to my expectations, our relationship has not withered with separation. Instead, a constant stream of passionate letters, coupled with my isolation from all things female, has strengthened our mutual interest. In the hope of getting a chance to see me, Julie is spending her spring break from college at my folks' place an hour north of here.

Captain Jackson, who has until now felt no compunction to grant his company any type of leave, has inadvertently granted my most fervent wish by releasing us for the entire weekend.

I stand with my toes hanging over the edge of the curb, balancing on the balls of my feet, waiting. I wish my hair had had a chance to grow a little more. I feel like a nervous kid waiting for his first date. Before today I have always been able to maintain enough distance in my relationship with Julie to keep it from becoming too serious. After all, she may be the most desirable girl I have yet dated, but she is far from perfect. I wish she would hurry up and get here.

As if summoned by the power of my desire, a car pulls to the curb. The delicious blonde behind the wheel bounces out of the car to clap me in a bear hug. My God, she feels good.

My hand presses a tantalizing thigh as we drive the short distance to Moss Landing where my father's little sloop is moored. We sail the bay, run on the beach, and toast the sunset. Everything is perfect between us. The laughter and loving rejuvenates my faith in life. It is increasingly tempting to steal Mr. Strindberg's daughter and Mr. Shook's boat, and sail off into the proverbial sunset, never to be heard of again.

Sunday night I pry my mind from the western horizon to apply it to more realistic matters. Although my restless urges have been subdued over the past two days for me to grudgingly return my body to the Army, I am not willing to accept this one weekend of bliss as my total allotment for the next several months.

Plans must be laid.

The Monday evening formation is dismissed for dinner. Instead of getting in line for chow I return to the barracks and slip out the side door. No one is in sight. The mighty military machine seems totally occupied with its refueling. Trainees are not allowed out of their company area without a pass, but if I act naturally and appear as if I know where I am going the chances of being checked are slim. I hope.

At the parking lot I begin the difficult chore of pretending to be on an errand while walking in a circle around the scattering of parked cars. Ten minutes past the appointed hour my car hoves into view. I direct Julie to park between two cars, with the trunk end pulled tight against a bush. With a quick look around, I open the trunk and crawl inside.

The car slows for the MP at the main gate, then accelerates into the world of normal people.

Julie brought steak, cold beer, homemade cheesecake, and best of all, the gift that brings intense pleasure with every unveiling—herself.

By the time we have eaten and loved and talked and loved again, it is 0330—time to wake from our dream. Reversing the trunk-smuggling operation, I am back inside the fort at 0400, in my bunk by 0410, and startled by the sound of reveille at 0500.

For the remainder of the week we continue our rendezvous. By week's end notions of love for this girl have escalated sharply. But love cannot stay. It takes itself back to Oregon, and I miss it all the more.

Saturday morning I discover that my squad leader has

been sniffing around the edges of our little escapade. He has noted me sleeping in the chow line, dozing during morning formation, and slumbering during lectures. Further, he has twice seen me up and fully dressed at 0400, an obvious indication of deviant behavior as no soldier would rise at 0400 when he could sleep until 0500. He informs me that in view of my recent behavior he is harboring serious doubts about his ability to support my nomination for soldier of the week.

I don't care any more about being soldier of the week than I did when nominated for soldier of the month. Besides, I'm too tired to deal with this gung-ho bullshit. The sun isn't even up yet. "Listen, you'll have to do what you think best," I offer lamely as I try to move around him.

He stands there looking at me like he is waiting for a confession. When the truth fails to come welling out of me, he demands, "I order you to tell me what has been going on."

"Take it easy, will you? I've been having trouble sleeping at night, okay? What's the big deal? All my Army stuff is up to snuff, isn't it?"

"That's not the point."

"What the hell *is* the point?"

"It's your attitude. You're getting a bad attitude."

"Oh, bullshit. My attitude has always been bad." I would not talk this way to a real corporal, and I usually have more sense than to talk this way to my acting leader, even though his stripes are merely pinned on and will be unpinned at the end of AIT. Most of all, I do not feel he has any basis for his complaint—unless he knows the truth, of course.

Still he persists, and I dismiss him by saying that he is making an ocean out of vapor and that perhaps he is taking his acting corporal stripes a bit too seriously. This last bit I should have left off, for he does take his pretend corporalship seriously. Off he goes in a huff to report to his superiors.

During afternoon formation I am called before the first sergeant. He instructs me to wait outside the orderly room until the captain is ready for me. Standing on the edge of a patch of grass, I begin doing what the Army has spent most of its time training me to do. The passing minutes and the weight of drowsiness drags me closer and closer to the ground.

After something more than an hour the first sergeant leans out his window to scowl at the man sleeping in his front yard. "Private Shook, get in here," he growls. "Leave your rifle where it is."

"Out here, Sergeant?"

"I'll look after it for you—now get in here."

Pulling my sagging cells to attention on the visitor's side of the captain's desk, I report. "Private Shook reporting as ordered, sir."

"Private, where is your rifle?"

"Outside, sir."

"No it's not. It's gone. You have lost your rifle, Private. A soldier without his rifle is a detriment to his company, an endangerment to the accomplishment of mission. A soldier never lets his rifle out of his sight. Do you realize the seriousness of the offense you have just committed?"

What *is* this shit? I thought he wanted to see me about that tiff with the acting corporal or something to do with OCS. Instead, he has set up a catch-22 with the first sergeant. Disobeying the sergeant would have landed me in trouble. Now obeying him makes me guilty of abandoning my rifle. Well, I am not going to let him nail me this easy.

"Begging your pardon, sir, I didn't lose my rifle. I gave it into the care of the first sergeant as ordered. If the rifle is missing, then it is he who has lost it."

"You presume to tell me . . . ," and off he goes carrying on at length about all the mean, nasty miseries he can subject me to for my crime. After several minutes he pauses in an apparent effort to judge the effect of his speech. "Is my meaning coming through to you, Private?"

"Absolutely, sir. You're saying that this is your game, played by your rules. You can do virtually anything you want to me. I understand that, sir, but why me? What's the point?" Whoa. Let's be careful here. This guy really can crucify me.

There is another thoughtful pause while the captain rattles the papers on his desk, and I stare resolutely at the wall as is correct and proper.

"Private Shook, it has been reported to me that your attitude toward military training is not what it should be. In fact, your attitude is so bad that I don't see how I can recommend you for OCS, do you?"

So that's it. The little twit of a squad leader has passed his bad-attitude theory all the way to the top. What a joke. If they're willing to go to all this trouble for a reported bad attitude, I hate to think about what they'd do to someone who went awol five nights in a row. And it all comes down to threatening to cut me out of OCS. If he knew how little I

care about going to OCS. . . . No, that would just open up
more trouble. I'd better defend myself as expected.

· "Well, sir, since you haven't told me who gave you this
report, I don't know precisely to what you refer, but if you'll
check your company training records I believe you'll find my
name at or near the top of every category. I therefore feel the
report you received must be somewhat inaccurate."

Apparently, he hadn't previously bothered to check my
standing in his company because when he receives the information from his first sergeant he becomes more subdued,
contenting himself with several more admonitions that I
am careful to answer with the proper penitence and respect.
The matter dissolves itself in a sense of duty done and dwindling interest.

The trucks sit with their engines idling, waiting for the
flare that will send the troops in the back scrambling for
cover. It is a dark night, cloudy, with the moon not due for
hours.

I have seen the snake pits and the toy electric chair and
the confinement boxes that keep a prisoner in a crumpled
crouch with no way to change position. I have seen the eager
faces of the interrogation teams fresh from intelligence school.
I have seen enough not to want to play their game.

A white flare bursts overhead. The platoon crashes into
the underbrush as if sheer speed would carry them past the
opposition waiting ahead. As I see no advantage in sharing
their eagerness, I drift to the rear of the pack. When the
flare burns out, I veer sharply for the left flank. With the
return of my night vision I begin to move more cautiously. I
have less than two minutes to find a thicket dense enough to
conceal me before the troops stationed before us and those
stationed behind us are scheduled to begin their pincer
movement.

In the renewed darkness, the general din is reduced to
the periodic bursts of bodies through brush. Considering that
there are some 200 men sneaking around this plot of land, it
is surprisingly quiet—except for the bursters, of course, who
are too excited to creep.

Fifty yards behind me there is a sudden outburst of
shouting and frantic movement. The enemy has been met.
And they cheat, for surely not even one minute has passed
since the firing of the flare.

On hands and knees I crawl to the center of a clump of bushes. It isn't the jungle I was hoping for, but it's the best cover I have come across. I'll lie here until the opposition sweeps by.

Several minutes pass with only the rare grinding of pebbles beneath boots, and once, the snap of a twig. It's time to move. Slowly, I crawl at right angles to our objective until a faint noise freezes me in place. Silence and time expand uninterrupted. Perhaps it was not a human sound—or is he just waiting and listening like me? The soft, slow sound of stalking footsteps comes. He's moving. I try to match my crawl to his stride. I must reach the bush between us before he does or be caught here in the open. Unable to hear his noise over my own, I move on, trusting the rhythm I began with, tensing for the explosion of sound I imagine he will make when he spots me. I stop at the edge of the bush to listen. Nothing. He has stopped as well. Then the footsteps begin again, very close. Staring through the base of the bush, I see his pant leg come to a stop within reach of my hand. My instinct is to leap up and bash him in the head with my rifle, but I don't suppose that would be considered fair play. He stands suspended over me as though he has nothing better to do with his evening. When I'm almost convinced that he has known where I am all along, that he's amusing himself by seeing how long I'll remain in the position of a turtle, he walks away.

Our objective lies a mile north of our starting position. The area we are to travel through is bordered on each side by a dirt road. Crossing the road is strictly against the rules, which means the punishment for being caught will be greatly increased while the chances of being caught will be greatly reduced.

Crouching at the edge of the road, I wait for a passing truck to shine its lights into the watching eyes, then spurt across the road and roll into the ditch. Whooee! Just like in the movies. I get up and run partway up a ravine before slowing to watch and to listen.

There are sounds coming from the ravine, then the silhouettes of two men as they crawl over the top. Friend or foe? I cannot ask, so I slow my progress to give the distance between us a chance to expand.

Peeking over the ridge I am dismayed at how much lighter it is up here and how much less cover there is. The clouds are clearing to allow clusters of disgustingly bright stars to light the plateau I must move across. The only compensation is that I can see my enemies as well as they can see me.

Moving from cover to cover at a crouching jog, I am three fourths of the way across the plateau when I spot a soldier coming towards me. I hit the ground and crawl rapidly from the spot where I went down. I don't think he saw me. His walk remains casual, but if he maintains his current course he'll intersect my trail of footprints in the sandy ground.

The vegetation is low and sparse. I lift myself up from my belly crawling to relocate the soldier. He is getting close enough to make further movement risky. I am still watching him long after I should have hidden my face. There is something about him. He looks familiar. Christ—it's my platoon sergeant. What's he doing here? He should be at the interrogation center drinking coffee and tormenting the troops. All he has to do is look ninety degrees to his right and I'll be in a front-leaning rest position until Jesus' revisitation. But he keeps looking straight ahead and keeps walking, a man strolling through a pleasant evening, the starlight reflecting off the sand to ease his path.

The remainder of my route to the north road is clear. Still cautious, I approach the assembly point from the north. According to the rules I am safe here, but they do not play by the rules any more than I do. I wait until the men gathering below make it clear by their conversation that they have been interrogated before I slip out of my hiding place to join them.

The only other man to complete the course uncaptured also cheated. He violated the boundary on the east side, as I violated it on the west.

The platoon sergeant stops by to ask if we have all been interrogated. A universal groan is given in reply. Satisfied, he loads us on trucks to be sent back to our barracks and a few hours' sleep.

We clean and polish everything we have touched during our eight weeks of AIT. Every piece is inspected again and again until each man's effort is approved and the gear can be returned to the supply room shelves. With our personal allotment of underwear, fatigues, and boots carefully rolled into our duffel bags, we put on our dress greens for the last inspection of them all.

An hour later we are declared acceptable and more. The men gathered on the raised podium claim they are proud of us, and they charge us with the responsibility of bringing honor to our service, to our country, and to ourselves. They say we are ready now. Ready to fight, ready to lay down our lives for our country and the principles for which it stands.

I wonder, who among us is ready? Vaulted or mud-spattered principles aside, none of us have received any training in guerrilla warfare. None of us have even seen an M-16. The only thing we are prepared for is marching, in temperate climates, back to World War II.

The speeches are few and short. Praise comes hard to these men so practiced in slander. Soon the two words we have all been listening for sing crisply over the assembly.

"Company, dismissed!"

Within minutes men eager for cold beer, family, friends, and thirty days beyond the sight of olive drab are gone. Their excited voices are replaced by a silence that slips into the company area with the wariness of an alien.

I walk across the high gloss of the barracks' floor, my steps echoing through the space where fifty men once slept. The men whose constant yelling filled this hollow wooden structure, the men who stood tense and beleaguered here, are all gone now. All headed for Vietnam. All except me.

Last week when I was offered an OCS class date beginning two days after AIT, I did not know what to do. I had had two months to make up my mind and still I had not decided. Suddenly, there was the form before me with the first sergeant handing me a pen. I did not want to stay in the Army an extra year. Then again, I would rather accept a probable tour of Vietnam later than a certain one now. Both options seemed as obnoxious as making any choice seemed pointless. But decide I must. Perplexed, befuddled, and pressed, I fell back on the stale mottoes that had so far guided my military career: keep a low profile, go with the flow, don't make waves, and sign the damn paper. I left feeling that I had done the right thing and that I would be sorry for it.

Enveloped in the quiet of the latrine, I sit on a white table in the corner watching water leak from a crack in the bottom of the urinal, run across the concrete floor, and disappear down a drain. I am free to go like the rest of them, but it is peaceful here, and I am not anxious to hurry the future. To the east lies six months of OCS; to the west—a year of killing.

OFFICER CANDIDATE SCHOOL

Swinging the heavy duffel bag off my shoulder, I wipe the sweat from my eyes, and check the number on the four-story, concrete barracks against the slip of paper in the pocket of my woolen dress greens. This is it. Officer candidate school at Fort Benning, Georgia. Six months of the strictest discipline the Army has to offer. Maybe I should go somewhere to savor a last beer before taking the plunge. Maybe I should go into town for a last night of freedom. How about an extended tour through the taverns of Georgia?

Oh hell, I might as well get on with it.

On the landing between the first floor and the basement, a private greets me with instructions to sign the ledger on the small table between us. As I fill in the last line of the form, someone who has stepped up quietly behind me remarks, "So you come to us all the way from California."

"Yes, that's right. Fort Ord," I reply without turning around.

The volume of the voice rises abruptly. "Is that the way they taught you to address an officer at Fort Ord?"

Oh, shit. It starts already? "No, sir," I reply, coming to attention.

"Wrong," shouts the crisp military voice. "What's your name?"

"Private Shook, sir."

"Wrong again. Your name is Candidate Shook. There

33

aren't any privates or corporals or sergeants in OCS. Only candidates and officers. Is that clear, Candidate Shook?"

"Yes, sir."

"What? What did you say?"

"Yes, sir. That is quite clear, sir."

"Nothing is quite clear to you, Candidate. Drop and give me ten, and you will keep giving me ten until you learn how to address me properly."

What kind of game is this? I wonder, finishing the push-ups and returning to attention.

"Nobody told you to get up, Candidate. Give me ten more."

Knocking out another ten, I lock in the up position known as the front-leaning rest, which is a misnomer because there is no resting involved.

"Are you ready to address me properly now, Candidate?"

"Yes, sir."

"Give me ten more."

My arms begin to tire.

"Well, Candidate?"

"How would you like to be addressed, sir?"

"Get up, Candidate," he says quietly. "When you address an officer you say, 'Sir, Candidate Shook,' and end your statement with 'sir.' Is that understood?"

"Yes, si . . . ah . . . sir, Candidate Shook, yes, sir."

"Louder."

"Sir, Candidate Shook, yes, sir."

"Good. Now follow me and I will show you to your room."

Hoisting my duffel bag I fall in behind him. At the next landing an officer descending the stairs stops to stare at me expectantly. I think I am about to learn another rule.

"Well?" he demands.

"Sir, Candidate Shook . . . well what, sir?"

"Get down and give me ten."

What kind of a stupid thing was that to say? I'd better start using my head, my arms are almost worn out.

"Get up. When an officer or senior candidate approaches you in a hall you brace up against the wall and yell 'junior candidates make way.' Do it."

"Yes, sir."

"What?"

"I mean, sir, Candidate Shook, yes, sir."

"You're disgusting. Give me twenty."

Straining hard on the last two, I surprise myself by completing the exercise. Locked in the front-leaning rest position my fatigued arms begin to shake. Are they going to let me up or wait until I fall on my face? Are they still here? I steal a look. Neither officer is within my restricted view. I take a chance and get to my feet. Where did they go?

The hallway above me is in chaos. The floor is littered with men doing push-ups. Other men are braced stiffly against the walls while officers harass them at full volume. I spot my officer standing over a man in the middle of the pandemonium. What a gauntlet to run with tired arms. I now know what to do when an officer approaches me, but what am I to do when I pass one of them?

I slip by the first officer when he turns his back, and am three steps beyond the second when: "Hold it right there. What are you trying to pull, Candidate?" The officer steps over one of the bodies on the floor to bring his face within a foot of mine. "What are you smiling at, Candidate?"

"Sir, Candidate Shook, nothing, sir."

He studies me for a moment. "Yes you are, you're smiling at me. Do you find me amusing, Candidate?"

"Sir, Candidate Shook, no, sir."

"You think this whole thing is a big joke, don't you? You think this is real funny. Well, I assure you there's no humor here. I'm going to keep an eye on you, Shook. I'm going to wipe that smile off your face for you. Now drop and give me ten."

While I am shakily pushing out my seventieth push-up, I try to recall if there actually was anything that could be construed as a smile on my face. Certainly the behavior here is ludicrous, even perversely humorous. Most likely he is just baiting me. Or *was* there a hint of a grin? I need a mirror. Regaining my feet, I resolve to show a blank face, but now I am not sure that I can.

"You're still smiling, Candidate."

"Sir, Candidate Shook, not intentionally, sir."

"I promise you that before this week is out I will wipe every trace of that smile off your face. Do you believe that, Candidate?"

"Sir, Candidate Shook, absolutely sir."

He leaves me still not knowing the proper procedure for passing an officer not approaching me—and in no shape to find out. I scan the hall for my lieutenant. He keeps drifting ahead of me, stopping to harass the men around him when I am stopped, moving on when I am released. At last he retrieves a man off the floor and ushers us both into a nearby room.

The room is furnished with two chairs, two desks, one bunk bed, two footlockers, and two standing lockers. The floor is polished to a deep shine that no machine could hope to duplicate. The lieutenant informs us that he is our TO and that he is going to devote the next sixty seconds of his time explaining a few of the rules to us. There are to be no footprints on our floor or on either side of the plastic runner in the hall. There is to be no walking on the furniture, no sitting on or touching of the bunk before taps. The bed will be made in such a way that a dropped quarter will bounce off the top blanket. We are to have our names stenciled on the front of our fatigue shirts and undershirts. We are not to leave the company area unless so ordered, or accompanied by a TO. Any infraction of these rules will result in demerits that will be worked off by walking guard tours during our only free time: Sunday afternoons. The minimum alternative punishment is low crawling the 330 meters around the building.

"You now have seven minutes to get out of your dress greens into your fatigues and join the formation at the west end of the building."

Removing his jacket and tie, my roommate introduces himself. "Hi, I'm Mark. Which locker would you like?"

Glasses, six foot, and slender. He looks intelligent and fit. Choosing the lockers closest to us, we hurriedly exchange our sweat-dampened uniforms for the fatigues and boots from our duffel bags.

"They don't believe in easing a guy into their program, do they?" he comments. "What I want to know is how we're supposed to get from the runner in the hall to our desks without stepping on the floor?"

"An officer in AIT told me he put Kotex on the bottom of the footlocker and slid them around to walk on."

"Kotex? Where the hell are we going to get Kotex? For that matter, how are we going to get our stuff stenciled if we can't go to the laundry to get it done, or to the PX to get the material to do the job ourselves?"

"All good questions. I am sure that after a few hundred more push-ups we will begin to learn the answers."

In the formation outside we learn that a candidate will run everywhere he goes with two exceptions: when returning from mess and when indoors. If a candidate intends to deviate from a straight-line course he will do so by making that corner a square corner. We are given a demonstration of the OCS method of eating, then we file off into a single continuous line that extends for a hundred yards to the base of the mess hall steps.

A new way to pass time in the mess hall line is explained and begun. A tactical officer taps the shoulder of the first man in line to bring him from parade rest to attention. The second man in line immediately copies the movement of the man before him as does the third and so on until a ripple of motion is traveling down the entire line. The first man is tapped again to bring him, and then each man in his turn, back to parade rest. Tap. Tap. Tap. Faster and faster the changes come. Men who disrupt the smoothness of the wave by being a fraction of a second too slow are dropped for push-ups.

By the time the mess hall doors are thrown open, there is only a ten-man separation between successive waves of motion. As each man reaches the top step he requests permission to enter. A TO scrutinizes the petitioner to determine his acceptability. The rejects are returned to the walkway for exercise. When they have completed their push-ups and chin-ups, they proceed to the end of the line to resume the crisp, precisely timed movement of legs and arms that produces that soothing domino effect for the observer.

The savory smell of well-prepared food permeates the mess hall. There is a choice of entrées, a variety of vegetables, and cake for dessert. Not knowing if the people on the serving side of the glass are military or civilian, or if addressing them incorrectly will land me back outside, I merely nod my head when they ask if I would like some chicken and beef and beans and potatoes and corn and squash and bread and salad and chocolate cake.

With laden tray in hand, I turn to face the noise blasting from the dining room. TOs prowl between the four-man tables, their voices ricocheting off the high concrete walls. Every few seconds a candidate is ejected from the room in a bath of angry words that describe his infraction and lack of merit.

I find a vacant chair amid the din and tension. Reviewing the proper procedures in my mind, I place my rear on the front two inches of the chair, press my knees and ankles firmly together, square my shoulders and back in a rigid set, fix my eyes on the acned forehead of the man across the table, and place my hands in my lap. Glancing down, I square my tray with the table, arrange the milk carton, the glass, and the coffee cup in a row across the front of the tray, sort and align my silverware, and return my hand to my lap. Now I can glance back down at the tray, pick up the fork, secure a morsel of food, return my eyes to the forehead across from me, bring the food to my mouth, return the fork to its place, return my hand to my lap, and chew. They sure know how to take all the fun out of eating.

Suddenly one of the shouting voices is directed at me. Too late I close the two-inch gap that has crept between my knees. I am sent outside to push myself from the pavement twenty times. At the back of the line I snap from attention to parade rest in fractionally delayed mimic of the man before me.

Finally at the door again, I am turned away to raise myself on the chin-up bar. Working my way through the line a third time, my diminished appetite is allowed to return to my overabundance of cold food.

Halfway through my lunch, in the middle of blaming myself for taking so much food and congratulating myself for having stayed seated so long, I hear my bunk mate ejected from the room. Unable to resist, my eyes dart in the direction of the disturbance. The shift of my gaze is so quick that I do not even have time to locate Mark before my eyes are back in their proper alignment. But nothing seems to escape the watchful TOs, who send me back outside to push the pavement twenty times more. Is this why I have never seen a fat OCS graduate? I am burning calories as fast as I am taking them in.

Without further interruption I choke down the rest of my meal, including the extra pat of butter and the leftover dollop of jam. Not a crumb of food taken can be left uneaten—it is a rule.

Returning to the barracks, I cross paths with Lieutenant White, who is black, and who does not like any number less than twenty-five. I give him a smart salute. He drops me for fifty. I must've left something out.

There's no way I can do fifty. He doesn't stay to listen to

me count them out so I begin to double and then triple the count. I reach fifty before I do twenty, but now I'm stuck in the front-leaning rest position with no one to release me. As far as I can tell from down here the company area is deserted. I can't stay here forever. It must be time to break another rule. I sprint for the door.

I make it to my room with fifteen minutes to rattle around in before the next formation. Mark and I sit on our footlockers polishing our boots and touching up the floor. We calculate that at the rate we are doing push-ups our daily average will be about seven hundred. This seems a staggering number, yet we are probably doing less than most of the men.

Although it is only late April, the gorgeous Georgia sunshine is already pushing the temperature into the eighties. We have gone only a mile on our afternoon run when our heaviest man's extra thirty pounds pulls him to the ground. With a man supporting him on either side, we pick him up and trot on. Within a half mile, he does more dragging than trotting. When a second and then a third man fall, we stop to pile them against a tree in the shade.

After two miles, we reach a grassy field where we are introduced to the OCS method of calisthenics. Five more men collapse from the strain and heat. When they revive they are told how many and what kind of exercises they missed while they were resting. If they pass out again—which they usually do—the process is repeated until they remain unconscious or complete the series of exercises.

I take a good look at the other men's uniforms. Normally, an OCS class consists predominantly of privates fresh from AIT, but this is clearly not the case here. A quick count reveals twenty Green Berets, fifteen Rangers, five warrant officers, twenty corporals, and eight privates, with the remaining bulk of the company made up of sergeants. It has undoubtedly been years since many of these sergeants have done regular physical exercise, and they are the men now falling on their faces in the sun.

By the time we have double-timed halfway to the barracks, we are dragging and carrying eleven men. By placing the victim's arms over our shoulders and pulling up on his belt with our free hands, we are able to maintain our position in the moving formation. As long as the man in the center can take a stride now and then, the burden is tolerable, but if he begins to drag his feet the load soon becomes exhausting. Without losing stride, we pass the eleven men around the company to share the load and to prevent adding to the number of casualties.

At first we resent these men, who cannot stand on their own, for adding to our burden. But when a man crumples like a bag of wet oatmeal, his face blotchy and clammy from trying too hard, too late, we just pick him up, drag him along, and feel sorry for him.

With the unconscious men placed in the shade of the barracks, the rest of the company stands at attention to receive instruction and scrutiny. It has been two hours now. Rigid little soldiers in the afternoon sun. Every fifteen minutes or so someone keels over and takes a nap on the concrete. Some topple like cut trees. Others sway until they collapse in a heap where they stood.

The TOs show no sympathy for those men malingering in untidy piles on the warm concrete. I do not suppose TOs are noted for their sunny dispositions at the best of times, but this lot is in a particularly foul mood. They graduated from this very building a couple of weeks ago. While the majority of their fellow graduates received assignments in Germany, these men were left behind to spend another six months in the very place they had surely hoped never to see again.

The two men not revived by their sleep in the shade are taken away in an ambulance. The rest of us start jumping back and forth, making human ripples in the chow line. Entrance to the mess hall is more frequently denied than before. Men are found guilty of allowing the grass they were crawling on to stain their uniforms. This crime is compounded by the discovery of candidates in existence with unbloused pants and disgusting scuff marks on the toes of their boots.

Forty push-ups and sixty-three wavelets later I am perched on the front two inches of a chair listening to the gut-wrenching bellow of criticism. As dining establishments go, this hall has a serious lack of the peaceful atmosphere recommended for good digestion. The vigilance of the TOs is astonishing. I find it hard to believe they can detect every deviation of form, but a quick glance at a sudden outburst on my left is all that is needed to prove their diligence and separate me from my meal.

After dinner we again congregate at the southwest corner of our building to stand in rank and file, waiting for the earth to rotate enough to block the sun so that our flag can come down from its pole. Having remained rigid for the required number of hours to accomplish this feat, the company divides into groups that separate and jog into the darkness.

As we trot about the bases of the airborne school's parachute towers, the TO literally runs circles around us delivering news and criticism. He is going to be presiding over this particular group for the next six months. He is our teacher, our leader, and our tormentor. The time we are now going through is dead time. Classes will not start until the company receives its full complement of men.

He stops circling to take over the lead of the column. Running backward as much as forward, he picks up the pace. Despite his repeated warnings to keep it closed up, several of the men begin to drop back. Soon there are six and then only two men keeping pace with the lieutenant. All the running we did in AIT had restored some of the endurance I had built up while on the college track team. Running is one thing I do well. When the last man fades from us, the lieutenant tells me to maintain the pace while he goes back to categorize his people.

He calls a halt to reassemble the squad, and we walk for a short distance before starting again at a slower pace. He falls in beside me chatting amiably about life and forms of punishment at OCS. By the time he completes his discourse, half our people have fallen out. The column is strung out over half a mile. We slow to a walk until the stragglers are collected and recovered enough to begin the run back to the barracks.

We reach our rooms in time to take a quick shower before falling into bed with the sound of taps echoing its melancholy notes off the walls of the buildings.

A riot of banging and yelling from the doorway startles me awake. I must have slept at attention, for the blanket lays as smooth as when I went to bed. With shaving kit and towel in hand, and eyes on the floor, I stumble toward the bathroom. Three steps into the hall I am dropped for twenty. I failed to yell "junior candidates make way," and I failed to brace against the wall for the TO I failed to see. Furthermore, I failed to attire myself in the proper going-to-the-bathroom-in-the-morning uniform, whatever that is. There is something particularly annoying about achieving such failure within the first thirty seconds of a new day. At least no one is accusing me of smiling.

It takes me sixty push-ups to reach the relief of the urinal. As I lather up for a shave someone yells through the door that we have five minutes to make formation.

The routine today is much the same as the day before. Push-ups, instructions, running, calisthenics, eating, and a plethora of personal scrutiny. Every twitch, wiggle, and blink is observed. Except for a short period after each meal, we are not left alone long enough to stifle a yawn.

At sundown a mobile barbershop pulls onto the broad concrete walkway that runs between the buildings. The neighboring classmen, who are only one week away from graduation, join us in the ritual of the biweekly haircut. Senior classmen are notorious for the havoc they inflict on their juniors, but the harassment we expect does not materialize. There seems to be a moratorium on the transfer of misery.

The upperclassman standing next to me in line proves to be friendly and full of unsettling pity for the members of my class. The fourth time he starts a sentence with "You poor suckers" I ask him why he stayed with the program for twenty-three weeks if he dislikes it so much.

"By the time the eight-week drop date came, I had gone through so much shit that I didn't want to throw all that effort away by quitting. And then I kept hoping things would get better when I became a senior and got a day off once in a while."

"You mean things don't get any better?"

"After classes start the TOs won't have as much time to mess with you. Studying will take the place of a lot of the bullshit you are doing now. But things don't ever really get any better. My days off usually turn into a few free hours once a week. All there is to do is drink a couple of beers and shoot a little pool."

"Tell me, if you had to do it over again, would you go to OCS?"

"Hell, no."

"What about your classmates—do most of them feel the same way?"

"You're damn right. Unless you intend to make the Army your career, it's just not worth it."

There it is again. I asked the lieutenants in basic and AIT the same question, and received the same response.

* * *

My third day of OCS. Life is not going any smoother. Every time we get a handle on the rules as we know them, we trip over a new one. But today the usual postbreakfast quiet is violated by excited candidates running around in the halls, stopping occasionally to converse in hushed voices.

"What's going on?" I ask a guy hustling past me in the hall.

"I'm quitting," comes the reply as he disappears around a corner.

"What? How can you do that?" I ask the empty space.

At the door to my room I am almost bowled over as Mark blasts by under full steam.

"Hey! Wait a minute. What's going on?"

He does not stop. He just waves a piece of paper over his head and says, "I'm turning in my resignation."

"But—but—" I say, and hurry after him. I catch up with him in a line in front of the commanding officer's door.

"I thought we couldn't quit until the eight-week drop date."

"I know, I know. But the CO is letting anyone who wants to quit, quit now. All you need to do is write a letter of resignation explaining why you want out."

"And they will let us go? Just like that?"

"That's it. Twenty or thirty guys have turned in their resignations already."

Still not convinced this unexpected offer is legitimate, I run to my room, rip a sheet of paper from a notebook, and write down the words that will release me. I am eager to put my name to the letter and be off, but I force myself to stay a moment to consider what I am about to do. I am throwing away the chance to be an officer in the United States Army. I am trashing a boyhood dream, albeit a dream that has faded considerably over the years. I will be sent to Vietnam regardless of what I do, so that is not an issue. Still, since I must serve, I would rather do so as a lieutenant. Is six months of this kind of intense masochism, plus serving the required extra year, worth the difference between a private and a lieutenant? No. Then it all depends on whether or not I want to interrupt my rather aimless drift through life with a fifteen- or twenty-year stint as a career officer. Ten percent of me finds this idea appealing, the other ninety percent finds it revolting. I hate to quit on anything, but screw it. I want out of here—badly.

I sign my name with a flourish and run to join the growing line outside the captain's door. This may be a ruse, a trick to ferret out those less committed than deemed desirable, a discovery to be closely followed by swift and painful retribution. Even so, the possible reward is well worth the risk.

I am so nervous by the time I am called before the captain there is a barely perceptible shiver running through me. He scowls at my scrawled note, then asks why I have changed my mind so soon after having volunteered to come here. I reply with the comment given to me by lieutenants and soon-to-be lieutenants: "I don't believe the reward is worth the effort."

He asks if I came here in good faith and a few other bitter questions. I confine myself to yes and no answers as appropriate. He finishes with an unflattering appraisal of my character before sending me to join the formation outside.

The formation is split into two parts: the quitters and the nonquitters. The quitters' side is larger than I expected and still growing.

When the captain finishes reviewing the last resignation, he comes to deliver words of dismay and disappointment. He ends his short rebuke by asking us to consider what will happen to our country if men are no longer willing to offer their services when their country is engaged in conflict?

Yes, what would happen if they gave a war and no one came? I ask myself in silence.

As the captain retires, the tactical officers take a turn. My TO walks slowly down the line of men until he reaches me.

"I'm disappointed in you, Shook. Real disappointed. I thought you were going to be one of the ones that made it. Look at me! Look me in the eye and tell me you want to quit."

"Sir, Candidate Shook wishes to quit, sir."

"That hurts me, Shook. I cry a tear for you." And he does. That tough little fucker actually sheds a tear. Whatever remaining doubts I have about quitting vanish. This dude is crazy, or a fanatic at the least.

Fifty-seven men enter the deserted barracks for the last

time. Swiftly and silently they move through the halls, careful to preserve the quiet equilibrium of this delicate moment.

With unnecessary haste I cram my gear into my duffel bag. After a quick backward glance for anything forgotten, I steal down the hall and out the door. The assembly area is deserted. All the way across the thirty-five-foot space to the boundary of the company area I expect to be halted, to be informed that this is merely another test.

On the far side of the sidewalk, I risk a backward glance. The barrack stands in ominous silence, exuding the tensions of thousands of young men who struggled for that superior level of achievement where all but random punishment would pass to others. With a shudder of relief, I turn my back on OCS and walk on in the peaceful Georgia morning.

CASUAL COMPANY

The 1st Casual Company is an outfit that takes its name to heart. Here in the dustbin of Fort Benning are the rejects, the dropouts, and the lame from jump school, noncommissioned officer school, and officer candidate school. Some of the best and brightest quitters in the entire Army have been swept into this little corner of America in disgrace and placidity.

Some of the men rise at the sound of reveille. Some do not. Some men salute the raising of the flag with their right elbow resting on their neighbor's shoulder, while others opt for the left-hand variation, and a few demonstrate a preference for the salute they learned in Cub Scouts.

Roll call is carried out with maximum efficiency. There is no dallying between names to allow for a response. The list is read straight through without pause. However, since roll call would not be complete without the familiar cries of "here" ringing in the early morning air, the troops do their part by responding now and again. Those who are more enthusiastic about sounding off respond four or five times so that those who feel less energetic need not respond at all.

While a normal company consists of four platoons, 1st Casual is so popular that its platoons vary in number between eleven and thirteen. Two of these platoons consist solely of casualties—primarily men with broken and twisted limbs, gained by jumping from high places.

We have not seen much of the sergeant in charge of our platoon. When he is not awol he spends most of his time in his room smoking dope, listening to music on his portable stereo. He has recently returned from Vietnam where he picked up a Bronze Star, a Purple Heart, and the stripes of a staff sergeant. But he must have picked up or lost something else as well, because he is the epitome of the listless man with the faraway gaze. Although he is a strict loner, the men of the platoon do their best to look out for him and cover for his absences whenever possible. At first it was difficult to understand why the men should show any loyalty to a sergeant whose only contact with them is to read their names on those occasions when he appears at morning formations, but I think I am beginning to understand.

Ever since eighty plus candidates dropped out of an OCS class a little over a month ago, Major General Timothy, the commander of school, ordered all future dropouts to be sent to Vietnam. Previously, dropouts were considered undesirables to be stashed in Alaska, Greenland, and other noncombative areas. Since the rule change, all of us here are assured of being sent to the place that made our sergeant a man who does not seem able to find a reason to get up in the morning, or concern himself with the Army's displeasure.

I think the men look at the sergeant and wonder if they are seeing a reflection of themselves a year into the future.

The first time I saw the sergeant, he had just been demoted a grade because of a week's absence without leave. Only six days have passed since then, and already he is in the process of being demoted again—this time for smoking marijuana and repeated awol charges. I do not think he cares. The smell of marijuana still leaks from the seams of his room at the front of the barracks. He is only twenty-one years old, yet for him it appears over. I hear they are going to kick him out of the service as soon as they can process the paperwork.

Despite the veil of decay maintained by this battalion-sized company, the men loosely contained in its ranks are the most intelligent, individualistic, contented group I have served with. It appears, at least for the short term, that the rewards for failure are greater than those for success. We are only required to pack books, set up classrooms, move furniture, wax floors, clean garbage cans, and dig holes nine hours a day, with night guard duty coming only twice a week. No one feels compelled to yell at us all day long, or to suggest that we smile too much or need an attitude adjustment. We even have most of the weekends off to go to the movies, swim in the outdoor pool, or go to the EM club for a beer.

On my second Saturday night as a regular soldier our platoon is given off-base passes. Eight of us head into Columbus in search of women and high times. We soon learn, however, that white soldiers and black soldiers must drink in separate bars, and that there is no big demand for bald-headed Yankee boys among the women of the town. Having been dissuaded from starting a race riot by the two black guys who had been with us, and having been told repeatedly to get lost by the girls on the dance floor, we content ourselves with watching and drinking until the boys are drunk and discouraged enough to return to the base, leaving me to wander the streets alone.

Three miles of sidewalk later, a man lurching out of a recessed doorway, his head turned to yell an incoherent slur at the muted voices in the bar behind him, slams into me and ricochets into a parking meter. With both hands clasping the meter and legs spread, he brings himself into a position of controlled weaves and bobs. "Merciful mother, what did I run into?"

With a concentrated gaze he studies the space between himself and the bar. Finding nothing, he extends his search up the side of the building. Having viewed the structure all the way to the fourth floor, he swings around on his support to bring the southern portion of his world into view.

"A-ha! There he is," he proclaims when he discovers me watching him from ten feet away. "I presume I owe you an apology, sir. I hope you will forgive my clumsiness. Fact is, I'm a bit intoxicated. No, that's a lie. What I am is drunk. You are undamaged, I trust?"

"No harm done."

"Are you sure? Here, let me give you something for your trouble." He takes some bills from his wallet and extends them toward me, dropping the wallet in the process.

While retrieving the wallet, I turn down his repeated attempts to give me money. "Can I call you a cab or something?"

"No cab. Live too far away. But I would be grateful if you would help me find my car. I left it around here somewhere. It's a white Cadillac with a cracked windshield."

"You sure you can drive?"

After a moment's thought he says, "No, I don't reckon so. I guess you'd better drive. You *can* drive, can't you?"

"Well, sure, but I was planning on having one more drink, then I have to get back to Fort Benning."

"Good enough. We'll stop by my club for that drink, then take you back to your base. What do you say?"

"Why not?"

At his private club, Lewis disappears into the back room to reappear a few minutes later with a woman on each arm. The women are attractive, friendly, thirtyish, and thirsty. After several more drinks Lewis and the ladies decide to move the party to his house. Since it is already past the hour when I could return to the base without awol charges, I agree to go along.

As I weave the Cadillac along a tree-lined country road, the woman snuggled beside me provides directions while moans of passion issue from the darkness of the rear seat. A few minutes later the sounds of desire are replaced by those of snoring. Lewis has passed out during foreplay.

By fate's allowance we reach the little town I was aiming for. From here on only Lewis knows the way. When the women's efforts fail to rouse him, I stop the car to give him a more vigorous shake. I rattle him harshly, but his flopping head shows no signs of consciousness. Finally, I lift his wallet to get his address from his driver's license.

When we stop at an all-night gas station to ask directions, the women calmly get out of the car and start walking from the station's pool of light.

"Wait a minute," I cry in dismay. "Where are you going?"

From the darkness beyond the light I hear their laughter and a faint, "Good-bye, good-bye."

With Lewis still snoring and wheezing on the backseat, I pilot the car to Elm Street. One house light a quarter of a mile away offers the only illumination beyond the Cadillac's headlights. I drive to the light to read the address: 2752. I want 2740. Putting the car in reverse, I count back six houses, shut the beast down, and give thanks for my arrival without mutilation.

Another attempt to revive Lewis merely results in a reaffirmation of his total success in achieving oblivion. Tired of trying to bring a spark of life into his alcohol-infused system, I stumble to his house to find a warm place to sleep. The front door is unlocked, but despite diligent groping I am unable to locate the light switch. Oh, well, who needs lights? I'm not here to inspect the decor; what I seek is one of those broad flat things with blankets on top. With one hand on the wall to steady the room, I move onward three steps before colliding with something at knee level. Skirting the obstacle, I move down the hall to its end, then slip left around the corner to an open door.

A-ha. A big, flat, horizontal object raised off the floor. Just what I need. Four steps to peace . . . ohhhh, shit. Quickly placing a hand between two elongated lumps in the covers, I struggle to keep from pitching forward onto the recumbent forms.

"Who's that?" comes a deep groggy voice.

Gaining control over my momentum, I straighten, then stagger back a step. What's going on here? Why is there a man in bed with Lewis's wife? She isn't due back until tomorrow night.

"Who's there?" comes the voice with growing alarm. "What are you doing here?"

"What am *I* doing here? What are *you* doing here?"

The voice takes on an angry edge. "I live here."

"You do?" This is getting to be too much for my muddled mind. Lewis should have filled me in.

"Who the hell are you? And what the hell are you doing in my bedroom?"

"*Your* bedroom? Isn't this Lewis's house?"

"Who?"

"Lewis," I answer, pointing toward the street. "Passed-out-in-the-car Lewis."

"Lewis? You mean Lewis Crampton?"

"Yeah, I guess."

"Lewis Crampton lives next door."

"Oh, oh. Listen, I'm real sorry about all this," I say, backing up, desperately hoping there isn't a gun within his reach. "This is terribly embarrassing—my mistake—I'll close the door behind me."

"Wait a minute!"

"Good night." Slamming the door, I sprint, stumble, regain balance, and walk rapidly to the car.

Having moved the car one house down, I attack the problem of Lewis's unconsciousness. This time he's coming with me if I have to carry him.

The neighbor's porch light comes on. The front door opens.

"Lewis, you fucking drunk. Wake up!" Jerking him upright, I shake him hard enough to rattle his ancestors, but the evidence of my innocence remains inert. Desperate, I grab a handful of his shirt to line up a stinging slap. He comes to life sputtering curses. Before his mind can short out again, I drag him out of the car onto his feet. Arm in arm we crash into his house, colliding with furniture and walls all the way to the bedroom. I dump him on a bed, cover him with a blanket, then find a second bedroom for myself.

Knowing that someone is looking at me, I awake into a world of pain. I venture up an eyelid. The pain increases. Lewis is propped against a doorjamb, studying me with intent.

"Goodmorning," I croak out of a bone dry throat and around a swollen tongue that threatens to stick permanently to the roof of my mouth.

Standing there with his arms folded across his chest, looking rumpled and grumpy, he says, "I don't mean to appear inhospitable, but who are you, and what the hell are you doing in my wife's bed?"

"Jesus, Lewis," I groan, pulling the blanket over my head. "Don't you remember anything?"

I received my alert for Vietnam today. I have been expecting it, yet somehow its final substantiation is more ominous than I had expected. I knew I was going, knew that they would not send me anywhere else, but until now there was always that last shred of hope. With the disappearance of all chance of reprieve, I am left with the reality of their intentions. They really are going to ship me across the Pacific Ocean to that strange little country whose people they figure need some killing so they can be brought around to our way of thinking.

Most of the men in the group earmarked to go to Vietnam with me have never seen an M-16 rifle. Since the M-16 is to be our primary weapon in the year ahead, our leaders have decided it is time for an introduction.

A hundred men assemble in the hall to receive instruction. With the plastic contraption placed before me, I disassemble it to the cadence of the instructor. My partner then reassembles the varied parts to the reverse cadence. He finishes with a spring left behind on the tabletop. Not to worry, we are told. The instructor's assistant will put things to rights in the armory. I ask the assistant if he is going to accompany me to Vietnam, as I have virtually no idea how to properly assemble my weapon and will surely require further aid. He tells me to get my butt out to the rifle range where an M-16 in working order awaits me. In spite of his indifference, the fact that I do not know how to perform this primary task, coupled with the suspicion that the Army is not going to bother teaching me, does nothing to alleviate the lack of confidence I am beginning to feel in both of us.

Somewhere there exists a rule stating that every man being sent to Vietnam must first qualify with the M-16. This means shooting down a certain number of the pop-up targets on the rifle range. An official scorer, seated at a lecture-hall-type desk situated at the rear of a firing hole, directs me to stand in the hole. He explains that when the siren is sounded, I am to pick up the M-16, insert the magazine, and begin firing at the targets that will pop into view on the brushy hillside before me.

At the sound of the siren, I begin my first experience with fitting a magazine into the rifle. Obviously, the bullets should point toward the barrel, with the open end of the magazine fitting into the rifle. Right. Now this pistol grip must fit into my right hand while my left hand supports the barrel. That feels right. Okay, now sight in the target. . . . Wait a minute. What's this handle-looking thing on top of the barrel where the rear sight should be? Oh, there's the rear sight on top of the handle. That doesn't seem right to have it way up there. Oh well, it must be right. Squeeze off a round . . . nothing. Hmmm. The safety must be on. Let's see, where would a safety be? Ah, here's a switch. No, that's the selector switch to change from semiautomatic to automatic—I know because it says so right under the switch. Not finding any other likely looking buttons or levers or switches, I turn to my scorer in frustration. "Hey, where's the safety on this thing?"

"I'm not supposed to help you, just score you," he says.

With this rebuke I take the time to look more closely. I find the button almost immediately. I'm ready now, just wait for a target and . . . nothing. Now what?

"Are you sure this thing works?"

"It worked a few minutes ago."

"Well, it doesn't work now. How am I supposed to pass this test if I can't even fire one round?"

My scorer cracks a sly smile. "Don't worry, you'll pass,"

he says, continuing the methodical movement of his pencil over my score card.

Well, hell. What do I care if I pass this stupid test without firing a shot? Plenty. The targets where I am going shoot back. It would make me feel a lot better if I could fire this thing just once before that happens.

"Look, since you already have my score figured out, what is it going to hurt if you tell me how to work this thing? I mean, we are on the same side, right? You could be helping to save a life here."

He looked down at me in disgust. "Did you cock it?"

Ah, yes. Rifles need to be cocked. I should've thought of that. If they would leave me alone with this thing for fifteen minutes, I could probably figure it out for myself, but with the clock running, and the sporadic firing up and down the range, it's hard to concentrate. Now let me see, I haven't had much experience with guns, but I know how to cock a .45, I know about bolt-action, lever-action, and pump-action rifles. Unfortunately, none of that kind of stuff is on this plastic wonder.

"How the fuck do you cock it?" I yell, beginning to get hot.

Hearing the threat of continued disturbance in my voice, he chooses to reveal the answer. "You see that little T-shaped thing under the rear sight? Put a finger on either side of the T and pull it toward you."

I follow his instructions, sight in a target, and fire. Missed. I fire and miss again. A target appears beside a bush on my left; I swing the rifle on line and fire. The target drops with the bullet's impact.

The siren sounds the end of the test. My scorer, with fabricated hit chart in hand, informs me that I have passed. The United States Army has cranked out another superbly trained marksman.

Today we are being introduced to the art of guerrilla warfare. Unfortunately, somebody's schedule does not allow us more than an introduction. We are given an hour's instruction on such things as heat prostration, phosphorous burns, and snakebite. We are told that when we are on patrol, exercising heavily in the tropical sun, and a man collapses from heat prostration, the solution is to throw water on him and to stop exercising heavily in the tropical sun. We learn that a piece of phosphorus burning its way through our arm cannot be extinguished by submersing the arm in water, but mud might do the trick. If one of the many varieties of poisonous snakes bites us, we had better be within a hospital compound when it happens—or not get bitten at all.

Thus enlightened and assured, we are taken on a tour where we are shown a Vietnamese hut (that's where they live); a man dressed in black pajamas (that's what they look like); and various traps, pits, and homemade bombs (that's what they do).

Armed with an hour and a half of guerrilla training, the proven ability to fire the M-16, four months of practice at standing in one place for hours, the competence to march in rank and file, a smattering of information about what to do should World War II need to be refought, we are now ready to kill those rotten little people over there in Asia—whoever they may be—for whatever reason our government deems they need to be killed.

God, I wish I had the necessary conviction to flee this insanity.

A thirty-day leave is granted to those designated for participation in America's "holding action." I take the long flight to Oregon and the loving arms of my girl. Our reunion is complicated by the necessity of Julie's attention to the completion of her junior year in college.

I had fantasized and longed for this moment so intensely that no girl could possibly equal my dreams, but Julie comes close, very close indeed. We treat each other with kindness, with gentleness, and with a respect unknown to us before. We are constantly thoughtful of each other's needs, and we are frequently consumed in the satisfaction of each other's desires. I accompany her to some of her classes just to be near her. I even summon the willpower to leave her alone for an hour or two each evening so she can study.

Our time together is a continuum of peace and satisfaction, often punctuated by intense pleasure. It is a unique experience for both of us, a cherished feeling to be nurtured and extended to the limit. At the end of the month the subject of marriage naturally slides into our conversations without complication or commitment. But I feel strongly that marriage, followed directly by a year of separation, is unfair to both of us. Besides, the very idea of inflicting the debilitating institution of marriage upon myself in the foreseeable future (or at least until I am thirty) has been unthinkable—until now. It will take me a while to adjust to the whole radical idea.

But now I must catch a plane to Oakland, California, with connecting flights to Asia. Duty calls and I must go, for this is how it has always been. With pledges of fidelity, and silent screams of emotional agony, we part to attend to our separate lives and to dream of a future together in a time that seems so distant as to be almost beyond hope.

ON THE WAY TO THE JUNGLE

I stop by my father's home in California to say good-bye. I have never been in his new house. He had it built two years ago to go along with his new wife. It is a nice house with a fireplace in the master bedroom, speakers hanging from the cathedral ceiling in the living room, and teak on the floor in the dining room. On the west side of the house there is a swimming pool. On the north side a deck has been built around the oak trees, offering a grand view of the San Francisco Bay area far below. It is one of those houses that says, "Hey, look at me, I made it." And why not? My father has worked hard for it.

I spend the afternoon hanging around the house looking at things, feeling nervous and all jumbled up inside. I don't know what to do with myself. I don't even feel like getting drunk.

I take myself for a walk.

There's no question about my going now. I've put aside my dreams of running away. I guess I feel I have to go through with it—to do it their way so I can earn the right to rebel. After all, they've lived more than twice as long as I have. Knowledge and experience are on their side—and wisdom too—if they aren't lying. But someone's sure as hell lying, and it looks more and more like it's them. Not an occasional little white lie—but big lies, all the time. That's what makes it hard to believe.

Turning toward the house, I meet my father searching

for me. We walk together, not saying anything. We have never been good at talking to each other. No animosity—just not close—not comfortable with each other.

After a time, he says, "Well, keep your head down while you're over there."

I say, "Sure, I will," and we continue in silence. Somehow I expected something a little more profound from a man with a Ph.D. in nuclear physics—a dissertation on duty to country, or an attempt to explain the mess our government has gotten me into. But by the time we reach the house it seems that for a father to tell his son, who is going to war, to keep his head down is about as good a thing to say as anything else.

I walk into the house and call Julie to ask her to marry me. I can feel the love coming over the wire with her answer, "Yes, oh, yes."

The base at Oakland is an overseas staging area, a place where uneasy strangers wait. We spend our time standing in formations of one hundred to three hundred men while long lists of names are read over the PA system. Each day I stand for hours, staring at the guard towers and the chain-link fences topped with barbed wire, wondering if they are there to keep us in or to keep some nameless enemy out. The fact that this place so closely resembles a prison yard does not help my perspective.

On the morning of the second day, with the pale orange of the sunrise illuminating the guard tower, my name is called. I am sent to fill out forms and do some serious waiting for a flight time.

In the middle of the night a dozen of us are hustled off to San Francisco to catch a commercial flight to Anchorage, Alaska. As the moment of our departure draws near, I cannot help feeling that there is something missing in the quiet, detached way we are moved about. Maybe it is because of the movies I watched as a kid, the ones with people cheering and women crying as their men go off to war. Then again, perhaps it is fitting that we should sneak to this war in the middle of the night.

We fly from San Francisco to Anchorage, to Yokotaamt, to Bien Hoa in a twenty-two-hour marathon of enforced sitting. My capacity for sitting comfortably in one place is limited to a single hour. After twenty-two hours, little spasms of jerks and twitches betray my body's displeasure with the Army's scheduling.

Somewhere past patience and isometrics and reapplied endurance, somewhere well into eternity, the pilot calls our attention to the smoky mist rising off the Mekong Delta. Lush green and mud brown filter through a liquid haze. The plane makes a steep dive for the north side of a large river carrying a saturated load of Vietnamese soil to the sea.

As I step from the alien atmosphere of the air-conditioned plane, I am hit with a blast of thick, hot air pungent with the odors of decomposition and lingering smoke. By the time I reach the bottom of the ramp, every pore in my body is off-loading water.

Well, here we are. July 3, 1968—day one of a year of free, continuous steam baths. I feel sick.

After two hours in the shade of a corrugated metal roof, we are loaded onto a bus with iron mesh over the windows. We are taken to the Long Binh Replacement Station. Long Binh is the biggest U.S. Army base in the country. It covers an expanse of gently rolling hills a few miles beyond the outskirts of Saigon. Perched on the highest hill, looking down on the expanse of reddish brown dirt streaked with lines of one- and two-story metal-roofed wooden buildings, are the modern, four-story, concrete, air-conditioned offices of the generals.

The base has been stripped of its plant life, leaving square mile after square mile of sun-baked earth that transforms into a sea of mud when the rains come, and a reservoir of heat and dust when it dries.

On my second day in-country I discover the origin of one of the ever-present odors of the base. Four of us are selected at random for what must surely win the prize for the lowest of Army details. From a hatch in the back of a latrine we carefully extract two cut-down fifty-gallon drums from their alignment beneath the corresponding derriere holds. The drums are filled to the rim with a sloshing combination of toilet paper, that which came before the toilet paper, and urine. Having dug an appropriately sized hole, we drag the fertile containers to its edge and dump the contents. The barrels and their contents are liberally doused with diesel fuel, sprinkled with gasoline, and ignited.

A vast plume of black smoke rises eighty feet. The smell

of raw sewage is bad, but the smell of it roasting in diesel fuel is truly disgusting.

I spend the evening filling sandbags in the rain. It is not the way I would choose to celebrate Independence Day, but we are not without the usual symbols of the holiday. A local band blasts a semblance of "Shake It Up Baby" at the nearby NCO club, and flares illuminate the sky to our northeast and west. Artillery thunders sporadically throughout the night.

At 2100 we are released from our labors. One of my fellow workers, Allen Gillis, and I head for the EM club to join the last hour of revelry before the club closes for the night. A single bare bulb, shrouded in cigarette smoke, casts a murky light on the crowd of drunken, yelling soldiers. All the seats around the beer-can-cluttered tables are occupied. The concrete floor is awash with a mixture from spilled beer and muddy boots belonging to the men clogging the remaining space between the chairs. A three-piece band belts out rock and roll from a corner.

Allen and I push through the crowd by the bar to buy three beers each at the surprisingly low price of ten cents apiece. Since we are already covered with mud from our labor, we settle down on a small section of the floor near the wall where the dirt has not yet turned into mud. Although the beers are as warm as the sweltering room, we down them quickly in the hope of joining the mood of celebration already so well embraced by the other men.

By the time we have each quaffed six beers our frame of mind is somewhat improved, yet we remain spectators of this wild pack of men. About them there is an air of reckless abandonment, a teetering on the verge of danger. Their yelling and hunger for drunkenness seem closer in spirit to that of an angry mob than to that of a social gathering. Allen and I stay on the floor by the wall until the bar announces its closure to a loud chorus of boos.

In the morning Allen and I conspire to avoid the days of work parties that lie before us while waiting to be assigned to our units. We scrounge up some old, faded fatigues and bush hats to replace the shiny new fatigues and caps that give us away as new arrivals. Then, instead of joining the hundreds of new men standing in formation, we hide in and around the nearby barracks to listen to the list of names being read over the loudspeakers. Three times a day the formations are held, and after each one the men not being shipped out are mustered into work parties.

While the rest of the men are doing KP, building bunkers, and burning shit, Allen and I visit the PX, the movies, and the EM clubs. We feel a bit guilty, but we easily console ourselves with the belief that the Army is only fulfilling its mandate to keep the men busy, while we are accomplishing the same task without their aid and without the monotony.

On the sixth day our names are called. Some frowns are cast our way by sergeants who hear us answer the call from well beyond the formation, but no action is brought against us as they are to be rid of us immediately in any case. Allen and I are both assigned to the 1st Division.

We are loaded onto trucks to be transported to Di An (pronounced *Zee On*). We travel north and then east, past hovels the like of which I have not seen since I looked upon the hills above Tijuana. Dirty-floored huts constructed of cardboard, tin, and palm fronds stand in clusters at the edge of the road or lean against the ruins of older, more permanent buildings. The original buildings of hollow brick and plaster have been left in various stages of destruction by the Tet offensive of five months ago, and the battles and skirmishes that had come before. While some of these buildings stand in good repair, most have bullet-riddled walls, and various sections of many have been reduced to rubble.

We pass through the small town of Di An with its starving dogs and gaggle of children playing in the stretch of dirt between the buildings and the road, or hawking anything sellable to GIs who have slowed their vehicles enough to do business. Beyond the town and a field of rubber trees, we come to a wide, freshly graveled road that leads into a vast circle of barren ground. Squatting in the center of this expansive wasteland is the base camp of the 1st Division.

We have spent the last five days doing details while waiting to begin our in-country training, which is scheduled for tomorrow. I have been assigned to Delta Company. Allen is with Alpha. We are living in a four-barracks complex designated for the four field companies in the battalion when they have occasion to stay overnight in Di An. The area is a plane of bare earth interrupted by an outhouse, various bunkers, and the four barracks. The floors of the buildings are concrete, the sides are wood on the bottom half with screens on the upper half. The roof is corrugated metal. When it rains it sounds like we are living on the inside of a snare drum at a rock concert.

In my barracks there are fifteen metal bed frames with springs, four mattresses, three footlockers, and six upright lockers. Fortunately, there are only four of us in residence, so the odd assortment of furniture is more than adequate.

Without preamble, a silent string of men from a combat outfit enter the U-shaped area formed by the four barracks and settle into the dust. The new men stand quietly in the shadows to watch the quarter-mile-long double line of grunts complete the last steps of a long journey. These are the 118 men of Delta Company. They do not look anything like the rear echelon personnel we have met in the base camps. There are no sergeants yelling, no officers preening, no apparent rank or communication of any kind. Unburdening themselves of steel helmets, rifles, canteens, bandoliers, grenade launchers, ammunition boxes, flares, hand grenades, radios, poncho liners, and machine guns, the dirt-streaked men in ragged, sun-faded fatigues sit nearly motionless. The talk is low and infrequent. They seem to be looking at something unseen in the distance.

A half hour later a captain drives up in a jeep towing a trailer full of beer and ice water. Apparently, this is the first beer the company has seen in over a month, but the stampede I expect does not occur.

"Well, come on," the captain urges. "This is supposed to be a bon voyage party. There is enough beer in here to set the whole company on its ass."

The only response is a skeptical "Ha!" from one of the men stirred enough to go and have a look. After he has passed out an armload of beer, one by one others begin to do the same.

I continue to study my future comrades from the barracks' doorway. They do not look at all friendly. I am not even slightly tempted to walk over and say hi. It is hard to comprehend one hundred and eighteen thirsty men who do not seem to care enough to walk thirty feet for a cold beer. I keep looking at them, trying to read something in their faces, but there is only fatigue and that glazed distant look in their eyes.

After three or four beers the assembly begins to move about. Men store equipment in the buildings or stroll to the neighboring compound to use their airplane wing tank shower.

The captain returns from a second jeep trip with three cases of liquor and enough chicken, steak, and beans to feed his army.

With daylight waning, a barbecue is set up in one of the barracks. The first sergeant does the cooking himself, swearing that if an army cook comes within reach of his barbecue he will butcher him and put him on the spit for the second course.

By now the men have loosened up enough for me to feel safe drinking their beer and wandering among them. I learn Delta Company was shipped here as a unit just over a year ago. This party is in honor of the last of that original group.

By the time dinner is finished, the party is well under way. Energy and loud voices have returned to men determined to make the most of this rare opportunity to live and celebrate in safety. Some of the men head for the big EM club to listen to the band that plays on Sunday nights. Those who stay behind sit on the ground in circles of ten to twenty men, passing cigarettes and joints around in a continuous cycle. The idea seems to be to get as drunk and stoned as is humanly possible.

At 0530 the next morning, the ground between the barracks looks like the aftermath of a battle. Bodies are strewn everywhere. Most are still in their circles, sleeping where they once sat. Others have come to rest in the most unlikely, uncomfortable positions possible. One guy lies half in and half out of the barracks' doorway; another lies head down on the stairs leading to a bunker. Several of the men are draped over stacks of sandbags as if they fell asleep halfway to the other side. Only a few men actually made it into one of the barracks, but once inside they seem to have lost direction, collapsing in random heaps on the floor. Excluding the four new recruits, only one man spent the night on the bare springs of the available beds.

By 0600 the company is on its way back to the field with only the fifty-gallon drums full of empty beer cans and dirty paper plates to tell of their passing. Those of us who are new take our hangovers to a small outdoor bleacher that has been set up for the in-country training school. Most of our instructors are recent combat veterans. Their lessons are fresh and vivid. When they talk about dung-covered pungy sticks, booby traps, little kids and old women with hand grenades, and spider holes and tunnels, we listen, trying to glean something that might allow us a better chance of survival.

At the end of the day we are supplied with M-16s for the first time. Now that we are armed, we are charged with the additional duty of guarding the perimeter every night.

Di An is approximately three miles wide by five miles long. It is surrounded by eighteen rows of either barbed wire or the new concertina wire with small razor blades hooked at the ends to snag anything brushing against them. Scattered on and between the wire there are various types of mines and trip flares to warn us of infiltration. Inside the wire is a line of bunkers that encircle the base. These are the bunkers we man for night perimeter guard. We set out five claymore mines and settle back for the night.

I can hear the chatter of small arms fire in the distance. Flares are constantly going off in a 180-degree arc around our sector. The big artillery pieces, one hundred yards to our rear, pound out a few rounds every ten minutes. Every time the big guns fire to send their shells whistling over our heads, the ground, the bunker, and even my shirt shakes with the vibration of the launching. If I could stop being startled by each reverberation, I might be able to enjoy the cool breeze and the clouds drifting across the moon.

In the morning, we again take up the challenge of the mysterious M-16. Outside the wire, at a makeshift range, we

M-110

sight in the rifles we have been given. I remember well the safety switch and the T-handled cocking rod; it is after these steps that the trouble begins. Only two rounds are coaxed from the weapon before the dreaded happens. My M-16 jams (just the way it did in *Time* magazine). I dislodge the spent cartridge that has jammed in the ejection slot. Repeated efforts produce the same results—two rounds and a jam. Tomorrow I go to the field. I will not have another chance to sight in my rifle.

I take my problem to the instructor, who advises me to see my supply sergeant, whom I am unable to find before I am put to work again.

Tonight we are due to return to the range for night firing practice. After dinner, I persuade strangers to show me how to disassemble, clean, and reassemble my faulty rifle. I clean everything, including the ammunition and the magazines.

Back on the range the jamming persists. The instructor excuses me from the mock ambush to follow, not wanting a defenseless man in an area where a mock ambush occasionally becomes the real thing.

The next morning eight of us wait by a truck to be taken out to Delta Company. Everybody is ready to go except me. I try to convince the supply sergeant to give me a different rifle. He tells me to take the weapon I have out to the field to be repaired by the weapons truck that comes by every few weeks. This sounds like a supremely stupid idea to me. The other seven guys are hanging off different parts of the truck listening to the argument, in no hurry to reach their destination. The supply sergeant is a stubborn man, accustomed to his independence. He gets more and more angry at my impudence, but I am determined and press on.

One of the guys waiting for the resolution of this argument is an eight-month veteran of the field, just returning from R and R. He walks up close to me and says, "If you go to the field with a rifle that doesn't work, you've got shit for brains." He points a finger at the sergeant without looking at him and says, "That son of a bitch doesn't give a damn about your life."

The sergeant explodes. With reddening face and quivering beer belly, he launches into a tirade.

My new ally calmly locks and loads his M-16, and slowly brings the rifle and his eyes up to meet the sergeant's. When their eyes meet, the sergeant falls silent. For a moment no one moves, then the sergeant begins to back his way into the supply room.

It is deathly quiet now, but I still do not have a working rifle. Screwing up my courage, I step into the supply room, hoping I am not met by a gun barrel. The sergeant is around the corner, standing very still against the wall. Quietly, I urge him to exchange my rifle. A few steps away there is an M-16 leaning against a counter. He grabs it and thrusts it towards me, yelling for me to get out.

I am not going to have a chance to sight this rifle in, nor assure myself that it works, but I feel a lot better having it just the same.

M-16

DELTA COMPANY

The truck heads west on the only road from the base, then north on Highway 13. We travel over rivers, through villages, past old plantations, rice paddies, and jungle. A half mile short of a small village the truck turns west onto an elevated single-track lane. A hundred yards down the lane, squatting on the edge of a swamp, is Delta Company's NDP.

No flag or pennant flies at the gate; instead, a bamboo pole has been rammed into the vacant cranium of a human skull to stand in that place of honor. The NDP is a 150-foot-square pad elevated a foot above the water that surrounds it on three sides. A three-foot wall of sandbags rings the outer edge of the raised pad. Because of the high water table, the conventional six-foot-deep bunker has been replaced by covered positions built from the ground to the level of the outer wall. Just behind the covered positions fronting the water are four tin huts, their walls and roofs perforated with bullet holes. In the center of this small peninsula of mud are six mortar pits, an ammunition bunker, and the company's water supply held in a small trailer tank and in a dozen or more jerry cans.

We jump from the truck into mud. The four of us who are new to the company are instantly recognized as such. A man dressed in green drawers and unlaced combat boots hurries up to me.

"How you like to carry gun?" he asks in a heavy Spanish accent.

"What?" Who is this guy and what is he talking about?

"Machine gun. How you like to carry machine gun?" Drawers elaborates.

"I wouldn't, thank you. Why?" I may be new, but I already know about the machine gun. I was elected to carry it for two days during in-country combat school. The M-60, with one hundred rounds of ammunition in its assault pack, is heavy and awkward to carry, not to mention that the machine gunner and the radioman are prime targets for the little guys in the bush.

Disappointed, Drawers slogs off through the mud. I am standing there waiting for someone to claim me when another shirtless, rankless, nameless guy comes to ask if I would like to carry the machine gun. I tell him not really, and he too goes away. Within a minute, a third man approaches me. This one looks like he has some authority.

"Welcome to Delta Company. I'm Sergeant Norris. You're the new machine gunner for my platoon. Follow me."

Well, what can I say? I guess I wanted to carry the gun all along. At least I won't need to worry about the unknown qualities of this M-16 anymore. I follow the sergeant into one of the huts. Indicating the M-60, he asks, "Do you know how to clean one of these?"

M-60

"I'm afraid not, Sergeant," I say, knowing what he really means is can I take apart every piece that can be taken apart, clean it, and put it back together without the slightest doubt that it will function perfectly.

"Hey, Gomez. Fill our new man here in on the 60," says Norris before turning his attention to me. "That gun is to be cleaned every morning and evening. You are to know where it is at all times and never be more than five seconds away from it." His orders are emphatic; no room is left for doubt or variation.

Gomez saunters over with a look of guilty relief. He was the first man to offer me the gun while I stood at the back of the truck. It is from his shoulders the weight of the M-60 is lifted. With well-practiced movements he breaks the gun down, then stands aside while I put it back together. Before leaving me with his burden he puts a hand on my shoulder, saying, "You big man, you carry gun no problem."

The rest of the day is spent passing time. Since it is the monsoon season it rains hard·at least once a day, usually about 1500. Some of the guys take advantage of the downpour by soaping up and letting the cool rain rinse them clean. Letter writing is quite popular, and books are big if you can find one not already in use. There are card games, too, but in the eighty to ninety percent humidity a deck of cards does not last long. A half hour after starting a game, a new deck is so swollen you cannot get all the cards back in the package. The majority of the platoon passes the day in languid conversations, resting from yesterday's patrol and last night's ambush.

As the sun sets over the swamp, boredom is replaced by irritation. Hordes of mosquitoes rise from the swamp to feast on the bounty of their neighbors. There is no protection and no escape. The blood-crazed vampiress bites through the light jungle fatigues wherever the cloth is flattened against the skin; she buzzes persistently an inch from faces and arms waiting for a droplet of sweat to clear a path through the repellent, then to softly alight, regurgitate anticoagulent, and plunge her snout in to gorge on government-issue blood.

Placing my new air mattress just outside a bunker, I lie down to sleep. Within seconds I am covered with a thin layer of mosquitoes. The bites come at average intervals of one every five seconds. Dressed in shirt, pants, and boots I am already sticky with sweat, but in desperate hope of escaping the bugs, I cover myself with a poncho liner. Within minutes my clothes are soaked with sweat and the damned mosquitoes are still at me, buzzing hysterically inside my ears, finding access through the folds and wrinkles of my cocoon.

I persist for an hour before jumping up in a fit of irritation. I can't stand it anymore. Pacing to cool my sweat in the hot night air, I run into two other new men suffering from the same plight. Together we lean against a bunker and talk away the night. I will need to be far more desperate for rest before I can sleep while being the main course of a blood feast.

By 0800 the men who have spent the night on ambush return to the NDP. I take the opportunity to watch the machine gunner. A black about my size comes down the dike with his gun balanced across one shoulder, holding onto an extended bipod leg to steady the load. As he strips off his gear, I go to talk to him. I am about to ask him if the towel he uses for padding is necessary when he takes off his sweat-soaked shirt to reveal a large pink patch on each shoulder where the top layers of pigmented skin have been worn away. The center of each patch is scarred and bloody. He tells me that when he first carried the gun he didn't use a towel and that is why his shoulders are such a mess. Once a scab forms, he says, it won't heal. The skin stays so moist that the scab won't harden; it remains soft, to be wiped away the first time something brushes against it.

Coming back from a successful search for a towel, I find the platoon digging through three cases of C rations. When I ask what is going on, I am told to grab two meals, we are going out in fifteen minutes.

With my weapon in one hand, my poncho liner in the other, and two boxes of rations at my feet, I stand at the edge of the activity wondering what to do next. I notice men tying their cans of food in a sock, so I get one of the green wool socks and do the same. My squad leader, Sandy, hands me some web gear with two canteens on the belt. He returns a minute later with some hand grenades, flares, and a claymore mine. I am still figuring how to attach all this stuff to my person when I look up to see the rest of the platoon standing in two lines and making their last adjustments. Someone drops a set of shoelaces onto my pile of gear. Taking the hint I roll the food sock in my poncho liner and tie the roll to the back of the web gear. I am down to stuffing grenades into my ammo pouches by the time Norris appears to lead the platoon out of the NDP.

The patrol moves through the countryside on a zigzag course to obscure our intended line of travel and to reduce the probability of ambush. We proceed in a single file with a thirty-foot space between men so a mortar round or burst of small arms fire will hit as few of us as possible. The land in this area is flat and wet. Our feet are in water as often as they are on solid land. The terrain varies from paddies, to forest, to fields of fruit trees, to bamboo thickets, to cane fields, to wet grassland with scattered trees, and back to forest again.

At 1400 a halt is called in a grove of small date palms. Two-man observation posts are set up front and rear. The remainder of the men spread out under the palms. As I lie down to rest, I wonder about the shortage of men in this platoon. I think all the platoons in the company are about the same size, and they are all short of men. A standard stateside platoon consists of fifty men. We have twenty-five men, none of whom, except for Norris, have been in the field for more than five months. And where the hell are all our sergeants and our officer? We have one sergeant and two recently promoted corporals. What happened to . . . Ouch! Now what's eating me?

Reaching under my shirt I pull out a red ant, and then another. A quick survey of the ground brings me to my feet in a hurry. This place is alive with ants. After shaking out my shirt and pants I join the other men walking around in a stoop and looking for a piece of ground less populated. The dates must provide a powerful attraction, for the entire orchard is an ant mecca.

Following the example of my more experienced companions, I perch my behind on my helmet. With stick in hand I flick ants from my boots. The more I flick, the more determined they are to gain my pant leg. I soon find it necessary to arm myself with a second stick. The determined onslaught of my multilegged attackers steadily increases until the battle of the boot tops has escalated to a fevered pitch. The dead and wounded pile up around me. I am barely holding my own, with only the occasional breach into the pant line, when a sting to the rear alerts me to a flanking movement up my helmet. The situation is desperate. Geneva, avert your eyes— this calls for chemical warfare. I squirt a line of insect repellent around the bottom of my helmet and the soles of my boots. The red army staggers back, aghast. Foul! Foul! they cry. I have them at bay. They swarm to the edge of the line, but they will not cross—not yet, at least.

An explosion of small arms fire comes from our front. The ants forgotten, we sprawl on the ground, grabbing for weapons. Two rifles of different sounds have gone off simultaneously. The one I recognize as an M-16 fires again. It comes from the forward observation post. Sergeant Norris motions me forward to a position where I can lay down covering fire if needed. He turns to the nearest man with an M-16. "Follow me. Stay well behind me, but keep me in sight at all times."

Five minutes pass. I roll on my side to unbutton my shirt so I can deal with the mass of ants I have infuriated by squishing their bodies beneath me. The man next to me and I sweep the angry, biting buggers from each other's skin.

A half hour passes before Sergeant Norris and his rear guard return with an explanation of what happened. A lone VC came within thirty feet of the observation post before one of our men and the VC simultaneously spotted each other. They were both so startled that for a second they just stared at each other, then they both swung their rifles around and fired a burst while diving for cover. Both sides missed. Norris and his man pursued the lone guerrilla into the jungle, but could find no trace of him.

Charlie will soon be telling his buddies where we are, so we leave the date palms to the ants and move into the trees. For hours we wander through the jungle, avoiding open places, looking, and watching.

Shortly before the end of daylight, we move into a grove of bamboo where we are motioned to a halt. Men break out their ration cans; it must be dinnertime.

With the last of the light we move again. The darkness that comes so swiftly to the tropics requires us to reduce the intervals between men to ten foot for the last five minutes before we stop again. We crouch in silence for fifteen minutes before the line moves on. Just inside a tree line, at the edge of an open field, Norris touches each man in line, pointing to the spot where he is to lie. The spacing of each man is such that we can reach out and touch our neighbor to eliminate the need to whisper.

Five boxes of machine-gun ammunition are quietly placed at my side. I open the cans and link the belts together, giving me a total of eleven hundred rounds ready to be fed into the gun. I then crawl thirty-five feet into the grass to set up my claymore.

The front of the mine is slightly convex so I can tell which way to point it in the dark. I unfold the four little legs on the bottom of its plastic case and stick them into the ground. Next the blasting caps are inserted into their slots and held in place with a plastic nut—this part makes me nervous. I am afraid something is going to set off the blasting caps, which will ignite the plastique explosive, and blow all those ball bearings and the plastic casing in my face. Feeding out the wire attached to a little generator that fits into the palm of my hand, I low crawl back to my position.

Now, the way I understand what we're doing is that we're to lie here as silent and still as death so that we can ambush Charlie instead of letting him know where we are so he can ambush us. That seems simple enough. Oh, shit! Here come the mosquitoes. It's a good thing I only used a fourth of my repellent on the ants. I liberally douse my face, neck, and hands with the potent oil and lie back to gauge the results of my efforts.

Except for one small problem, it is working perfectly. I am not getting a single bite on my face and hands; the problem is that the rest of my body is getting eaten alive. The mosquitoes fly through the openings in the front of my shirt, they fly between the buttons of my fly, they bite through the hair on my head. Those that do not wish to risk the dangers of flying inside my shirt and pants content themselves with the more laborious task of biting through the material. This isn't fair. I can't even slap back—the noise, you know. I lie in torment, running my hands over my body, quietly squishing mosquitoes by the tens, the hundreds, the thousands. They're slowly driving me crazy. My body itches in every part, in every inch of every part. I'm a piece of fresh meat being fed to the critters of the jungle.

I dab more repellent on my skin at the entry points of my shirt: the sleeves, the neck, the front. Maybe it helps a little. My God, when will this night be over? I don't believe these people can actually sleep through this. I thought I was reasonably tough. Whatever other men can endure I can endure right along with the best of them—but I can't take this. I'm turning into one solid bump.

I wrap myself up in the light nylon blanket they call a poncho liner. The night air is still over eighty degrees, the humidity close to 100 percent. I would rather have my blood boil than have it all sucked up and flown away.

After half an hour in my cocoon I lie in a pool of my own sweat. This is insane. Tomorrow I'm telling the captain I quit. I don't care what he does to me, nothing can be worse than this. Court-martial me. Throw me in prison. I don't care, as long as there aren't mosquitoes where they send me. I swear to God, my body is humming on its own—the same damn frequency as those damn mosquitoes. Jesus!

I jump a foot at someone's touch.

"Take it easy, man," comes a low whisper. "What's the matter with you?"

"These fucking mosquitoes are driving me nuts."

"Shh. You have repellent?"

"Yes."

"Put more of it on. It's three o'clock. Your watch."

Outside the poncho liner the night feels cool. I can see a light mist in the moonlight. It is cooler. The wrapping of tension loosens. If the twenty-four other guys here can take this, then surely I can, too. What did that guy say? Put more of it on? I've been putting more of it on. I'll put more on the more.

I spend the next hour spreading repellent. I put it on the mosquitoe bites, rub it into my hair, soak it into my clothes. Wherever there is a breach in my antibug armor, I add repellent. It makes the bites feel better, and the new ones are produced at a slower rate. Put more on my shirt. Put it all over my shirt. Rub more· in my hair. It's working. It's a revelation. It's the greatest discovery since sex.

The bottle is empty.

I hope somebody's been watching for Charlie.

The gray of first light seeps through the low mist blanketing the stretch of grassland before us. The air is so cool that the sweat no longer flows. The clouds of mosquitoes have settled down to rest from their night of frantic labor, leaving a scattering of nonconformists still intent on securing that one blood meal that will allow their propagation. It is far too still and peaceful for violence. We retrieve our claymores and saddle up.

Ten minutes after the rays of the sun reach our column, perspiration returns to soften our skin and trickle down our rib cages. We take a straight-line path back to the NDP. With the zigs and zags eliminated it takes us a mere two hours to return to our home at the swamp's edge.

The smell of frying food greets us as soon as we cross the outer wall. No can of heated C rations ever gave off a smell like this. Something strange is afoot. Inside our platoon hut we discover four cooks preparing breakfast on a field stove. We are told that only men coming in from ambush are entitled to a hot breakfast. The other half of the company must get its ham and eggs out of a can, as usual.

Our special treat consists of powdered eggs, oatmeal mush with sour milk, sausage of unidentified animal, toast with rancid butter, and clotted chocolate milk. I take an exploratory bite from each foul food group before carefully placing the lot of it in the garbage. I have never been one to complain overmuch about army chow, but this is an insult.

I give myself a shave with a helmetful of cold water and a bar of soap. There must be a better way. I finish by pouring the water over my head and calling it a shower. There aren't any clean clothes. What's the point of getting carried away?

In the shade of the hut, I break down the machine gun. Men stop by to watch a moment, or to merely nod their heads in passing. When I am done, those who did not drop by earlier ask if I have cleaned the gun. It seems to be an obsession. I think every man in the platoon has personally paused here to assure himself that the gun has been properly cleaned. It appears I will be changing my daily greeting from "Good morning" to "Yes, I have."

The weapons truck pulls into the compound at midday. Since I have been issued a .45 pistol that does not fire, I ask one of the gunsmiths to look at it. He determines that the firing pin is broken, a problem he claims he is unable to resolve with the tools in the truck. He will need to take the pistol back to the armory in Di An for repair.

One of the guys from my platoon who has been listening to the conversation from his seat against a wall of sandbags says, "You give that guy your weapon, you'll never see it again."

"He's giving it to you straight," says another guy who comes over to lean on the side of the two-and-half-ton truck. "These dudes have a little business going on the side. That .45 will be cash in their pockets before the week is out."

He talks loud enough so the three men inside the truck will be sure to hear. He stands glaring up at the faces in the

Colt .45 Automatic

dark interior, daring them to challenge him. But the gunsmiths return to their work without a word.

"What you say may be true enough, but what is the good
of my hanging onto a .45 that doesn't work?"

He shrugged as if to say it's up to you, and walked away.

I ask the gunsmith if I can trade my pistol for one in working order, or if he can bring a firing pin with him the next time he comes. He assures me that the only way I can possess an operable .45 is to turn the one I have over to him and wait for its repair. An answer like this makes me very suspicious, but I am tired of hauling a heavy .45 that is no more use to me than a rock. I sign the necessary paper and give him the pistol and holster, reasonably sure I will not be troubled with its return.

A light evening rain begins to fall as the winged hordes gather strength for their nightly assault. Since we are not allowed to sleep in the huts, I crawl into the damp darkness of my bunker. This rectangle—six and one half feet in length, three and one half feet wide, and three feet high—offers some protection from rain, but not from wetness. Water trickles between the sandbags to drip upon the floor made from the wood of old ammo crates. Having slept only one hour in the past two nights, I am eagerly looking forward to crawling onto my new air mattress to float the night away on the incoming waters. Groping in the blackness I find only wet boards where my air mattress should have been. More groping reveals the absence of my boots and shirt as well.

I can almost understand someone taking a new guy's air mattress. Air mattresses are doomed to a short life in the field, anyway. A week or two at the most will pass before they develop a leak. When they go flat, that is the end of a somewhat decadent comfort, for there is no replacement issued.

Foolishly, I did not write my name on my mattress so I could identify it in a thief's collection of goods. But I will find the son of a bitch who stole my boots and shirt. Those thefts are the acts of a low and stupid man. Who would steal from the men who directly help preserve your life?

I cover my bare upper body with repellent, wrap myself in the poncho liner, and lie down on the wet boards. The mosquitoes are almost as bad as usual, but the rain is refreshing and cool, and the crickets and frogs are singing a lullaby to the beating of the rain that is hypnotic and vaguely reassuring.

After a good night's sleep my vengeful spirit has mellowed. I squish through the mud hoping my vanished belongings will miraculously reappear. But there are no pleasant surprises this morning, unless the departure of the cooks can be taken as a good sign. After the rubbery water buffalo they served for supper, it was prudent of them to take themselves back to Di An where they can feed their rotting goods to the garbage dump instead of us.

In the middle of a can of breakfast, Sergeant Norris asks, "Have you cleaned the gun today?"

"Yes I have, Sergeant."

"Good. Get your stuff together. We're moving out at 0900."

Okay, no more misguided hoping for divine deliverance. I'm not going out in the bush without my boots and shirt. I ask the members of my squad if they've seen anything of my missing equipment. I don't believe any of them are guilty, but they may be able to point me in the right direction. Their response is to say, "Ask Jesse," and to walk away as though they don't know anything about it, and don't want to know anything about it, but if something's missing Jesse is likely to have it. Jesse's bunker is pointed out as the one across the NDP entrance from the skull pendant, the one with the three black guys lounging around the inside of a small ring of sandbags shaded by two ponchos.

"Is one of you guys Jesse?" I ask, noticing that they look stoned. Nothing like getting a different perspective on your morning.

"Who the fuck wants to know?"

"I do. I can't very well go on patrol without my boots, now, can I?"

"Hey, gray meat, why you come snooping 'round here for your boots? You accusin' us of being thieves? You call me a thief, I'll cut your guts out."

While he talks I look over the gear inside their circle. Boots never get polished in the field, so a new pair stands out like a crow among gulls. There's a new pair placed against the inside wall, not three feet away. They look like size twelves. I figure Jesse and his boys aren't angry enough yet to penetrate their morning mellow. Despite their rough talk, none of them are even sitting up straight. I reach into their shade, grab the boots with my right hand and liberate one of the shirts on the sandbags as I straighten up. "Nice talking to you, gents," I say, backing up.

For a moment, it looks like they are going to come after me, but a "Hey, mother fucker," and a forward lean by the guy who was doing the talking is as far as things go.

By pure chance the shirt I snatched is my own. As I slip on my jungle boots the platoon is assembling its gear. Ammunition clips are checked, hand grenade releases taped down, canteens filled, pack straps and belts checked for wear, flares passed out, strobe lights and machine-gun ammo assigned, claymore mines counted, first aid kits checked, mosquito repellent obtained (better take two), two meals' worth of cans tied up in socks, poncho liners rolled up, P-38 can openers dropped into shirt pockets, weapons checked, cleaning equipment, helmets, helmet liners, and camouflage covers secured, and we are ready.

One hundred six men walk out of the NDP, leaving behind the mortar section to guard the home base. The company moves in double file, the men spaced thirty feet apart. Point, flank, and rear guards are sent out as soon as we clear the local swamp. We spend most of the first two hours slogging through rice paddies and bogs. We could walk on the dikes that enclose each paddy like the villagers do, but if the VC hear we are using the dikes it will not be long until these natural walkways are mined. Sloshing through the paddies makes progress more difficult, but it also makes booby trapping impractical.

An average rice paddy consists of one foot of soft mud covered by one foot of water. Walking through a paddy is a lot like wading through water with a thirty-pound weight attached to each leg. After two hours I am carrying on a silent conversation with my feet.

"All right, left foot, big pull now. Good. Okay, right foot, here we go."

"Oh, no you don't," says the patch of particularly obstinate mud, nearly sucking my boot off before pulling my foot back to the bottom.

"Oh, yes I do," says I, giving my leg a mighty jerk forward. The boot is raised almost to the top of the mud before losing momentum and being sucked back to its starting point. Once started in a backward direction I am unable to extradite my left foot in time to catch my balance. I land on my ass with a splash. I am up to my armpits in brown water, but my landing site is comfortable and I have managed to keep the gun out of the muck. Someone grabbing my web gear from behind says, "What is this? Taking an unauthorized break, are we?" The captain smiles down at me, pleased with his wit.

"A break? Oh, no, sir. This here's your basic recreational swim, sir," I say, doing the side stroke with my free hand.

He chuckles and helps me to my feet.

A little further on we climb from the paddies onto higher ground. The land here is covered with knee-high grass and trees of every description. There is still plenty of water, but it is confined to a system of grass-choked ditches. Jumping over these ditches with the machine gun on my shoulder presents a problem. Since I weigh more than the gun, I land first, with the weight of the gun crashing down on my shoulder a second later. I soon find that on small jumps I can hold the gun in both hands over my shoulder, using my arms as shock absorbers. On longer jumps I swing the gun by the fold-up handle on top of the barrel; when it begins its forward arc I jump with its momentum. The first time I attempted to leap a ditch with the gun still hanging at my side, my body was well on its way to clearing the ditch when I was pulled back by the lagging gun to land sideways in the water.

With eighteen men walking before me I am not too worried about stepping on a booby trap. But then I do not really know what to worry about. I look at the thick stands of trees, the high bushes and the low, and the long grass. Hundreds of people could be hiding on each side of us, waiting, watching. I look at the faces of the other men. Are they checking the bush for something out of place, a glint of steel, an unnatural shape? The faces I see concentrate on the ground before them, the bush they are about to walk through, and the man in front of them. Their faces are wet, tired, and blank. Maybe they feel if the flankers and point men walk the company into an ambush there is nothing they can do until it happens. Or maybe they are more concerned about where they are putting their feet than they are about looking for something they cannot see.

We come to a ditch running full with water that is too wide to jump. Some of the men wade in, while others search downstream for a crossing. A hundred feet down the bank a log of small diameter bridges the ditch. The first man to attempt the crossing loses his balance halfway across and falls full length into the stream. His fall wets the log, makes it more slippery for those who follow.

The log crossing becomes a challenge only a few can master. The discipline of silence is repeatedly broken with small cries of alarm as men tumble into the water, then thrash and curse their way out. I opt for the direct water route. When I reach one side of what seems to be the center of the stream, I jump over what I hope is the deepest section and climb the far bank, getting wet only shirt-pocket high.

The captain, walking three men behind me, takes one look at the fiasco downstream before asking, "How deep is the stream here?"

Holding my arm over the high water mark at the top of my shirt pockets, I reply, "Chest deep, sir."

The captain, just under six feet, is four inches shorter than I, and if he doesn't jump the center section I will get the chance to see if his helmet floats. The captain is waist deep when he catches a faint smile on my face.

"What are you smiling about?" he asks with suspicion on the rise.

"Nothing, sir," I say, trying to get that troublesome smile off my face.

When the water reaches his chest he stops again. "How deep did you say this is?"

"I didn't get wet above the chest, as you can see."

He studies my grin for a moment, then moves forward. He slides to a stop when the water laps at his chin. "Whose chest is this stream chest high on?"

"Why mine, of course. And don't forget to jump over the deep section."

With a laugh he disappears from view, to come bobbing up a few feet away still laughing. As I give him a hand up the bank, I admit to myself that I am impressed. I never met an officer with a sense of humor.

A few hundred meters further, we enter a large grassy area surrounded by trees. A shot rings out from our right flank. The company is on its belly before the second bullet leaves the sniper's rifle. He is in the trees, two hundred meters out. There is no chance of spotting him. No one speaks. No one returns fire. We wait two minutes—no more—then we are on our way again.

I turn to the man behind me. "Why didn't anyone fire back?"

"It's an old VC trick. There's a friendly village just beyond that tree line, directly behind the area where the shots came from," he explains.

We go on without further harassment.

An hour later we come to the ruins of an old French

plantation. The buildings are burned and bullet riddled, but the fields and paddies are still worked. A grassy lane, bordered on each side by a row of majestic palms, leads to the main house. In the shadow of three coconut trees growing at the edge of what was once a yard, the captain calls a halt for lunch.

Sitting in the shade of the veranda, I open a can of beans and franks, and wonder about the Frenchman who once lived in this grand setting. What history of terror has reduced this place to a charred shell with killers on the front porch eating beans?

It is not a fancy house built to impress; it is a practical house made to last. It has foot-thick masonry walls that stay cool through the heat of the day. Its wooden roof is gone, burned years ago, and the locals probably scavenged what good timber remained, along with the screens that covered the windows and enclosed the veranda. Both the outer- and inner-wall surfaces are heavily pockmarked with bullet holes. No doubt this house was used many times as a refuge. I wonder what draws soldiers to this place when they know they would be safer concealed in the jungle. Maybe it is the feeling of permanence and security in the heavy old walls that makes a man without a home take shelter in such a conspicuous place, or maybe it is just a shady place free of ants.

But the value here is not in this old house, it is in the surrounding land. Here is a land that abounds in the richness of nature, a place where a family could live and grow contentedly—if the wars would stop, if the humidity didn't rot your body, if the jungle didn't kill your children.

The men are beginning to collect their gear. It is time to move on. In and out of the tropical forest and rice paddies, up to our knees in water and sticky mud, always on a zigzag course to confuse the watchers.

Four hours later we come to a small river spanned by the remains of a wooden bridge. The signal to take a break passes down the line. Tired men sink to the ground with a moan of relief.

From where I sit, I can see Sergeant Norris checking the underside of the bridge for booby traps. It is evident by the damage to the bridge that this crossing has been the scene of several previous engagements. The timbers are splintered and shattered. All signs of the guardrail vanished long ago. So many holes have been blown through the four-inch-thick planks of the road surface that the only section now capable of supporting a man's weight is over the main beam on the right side of the bridge.

When Norris finishes checking the lower portion of the bridge, he starts searching the roadway for trip wires. At the center of the bridge he turns and signals us to follow. Reluctantly, we resume our patrol, crossing the bridge to a low, open, marshy land beyond. When the platoon is well into the marsh, I look back toward the bridge. No one follows. It looks like the rest of the company is staying behind.

A kilometer beyond the first river we come to a second, smaller river. I wade into the warm, sluggish water, my feet sinking deep into the mud bottom. When the water reaches my chin, I resort to a one-armed paddle walk to reach the other side. Those men whose mouths nature placed closer to the ground must swim, but swimming fully clothed with your arms raised in the air to keep your weapon dry, weighed down with all your gear and wet clothes, is a struggle for even the most confident swimmers. Those men unlearned in swimming thrash across as best they can with the help of extended arms and rifle barrels. Most of the men cross the deepest section using the hippopotamus method. They take a big breath and walk across the bottom, careful not to get a foot stuck in the mud.

Reaching the crest of the steep, slippery riverbank, I am met by the sight of nine GIs with their pants around their ankles and their bare asses in the air. I walk to the nearest man with his pants on and inquire, "What is this, a group BA?"

"Leeches," he says with no trace of amusement. "Best pick them off quick before they get too well attached."

"Leeches!" I echo, my pants falling to my knees. Sure enough, leeches. With growing revulsion, I pick a half dozen of the fat, black, slimy suckers off my legs. There is something unreasonably repulsive about these sluglike parasites secretly stealing my blood. The NVA, the VC, our own government, the mosquitoes, and now leeches—our blood seems to be a popular commodity.

After being assured by a rear observer that I am leech free, I rebutton my pants and begin slogging through the expanse of rice paddies ahead. I wonder what the rest of the company's doing? Probably sitting on their butts. Sure wish I was there helping them. I'm tired. Why is our platoon wandering out here by itself, anyway? I never know what's going on. I feel like the donkey loaded up every morning to be led around all day, never stopping where the grass is tender or the water cool or doing anything else that makes any sense.

Climbing from the last paddy, Norris walks a hundred meters into the bush and sits down to open a can of C rations. It must be dinnertime. I sit my weary body down to a succulent dinner of lima beans and ham, heated by the sun to exactly 91 degrees, with a side dish of peanut butter and jelly on crackers. As I eat I watch storm clouds gather overhead and resolve to avoid canned lima beans in the future.

The day darkens before its time. The rain will be coming soon to wash the sweat from my body and flood the land. The platoon starts back the way it came. You can hear the rainstorm approaching from the southeast, its front edge sweeping through the forest, rattling down on millions of leaves, creating a roar of steadily increasing volume. Before we reach the bank of the smaller river, big isolated drops begin to fall. I can see the wall of rain moving toward me over the open ground. Men hunch their shoulders in anticipation. Suddenly, the front is before me. My next step takes me into the full force of the storm. Visibility decreases to forty feet. I didn't know it could rain this hard.

Having rejoined the company on the east side of the bridge, our platoon is dispersed along the edge of a single rice paddy that has been carved out of the forest. I sit at the base of a palm tree, leaning my back against its slightly inward leaning trunk, seeking the slight protection it offers against the rain. My poncho liner is still partially dry, so I put my steel helmet on my lap and stuff the poncho liner inside to preserve the only piece of dryness within miles. I have taken care to keep it dry through the rivers and ditches and rainstorm. I know it does not make any sense; as soon as I wrap myself in it to lie upon the wet ground it will be as soaked as if I had dunked it in the first ditch this morning. But keeping it dry is something to do, something to focus on, a small accomplishment that gives my mind a touch of peace.

Now that I am motionless and soaking wet I begin to feel the cold. My poncho liner would keep me warm, but this would mean giving up and I cannot bring myself to do that. Besides, I am so often hot and so seldom cold that shivering feels good. I concentrate on the rain falling in the paddy before me. A raindrop impacting with the water's surface makes an impression the diameter of a nickel. The rain keeps every inch of the water's surface dancing, sending its own water in small leaps back into the air. I watch the rain striking the paddy water a long time before I realize I can actually see the water level rising. A green snake swims by with its head raised two inches out of the water, gazing about, but not seeming to notice the soldiers a few feet away, motionless in the rain.

The vast quantity of water falling between myself and my nearest neighbor twenty feet away renders his outline fuzzy, his image vague. Just when I am convinced that this is a world-record rainstorm, it begins to rain harder. The downpour is impressive, but this is not merely a one-act show. As the last of the evening's gray light fades to black, multiple streaks of lightning slash through the sky, six bolts hitting the earth simultaneously, momentarily flashing brilliant light through the darkness. The shattering explosions of thunder are not like the explosions of man; still, the similarity in flashing light and sound is near enough to set nerves on edge.

As the company moves to its ambush site, I notice during a lightning flash that the water in the paddy is a foot higher than it was when we first arrived. The ground is under two inches of water or more.

The company deploys in a tight line adjacent to the path leading to the bridge. After putting out my claymore and setting up the machine gun, I kneel in the water that is my designated place to rest and consider the situation. I have succeeded in bringing a dry bedroll to my place of sleep—now what? I could fold it up and use it as a thin submerged mattress—it is unfortunate that air mattresses are not allowed on ambush, I could float all the way to the South China Sea on a night like this. I could carefully place it on top of me and keep it from getting completely soaked for another two or three minutes in the now easing rain.

While I contemplate this weighty problem, the local coalition of mosquitoes finally zeros in on our scent. Their tardiness is no doubt due to the wind and rain masking our odor. One of these raindrops weighs several times more than a mosquito. I had held some faint hope that the little bastards would stay home instead of risking the heavy bombardment. But no. Rain does not seem to hamper mosquitoes in the slightest. To make matters worse, all this rain is washing away the repellent I had soaked into my clothing. Without further consideration, I wrap myself from head to foot in my poncho liner and sink into my watery bed.

In the morning my body looks like it has aged a hundred years. I have seen my hands wrinkled from being submerged in water for an hour, but that experience was a poor representation of what more than eight hours of submersion will do to the skin. I am a prune. My wrinkles have grown wrinkles.

Cold and stiff from my night in the water, I am eager to begin the long march back to the NDP so I can stretch the muscles and warm the body that is already anticipating the food at the end of the trail. We are packed up and waiting for the order of march to be given when an order to wait arrives instead. Ten minutes later our thoughts of food and rest are swept aside. Battalion HQ has decided to extend our patrol. It looks as if we are going to go hungry awhile.

The rain has stopped but the sky is still thick with clouds that allow the coolness of morning to linger past its time. Just beyond a small, carefully tended banana orchard, we enter a fog bank caught in a bamboo thicket. The men before me disappear into a nether world of eerie white clouds that lazily whirl with their passage. I emerge from the fog-enshrouded bamboo at the edge of a series of neat, rectangular rice fields. Across the paddies, a small village perches on wooden posts above a finger of land that extends into the surrounding wetlands. A dozen huts thatched with palm fronds cast their reflection on the water's mirrored surface. A thin mist rises to ghost across the paddies and eddy at my feet before congregating in the wall of bamboo behind me. Villagers in conical hats and rolled-up pants stoop to the water in their early morning labor. The sun sends thin beams of light streaming through the clouds to streak the mist with luminous rays, as if to set the scene for a divine visitation.

The picturesque village before me contrasts so sharply with the line of armed men slogging through the mud and water that I know it will be one of those rare sights that will stay imprinted on my mind forever.

A halt is called as I reach the approximate center of the series of paddies. It is a strange place to call a halt, with half the company knee deep in water. The point element must have run into something in need of investigation.

Being near a dike, I climb the bank to sit on a small mound of soft dirt. I make a beautiful target of myself up here, but violence seems distant from this place, and I'm already too tired to care about vague dangers—of course, if I get shot . . . oh, the hell with it.

A small boy comes down the dike to ask for chop chop, but I have none to give him. He is almost as disappointed at my lack of chop chop as I am. He makes his appeal to several other men and is finally rewarded with a single can. He takes his prize to one of the huts where I swear I hear the sound of one tin can clinking against others.

After a ten-minute rest we move on. Leaving my comfortable seat, I am vaguely aware of some sharp stinging bites, but I am always getting bitten so I pay them little mind. By the time I reach the next paddy whatever is biting me has gained my attention. The more I move the more I am bitten until the sharp stings feel like a fire moving across my back, chest, and hips. I rip open my shirt with my free hand. My upper body is crawling with red ants. Splashing through the water to the nearest dike, I drop the machine gun on dry ground, tear off my shirt, and flop full length into the water.

After considerable splashing around and brushing off, and some strange looks from passing men, I return to the soft hammock I had so comfortably rested upon. Just as I feared: my posterior had been squarely placed atop the home of several hundred furious fire ants.

I hurry through the paddies to resume my place in line, stopping occasionally to submerge my body in water to cool the burning bites. Within fifteen minutes a rash has broken out under my arms and around my waist. When I check a few minutes later, the rash has spread over most of my chest and is beginning to move down my arms. A burning itchy sensation crawls across me from my knees to my neck. Only repeated scrutiny of my clothes assures me that I am not still being bitten by a horde of fire ants.

As noon comes and goes, other small mishaps occur. Four spaces up the line a guy falls off a log while crossing a stream, ripping the crotch out of his pants on the stubs of a broken branch. The rip exposes the man's right buttock and genitals to general view. He hitches the remains of his pants so they are reasonably comfortable and he continues unconcerned until we reach the next village. The women of the village seem to think our risqué man is the best show they have seen for many a week. Pointing and hooting and whistling, they yell, "You boo coo number one GI," and giggle behind their hands.

Because Caucasian males are more generously endowed than their Vietnamese counterparts, the women react more to the size of the exposure than to the exposure itself. They carry on just like a bunch of beer-swilling loggers at a strip joint, hooting it up over a big-breasted blonde.

Meanwhile, Vareck (a strong, very bright guy who joined the company the same day I did) is learning about the hazardous side effects of mosquito repellent. Sometime during the day the screw cap on the repellent bottle he was foolishly carrying in his front pants pocket worked loose, spreading its contents drip by drip across the front of his pants. A drop of repellent not spread out on the skin will begin to dissolve the skin just the way it will dissolve plastic. By midafternoon Vareck is in agony. His walk becomes more and more straddle legged as his groin becomes more and more tender, and finally begins to bleed.

Late in the afternoon word is passed down the line that we are approaching Bravo Company's NDP. A few minutes later we enter a clearing covered with short grass. In the center of the clearing are the typical rows of concertina wire, bunkers, trenches, and sandbags of a defensive position. A few of our men have friends here and quickly disappear under poncho awnings or into bunkers. The rest of us, being greeted with blank indifference, settle on an unused patch of ground close to the wire.

Hungry and tired, Delta Company slowly inspects itself for damage. Several men have blood-filled leeches clinging to their legs, a dozen more have a swollen rash that is apparently the consequence of spending the night in the water. I take off my shirt to examine the result of my encounter with the ants. My upper body has expanded by an inch. My left arm and the little finger side of my left hand are as swollen as my chest. My right hand is puffed up so tight I can hardly wiggle the fingers.

I locate a medic in the hope of getting an antihistamine. The medic takes a glance in my direction and diagnoses swelling due to sleeping in water. It will go away in time, he assures me, and returns to wrapping gauze around Vareck's bloody prick. Oh, well, he doesn't have any antihistamine anyway.

I remove my boots to look at the fish-belly white, convoluted wrinkle that are my feet after being wet for thirty-two consecutive hours. Then, following the example of the other men, I remove the rest of my clothes and lay them beside me on the grass so that we both may dry in the newly arrived sunshine.

My skin is well on its way from soggy to clammy when a helicopter comes roaring over the trees to hover fifty feet above us. The downdraft from the rotor blades sends pants sailing over bunkers to roll across the ground until they find a pool of mud in which to anchor themselves. Shirts are snatched from the grass and hurled into the air, fluttering down at last to snag in the concertina wire, three rows out, between a mine and a trip flare. When the last sock is swept from the reach of the scrambling company of naked men, the pilot maneuvers his craft through a short circuit of the NDP, leaving flattened awnings and ripped ponchos in his wake. His tour complete, he touches down on the landing pad two hundred feet from his starting position above our heads.

In a ten-second flurry of activity, bags and boxes are heaved and kicked out the side door before the chopper lifts off again in a hail of flying grass and dirt and pebbles. One hundred six naked armed men watch as the straining engine angles the Huey steeply upward into the freedom of the sky.

We continue to watch until our view of the chopper is blocked by the surrounding trees, then turn our attention to the ejected baggage. There are cases of rations and bundles of clean clothes. We tear into the cases of food as if afraid someone will try to take them away. I grab a meal and move a comfortable distance away from the mob gathered around the new supplies. Scared and dirt-streaked bodies snatch food and clothes, arguing over the choice meals. Life is getting very basic.

In my haste I have taken a can of scrambled eggs. I strongly suspect these eggs are powdered before they are reconstituted and canned. The results of technology's encounter with the egg is thoroughly revolting. It is only because I am starving from not having eaten for the past twenty-four hours that I am able to hustle these high tec eggs past my taste buds and control my stomach's efforts to purge itself of the experience. I upend the meal packet to see what else is on the menu: caraway cheese, crackers, and a can of fruit cocktail. That's better.

Having satisfied my hunger, I select a shirt and a pair of

pants from the scattered collection. Clean, dry clothes feel so good I am already looking forward to next week's shipment. Of course, I will need to soak them with mosquito repellent, but that can wait. For now I am just going to enjoy their dryness while I take a nap.

I pass a half hour in the comfort of the grass before the rain begins. It is another tropical deluge. Visibility closes down to forty feet, then thirty.

By the time Sandy drops by to announce that we are going on night patrol, the sun is already beginning to set. At least I think it is beginning to set—either that or it is raining even harder.

Ten minutes later Bravo Company is on its way out the gate, heading west. Delta Company follows, but once outside the gate we head southeast. Naturally, I do not know why we are going for a walk in the dark, but I do know that walking around at night is a good way to get shot. There is a dusk curfew in force all over South Vietnam. Any man, woman, or child outside his village after dark is shot without question. The curfew greatly simplifies enemy identification. Unfortunately, for this night at least, the curfew rule makes us fair game for anyone with a gun.

We must rely on battalion HQ to communicate our intentions to the ARVN forces. Every unit whose patrol area encompasses part of our route must be notified if we are to prevent friendly forces from firing at us. Unfortunately, the man we rely on to perform this task is Major Barlow. It is the strongly held opinion of my comrades that Barlow's sole purpose in Vietnam is to get himself promoted to lieutenant colonel. If the major lets the informant-riddled ARVN outposts know about movements, it is likely that the VC will have the same intelligence shortly thereafter, causing them to alter their plans for the night and to deprive the major of increasing his body count, thereby slowing his progress toward promotion.

Whatever trouble the major is brewing, he has at least lucked upon a night sufficiently dark to conceal our movements. Heavy cloud cover combined with torrential rain has reduced visibility to less than three feet. The company proceeds in single file, each man holding onto the web gear of the man in front of him. I cannot see the hand at the end of my arm, but I can distinguish the outline of the man who leads me through the blackness. The muddy ground beneath our feet gives no hint of its dips and rises. Our human chain is constantly broken as men slip into unseen holes and trip over invisible projections. While a man scrambles to regain his feet, the line of men before him vanishes into the darkness, leaving him and all those behind him hurrying forward in a blind effort to reestablish contact. Men call to each other through the roaring downpour. "Mike . . . Mike . . . where are you?"

"Here. Over here."

Contact is broken and reestablished and broken again. Our progress is slow and far from quiet, but the rain drowns most of our noise—most, but not all. A flare pops overhead, flooding the area with harsh white light. I am halfway to the ground before the first burst of fire comes. Landing with a splash in the water and mud, I turn my head to see the tracers coming close and thick overhead. Staying as low as possible, I push through the mud toward the protection of a tree trunk silhouetted by the light of the flare. A long burst from a machine gun freezes me in place. When it stops, I slide behind the tree and bring my M-60 to bear on the source of fire. Their machine-gun fire is coming in shorter bursts now. I feel secure enough behind my tree for my mind to expand to the men around me. None of our guys are returning fire. What the hell's going on?

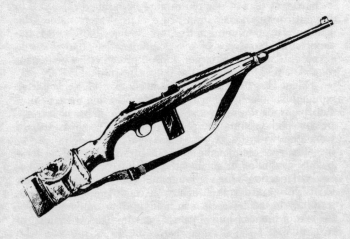

.30 Caliber M-1 Carbine

As I listen, the answer slowly dawns on me. No doubt the men with more time in-country instantly realized the significance of what I'm hearing. That machine-gun fire is coming from an M-60. And there—that's an M-16, not a Russian AK-47. And those—those are American carbines, I'll bet. The people shooting at us are our allies. And American troops don't carry carbines anymore. The ARVNs do.

Thanks, Barlow. You didn't call them, did you, you bastard.

The ARVNs continue to fire for twenty minutes before someone convinces them to stop. Luckily, no one is hit. The majority of the company has taken cover behind a dike; the rest of us are on low ground where the ARVNs are unable to bring their small arms fire closer than a foot above our heads.

I slowly get to my feet, feeling a little shaky from the rush of adrenaline. Dripping with mud, I move to the area where I had last seen Sandy in the light of the flares. In a few minutes we have our squad assembled despite the blackness of the night. In a few more minutes the men are linked up and the company is on its way again.

I have a hard time understanding how Liem can effectively lead us through country he cannot see. Liem has been with the company for three months now. Despite his being Vietnamese, most of the men have learned to trust him. The captain recruited him as an interpreter, but he does much more than interpret. Right now he is walking point. He knows this part of the country well because he was born and raised in this section of Vietnam. Nevertheless, I would think he would have trouble finding his way across his own backyard on a night like this.

Liem first became actively involved in the war against communism two years ago when the VC killed his father. In the traditional style, Liem took the place of his father. His personal vendetta proved so successful that he soon earned a reputation with the VC who retaliated by placing a price on his head. As Liem persisted with his private war and the bounty continued to go uncollected, the VC were forced to take other action. One night when he was gone, the VC came to his village and took his sister. A week later her head was sent back to the village as a warning of what would happen to the rest of Liem's family if he did not stop fighting against the revolution.

The death of the second member of his family only

succeeded in making Liem more dedicated to his pursuit. After hiding his mother and remaining sister in Saigon, he set out in search of the men who had committed the disgraceful murder of his sister. Within a month he had found and killed four of the men involved.

By the time Captain Wilkins had heard about him, the bounty on Liem's head was up to five thousand dollars. After checking his background, the captain hired him without the approval or financial aid of the Army, which prefers that its field units use captured enemy soldiers for interpreting and scouting. At the end of every month a helmet is passed among the men of Delta Company so that each man may donate whatever he wishes toward Liem's salary. The collection usually amounts to about two hundred forty dollars—which is more than the Army pays us.

Liem does not live with us, he just appears on those mornings when the company is going out on patrol. Sometimes he walks with the point element, sometimes on the flank. Usually he wanders up and down the column or slips off to gather information from a nearby village. He does not talk much, and he never smiles. Whatever type of man he was two years ago, circumstance has replaced with a highly dedicated and skilled killer. Outside his family he seems to have only one interest—killing VC.

At the head of the column of men struggling to maintain their hold on the man before them, Liem continues to lead the company from the ARVN outpost. After an hour the rain slackens, but visibility is little improved. We are walking along a dike that separates two paddies when the line accordions to a stop.

We stand ten minutes before the words "sit down" pass down the line. I sit astride the dike wondering what comes next. Where am I being led on this night, in this new life in which I have so little control? There is no answer. My life is in the hands of the U.S. Army. I shiver inside my wet clothes.

The noise of the rain falling into the water around us washes away all other sound. After a while each man lies back on the body of the man behind him. The warmth of the bodies I am sandwiched between stops my shivering. I lay the M-60 on my chest between my chin and the helmet of the man before me.

Someone whispers to me but the words are unclear. I

listen more intently, I need to understand. The whisper comes again. "Hey, wake up. We're moving out."

My eyes spring open. Have I been asleep? For how long? The rain has stopped. The cloud cover is breaking up. I withdraw my right hand and foot from the water of the rice paddy where they have taken rest. My left hand still clings to the machine gun balanced on my chest. I prod the man behind me and help him to his feet.

The starlight shining through the open patches in the drifting clouds gives off enough light to allow us to continue our mission at a reasonable pace. We walk through the paddies, the orchards, and the jungle hoping we will not stumble into an ambush, or another ARVN outpost. We should not need to worry about the enemy tracking our movement. It would have been difficult for anyone to follow us through the blackness of tonight's rainstorm.

In the hour before first light, the company is brought to a halt. Norris gathers the men of his platoon around him. We squat in an old orchard, knowing we must be close to our objective, expecting to be finally trusted with the particulars of our mission.

"There is a village half a kilometer to our south. We are here to put a seal on that village. Nobody leaves the village until it has been thoroughly searched. Anyone who insists on leaving will be shot. Be ready for trouble. Your squad leaders will show you where to set up. There will be no talking once we leave the orchard. Stay low, keep quiet, and move fast. Let's go."

We run in a crouch down an elevated dirt road leading to the village. Men peel off the front of the line as squad leaders tap their shoulders. When Sandy and I reach the front, we drop behind the three-foot berm on the left side of the road, ready to provide covering fire for the next squad taking positions further up. We aim our weapons at the village we can see only with the help of our imaginations—a black mass against the gray-black sky.

With the next squad in position, Sandy and two others jump the berm and slide down a twelve-foot bank to a narrow muddy flat at the edge of the paddy below. While I keep watch they scoop mud with their hands to fill the sandbags each of us has been assigned to bring on this patrol.

We wait about an hour at the edge of the sleeping village for the night to lift. Small circles of light appear in huts as early

risers light their candles and oil lamps. Slowly the outline of
the village emerges. There must be at least fifty hooches on
the plateau jutting at right angles from the road. Twelve feet
below the village, rice paddies fan out for 150 meters,
extending from the elevated dirt road to some distant point
on the far side that I cannot make out.

Feeling more and more vulnerable in the growing light,
I look across at the village, and then down at the three men
huddled behind a stack of sandbags less than two feet high.
From the height of the village a rifleman has a clear shot at all
three men. I look around for a more secure position, noticing
again the flicker of candlelight coming from a hooch set off by
itself to my right rear. The berm provides good protection
from the direction of the village, but my back is completely
exposed. There are no better positions, not down in the
paddies nor along the dirt road. The only good cover is fifty
meters away in the jungle, and no doubt there are men
already stationed there. It is getting light. The villagers will
be trying to leave for the fields any second now. I feel
trapped and exposed. There is movement in that hooch behind me. I want to move, but where?

Shouting comes from the village gates. I can see Liem
directly across the road from the gate arguing with some local
men. The entire upper half of Liem's body is exposed to fire.
That guy is going to get himself killed. More voices are added
to the confusion at the gate. Liem points his M-16 in the air
and fires. His shot is answered immediately by a rapid succession of single shots from the gate. A burst of automatic fire
comes from high in the branches of a large tree to the right of
the gate. Our men in the ditch across the road from the gate
fire back in short bursts. Like an electric shock, automatic
rifle fire erupts from behind me, the bullets digging into the
berm a meter to my right. I dive over the berm, sliding and
rolling down the bank, coming to a stop at the feet of my
comrades. The three of them, lying side by side on their
stomachs, take up all available room behind the pitifully small
wall of sandbags.

The automatic rifle high in the tree sprays a loose pattern of bullets down the flat at the edge of the paddies.
Scared and angry at my exposure, I jump on top of the slot
between two men, throw the gun across the wall, and unleash
a sustained string of fire at the center section of the tree.
Twigs and leaves fly in all directions. By the time I let up on

the trigger I figure I have at least frightened the man half to death. With the sound of my fire still ringing in my ears I realize the rest of the shooting has stopped.

As the men beneath me wiggle out from under, I feel a twinge of guilt. Maybe I overreacted. Then again, maybe I did just the right thing. Anyway, it seems to have put an end to the skirmish and that is the important thing.

Bravo Company advances from the far side to sweep the village. They find two dead VC at the gate. Two more are killed in the tunnels under the village, but we have missed the company of NVA. Apparently, they moved out sometime during the night.

By 1000 we are back in the bush, not heading north toward our NDP, but south and east toward God knows what. We walk all morning and into the afternoon. The sun is not blocked by clouds this day. It bakes the ground dry and sucks the water from our bodies faster than it can evaporate.

I keep thinking about the can of scrambled eggs I ate yesterday and wondering if I will eat today. There are coconuts, bananas, grapefruit, and sugarcane in the fields we pass, but it is too early in the year for anything to be ripe. I try to think about this problem the way the Army would. Feeding its men one can of food a day would be considered a hardship and therefore acceptable, while not feeding the men at all would have to be termed a failure, which would look bad on Major Barlow's record. Obviously, I have nothing to worry about. Food will be forthcoming.

We emerge from the jungle into an expanse of moonscape. A holocaust has visited the land before us. Everything that lived here has been annihilated. Large craters pockmark an area one kilometer long by half a kilometer wide. Within this area not even the smallest bush has survived. Yet the jungle persists. The pale green of new plant shoots are coming up here and there, and the ants have come back—and the mosquitoes, too, who are now busy breeding new millions in the water-filled craters.

The next bomb crater on my left is being used by Liem as a bathtub. Standing there with his shirt off, submerged to his waist, splashing water over himself in the middle of this desolation, he looks extremely out of place. This is a dead place; not a place most men would choose to linger.

At 1700 we are informed that our destination is Di An. This is the best possible news. Two trips to Di An in the

same month. Our spirits lift and might have actually soared if
we were not so tired. Fifteen minutes later we connect with
the road leading south from the base camp. In the distance I
see the trucks waiting to take us the last half kilometer to the
gate. If they are going to waste the men and gas to give us a
token ride, why must we walk this last kilometer of road for
the privilege? The sight of those trucks waiting on the side of
the road, twice as far from us as they are from the base camp
gate, becomes more irritating by the step. This must be one
of Major Barlow's stupid ideas. Only because the captain
finds the situation humorous are tempers cooled enough for
us to physically restrain two of our more hot-headed members threatening to commandeer the trucks.

Just inside the gate the trucks stop to let us off. They are
not going any further out of their way on our behalf than is
required. Muttering curses at the drivers and the Army in
general, we walk the last half klick to our collection of deserted barracks.

Before I notice he is gone, the captain shows up with a
jeep trailer full of beer and ice. I am told this is done in an
effort to keep the boys drinking free beer here instead of
going to the EM club and getting into trouble. However,
there is no question of anyone leaving just now because our
water buffalo cooks have arrived with fifty authentic American chickens and a large pot of beans. The two tables that
hold the food and grills are quickly surrounded by hungry,
silent, staring men. Growls from the mess sergeant to stand
clear are ignored. We watch each chicken as it is transferred
to grill or plate as if to ensure that these rare birds do not get
canned, dehydrated, or replaced by rubber imitations. Despite the frayed nerves of the cooks, each of us finally receives his first meal of the day. Major Barlow's record is
clear—officially, at least.

With the excitement of dinner over, it occurs to someone that this is Saturday night. On such a night there is likely
to be a band at the main EM club. This thought spreads
around and settles in until the sun goes down; then men
wander off in groups of threes and fours.

A few men have fallen asleep with half-finished beers in
their hands; one or two others have decided to write letters
home while they are still sober enough to do so. Some of
the groups stop in dark secluded areas to share a joint and
some quiet conversation. But the majority of the company

finds its way to the EM club where a Philippine band is setting up its equipment.

By the time the band begins to play every chair in the club is occupied. Five of us sit at a table covered with beer cans bought by the armful. The electrified rock and roll shatters any attempt at conversation. Smoke-filtered light reflects off the sheen of perspiration on alcohol-flushed faces mesmerized by the thundering beat of the band and the pulsating bodies of the two women dancing on the stage.

Garbage cans fill with empties as new lukewarm beers are brought in replacement. Tonight the more moderate-drinking rear echelon personnel who normally occupy the club have been supplanted by at least fifty men from a field company of the 109th, and the seventy-odd men of Delta Company. Late arrivals stand between tables and against walls. Eyes and energies are consumed by the gyrating, sweat-slicked, bikini-clad bodies of the dancers. Men yell obscene suggestions into the roar of whoops, yahoos, and whistles. Sex-starved men are held in hypnotic fantasy of the voluptuous, glistening young bodies lustily making love to the air until the spell is broken by a man bursting from his chair with a primal yell. Charging the stage, he leaps for the space between the arms of the waiting bouncers. One flying foot reaches the stage before a strong hand seizes his shirt and an arm brings a club down upon his head. He crumples in a heap on the stage. The band stops. Men freeze in disbelief. Ten more bouncers with clubs rush to the stage front.

The burly sergeant in charge of the bouncers shakes his club at the crowd, yelling for the room to be cleared. Two men from the 109th argue with a bouncer over the fate of their buddy lying unconscious on the stage. One of the men makes a move to recover his friend. The bouncer pushes him into a stage side table. The second man gives the bouncer a hard two-handed push in retaliation that sends him crashing against the stage. Down comes a club. A right fist smashes into the side of a face. Another club comes down and the brawl is on.

The men of the 109th might have tolerated one of their men going down under the club for his misconduct, but men who risk their lives for each other cannot tolerate their people being clubbed for trying to retrieve a fallen friend. With fists and chairs and hurled beer cans they swarm the men

with clubs. The bouncers are beaten back against the stage
and are quickly pounded out of view. The mob spills onto the
stage. A few men swept up in the excitement grab the dancers while others wade into the band equipment, flinging
guitars and kicking drums. A girl screams as her bikini top is
thrown to the crowd and a hand cups her breast.

Angry yells of warning are heard from the right side of
the room where Delta Company sits en masse. We will not
have our Philippine beauties mistreated. While the men on
the stage turn to face this new threat, the girls wiggle free to
join the rest of the band escaping out the exit at the rear of
the stage. The two field companies face each other, exchanging threats. Some of the men from Delta who have been hit
by stray tables and chairs are already engaged in isolated
fights. Men at the edges of the fights are sucked by ones and
twos into the melee.

One of the guys at our table leaps into the fray. Another
goes to retrieve the first. The three of us remaining scoop up
all the beer on the table and head for a side door. A half
dozen like-minded men reach the exit on our heels before the
brawl spreads to encompass all who remain.

In the lee of the doorway we are swilling beer, ducking
flying debris, and generally enjoying the foolishness going on
inside, when two dozen MPs storm through the main door.
Without forewarning of whistles or commands to cease, the
MPs form a line abreast and wade into the mob with night-
sticks flying. They beat men to the ground, step over the
fallen, club the next man regardless of his attitude of belliger-
ence or surrender.

The MPs have only the opportunity to crack the back of
a few skulls before the mob becomes conscious of their presence. There is a pause in the general calamity as the men
stop punching each other to look in wonder at this latest
threat. Hesitantly drawn into the room, I, too, pause in the
hope that my help will not be needed against the MPs who
continue their bludgeoning, unaware of the men's changing
mood. A cry wells up from the mob as it speaks in one
terrifying voice. It turns on the MPs, surrounding and engulf-
ing them in seconds, beating them to the floor. It is over so
suddenly that men are left with cocked arms and wide eyes
shooting glances around the room in search of someone new
to hit.

With nothing left to do except clean up the mess, the

men pick the MPs off the floor and throw them out the front door to land at the feet of a stunned MP lieutenant. This is not the way it happens in the manual. Not knowing what to do or say, he stands there with his pistol pointed in the air, watching the growing pile of MPs at his feet.

People begin to drift in all directions. It will not be healthy to be here when reinforcements arrive. My friends and I take our beer and shuffle through the dust to the small battalion EM club. Not long ago it had been a barracks, and from the outside, it still looks like one. There is a wall in the center of the building now to provide a bar for the noncommissioned officers on one side and a bar for the enlisted men on the other.

The place is nearly deserted when we arrive, but before we finish the first round we are joined by six more men from our company. Rounds are bought and downed as we talk of women, the world, and future dreams. Only one topic is forbidden—the military or anything connected with it. Every man at the table hates the war and despises the Army. If those subjects have to be discussed, we can do so when sober and already depressed. This is party time. A rare opportunity to enjoy ourselves, an opportunity not due to be repeated for at least a month. We drink and talk and laugh until, one by one, the men go face down on the table. There are only three of us left upright, spewing jokes and garbled wisdom when the bartender closes the bar.

Slapping backs, pounding tables, dragging unwilling bodies to their feet, we manage to get everyone moving except for the two lads passed out on the floor. With every man lending his unstable support we pick up their Jell-O bodies and carry them from the club, struggling to contain the limp legs and arms that keep oozing from our grasp. Even when we manage to maintain our grip, we are all too drunk to walk more than ten steps without falling. We carry and drag and drop our charge, landing in a heap of uncontrollable laughter. We pick him up again to lurch forward a few more steps before collapsing in another pile of hysterical merriment. Our progress is extremely slow until someone emerges from the darkness with a stretcher. We pile both men on the stretcher, one atop the other. This is a much-improved method of carrying limp bodies, but the top man will not stay put. He keeps sliding off until two men pick him up and drag him along between them, which is a fine method except that the

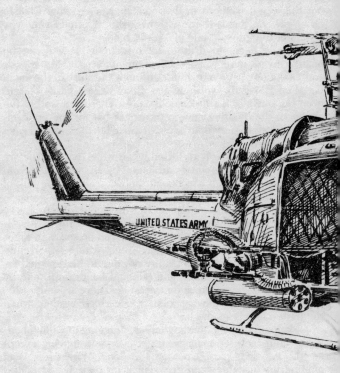

Huey

two conscious men are unable to maintain a vertical attitude. The man on the stretcher does not fare any better. We constantly dump him onto the ground or roll him into a nearby ditch. It takes an hour to get all nine drunks to our final resting place in the dirt of the company area.

I awake to stare at the steel blue of an early morning sky. My body is stiff from exercise and abuse. It is 0600. I drag myself off the ground to join the preparations to move out. We pick up C rations, give our weapons a quick cleaning, and haul our gear to the truck pick-up point. There are many

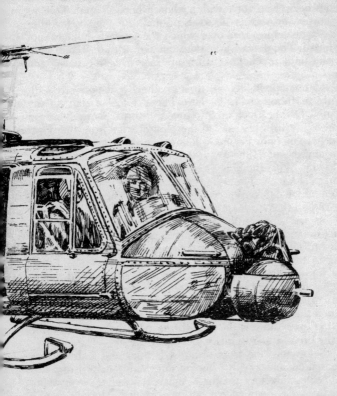

bruised, stiff bodies as a result of the fight. There are even more throbbing heads from the alcohol. But these things are small pains, soon to be outweighed.

The trucks take us to the helicopter port. There is the normal confusion, but I reside more comfortably now in my ignorance. I sit on the ground next to my machine gun, hoping they will overlook me this time, hoping no one will come by to tell me what to do, praying they will leave me sitting on the ground.

The Huey helicopter pilots start their engines with a

quiet whir that slowly increases in volume until the rotor blades begin to revolve with a whop, whop, whop that comes at shorter and shorter intervals until all the engines together make a deafening roar over which the loudest shout cannot be heard. The down wash stings our skin with dust and sand. I hang onto my helmet, turn my face from the blast, and wait.

One chopper lifts off, then another. I sit perfectly still, trying to think small. Is there hope? I feel a slap on my helmet. Damn! I look up into the sandstorm. Sandy stands in front of me with his back to the blast of wind from the down draft. He motions for me to follow him. Why should I follow him anywhere? Huh? Why? I tumble into the chopper behind him. What the hell, I've never had a ride in one of these things. The view should be terrific since the doors have been taken off for quicker entry and exit. There's nothing between me and all that fresh air.

As we gain altitude the view below reminds me of the coast range in Oregon. In both places the forests stretch for miles in all directions. So much lush green vegetation running to the horizon staggers the imagination. A man could lose himself down there forever, or at least he could before the machines were brought in. On the coastal range the millions of acres of trees have been divided into plots. In one section the trees are forty years old, ready to cut. In the next section everything is dead, with the trees lying in a jumble on the ground like so many pick-up sticks.

Below me, the tropical forest is thick and lush up to a line that coincides with a line on somebody's map. From this line, extending forward for a square kilometer, everything that lived has been blown out of existence. The alternating patterns of lush growth and barren land repeat themselves like a giant irregular checkerboard. Our government seems to be doing its best to convert this country into one vast expanse of wasteland. I can see the State Department's advertisement now: land clearing done free of charge—let the U.S. government be your buddy. But I must be fair to my government. It is doing a great deal with the starving people in this region. It has eliminated a few hundred thousand of them already. So it all equals out—in a way.

The helicopter accelerates as it dives to tree level. Skimming over the treetops at full speed is both thrilling and mesmerizing. The door gunner in his seat to my left is getting fidgety. He nervously rechecks his machine gun and ammunition belt. He zips up his flak jacket, fastens his helmet strap, and adjusts his seat belt. He is making me nervous. Whatever he is afraid is going to happen to him is going to happen to me as well. He looks right at me and gives me the thumbs-up sign. Great, what the hell does that mean? I look at the other guys sitting on the floor with me. They are strapping down and tightening up. This must be the end of the ride. Maybe I should go up and thank the pilot. Helicopter rides are so much nicer than walking.

I'm the only one here who hasn't done this before, but it looks like I'm going to be the first one out because I'm the closest one to the door—or the open space where the door used to be. What do I do when we land? I try to remember my in-country training. You hit the ground running, go about thirty yards, and assume a prone position ready to direct fire to your front. Then what? Oh, yes, then the sergeant blows a whistle and the exercise is over. I hope our sergeant has his whistle with him.

We clear the last tree at the edge of an open, grassy area. In seconds the helicopter swoops down to hover six feet above the ground. I poise in the doorway ready to jump the instant the ship touches down. A hand slaps my back, urging me forward. I guess this is as close as they are going to get. The door gunner's M-60 erupts in a long series of explosions as I jump to the grass- and tree-stump-covered ground. I sink into muck up to my knees. The noise is incredible. Weapons are being fired everywhere. The chopper is off before I can pull my right foot out of the mud. There is a tree line fifty yards away. I lurch forward. The heads and hunched shoulders of the men appear above the long grass. The forms stagger over soft ground, fire into trees, then vanish again. Powerful engines roar behind me, sending a gale across the meadow. Automatic rifle fire screams into the trees. A machine gun fires a long burst close overhead. I dive into the grass. What the hell is everybody shooting at? Some of our people are already into the tree line. I stay down until the machine gun behind me stops. I run for the woods in a nightmare of slow motion, my back tingling in anticipation of being struck by friendly fire.

I reach the protection of the woods and fling myself behind a tree. Listening intently, I still can't distinguish any enemy fire against the diminishing barrage of our own. I

crawl forward until I spot two of our people. I'll watch them
and move when they do. I hope they know what they're
doing. We lie in our places listening to the firing slowly fade.
After a few minutes it stops.

The company sorts itself out and begins walking west.
Cambodia is to the west and north, though a long way off by
foot. We flew to the northwest for about half an hour. Now
we are walking west. I wonder how many days it would take
for us to walk to the border? It's no use trying to figure it out,
I've only a vague idea where we are. Someday I'd like to get
hold of a map.

From what I have heard, the area northwest of us,
where Cambodia's border bulges into Vietnam, is a major
infiltration route for the NVA. In the opinion of the men I
have heard talking, the North Vietnamese soldiers are tough
and dedicated. Well, there's no sense worrying about it—we'll
either run into them or we won't.

It suddenly occurs to me that during all that shooting
back in the clearing nobody seems to have gotten hurt. What
was all that about, anyway? Was that just cover fire or was
there really somebody in those trees? Since I've been with
this unit, it has never fired its weapons indiscriminately. I
was impressed by the company's discipline two nights ago
when every man held his fire when the ARVN's opened up
on us. Why all the shooting today? I must find out. I must
learn quickly before it's too late. I increase my pace to close
the gap with the man in front of me.

"Hey, Dryden, what was all that shooting about back
there?"

"I don't really know, but the word I got was that the first
set of choppers that sat down took some fire. I guess Charlie
took off when we started giving him a lot of heat."

How'd he find that out? He was in the same chopper as I
was. How come I always seem to be the only one who doesn't
know what is going on?

Three AKs open fire on our left flank. My knees send
me to the ground in automatic reaction. A barrage of M-16
rounds pours into the jungle, discouraging our attackers from
delivering a second volley. But for one man, it is already too
late. A few more scattered bursts are fired into the bush
before everything is still again, except for the quiet voice of
the medic at his work.

It happened suddenly. I didn't even fire a shot. I'm still

lying on the ground deciding whether it is safe to get up when Liem and Norris slip into the jungle.

Poles are quickly cut to make a stretcher for the wounded man. In a few minutes the company is moving again. I pass the prone form on the stretcher. It is the third platoon's radioman. One bullet hit his radio, another went through his upper arm. He looks numb. It is probably shock as well as the morphine the medic pumped into him that is keeping him so placid.

Moving on, I find myself continually looking for cover. If we get hit here, I can drop behind that log. Now I can still make it back to the log—no—now the boulder's better, at least from the left. There's a dip in the ground up there that'll be good when I get closer, past that is a bad stretch, except for those small trees on the right. Okay, now that bank's good if it comes from the left and that stump'll do if it comes from the right.

Twenty minutes go by before we come to an open area large enough to land a medivac chopper. We stay in the trees along the edge of the open clearing, but Charlie has anticipated our actions. He fires at us from the other side of the clearing. We hit the ground without returning fire. Liem and Norris are over there somewhere, crawling through the bush, putting their lives on the line. There is too much chance of hitting them accidentally. Besides, if Charlie keeps firing at us the noise will lead our people to him as well as mask the sound of their approach.

The cover here in the trees is good, but if we give Charlie long enough he is going to hit one of us. What amazes me is how these guys know when to fire and when to hold back. No orders were given to hold our fire; there wasn't time. How come at least one guy didn't automatically return fire?

I wish Norris and Liem would hurry. I don't like being a decoy.

After what seems like ten minutes—but is probably only one or two—we hear two M-16s fire, answered by one AK, and then one 16. Quiet. Time is suspended as everyone strains to hear a sound that will tell them the results of the skirmish on the other side of the field. There is no sound. No clues.

I begin to relax and look around. Bill Dryden is curled up in a ball fifteen feet to my right. Something is wrong. I crawl over to him, saying his name before I touch him. His arms are protectively wrapped around his helmet, his knees drawn to his chest. Every few seconds a tremor passes through his body.

"Dry, are you all right?" He doesn't answer or move except when another tremor racks his body. I don't see any blood along his back. I look over the rest of him and the ground. No sign of blood. "It's okay, Dry. It's over. You're not hurt, are you?" He looks at me for a couple of seconds, then gives his head a shake no.

I sit by him awhile, talking to him in a low voice. After a time his body begins to unwind.

Dryden lives in the bunker next to mine back at the NDP. I don't know too much about him except that his father is a general, and that story about the time the platoon got hit outside Lai Khe. General Dryden could've had his son posted to noncombat duties, but he must've felt combat would be good for his son. Looking at Bill now, it is hard to believe he has a father called General Bill "Bulldog" Dryden, Sr.

Bill, Jr., is so quiet and soft spoken you hardly notice him. He is nineteen, of medium height, and thin, like everyone in the field. He is still a PFC but will be promoted to Specialist Fourth Class as soon as the paperwork sent to the rear two months ago is processed. He is too withdrawn to ever be a leader of men like his father, but he always does what he is told and never gets into any trouble. With five months in the field he is one of the old-timers in the company, and he was doing fine until Lai Khe when a guy walking in front of him got his belly ripped open by mortar fragments. The man tried to hold his insides together while Dryden dragged him to the cover of a nearby ditch, but his intestines kept oozing out between his fingers. They were trapped together in that ditch for over an hour. By the time help arrived the wounded man was dead and Bill had dropped into a spell of silence that lasted nearly a week.

After Lai Khe the bands of sanity around Dryden's mind began to snap. I think his nerves are shot. Shell shock or battle fatigue is what they called it in previous wars, but the Army has done away with the troublesome disorder. Officially, it no longer exists. Some days Dryden does not talk at all, other days he seems as sane as anybody else out here. He might be able to deal with this life better if he could scream or cry or even get wildly drunk. But Bill has never been drunk, and I believe he is afraid of what will happen if he lets his emotions go. The only thing that can save his mind now is peace, but peace is not likely to come to General Dryden's boy.

Bill is more relaxed by the time Norris and Liem rejoin the company. They killed two of the VC, but the third escaped.

The helicopter arrives to pick up our casualty. I wonder if they'll be able to save his arm? This has been just another day in Vietnam for the rest of us, but it's a day the third platoon's radioman will never forget. I am glad I don't know him.

It is past time for lunch and way past time for breakfast, but we move on again. It is no good having Charlie know exactly where we are. We go deeper into the jungle. After two hours the line stops. I sit with Sandy, Dryden, and Gomez facing a thick growth of bamboo. We sit without talking, trying to work up enough energy and enthusiasm to open a can for breakfast or lunch or dinner or whatever meal this first food of the day at 3:00 P.M. represents. Christ, was it just this morning that I woke up in the dirt of Di An with a hangover?

After a few minutes Gomez begins to reminisce about the fight in the EM club. Sandy is reaching for a cigarette when Gomez suddenly interrupts his dialogue to whisper a harsh, "Don't move."

My right hand inches toward the trigger of the machine gun as my eyes search through the bamboo for Charlie. I don't see anyone. Without moving anything but my eyes I look past Sandy and Dryden to Gomez's eyes. He is looking straight into the bamboo. I search the bamboo again. Nothing. Gomez carefully slides away from us. "Snake. Do not move."

With relief I scan the ground for a snake. I don't see the snake even though it must be near, within striking distance, or there wouldn't be urgency in Gomez's voice. I shift my eyes to Sandy's motionless form a foot to my left. He's staring straight ahead as if mesmerized. I follow his gaze to the bamboo—then I see it. Three feet above the ground, two feet from Sandy's head lies the snake, half coiled among the bamboo stems. Men and snake stare into the eyes of their deadly enemy. The only movement is the snake's thin tongue flicking in and out, tasting air. I hear the rubbing of plastic against metal as Gomez picks up his rifle, the click of the safety, and at last the explosion of gunpowder. At the sound of the shot we dive away from the snake, but Gomez's aim is good.

We edge back to the bamboo to examine the kill. Though it is only slightly more than two feet long, it is proclaimed to be a deadly bamboo viper. I study the snake so that I will not forget what it looks like. When it was alive I saw only its head. I have much to learn.

Because of the rifle shot we move east another kilometer. When we stop I waste no time shoveling down a can of turkey loaf. We will probably stay here until dusk, but one never knows, and last night's chicken is only a memory—or at least it should be only a memory. An unusually large number of men are trotting off into the bush. I think the water buffalo cooks have done it to us again.

Gomez comes over to see if I want my instant coffee. I am not enthusiastic about cold instant coffee, so I bequeath to him all the instant coffee I now have or will ever receive. He returns to his place a few feet away to select a C ration can to use as a cup. As he is about to pour some of the valuable water from his canteen into the makeshift coffee cup, the first drops of a rainstorm fall into the dust. After we drape our poncho liners over our heads, he comes back to ask me for the two empty cans in front of me. He places all five cans upright in the dirt before him to catch the rain. This is like watching an eight-year-old kid at play on a sunny Saturday afternoon.

Gomez fiddles with his cans for half an hour before he has enough rainwater to mix with the instant coffee. He then takes the four-pack of cigarettes found in the same airtight plastic bag as the coffee, the cocoa, the chewing gum, and the single serving of toilet paper (currently at a premium), and with great care and skill lights a cigarette despite the downpour. In an exhale of smoke he turns to me with his can raised in salute, reeling off a Spanish salutation that I cannot hear through the rain. I smile and nod as we both return our attention to the three-foot semicircle before us that comprises our private worlds.

The rainstorm passes in an hour. From Sandy, I learn we are here to find a company of NVA reported to have moved into this area. We exchange the hope we are unsuccessful in our search.

Ambush this night is tense but uneventful.

At first light the company heads out at a forced pace. Rumor has it that a large contingent of NVA has been spotted south of us. For three hours the rate of our march does not slacken. Men periodically break into a jog to maintain their intervals. It feels like we are a pack of migrating lemmings, rushing mindlessly toward a cliff at the edge of the sea.

We stop on the fringe of a large clearing. Helicopters are to pick us up to speed our intercept with the elusive northern army.

Minutes later the thrashing of rotor blades barely precedes the sight of choppers swooping in at tree level. Three of them hover two feet off the ground as if impatient and quivering with nerves. There is a rush of movement and noise as those of us assigned to the first flight scramble for the doorless openings. Not wanting to push with the pack, I am the last one aboard. All the floor space is taken up with sprawled bodies and weapons and equipment. I have one knee on the door sill and a hand on the wall when the pilot takes us up. I am pitched forward by the increased gravity of our vertical climb. With both knees now on the lip of the door and feet dangling in the air, I push myself upright at the same time the pilot banks his ship 45 degrees to starboard. While men scratch for handholds to stop their slide in my direction, I slam my right hand against the edge of the doorway, my left side pivoting out into space. Below me is three hundred feet of air. The force of the wind against the machine gun still laying across my left shoulder adds its weight to the forces pulling me into the air.

Seeing my plight, Sandy grabs my shirttail, but he can only exert a slight pull for he is in danger of sliding out as well. There is nothing on the floor to cling to. Half in and half out of the helicopter, an eternity of seconds pass while I pit the strength in my right arm against the pilot's determination to fly with a 45-degree list. If I dump the machine gun I may be able to pull myself back inside the chopper, but then Charlie would get the gun and I would be defenseless.

At last the pilot completes his sweeping right turn and brings his ship back on an even keel. I fall into the crowd of bodies on the floor, my right arm shaking with fatigue. Damn! That was much too close. Next time I jump in a slick I will be less timid about the body parts I may bruise in the process. Being polite could be fatal. Better yet, I'll hang onto the pilot's neck; that way he'll know when his passengers are less than satisfied with his flight plan.

We fly southwest for fifteen minutes before we are again skimming the treetops on our landing approach. This time there are no fireworks at the landing site. We touch down in another area cleared with the compliments of Uncle Sam and a few hundred thousand dollars' worth of munitions. The choppers lift off, leaving us standing in the quiet and desolation.

Again we walk. The direction remains south by west. Every fifteen minutes my shoulder tires. I shift the gun and padding to the other shoulder, making sure the towel lies smooth so that my continually moist skin will not be rubbed raw. Although both shoulders are sore by the end of the day, I have been careful not to wear a hole in my skin that will not heal.

The air is heavy with heat and humidity as I move along looking for cover, always and forever, looking for cover. Sandy works his way down the line, walking awhile with each man in turn. When he comes to me he gives me the usual, "How are you doing?"

"Well enough," I say, noticing that he looks a bit worried. But he often looks worried because he takes his job seriously, and I am glad he does.

"We are going to be hooking up with Charlie Company in an hour. They will be coming in from over there," he says, pointing west. "Keep a lookout for them. You will be kept posted as they get closer."

When we arrive at the preselected meeting place, Charlie Company is still half an hour out. We sit down to eat and to wait. I inspect my food supply. One can of beef stew, one can of peaches. I decide to eat the stew and save the peaches for a hungrier time. The news passes up and down the line that Charlie Company's point unit should make contact with our line in five minutes.

Gomez sits on his helmet in a small clearing forty feet up the line from me. I ask him if he wants my coffee. He says, "No, not today." I can understand that. Water is scarce. Many of the men already have empty canteens.

Charlie Company's point unit is in visual contact with our line. Apparently, they are intersecting our line close to its center, about two hundred feet behind me. Good navigation, boys. Actually, we sent up some green smoke, all they had to do was walk toward its source. I hear the next message passing up the line, "Point unit coming in."

A burst of rifle fire comes from my right front. I see Gomez's head snap back as he falls backward off his helmet. Shooting breaks out all along our right flank. Men on both sides of me return fire. I hesitate. Something's wrong. Very wrong. VC attacking two American companies in daylight? NVA attacking between two companies? A burst of fire rips through the bush inches above my head. It doesn't matter who's trying to kill us. We must stop them, I fire wildly into the dense foliage, left to right and back again. Make them stop. Make them stop. I let up on the trigger. My ears ring in the quiet. Someone shatters the silence with a yell, "Medic." The spell is broken. The shooting starts again.

Where are the three guys who carry the boxes of machine gun ammunition? Not risking their lives in this barrage to get it here, I'll bet. Damn! I don't even know if they're up or down the line. What's that? There. Someone yelled, "GIs." There it is again. "GIs." Shit! That's Charlie Company. Those stupid mother fuckers.

My body shivers now and then as if it were cold, but I know it's the adrenaline and anger. I walk to where Gomez sat eating his lunch. Our medic is kneeling over the body, working with practiced efficiency.

"How is he, Doc?"

"Dead," answers the medic without looking up. He will have to answer that question twenty times more before everybody is sure. He finishes wrapping gauze around Gomez's head and lays him back on the ground. "One little hole in his forehead. Blew his brains out the back of his head."

Abruptly the moist, gray matter mixed with the blood on the sand behind Gomez comes into recognizable focus. I quickly look away to control the rush of revulsion. What a stupid, pitiful waste.

Later we piece together what happened. Someone had neglected to inform Charlie Company's flank man that the two companies had made contact. Apparently, the green smoke, and the consideration that he would soon be meeting with a friendly force, also escaped his attention. What he did notice was a soldier with black hair and brown skin sitting in the jungle. In panic he fired all eighteen rounds in his magazine at the lone man. Only one bullet struck Gomez—the one that passed through his brain.

The other men in Charlie Company assumed their flank man had run into a nest of VC and poured more fire into the area. Believing themselves under attack, Delta returned fire. When a pause came in the shooting, Charlie Company heard the call for a medic coming from their attack area and realized they were having a firefight with another American unit. Gomez was the only casualty.

Feeling sick and angry, all I can think of is strangling the idiot who killed Gomez. I set out on a halfhearted attempt to find the man, but before I get far I learn he is being flown out with the body. A wise decision.

Black thoughts drag my mood into a mire of resentment. Damn this stupid, useless war. Damn the people who sent us here.

We walk on, hour after hour, the heat, the fatigue, and the sameness wearing my anger. Eventually, I cease to think at all. My eyes watch for cover, my feet move over the ground, and my arms shift the gun from shoulder to shoulder.

When the light begins to fade the two companies take a welcome rest in a grove of large trees. Three times men come by asking for water. I shake my head no. I only have a few swallows left—besides, we all started with full canteens.

I watch the ants hurry on their erratic path across the jungle floor. What motivates an ant? What keeps him working so hard all his life? Is it mindless instinct? Fear? How come I never see a fat, lazy ant just cooling itself in the shade?

There is a spider's web in a bush near my side. What an intricate, delicate creation the web is. There is the spider, motionless at the edge of his web, waiting. I flick an ant into the spider's lair. The spider runs lightly over his silvery web to see who has come to be his dinner. The ant's struggles are to no avail; the sticky threads will not come free. The spider wraps his prey. . . .

"Be ready to move out in five minutes."

I'm ready. I'm ready. I roll back beside my gun. I poke around a little, looking for dirt that might cause a jam. My gaze falls on the ammunition belt hanging out the side of the gun. I realize with a start that there must be very few rounds left in the assault pouch. I rip the cover off. Thirteen rounds are all that remain on the belt. Terrific. You stupid shit. I search for a can of machine-gun ammo. Get your act together,

Shook, or you're going to leave this place wrapped in a green rubber bag.

I find a can next to a guy puffing on a cigarette. I pick up the box and walk off. I know he will not object to its loss. I put a hundred rounds into the assault pouch and wrap the remaining hundred rounds around my shoulder like a Mexican bandito. Now I am ready.

We walk for half an hour in the deepening twilight, stopping at the edge of another large clearing created by the war. Our combined force crouches under the trees waiting for the darkness that will conceal our movement across the bomb-cratered land before us. Two kilometers to the southwest a battle rages. The sounds of rifles, grenades, and mortars grow and fade and grow again, the rattle of war increasing in intensity with each oscillation.

Sergeant Norris gathers his men around him. His voice is tight, his manner demanding. "In the trees across this clearing there is a battalion of NVA. They are surrounded by two battalions of the 1st Division. Our job is to seal off this corner of the encirclement. The bulk of the NVA are now about one kilometer beyond the far tree line, as you can hear. However, if they don't break through on the west side they will be pushed into our position. From here we will proceed south to the edge of the trees. Delta Company will then turn west along the tree line while Charlie Company continues south. We have very little time. Are there any questions?"

"Yeah, Sarge, can I take my R and R now?"

"Shut up, Lansky. I want absolute quiet going across this clearing. Squad leaders, have your men jump up and down to make sure nothing rattles."

While we are jumping up and down and tightening each other's gear, Norris arranges the platoon in the order he wants it to cross the clearing.

"All right. Move fast but don't run. We must reach the far edge of this open area before the NVA. Move out."

Not until now does it dawn on me that our platoon has been assigned to walk point. I guess we just tiptoe out here and see if anybody shoots us. You sure you wouldn't like to ask for volunteers? This is just terrific out here in the open. Don't shoot the tall guy with the machine gun. Why does our platoon leader have to be the man most relied upon by the captain? Where are all those eager lieutenants? How do we know Charlie isn't already at the edge of the tree line? Easy.

If when we get to the middle of this open area we get splattered all over Vietnam, then we'll know the NVA reached the tree line first. Why does it have to be so clear tonight? Where is a good monsoon when you need one? I wonder if anyone would notice if I sort of veered off to the east here? Why don't we wait in our trees for them to cross the clearing? Oh, Jesus, how I wish I were anywhere but here.

We hit the ground in response to a series of explosions. It is just an air strike a kilometer in the distance. We hear the screams of jets, the explosions of their rockets. The rattle of gunfire is louder now. Can't we go any faster?

We reach the corner. I am the eighth man in line as we turn the corner at the edge of the tree line heading west. The point man skirts the trees at a crouch, followed by Norris, then the radioman followed by two others, then Dryden, Sandy, and myself. We hear the *braaaaah* of a Minigun firing six thousand rounds a minute from a C-47. Every fifth round fired is a tracer, creating a solid, wavy red streak through the sky. Thank God everything that flies is ours.

We make a hundred yards on our western leg before we receive scattered fire from the trees. I find myself lying on flat ground with no cover. The memory of being caught in an exposed position during the village seal makes me determined to find some kind of shelter. As the platoon launches its first volley into the tree line I crawl forward on my belly toward a depression I can see thirty feet up the line. As I crawl behind Norris he yells, "Where the hell are you going?"

I can't stop to explain. A few more meters and I slide into the protection of the shallow crater. Without exposing any body parts, I slide the gun over the lip of the crater and fire blindly into the jungle. The fire from the trees is heavier now. I look back the way I have come. I see prone forms firing and moving over the ground, seeking any kind of cover. Dryden moves into a hollow to my right front. I can make out another form that must be the point man further up our line moving toward the trees. A burst of fire comes from the trees, not more than ten meters ahead of the point man. The air is rent by a blood-chilling scream. I shrink into my hole. Point has been hit. His screams are horrible. I grab the gun, peek over the lip of my crater, and fire a long burst into the woods. Don't be stupid and fire all your rounds. Controlled fire. Controlled.

The urgent roar of battle surrounds me. The explosions

of hand grenades and M-79 grenade launchers are mixed with the rifle and machine-gun fire. But those cursed screams pierce all other sound. It is the scream of pure animal terror that shatters the soul. It is unbearable. Dryden is yelling hysterically, "I can't stand it! I'm going to get him!"

"No! You stay put!" bellows Norris, now within two body lengths of me.

I risk a look over the top of my hole. I see Dryden crawling toward the screams. He must have lost his mind. He is going to get himself killed.

"Dryden! No!" I hear the shouted words distantly reverberating in my mind together with the clatter of machine-gun fire. Stop Dryden. Stop. Come back.

My body stops vibrating. The gun is still. For a second I stare at it, not comprehending. I only vaguely remember firing it. Now it's empty. I drag it down from the lip of the hole. With fumbling fingers I hurriedly engage in the eternal task of taking the belt from around my chest and fitting it into the gun. Oh shit, hurry. Hang on, Dryden. Get lucky, you crazy fucker. Concentrate on what I'm doing. Do it fast— carefully. Please, don't get shot for another second. There. I throw the gun back over the top of the hole, firing as it lands on the lip of the crater.

Dryden has reached the foot of the point man who is still screaming in stark terror. I fire at the muzzle flashes in the woods, but as soon as one source dies it is replaced by two or three more. The North Vietnamese must have been waiting for someone to try to rescue the wounded man, hoping we were too soft to ignore his anguish. An independent firefight has developed over the two men pinned between our opposing forces. The four or five GIs close enough to be aware of Dryden's desperate efforts frantically try to pour enough fire into the tree line to provide him cover.

Suddenly, the screams stop. Then the fighting nearby stops as well. For a few heartbeats we are still, listening intently to the void that was filled with horror—the void that is the silence of death. A shudder runs through me. The firing starts again, breaking the spell, walling off thought. Through the darkness I see Dryden's motionless form, his arm outstretched for the boot of the man whose soul-shattering screams he could not endure.

Slowly I slide back into my hole, my ammunition nearly gone. What now? I finger the foot-long belt that hangs from the side of my gun. Should I crawl down our line in search of the boxes of ammunition that never seem to be where they are needed? Should I wait here for a hand grenade to find me, or will the tangle of jungle growth prevent their use?

Something heavy lands on my legs. I spin to find our medic with the barrel of my gun in his chest.

"Jesus, Chandler!" I explode.

"Easy with that thing," pants our platoon medic, carefully pushing the machine gun barrel to one side. He must have crawled behind me and then flung himself into the crater.

"Is there any chance of getting to that wounded man who was screaming up there?" He shouts at me from two feet away to be heard above the din of the battle. "I would have been here sooner but I had some work to do down the line, and then with all this shit flying around I thought I was never going to make it here."

"You're fucking crazy, crawling up here."

Outside of Norris, who has been in the war too long to be actually sane, Chandler is the bravest man in our platoon. He will go after a wounded man anywhere unless he feels he is sure to get shot.

"There is no chance, Chandler. There is another man lying out there who just tried. Besides, I think they are both dead."

He slides up to have a look over the top. I am ready to grab his leg in case he gets any foolish ideas. He slides back down. "I think you're right."

We settle into the hole, wondering what to do with ourselves. Everybody must be running out of ammo by now, even Charlie. I wish a man like Chandler was carrying my machine-gun ammo, then I would have something to do. At least he has an M-16, that helps, and so does his presence in the crater. Every minute or so, one of us peeks at the tree line to make sure no one is sneaking up on us. After a while he nods toward the silent gun and asks, "What's the matter? You resign from the war?"

"I wish. You didn't see anybody back there with a couple of boxes of M-60 ammo, did you?"

"I didn't notice," he says taking a look around. "I think the gooks have didi maued."

We are both quiet as we listen to the dwindling gunfire. Once again I become aware of the air strike raging in the jungle. So this is how tropical forests are turned into waste-land. The might of our air power is impressive. The trouble is, I don't think the NVA are in these woods anymore. The small arms fire is scattered and distant. Only the thundering reverberations of the big stuff continue unabated. I bet Major Barlow is flying up there loving every minute of this U.S. Army extravaganza coming to him complete with Panavision, Technicolor, and stereophonic sound.

After a few more minutes, Chandler crawls to Dryden and the point man to see if a glimmer of life still clings there. When he drops back into my crater all he says is, "I've got to get back. The chopper will be coming for the wounded soon."

I lie in my hole and stare at the sky. I feel empty and exhausted and sickened. I try to let my mind escape into the vision of sparkling peacefulness above me, but I know its apparent calm is a lie, just as the stories of my youth were a lie. What glory lies here among these dead and frightened men? Where is there found anything of honor? And how started the myth that the shooting of another human being is a soul-rending experience? Shooting at men is frighteningly easy. It is dealing with the remains that sickens the heart, regardless of who produced the corpse.

After a time, I crawl down the line to round up the remaining four cans of M-60 ammo. I set the gun in a different hole closer to the remainder of my squad. I drink my last mouthful of water before remembering the can of peaches tied up in a sock on the back of my web gear. Their thick, syrupy sweetness is a luxurious treat. I think I shall always love peaches.

We maintain our positions through the night. The dead are left where they fell. In the morning we sweep the woods for the brass's precious body count. The last thing in the world I want to do this morning is to go on an Easter egg hunt for dead, mangled bodies.

The Vietnamese are fanatical about carrying off their dead and wounded. It has something to do with their belief that a man must be buried properly if he is to reach heaven. After many a firefight the only evidence of the enemy's presence the night before is some abandoned equipment and blood-soaked patches of earth.

But last night they left the dead behind. They had to move fast, with stealth, to escape our trap. They could not

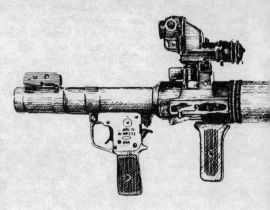

RPG 7

save their lives and the souls of their dead, so they left the
dead and the dying where they fell, their souls unattended.

If I had my choice, I would have wandered through the
woods avoiding anything that resembled a body. But some of
them could still be alive, still harboring a desire to kill the
hated American. It is because of this that I search carefully
and remain alert.

I see a foot, then a pair of legs, protruding from behind a
tree. He lies on his stomach with his limbs splayed at unnatural angles. I swing to my right to approach him from the feet
where it will be more difficult for him to roll and shoot at me.
There is blood splattered across his back, an AK-47 still
clutched in his right hand. I stop ten feet short of his sandaled feet. "Sergeant, there's another one over here."

Norris comes straight to the body as if he could smell it.
He steps on the wrist of the hand holding the gun, leans
over, and jerks the gun free. He strips the body of its bandolier of ammunition, handing both the ammo and the rifle to
me. He might have kept the rifle for himself, but he already
has an AK-47 slung across his shoulder one way and two
bandoliers tied across his chest the other. He continues to
rapidly search and strip the body, removing anything of interest or of military value.

I rejoin the sweep, not wanting to look at death unneces-
sarily. I do not mind that the man is dead, but I have not yet

hardened to the sight of mutilated bodies. I wonder if I will ever become inured to the sight and feel of violent death. But I must adapt. I must become more callous or I will lose my grip on sanity. Yet what will be left of tenderness and compassion when I learn to rip out a man's guts without revulsion?

We count fourteen NVA bodies in our company's section. Someone imaginatively estimates twice that number wounded. From our radioman we learn that the total score for the operation is 120 NVA dead, 263 wounded. We have a good laugh at that. No doubt the fighting was heavier on the west side where contact was first made, but if that many NVA were killed and wounded it would mean that virtually every man who escaped was wounded, which presents some interesting logistics problems. As usual, each captain is trying to out-lie his competitors in the race for major. But our captain does not seem to be playing the game. It appears he has taken himself out of the race. I wonder why?

The helicopters are busy all morning bringing in officers and reporters, and taking out the dead. Pale-skinned men in pristine uniforms come from their air-conditioned offices in Long Binh to explain the exciting details of last night's action to other men who look half asleep with boredom.

"Over there, gentlemen, is the sector where I trapped the NVA battalion. Those rows of bodies are some of the one hundred twenty enemy dead that I caught and crushed as easily as I squash a bug between my fingers. You see, gentlemen, the NVA are really no match for the U.S. Army once they are forced to stand and fight."

"Yes, yes, of course. And is that bedraggled crew of men lying over there in the shade a part of your elite fighting force, Colonel?" asks a reporter, waving a hand in our general direction.

The colonel, clearly irritated by this interruption to the chronicle of his achievements, does a quick one-eighty in search of the offending troops. When his gaze falls upon our company, his face contorts in disgust. I suppose we have a military bearing that is about as far from the colonel's sense of the ideal as it is humanly possible to achieve. Men are sprawled in every conceivable position of rest. A lean, sinewy group, barely averaging twenty years of age, with the red-rimmed, vacant stare of old men. Dirt-encrusted, ragged fatigues hang loosely on sun-tanned, jungle-rotted bodies. Tired, dirty faces take in the ogling spectators with haunting indifference.

The colonel shudders. Turning back to his gaggle of cocktail-circuit reporters he dismisses us with a wave of his arm, "Oh, that's just the mop-up crew. They pick up the dead, collect enemy weapons, and other such menial but necessary tasks." Continuing his self-elevating commentary he leads his sleepy entourage from the offending sight to more pleasant surroundings.

After the VIPs are returned to the bars in Saigon and Long Binh, the helicopters return to ferry us to our patch of dirt at the edge of the swamp. The sight of the sun-baked earth of our NDP does not make anyone smile inwardly at memories of the beauty and serenity of home, but at least we feel somewhat protected here from Charlie and the prying eyes that come to gape at the spectacle of war.

We are greeted by the quiet solemn faces of our mortar unit. They had spent part of the night exchanging mortar fire with the VC. An incoming RPG round, which is a Russian-made, portable, ground-fired rocket, landed a few feet from a mortar pit, filling one man's upper back and head with metal splinters. The mortar men are glad for the return of our numbers to strengthen the NDP.

Inside the platoon hut hungry men tear open cases of C rations to still their long-neglected stomachs. Eager hands rip cardboard, frantic fingers grab for prized meals. But I am in no mood to compete for dinner—besides, I am not as sick of the limited selection of food as most of the men whose primary fuel has come from these cans for several months.

I find a quiet space along the wall and begin to clean the gun. Now, I want most of all to be left alone. In time perhaps I will take events like last night's bloody action in stride the way the rest of the platoon seems to, but for now I need some peace to let my emotions subside. I completely disassemble the M-60, laying the multitude of parts on a poncho. Meticulously oiling and cleaning each part keeps my hands busy while my mind sifts and mulls its jumble of excesses. Everyone here approves of thorough maintenance of the gun, so I am left to myself for almost an hour until Sandy drops a carton of Cs at my side, saying, "You better eat something."

"I will. Thanks."

He sits on his heels for a while watching me put the last few pieces together. "The platoon lost four men last night."

I nod: two dead, two wounded. Seven men in the company were wounded in total, but two of those were only minor and should return in a few days. It could've been a lot worse.

"They're sending up two new men tomorrow." After another pause he says, "I need an assistant squad leader to replace Dryden. How would you like the job?"

"Not particularly."

"Well, Sergeant Norris told me to pick a man to fill the position. When I suggested your name he agreed, so you're it. Okay?"

"Sure, Sandy, whatever."

"You will make Spec 4 in six weeks and before you've been in-country for six months you'll be a sergeant."

I nod again as he leaves. I don't like the idea of being responsible for other men's lives in a cause I don't believe is worth the inevitable sacrifice of those lives. I don't want to be associated with the ego-maniacal authority that won't or can't recognize the men in their own command. On the other hand, assistant squad leader isn't responsible for anything more than passing the word along, and by the time I am a squad leader I will have the experience to be competent at the job. Then, maybe, I can save those lives that can be saved. On the other hand, replacing a man who was well on his way to insanity before he got shot could be construed as a bad omen—if you believe in such things—which of course I don't.

They could award Dryden a Bronze Star for what he did. Norris wouldn't tell anybody that he ordered Dryden not to go after the screaming point man, and nobody else is likely to say that Dryden went after the man because his mind was on the edge of dissolution. Considering who his father is, there is little doubt that Bill will be awarded a Bronze Star posthumously. Driven mad and shot dead; an old man of nineteen. I wonder if "Bulldog" Bill Dryden is proud of his son now? One thing for sure—Bill Dryden doesn't care anymore.

Oh, the hell with this, I'm going to take a shower. I get the bucket that holds the two gallons of water each man is allotted for a shower. The water runs cool and clear from the 250-gallon portable tank that is our main water supply. The water's alien chill means that it was hauled all the way from that deep well in Di An late yesterday or early this morning. This is prime drinking water, but the best shower water comes from a nearly empty tank, warmed by a day or two in the sun. I could put my allotment in a jerry can and set it in the sun. Na, I don't want to wait the hours it would take to warm.

Inside the tin lean-to that serves as our bath, a canvas bucket with several holes in the bottom is suspended from the ceiling on a rope. I pour one third of the cool, precious liquid into the canvas shower. Quickly setting the metal bucket aside I jump under the bracing spray. Immediately the spray dwindles to a trickle and then a drip which is delivered into my quizzically upturned eye. A brown, muddy rivulet slides off my hair to wind its way through the dust on my chest. I consider my water supply and the apparatus overhead. Yep, a typical case of Army planning. I would need at least six gallons of water to bathe under this fine Army shower bucket. Clearly, the panel that approved the contract for these buckets didn't give them a field trial. Well, expecting some major to take a cold shower on behalf of the troops is really asking too much. Besides, there probably wasn't a two-gallon limit on water in Michigan, or wherever at the time. I take a sponge bath with the rest of my water. Except for making the towel brown, my first field shower must be considered a success.

Wrapping the towel around my waist I head for the bundle of clean clothes I noticed earlier in the platoon hut when I am brought up short by an unbelievable sight. There in the shimmering heat before me is a vision of four white American girls in short skirts and white blouses with a look on their faces like they just stepped off the bus in Harlem and realized they forgot to dress this morning.

I close my eyes. It is just the heat, a weird mirage, a mild hallucination. I'm okay—really. I'll open my eyes and they'll be gone. I take a peek under my lids. Damn! They're still there. I snap my eyes shut again. Okay, Scotty, beam me up, I can't take any more. All right, no shit now, what's going on here? Either my mind has time warped me back to high school or those chicks are really here.

Yep, they're real, all right. Just look at those sorry GIs gawking at those girls like they just dropped in from Venus. Bleak, grimy soldiers with the scent of death still on them stare in silence at bare legs, firm breasts, curls rigid with hair spray, pancake makeup faces, grease-red lips stretched in tentative smiles, and fearful eyes darting under pale blue and green lids.

For an insane moment I believe the great white father who lives the long freedom-bird ride across the ocean has sent us a gift for our victory in the field. But an embarrassed glance by one of the girls at my staring eyes, open mouth, and towel-clad body, brings me back to reality.

As men shake their heads in disbelief and wander to the seclusion of their huts and bunkers, I hurry off to search through the pile of clothes for pants and shirt that are of approximate fit.

"Where . . . why . . . who are those women out there?" I stammer as I successfully find pants that are only two inches short.

"Don't get excited, man. Those Red Cross girls aren't going to do you any good."

"What the hell are they doing here?"

"They come once every couple of months to cheer us up. It's a shitty deal all the way around."

I grab a shirt on my way back outside. The girls stand behind a card table that holds a big thermos of punch and several paper cups. The crowd of GIs, dressed in their usual green boxer shorts and shower shoes, has been replaced by a dozen fully clothed guys sitting on the ground in front of the table. One of the girls is pointing to a big folder resting on an easel behind her. They are playing some kind of game involving state capitals and flowers. Only one guy is participating in the game, the rest of the men are here simply to stare at honest-to-God round-eyed girls. The small group of females is embarrassed by the eyes that follow their bodies every move. The game repeatedly lapses into silence. I feel sorry for these young women with painted faces, vainly trying to hide the pimples of their youth. Here are four girls fresh out of high school trying to engage a dozen killers in a child's game while silently praying that they make it out of here without getting raped.

These people could have been classmates a year ago, but the gap that now separates them is so vast that it may never be bridged. Was the brilliant mind that dreamed up Red Cross girl visits from the same source that was convinced that a guerrilla war could be won using conventional World War II tactics? Perhaps next year we'll have hovering cheerleaders for our firefights, with death-by-death television coverage complete with instant replay. Sometimes I wonder if anyone above the rank of captain has any idea of what's going on out here.

After the girls safely escape in their helicopter, there is a slow, steady procession of men going over the north wall of the perimeter. In well-spaced groups of threes and fours, they shuffle along in olive-drab skivvies and unlaced jungle boots. In the shade of the trees of an old untended orchard, mama-san and six of her girls wait daily to service the men of Delta Company. Straw mats are spread in the knee-high grass, each nest separated by fifteen or twenty feet to give some semblance of privacy. The old mama-san is very obliging. If you don't like the girls she has brought she will send a boy to bring others who might better suit your taste. For a fifty-cent additional fee she will hold an umbrella over you and your girl if you can't wait for a drier day. A mere three dollars MPC entitles you to a short time—ten minutes on the mat. Afterwards, if you want to get mellow, you get yourself a three-dollar pack of American cigarettes that has been steamed open, filled with marijuana, and resealed.

It is part of the benefits of living next to a Vietnamese village. Every day the village daughters are sent to give a little pleasure to their American guardians of freedom in exchange for what amounts to five days of peasant wages a trick. At night the fathers and brothers get their vengeance by dropping mortar rounds on us. They are never very serious with their attacks—just a few poorly aimed mortar rounds once a week or so, or maybe a clip or two of small arms fire. They do not want to kill the golden goose, but they must do something to appease those nasty NLF boys when they drop by the village.

The good captain does not try to keep the men from their few small pleasures, but he has made some rules. No one can leave camp alone. One man in every group must carry an M-16 and stand guard while his buddies frolic under the trees. No marijuana smoking after dark or at anytime outside the NDP.

None of my information concerning the revelry on the shaded grass is from firsthand observation because I have not visited mama-san, although, God knows, I am tempted. Lying with a prostitute runs against the grain of my upbringing, and although my natural urges may soon enable me to overcome the tenets of my youth and ignore the perils of venereal disease, my sense of loyalty to the girl I intend to marry demands that I reserve my sexual passions for her exclusive enjoyment.

Most of my friends think my fealty is foolish. During the hot, boring days and the long, sleepless, mosquito-ridden nights, our conversation frequently turns to old adventures and the girls we knew back in the world. Since Julie is so much on my mind, my comrades soon learn of my plans to marry when my tour is over. My friends are skeptical of any woman's ability to remain loyal for an entire year. Vareck, with his 145 IQ, seems to think he has a corner on all the information pertaining to the behavior of the woman who was left behind. He began his lecture eloquently. "Don't be a jerk, Shook. No good-looking woman is going to wait a year for anybody—married or not. How could you be so ignorant and naive? Granted, even she may be convinced of her future faithfulness as she waves her last farewell, but that conviction will soon erode. She is accustomed to the pleasures of a man, and she will have temptations every day. The relief to all her frustrations is perpetually only a nod away. Her memory of you will slowly fade while her fantasies of that 4-F jock next door will grow ever more vivid. Why should she make herself miserable for an entire year waiting around for your shaved-headed, gook-killing, mind-fucked, jungle-rotted body? Heed my words, my friend, and save yourself the agony."

The gathering's agreement is universally, "Right on, man.

Say, you wouldn't believe the number of dudes around here that got them 'Dear John' letters."

What's so disturbing about their remarks is that they echo my words of old. How many times have I impressed upon others the uselessness of pining over a girl when she's likely to be married to somebody else before their two-year hitch is up? Nevertheless, I heed their advice no more than other men had heeded mine. This situation's different; Julie and I are different. The old advice surely doesn't apply to us.

I write to her every day I'm not in the bush and she answers with even greater regularity. We promise each other life-long love and devotion, discuss children and careers, describe the small events of our separate lives, and vent our building, pressing passions upon the indifferent pages. She says her greatest accomplishment in life has been getting me to love her and that she will be waiting for me when I return. I want her so desperately I get excited every time I think of her golden hair and sensuous, shapely form.

I recently found out that it is possible to get a Hawaiian R and R if you are willing to wait well past the minimum six months in-country. Julie and I could meet in paradise. Man, that would be pure heaven. Okay, I'm willing to wait. What choice do I have? I want her so much I can hardly stand it, yet the months I am required to wait stretch before me into the endless plane of eternity. The wait is many times longer than I can endure. Even this single day goes on forever. I will not think about time. I will not count the days. I will think of each day as number one; the one day I can barely tolerate. Tomorrow's day will be barely tolerable as well, and I will be able to endure it because it will be like the day I just endured. And I shall dream without reference to time. I will conjure erotic scenes on sandy beaches—and the pressure will grow.

I have learned to omit any mention of danger or death in my letters to Julie. Even a cursory description of the war evokes grave and unrealistic concern. In her letters she asks, "Are you in any danger?" and "Is there much shooting where you are?" I picture her spending a sleepless night with tear-filled eyes, and I tell her, "No, it's quite safe where I am." My conscience cringes at the lie, but I justify it by telling myself that I am saving her a lot of grief. Still, her display of alarm over the violence here surprises me. What does she think happens in a war?

I have not been so considerate with the letters I send to my friends and relatives. Their letters are mailed uncensored, with a little political commentary thrown in for color. But their reaction surprises me even more. They are not interested in hearing about the war. They seem to have their minds made up about what is going on over here. They will not discuss it and they certainly do not want to hear about it. This is especially true of my parents' generation. The way I understand their feelings—though this is pure conjecture because I cannot pry an opinion out of them on the subject—is that a man is honor-bound to shut up and serve his country and never mind the comments on the wisdom of his government's actions. It seems a very undemocratic view to me.

On Wednesday—I can tell it is Wednesday because a minister of one denomination or another usually visits our NDP on Wednesdays—our platoon is assigned a second staff sergeant. Actually, Sergeant Jackson is rejoining us after a six-week absence. His whereabouts during this period is somewhat a mystery, but the only circumstances I can imagine that would allow a man to be separated from his unit for that length of time would be an emergency leave back to the world to take care of some kind of family trauma or a stint in the hospital. He could have been in the stockade, but if he did something serious enough to get court-martialed and interned, he would also have been demoted.

At any rate, he is not telling and this makes the troops even more curious. "Come on, Sarge, where you been?"

"I've been dancing down the main street of life, tickling my taste buds with golden nectar, going where the night lights shine, living on good times, and filling my soul with sweet memories."

"Right, Sarge. Thanks for clearing that up for me."

"No thanks is required. That's what your old sarge is here for: to guide you on your way through the booby traps of life."

The high-spirited banter continues for over an hour. Jackson asks questions about everything that happened during his absence while interjecting a lot of nonsense to keep things light and friendly. His behavior is quite unlike any sergeant I have known and diametrically opposed to Norris's cool detachment.

Jackson is a tall, rangy black in his late twenties. He

walks among his men wearing a whimsical expression as if he is the sole possessor of an amusing secret about to bubble forth. There is so little humor here that men are drawn to the sound of it, warmed by the feel of it.

The reunion is interrupted when Norris ushers Jackson off to a meeting with the captain. I do not see them again until the safety of daylight is dissolving in the west. As the last rays of sunlight glint off the company skull perched high on its shaft, I spot the two sergeants and a Vietnamese sitting cross-legged on the bunker beneath the skull, their heads bent close in conpiratorial conversation. The third man is our elusive scout and interpreter. Why is Liem here at dusk instead of appearing as usual with the dawn? His presence anytime is foreboding. An uneasy feeling creeps over me.

I wake to the boom, boom, boom, boom of incoming mortar rounds. Crawling to the entrance of my bunker, with my poncho liner dragging behind me, I see the shadowy forms of men leaping into mortar pits. A voice calls out windage and elevation in a Puerto Rican accent. Men echo numbers to the shouted commands. Furious activity in the pits.

"Crew one ready."

"Crew two ready."

"Crew three ready."

"Crew four ready."

"Hang it in the hole."

"Fire in the hole."

Hollow thunks report from the tubes as 81-millimeter shells arch skyward. The jungle erupts in a rapid series of explosions.

An expectant hush fills the night. The creatures of the swamp are still. Bodies tense. Senses alert.

A mosquito roars to a landing inside my ear. A frog belches a trial croak. A cricket rasps and is answered by its neighbor. The swamp resumes its cacophony of racket. I pull the poncho liner around my shoulders and roll back into the bunker.

Sergeant Jackson doubles in agony against the outer wall of the platoon hut. He sits on his heels, clutching his stomach, rocking and groaning. I kneel down beside him. Beads of sweat stand out on his face despite the coolness of the pre-dawn air.

"You don't look so good," I offer, not knowing what else to say.

"I'll be all right in a minute," he replies between clenched teeth. He is dressed, ready for patrol, but the pain in his face tells me he is not going to make it.

"Anything I can do for you?"

"No, it's just stomach cramps from that damned Viet-namese wine." A shudder runs through him accompanied by another groan.

"How about if I get the medic?"

"No. If they find out I spent the night in the village I'll get busted."

The village! Christ! There is little doubt that the guys who dropped mortars on us last night live in that village. Besides, it is strictly off limits.

"Well, listen, Sarge, you've got to do something. You could have been poisoned in that fucking village. They might not have any fancy chemicals but there is plenty of excrement and poisonous plants for them to slip into a drink."

"Yeah, I suppose you're right. Get Norris for me, will you?"

I look around for Norris, hoping he is not in the same sorry state as Jackson. He is not. He is rushing around preparing the platoon for patrol in his usual brisk manner. I quietly inform him of Jackson's condition. He curses and tells me to keep quiet about it.

A medivac is not called because that would result in the filing of an official report and the subsequent demotion of both sergeants. Instead, Jackson is sent to the rear with the supply truck so he can produce any story that suits him. He certainly was not with us long.

Norris takes Jackson's second squad to the south while Sandy leads the first squad east. Second platoon sends its two squads north and west. The plan is to set up night ambushes around the NDP in an effort to catch the local VC mortar crew. Following Sandy's lead we head northeast, then south, then east, then southeast in an attempt to lose or at least confuse the unseen eyes that follow us. Two hours pass. We are far enough from the NDP. The squad looks for a dry, shady spot that is relatively free of ants and has a good view of its approaches. We settle in for the day under the branches of a thick grove joined on two sides by dry, abandoned rice fields.

It is a good place, and it sure beats walking around in the bush all day, but after taking in the scenery for an hour I am deathly bored. We have no cards, no books, no radio, no writing material. I roam, looking for something to do until the other guys tell me to park it somewhere: I am making a target of myself and drawing attention. In desperation I choose the ants to be my unwitting playmates. Although the ground beneath me is not the usual Calcutta of the ant world, it is not the Sahara either. There is never any fear of an ant shortage.

I break off a piece from a tropical chocolate bar and place it on the ground. As the ants approach, I flick them back with a twig. Soon the ants are rushing Chocolate Hill faster than I can repel them. Quickly I dig a moat, but I am too late. Chocolate Hill has taken flight on unseen legs. Bearing their prize aloft the red hordes are triumphantly returning to their home in the bowels of the earth when suddenly, a mighty force seizes the succulent trove and hoists it effortlessly into the heavens.

I return Chocolate Hill to its protected place and fill the moat with half the water in my canteen. The red horde races along the edge of the water. I have them at bay. But no, those devils are swimming the moat. I squirt bug repellent upon the water. Yes, yes. We have them now. Ho, ho. Hee, hee. But wait. The water sinks into the earth. My moat's dry. Still the bug juice holds them back. Oh no, a breakthrough on the right, a breach on the left. We are being overrun. Do not fear. We are not yet lost. A size-twelve boot should put a crimp in their day.

Whoa. How old did you say you were? Nanner, nanner, nanner. How many more months of this remain? Shit! Don't think about it. Look for Charlie or count the trees or dream of faraway places.

"Ants, I must go now. Enjoy your feast."

"Hey, Boston. What time is it?"

"Nine twenty-three."

Nine twenty-three! Oh-my-God. Maybe I'll have something to eat. No, then I won't have anything to do at noon. Relax. Take it easy. I know. I'll plan a boat trip to the South Pacific. Yeah, that'll be good.

My mind wanders the vast ocean reaches, it lingers in the fresh palm-scented breeze, losing itself in the vision of

M-29 81mm Mortar

grass-skirted wahines. Damn, I'm horny. I'd better think of something else.

I daydream every daydream I can conjure up until I can't stand it anymore.

"Hey, Boston. What time is it?"

"Ten forty-seven, and quit asking me."

Holy shit. If I had a joint right now I'd smoke it. Just think. A year of this. A whole bleedin' year. I sit at the edge of the steaming jungle and wait for a year so that I can begin my life again. My year has a long way to go, but my forbearance is all used up and I can't figure any way to get any more. I would welcome any kind of diversion—except a firefight.

I talk to all nine men in the squad, smoke all my cigarettes (even though I don't smoke), watch my instant coffee dissolve in a small puddle of water, shred my toilet paper, make a paper airplane out of the empty cigarette pack, chew my gum, and spend hours trying to make my mind like a clear, still pool of water through the practice of yoga, which I don't know anything about. At long last daylight begins to fade. Unfortunately, the change is brought about by clouds, not nightfall. We are soon awash in a torrential rain. Well, at least this is different.

We sit in the downpour for a long time trying to determine if what we are experiencing is twilight or just heavier cloud cover. When visibility drops to fifteen feet we decide the cause of the dwindling light is irrelevant—it is unquestionably dark enough to conceal our movement to the ambush site. As we walk through the roaring rain, darkness closes in. How Sandy can tell where he is going is beyond me. Perhaps he has been here before. After half an hour we come to a piece of land a couple of inches higher than the rest. This, Sandy decides, is where we will spend the night. We set the claymores in a line and lay down on the soggy jungle floor.

As soon as we arrange ourselves in our watery beds the rain stops as suddenly as if someone turned off the tap. The dark blanket of clouds breaks into individual puffy dollops that slowly dissipate to leave us with a standard starry night. By this new light we see that our ambush is directed at a formidable stand of trees while our left flank borders on a long, open section. This is hardly a textbook ambush. Grumbling to ourselves we crawl to our claymores and move them to cover the open expanse of long grass.

About 2300 a call comes over the radio reporting company-sized enemy movement in our area. At the end of the transmission they request the coordinates of our position. Sandy has to confess that he does not know exactly where we are. HQ replies that they will send up some white flares which we are to correct until they pop one directly over the open area before us. Their first attempt is nowhere in sight, but by the fifth effort they light the landscape before us. They pop three more flares in a scattered pattern after they have us located so as not to give away our position.

Intelligence reports enemy activity nearly every place we go, but the enemy is an elusive creature and rarely shows as scheduled. Tonight, however, my uneasiness keeps me scanning the waist-deep grass long after I should have gone to sleep. I keep spotting movement that further observation reveals to be nothing more than grass swaying in the breeze. Vaporous images of soldiers pass before me, only to disappear again as my eye shifts. A company of men could stand in the open at the edge of the jungle and I would never see them unless they moved. When I think I see something I stare at the spot for several seconds. If nothing reveals itself I continue scanning. Every time my scan brings me back to a spot under question, I stare at it for a few seconds, waiting for something to move. I might have two or three spots going at the same time, giving up on a location only after I have run out of patience with it.

Something moves to my far right, across the open area at the edge of the trees. I concentrate on it for a while, but I am unable to distinguish anything unusual, so I go on with my scan. As my gaze moves back across the area, I see movement again in the same place. After a couple of seconds I see a form change position while I am looking directly at it. Am I imagining things again? No, this is real. There it is again. And another. There is a third. I poke the guy next to me. He comes awake easily, quietly, without movement. I slide over and whisper, "Three VC," in his ear and point in their direction. He passes the message down the line.

Now there are four moving diagonally across the open space, bent over so only their heads are visible above the grass. Their line of travel will take them directly in front of us. The guy on my left whispers, "Hold fire until Sandy opens up." I pass the message.

I track their movement through the sights of the machine gun. They are fifty meters out now. Another twenty meters will put them in perfect position. Right—about—now. . . . What the hell's he waiting for? They're crossing right in front of us. I can even see their rifles. He's letting them go. I hope they don't spot us. I watch them disappear into the woods, then snap my attention back to the spot where they emerged from the brush on the other side of the opening. Maybe they're a point unit for the company we were told about; that must be what Sandy's thinking.

We watch the far side of the clearing. We listen for sounds behind us. The enemy unit in company strength never materializes.

Our section of Vietnam is quiet for the next couple of weeks. We go on ambush every other night as usual, but Charlie is taking a break, or regrouping, or something. He still snipes at us two or three times a day when we are on patrol, just to let us know he has not forgotten us. No one appreciates his absence more than we do, but it is not always good when things are quiet like this. People get edgy waiting in the silence. We know Charlie is going to jump us sooner or later. The longer he waits the more certain we are that something bad is going to happen soon.

One night I find a cot just inside the back door of the officer's hooch. It is almost midnight, yet the cot sits vacant and unappreciated. There are only eight cots in the entire NDP. It would be a shame to let this one go to waste. Since I have guard duty at 0100, why not enjoy an hour of ease until then? I tell the guy I am to relieve where he can find me before settling onto the piece of comfortable canvas.

I lie on my stomach, staying about half awake so I can enjoy the luxury I am wallowing in, when I feel something land on the back of my neck. Instinctively, I brush it off, but as my hand makes contact with the thing I feel a sharp sting about two inches below and to the back of my left ear.

Striking a match, I search the floor of the hooch for the intruder. A foot from the wall, standing perfectly still with his tail curled over his back, is a shiny yellow scorpion. Not wanting to risk stepping on him with my foam-rubber shower shoe, I end his life by flattening him with a sandbag.

I sit down on the edge of the cot and try to remember what I learned about scorpions as a child growing up in the Mojave Desert. As I recall, scorpions are more poisonous than tarantulas but somewhat less dangerous than rattlesnakes. I also seem to remember that it's better to get stung in the leg than in the neck. Not very many people actually die from a rattlesnake bite, so if I am remembering correctly my life should not be in any danger. Besides, I knocked the scorpion off my neck at almost the time it stung me so maybe I didn't receive a full dose of its poison. The one thing I do remember for sure is that the best thing to do in such cases is to remain calm. I lie back on the cot to await further developments.

Soon my head begins to throb. Sitting up produces marked dizziness. I decide it is time to talk to the medic. Steadying myself in the doorway of the hooch, I pause to focus the somewhat bleary scene before me. An explosion of fire erupts behind me. I drop to the ground. Bullets pass overhead. I try to think. My gun is set up and manned on the southeast corner of the NDP. That means that the man behind my gun has a rifle he is not using. Jesus, my head hurts, and the noise isn't helping. Here I am with nothing in my hands to fight with. I hate feeling helpless.

I low crawl toward the east wall. People scurry on their knees in every direction. Flares burst overhead. Everybody is yelling. I reach the outer wall, prop my back against it, and watch the confusion inside the NDP. I can't figure out what's going on. Some people are firing and some aren't; there's even one guy who's trying to convince people that the fire we are taking is from one of our own platoons.

I crawl slowly toward the southeast corner of the NDP where my gun is located. I do not know why. Just to be near it, just to have someplace to go. The flares have developed a beautiful halo of color. The long red streaks of tracers slash through the air to disappear in tin huts or the jungle beyond.

Somewhere someone is yelling for a medic, then above all the other sounds I hear the viciously angry voice of Sergeant Norris. "Stop firing, you stupid son of a bitch." There is more danger in that voice than in the bullets going over our heads. The firing along the east wall stops.

I bump into the sandbag steps leading into the raised corner bunker where my machine gun is positioned. The only thing I can see in the shadowed emplacement is a boot and pant leg protruding from the darkness. I watch the boot until its movement indicates that the man connected to it is healthy. Lying on my back I can see that the incoming is easing off. My head is a combination of numbness and throbbing pain.

Unable to think of anything constructive to do, I lie still. Chandler crawls past and disappears over the wall. He still hasn't any sense. There are people shooting at each other in that swamp. There is scattered fire near the other three sides of the perimeter, but I can no longer distinguish any incoming.

A helicopter descends to hover over the swamp. While I am listening to the beat of the rotor blades, a voice startles me.

"Are you hit?"

I pull myself up to a sitting position, slightly embarrassed. I don't suppose it looks too good, me lying on my back like that. I try to focus on the face that has snuck up on me.

"No. I'm okay."

"You don't look okay."

I can tell it is Sandy even though his face is too close to bring into focus.

"No, no, I'm okay. Oh, I got bit by a scorpion before all this shit started happening."

"Well, I'll have Chandler look at you when he gets back."

We sit side by side, leaning against the sandbag wall and listening to the last shots fade into the noise of the helicopter that alternately grows louder, closer, then more distant.

"Hey, Sandy, do you have any idea what just happened here?"

"Yeah. We had a firefight with our own platoon. Three Vietnamese, an old man, a woman, and a kid walked between the first platoon's ambush position and the NDP. Lassen blew his ambush without letting HQ know what was going on. His platoon fired right into the NDP. The captain is so pissed off he says he's going to put one of the acting sergeants in charge of the first platoon."

"Did anyone get hit?"

"The two guys on LP are pretty messed up. That's where Chandler is now."

The chopper still hovers over the swamp with its spotlight on. After a while it pulls up, the sound of its rotor blades fading into the night.

A minute or two later Chandler climbs into the NDP covered with mud and blood. Sandy tries to get his attention.

"Chandler, Chandler, I've got. . . ."

"Don't fuckin' talk to me, man. I'm so goddamned mad. I'd like to kill that fuckin' pilot."

"Hey, take it easy. . . ."

"Don't tell me to take it easy. I could've saved that man's life."

Chandler is yelling, pacing back and forth, waving his hands in the air. "I could've saved him. I know I could've. That arrogant bastard. I hope he and his chicken-shit crew get blown out of the sky."

He folds his arms across his chest to keep them from shaking.

If he walks away with all that rage in him something bad is going to happen to one of our best men. In the recesses of my foggy mind I know if he yells some more it will help.

"What happened, Chandler?"

He does not answer. He just paces. Abruptly he stops in front of us and begins a rapid-fire commentary.

"I get out to the LP and there's one man dead and the other one has taken a round through the neck that has collapsed his trachea, but he still has a pulse. So I'm doing a tracheotomy, trying to get an airway cleared when this son of a bitch comes in and hovers right over me. His down draft is spraying water and mud and shit in my eyes and all over my work. I'm trying to wave him off but he just parks it forty feet over my head so I can't see or do anything. Finally, I have to let go of the airway I have partially inserted to grab the radio to get this idiot pilot to back off. I'm yelling into the radio for him to back off, to take his ship up until I can stabilize my patient, but he can't understand me because of all the chopper noise and the down draft blasting into the microphone so finally I scream, 'Take-her-up-you-stupid-mother-fucker.' That he hears. By this time my patient is covered with mud and my airway tube has been blown away. I get his neck halfway cleaned off, get a good hole cut in his trachea, which I'm holding open with my fingers, and with my free hand I've got to call this medivac back on the radio, only now the asshole says he won't come back down because of the little bit of shooting that is still going on down there. Hell, he came down the first time when there was four times as much shooting going on. I keep telling him that it is all friendly fire, that nobody is going to shoot at him, but he says he doesn't give a damn whose fire it is, he doesn't have to land under fire and he's not going to. But after a few minutes the chicken shit comes down and hovers right over me again. I'm bent over my man trying to keep all that blowing crap from suffocating him and this asshole above me knows I've got this guy's throat opened up, but he just keeps hovering right on top of me so I grab the radio again and tell that fucking pilot if he doesn't set that ship down I'm going to blow his stupid ass out of the sky, but by now my man is choking to death and it's another five minutes before anyone comes out of that chopper to help me and by that time it's too fuckin' late.

"That man shouldn't be dead. He shouldn't be. And they just took those bodies and threw them on the chopper like they were two sides of beef. I'm on my knees out there, so mad I can't even talk to these guys and I've got this 16 in my hands and I want to blow them away so bad I'm shaking all over—shit, I'm still shaking. That pilot killed that man just as sure as if he had strangled him with his own hands—and do you know why? Because I called him a stupid mother fucker, that's why. He was getting even with me for calling him a stupid mother fucker.

"I don't know, man. I came over here to save lives, I didn't want to kill anyone, but I can't even tell who the enemy is anymore. One GI shoots another GI and a third GI lets him die."

A big empty space follows in the wake of the medic's last words as his rage sinks into helpless depression. There is nothing we can do for him. The trauma and the anger may ease in the hours or days or years ahead, or. . . . We can only hope that he does not receive another bad jolt before he has learned to deal with this one. I am afraid this is going to drive him even deeper into himself. He is an intelligent, good-looking guy who is well respected. But he is always serious. He does not joke or join the bull sessions.

Chandler only begrudgingly talks to us. You get the feeling he doesn't want to know you, and I think that's exactly what he has in mind. How can he be our friend and still deal with our shattered bodies spread over the ground? He did have one friend— the medic from the second platoon—but he got bit by a bamboo viper a couple of weeks ago. He was medivacked to the hospital and none of us has heard from him since. Maybe he died—I don't know. But Chandler stays completely to himself now.

"Listen, you're a damn good medic. Just keep being a damn good medic—that's all you can do."

Without comment he turns and starts to walk away before Sandy remembers there is something else. "Say, would you have a look at him? He was stung by a scorpion."

Chandler stares at me through twenty feet of darkness. "No . . . I can't . . . get somebody else."

Sandy looks at me. "How do you feel?"

"Not too bad. Big headache. Dizzy. If whatever was going to happen hasn't happened by now, maybe it's not going to. Let's just let it go for now."

"Well, I'll see if I can't come up with something for you. And don't worry about your watch, I'll find a replacement."

I lean back against the sandbag wall. This seems as good a place as any to spend the night. I close my eyes. Little star bursts flash in my mind. A hand on my shoulder.

"Here. It's all I could find."

"Thanks." Two white tablets. Aspirin? Well, why not?

In the morning I feel like I have been deprived of the pleasure of drinking eighteen bottles of beer, but have been rewarded with the hangover nonetheless. I eat a can of fruit cocktail with peanut butter and jelly on crackers and a tin of pound cake. It does not help.

The platoon is not slated to go on patrol until noon. In the meantime there are a lot of rumors passing among the men. The source of the rumors is the meeting being held between Major Barlow, who flew in this morning, and our officers. I have heard that we are going to be moving to a new NDP tomorrow. I do not know if that is good news or not. Certainly I will miss the mosquitoes I have come to know so well, but there are many places in this country where the fighting is far worse, which is, no doubt, why we are moving. Our major will never become a colonel at the rate we are killing gooks.

I understand that since we are leaving this area we will be getting a new Vietnamese interpreter. This is not welcome news. We would rather limit the Vietnamese in our ranks to the one man we have. Liem was carefully recruited and has proven his loyalty and ability. This new guy was hired by the Army, undoubtedly with their usual selective criteria; he is Vietnamese and breathing. We have no precedent for trusting the Army's judgment. Does it have the capacity or inclination to learn where this new man's loyalty lies? Is he motivated by a belief in a cause, or is he motivated by whoever is threatening him at the time?

And there is worse news. It is rumored that fourteen chieu hois are to join the company in a week or two. These are VC and North Vietnamese soldiers who have surrendered and then have volunteered to work as scouts for the South. "Kit Carson scouts" are what they are commonly called. The idea is for them to show us where enemy weapons, tunnels, and trails are located. Although a few of them may actually lead us to a weapon or two, they are just as likely to lead us into an ambush.

The politicians love this program. They bask in righteousness when enemy soldiers shun their errant communist ways to fight for the cause of justice, truth, and freedom. What horseshit. The Kit Carsons who are not outright spies go along with the program because it is the only way they can keep from being shot or put in a prison camp. It is hard for me to comprehend a VC or NVA soldier who is so sick of fighting, or who is in such fear for his life, that he is willing to take the tremendous risk of being shot when he chieu hois just so he can fight on the other side. Or maybe he saw his village annihilated by a B-52 strike and said, "Wow, that's the side I want to be on." I can imagine what will happen to his family when word gets back home that he has switched sides. And word will get back—nothing is secret in South Vietnam for long.

If a man is sick of war he runs away, he does not join the other side. The majority of American soldiers I have met hate this war. A lot of them feel we have no business in Vietnam. There are even a few who think the North's cause is more just than the South's, but I haven't met anyone who wants to fight for the NVA.

Granted, a man who wishes to stay out of the war may wake up one night to find himself conscripted into the northern army. He may find an opportunity to escape from this unwanted service by surrendering to a U.S. compound. Then, if his family has already been killed by the VC or NVA he might join the southern forces for vengeance and be a valued scout once the men he works with have learned to trust him.

But which of these men are to be trusted? The men of the armies of the south universally hate them and itch for an excuse to kill them. It is inevitable that some Kit Carsons will be foisted upon us, but I pray the number fourteen is an error of rumor. With that many possible Judases we will be in more danger from within our NDP than from without.

My rumor analysis is interrupted by a spray of bullets

ripping through the platoon hut. Norris yells for the second squad to be ready to move out in two minutes. Rolling off my side to resume my seat, I wonder if I should be doing something. I guess not. There is a flurry of activity as men find pants, lace boots, sling on bandoliers, and grab weapons. In less than two minutes they are out the door.

Quiet returns as I gaze at the latest ventilation holes in the corrugated aluminum wall. Neat little holes with jagged edges curved inward by the passing of the small lead projectiles. The light of the tropical sun peeks through the west wall in sixty or seventy places. I guess the latest addition to be those five in a line, almost seven feet above the floor. I wonder what happened the day those holes slightly more than three feet above the floor were made?

The two guys I was talking to are gone, but another man sits down beside me when I ask, "Why is it always Norris who goes out after those guys?"

"Because he is damn good, that's why."

"Yeah, but if he keeps doing it he is eventually going to get blown away. All Charlie has to do is wait behind a tree and zap him when he shows up. Why don't they spread the load a little?"

"He is halfway through his second tour. They haven't killed him yet. Anyway, I heard they are sending us a second lieutenant."

"Oh, shit."

"Know what else I heard?"

"What?"

"The captain has put Norris in for a field promotion to lieutenant."

"Is that right?"

"Yep. He did it a couple of months ago and they're expecting it to come through any day now."

"A field promotion to officer is pretty rare nowadays, isn't it?"

"Yes, but even the major is behind this one. Norris is the most gung-ho guy we've got."

"True, but at least he takes the risks himself. You don't find many officers like him. They all think they're too valuable to risk getting their asses shot."

Norris, at twenty-five, is the old man of the platoon, the one man everybody trusts to always know what to do. He, like Chandler, though well respected, has no one he can call a friend in the platoon. I believe the distance he maintains from his men has less to do with his rank and abrupt personality than it does with knowing too many dead men.

Although two new men joined us last week, we are still incredibly short of men and rank. I'll bet there isn't one unit in the rear that is this short of personnel or whose promotions are processed more slowly. It's not that more men or more rank is important to us, it's just that we're doing the dying and they're getting the consideration. It's almost as if there are two separate, jealous U.S. armies. One massive army with beer and clubs and movies and showers and hot food and safety; and a second army, less than one ninth the size, that is always short of food, water, sleep, and lives.

Second squad returns without finding the people who put the latest holes in our hooch; nobody expected they would, but Charlie shoots less and runs sooner when he knows somebody is coming after him. The squad is given a chance to eat and rest before the platoon packs up and heads west along the northern edge of the swamp. We wind our way through the tangled jungle growth to emerge on a stretch of spongy grassland. The point swings south down the length of the opening, then west before we reach the relative safety of the trees again. Never following the same route twice, we duck and weave through the trees, slog across the paddies, then back into the trees with muddy water squishing out the vents in our boots.

A dull ache throbs at the base of my skull while the top of my forehead floats six inches above its proper place. I fantasize glistening, yellow scorpion poison exuding from my pores. My skin has sprung a multitude of leaks. I pour water into my mouth just to find it oozing out of my body in a thousand places. I think I am slowly melting. I wish they would stop walking so that I could keep myself together in one puddle.

These damn daylight patrols. We are merely twenty-three pieces of live bait trolling through the jungle. The high command figures there is little chance of us finding the enemy, so they have us troop around out here until the enemy finds us. After Charlie takes his best shot, they believe we can stomp him with our superior fire power. The trouble is that we have not had much luck getting him to stay while we stomp.

In my lowly opinion, we should be sneaking in the bush

in smaller units. We should live in the villages to offer protection to the people and their crops, to prevent their young men from being conscripted by the NLF, and to gather information and accumulate trust. I realize that just because the Vietnamese have been extremely effective basing their strength on the rural village for more than a thousand years, that is no reason the mighty U.S. Army should pay attention to the ways of these inferior natives.

Now, now, don't bitch so much. What do you know about it, anyway? There must be thousands of America's finest working on this problem. Then why do I have the distinct feeling their combined intellectual output equals that of one retarded bully?

The patrol bunches up at the edge of a long series of paddies. A small hamlet hunches on the far shore. I check the jungle fringe for unfriendlies. I might as well look in my hip pocket. I hate paddies. I feel vulnerable standing in the open with both feet stuck in the mud. I look for the new man I assigned to carry my ammo. Never again do I intend to be caught in a firefight without at least one can of ammo at my side.

"Franklin," I say, noting the weary, pained expression on his face, "you're doing fine. Just stick with me."

"Yeah, I got it. I sure hope you shoot up some of this stuff pretty soon. It's not that heavy, it's just so damn awkward to carry."

"I know, but don't worry, you'll get used to it in a couple of days. Besides, you'll like it a lot less if I have to use those boxes."

"Great. Condition miserable heading for terrible. I can't wait."

We follow the dozen men before us into the boot-sucking ooze. As the last man steps into the paddy a succession of shots pops into the water. Men drop to their knees to reduce the amount of body area exposed to fire, while others desperately thrash through the muck to the protection of the dikes. We pour fire into the trees on our right flank, praying that these are only snipers we can scare off with a barrage of counterfire. Norris splashes forward toward our attackers. The rest of the platoon gains its feet and forms a scraggly line of attack. Firing and stumbling, we move forward.

By the time I reach the edge of the paddy the shooting has stopped and Norris has disappeared into the trees. Our attack line streams off to the left in a single file of men running to keep sight of the backs weaving in and out of the trees before them. We run, walk, jog, and run again until I am sure we have lost Charlie's trail as well as contact with each other. Sweat streams down my body, blurring vision and slickening hands; my arms burn with the strain of holding the machine gun in my arms. Franklin begins to falter. If I keep up with the men in front I will lose him and the rest of the platoon. He must keep up.

It has been some time now since I have seen more than one man in front or behind me emerging and disappearing again into the jungle. The man before me suddenly drops to the ground. I follow suit, without knowing why. We are in a small patch of foot-high grass at the edge of the trees. Fifty feet to my front I spot Norris looking back at me. He motions me forward. I crawl to his side at the top of a rise overlooking a meadow. Across the meadow, on the opposing slope, is a thatched-roof bamboo hut elevated five feet off the ground by stilts. A pool of spring water collects in a hollow at the upper end of the miniature valley. The water flows from the pool into a grass-covered creek that runs over the low ground between the two slopes to disappear in the dense growth surrounding the meadow. This is a place of calmness, a place where the tangled jungle will not enter, a place of simple beauty. My few seconds of reverie are broken by the sergeant's voice at my side, "Strafe that hooch at floor level."

I wonder for a second who might be within those bamboo walls, then shatter the hut with a stream of fire. A man jumps out the right side of the hut. He runs twenty feet up the hill before he staggers and drops under a barrage of lead. My fire splinters the left front support post, tilting the hut forward and to the left, catapulting a second man through the doorway. Bullets riddle him as he arches in slow motion to the ground.

Silence descends like a heavy fog. The smell of burnt gunpowder fills the air. Norris moves off in a crouch to inspect the bodies and the wreckage of the hut. With the sound of gunfire still ringing through my mind, I close my eyes in an attempt to regain the pristine image I had of this meadow only a moment ago, but the image will not return. I open my eyes. It is, after all, only another hot, humid clearing in the jungle.

Inside the sniper's broken hut, we find a large clay jar

Chinook

full of rice. Norris spills its contents onto the floor. An American-made hand grenade rolls down the heap of spilled rice. A second grenade follows in the path of the first. Norris feels inside the jar. His hand emerges, clutching a claymore covered with rice dust. "Damn. Nothing like equipping the enemy with our own stuff," he grumbles, kicking rice out the door to spoil on the damp ground.

"Did you find any papers on the VC?" asks Sandy.

"No, nothing. Just a U.S. carbine and an AK. I wish Liem was here. He might recognize these two. I'd sure like to know if they have relatives in our village. It would be interesting to know where they got this stuff."

Leaving the dead to the ants, the platoon begins the long, empty walk back the way it came. After several minutes we veer north off the snipers' route to avoid the possibility of walking into an ambush laid by their friends. We claw through the mind-numbing heat, the clinging foliage, the bugs that want a piece of us, and the ocean of very thin, hot water that passes itself off as air.

The rain comes with the falling of the sun. We grope our

way in the blackness to the ambush site Norris picked out an hour before. By the time we have rolled ourselves in poncho liners and settled into place, the rain is easing. With nothing else to occupy my time I slowly resoak my clothes, my hair, and my skin with repellent. The hordes have come to suck the blood that will perpetuate their maddening species. I hear that the monsoons will be over soon. I hope what the other guys say is true about there being fewer mosquitoes in the dry season.

By midmorning we are back at the NDP. The ground is covered with cases of C rations, crates of mortar rounds, and lines of five-gallon jerry cans of water. Our worldly possessions are ready to be moved to our new home somewhere in the jungle to the northwest. We will be spared the labor of dismantling the buildings, emptying the thousands of sandbags, and rolling up the concertina wire that would normally be necessary to keep the material out of the hands of the VC. Another company is arriving at noon to take over the position.

Two Chinook helicopters come to ferry us to our new location. The down draft from the twin rotor blades picks up everything loose and hurls it into the air. Sand projectiles sting the skin, clothes buffet against bodies, eyes are kept protectively downcast while clutched hands keep helmets from lifting into space. Lines of men hurry to load boxes of supplies, roasting in the blast of hot air emerging from the jet engines mounted on either side of the rear loading bay. Our job would be easier if they would shut this monster down, but Chinook pilots do not like sitting on the ground any more than Huey pilots do; they both leave their engines on to reduce lift-off time in case of attack.

Once in the air, we have a good view of the passing landscape through the open cargo hatch in the floor. The farther we fly to the northwest the thicker the jungle becomes and the less common are the patches of bomb-cleared land. At last we come to a clearing in the trees near no mountains, villages, or landmarks of any kind. We land in a place so nondescript, so exactly like the thousands of acres surrounding it, that I could never find it again on my own.

Our new home is a circle of barren earth bulldozed out of the jungle. In the approximate center of the circle stands a forty-foot tower offering a clear view of the surprisingly uniform eighteen-inch-thick tree trunks that surround the NDP like a massive picket fence. Normally, when a forest stops at the edge of a natural clearing the foliage tapers from trees to bushes to grass. But when a bulldozer creates the clearing there is no green at the edge of the forest. There are thirty-foot limbless trees standing stark below a canopy of leaves. We are encircled by hundreds of brown, barren poles backed by thousands and thousands of their identical brothers. We are on a bald spot on a gigantic hairbrush.

The land here is higher and drier than the country we left behind. We are somewhere northwest of Saigon, somewhere near Cambodia. There are no bunkers, no wire, no corrugated aluminum huts. We have the dubious pleasure of building this defensive position from the ground up, or in this case, from the ground down.

The second Chinook we unload contains shovels, sandbags, and metal fence posts from Di An. With these implements we begin digging in. Three men are assigned to each bunker. The bunkers are laid out around the perimeter to enable the firing slits of each position to provide cover fire for the adjacent positions. The firing slits are directed at 45-degree angles from the front so that you cannot fire at, nor receive fire from, men charging your bunker. You cannot protect yourself from inside a bunker, you can only protect your neighbors and must rely on them to do the same for you.

Boston, the new guy (Franklin Wagner), and I team up to burrow a home in the earth. Before we are down a foot Boston is called away on a detail. Franklin leaves soon afterward to help with the ammunition bunker. I continue to dig into the rich, red earth alone. There are few rocks, and as I go deeper the soil becomes moist and cool. This is not like the soil of western Oregon and Washington where only the top foot or two is loose enough to work effectively with a shovel. There, below the loam, is a depth of clay that adheres thickly to itself and clings tenaciously to the shovel. Crumbly, decomposed bedrock is next, followed by solid rock. All in all, it is a lousy place for bunkers. The digging here is more like it was in the Mojave Desert where you could dig forever without running into anything that would stop the progress of your shovel.

I was a great digger of holes when I was young. I would dig into the desert soil until only my fingertip could reach the surface. My mother was certain I was going to be buried alive. She periodically handed my father a shovel demanding he return the backyard to the smooth, level, tranquil place

she was determined it should be. Years later when I was in
high school I plagued my father for a swimming pool. After a
month or more of, "Look, here's one we can afford," he
finally lost his patience. He told me if I wanted a pool so
much I could go into the backyard and dig one. When I
pointed out that there was more to a swimming pool than just
a hole, he said to let him know when the hole was ready.
When he came home from work the next day there was the
beginning of a large hole in the yard, but he was not concerned since surely my energy would wane in the hot summer days ahead. As the weeks went by the level of our
backyard, as well as the empty lot behind us, rose with
excavated dirt. Each day he would peer out the window at
the growing hole and the wheelbarrow piles of dirt expanding
ever outward, until at last he realized I had dug another
dangerous pit he could no longer ignore. It would lie there
gaping at him until he filled it with something.

Where would we be without our daydreams to pass the
hours of menial labor? Once you are in condition there is
little difference between walking, or working at a measured
pace, and sitting still. The mind ignores the body as it wanders off to entertain itself.

Because of our extreme vulnerability here, no one is
allowed to eat or sleep until his bunker is dug and is covered
with at least two layers of sandbags. Since my social calendar
is clear for the entire day, and well into the night, I decide to
expand somewhat on the standard Army bunker. When I
reach the six-foot mark I start a tunnel at the base of the
sidewall, curving forward and down until I complete a ninety-
degree turn. I then begin hollowing out a cavern deep enough
in the ground to maintain the five feet of earth overhead. I
have a good start on my hidden burrow by the time Boston
returns from stringing barbed wire around the perimeter. It
does not take me long to convince him of the merits of my
cave. It will be cool during the day, I say, and unlike other
bunkers it might survive a direct hit by a mortar round.
However, I believe his primary reason for helping me is his
vision of the cavern as a place where he can smoke his dope
in peace.

I push dirt up the tunnel to Boston, who pulls it into a
pile in the main bunker. We steadily expand the cave until
there is room enough for us both. The air is cool and damp.
We talk in whispers in the dim light like two kids sharing a

secret. There are no sounds other than our own. It is as if we could shut out the realities of the world above. Perhaps we should live in caves like the VC, hidden from the ogre that is the U.S. Army.

Boston and I agree to stop all other work until we have a cover on our bunker to shield our cave from prying eyes. We emerge from the bunker to find Franklin wandering like a lost gopher trying to determine which hole in the ground is home. He looks tired and well baked. Perhaps a touch of heatstroke from working too many hours under the tropical sun. We park him in a shady corner of the bunker and put sandbags in his hands to hold open while we shovel in dirt. We are soon surrounded by bulging, green plastic sandbags. We position our firing slits, span the hole with metal fence posts, and cover the structure two bags deep.

Our day's work complete, we climb into our new home to settle cross-legged in the dirt. Boston pulls a bar of plastique explosive from his gear, tears off a piece the size of a quarter, and ignites it with his Zippo lighter. He drops the C-4 into an old date pudding can with vent holes placed around the bottom rim. The explosive burns with a cool blue flame. Holding our C rations by the lid we take turns warming them over the flame, stirring the contents occasionally with plastic spoons to minimize the inevitable scorching of the food at the bottom. To melt the congealed fat that floats on the top of our rations, to warm a potato or a carrot halfway through, to turn a gelatinous mass of brown goo into a sauce opens up a whole new world of culinary delight.

Several empty cans litter the ground as evidence of the meal just passed. The small piece of plastique explosive burned out well before the last ration can was emptied. As with primitive men, our light ends with the setting sun. Only our outlines are visible as Boston searches for his pipe and his two-pound bag of marijuana. He left the old NDP prepared for the future, not knowing when he would have a chance to resupply.

"I've got enough here to keep me stoned for a couple of months. And it only cost me twenty bucks," he says offering his pipe around. "What's the matter, you boys still not smoking? Man, oh man. You guys just don't know where it's at around here." He pauses to relight his pipe, fill his lungs with smoke, and hold it there. "Boy, I'd love to have a hundred pounds of this back in Boston," he says, still holding his breath, which makes his voice high and tight. When he exhales I am sure everyone within a hundred feet can smell the musky, sweet odor drifting out the entrance of our bunker. I poke my head up to have a look. Nobody is paying us the slightest attention.

"Hey, man, don't worry about those dudes out there. Nobody gives a shit about a little grass. What we've got to do is find a heavy-duty container so the rats won't eat all my dope. The damn rats love to eat this shit. They'll eat through heavy plastic, wood, anything to get at it. The only thing that will keep them out for sure is metal."

Barely pausing for breath he switches to a new topic. "By the way, who did you guys make the beneficiaries of your GI life insurance?"

"My parents. They spent a good deal of money raising me. I figured ten thousand dollars will be some compensation, should it come to that."

"My girlfriend. Why?"

"Those were reasonable enough choices when you were back in the world, but you're not in that world anymore. Look, we can divide people into four general categories: those who support their government and are willing to sacrifice our lives to save Vietnam from communism, those who support peace and hate us, those sent here with us to ensure continued death, and those sent here with us who help us stay alive. The way I see it, the only friends we have are the men who lend us a hand when we step into the shit. Now, I ask you, who deserves to benefit from your death more than the man who fights beside you, the man who is willing to risk his life to save yours?"

"That makes a lot of sense to me."

"You're damn right it does. This way at least some of us will leave the Army with more than our nightmares and spit for gratitude. What you guys should do is find a guy you trust, a guy who won't put a bullet in your back for the money, and make each other the beneficiary of your life insurance. I've already made my deal, but you guys should think about it."

"Sounds good to me. What do you say, Franklin? Do you trust me not to shoot you?"

"Shit, man, if I can't trust you I'm already dead. Where do I sign?"

"Good. Let's do it."

At 0700, Captain Wilkins announces that two platoons will accompany him on a survey of our new surroundings. We walk through tangled brush, over, under, and around the jumble of dying, rotting trees slanting at different angles as they slowly fall toward the molding compost of the earth that feeds the forest of bare tree trunks, ten feet apart, going up straight, going on forever.

I sink to the ground at the base of a tree, tired, hot, depressed. What I have seen I do not like. There are fewer mosquitoes here than in the swamp and there are as yet no rice paddies to mire in, but this place is dark, damp, and eerie. The tree branches and leaves form a canopy overhead that blocks out most sunlight, but retains heat and humidity. No breeze penetrates this jungle. The air is stagnant and heavy with rot. Our sweat does not evaporate. It runs in rivulets down our chests and legs, soaking our fatigues and collecting in pools in our navels and the inside of our elbows. A constant film of sweat softens our skin, allowing it to be easily cut by the brush. Everything that is not lush, vigorous growth is molding. I too am molding. The inevitable jungle rot has begun to eat at my skin. I first noticed it a week or two ago. Now I notice it all the time—a constant burning itch.

But worst of all is the natural camouflage of this jungle that makes it a daytime ambusher's paradise. A man lying on the ground or squatting behind a bush is not likely to be detected until we are within a few yards of him. The shadowy jungle floor, together with spots of dancing sunlight that come in wavering beams through the leaves above, confuse the eye and befuddle the mind. No wonder this area is one of the NVA's favorite infiltration routes off the Ho Chi Minh Trail.

Leaning against my tree in the jungle I stare at lunch. I am really sick of cold spaghetti and meatballs, and it is one of the better meals available. Maybe if I avoid it for a week I will reacquire my taste for Italian cuisine. I cram half a can of spaghetti into my mouth and swallow without chewing. Eating is necessary to maintain strength. I take a couple of big gulps of water, hoping everything will stay down.

So far the only human sign we have seen were the two footpaths we crossed this morning. Charlie must not yet be fully informed of our arrival, or at least not yet prepared to give us a reception. Our new interpreter tells us there is a village five klicks north of here. "Boo coo VC," he says, pointing north. "Boo coo VC." Apparently the captain does not want to deal with a lot of VC today because we swing to the east. This is my kind of military exercise. Find out where the enemy is and go the other way. Why, if everybody did that, we would soon have a cease-fire, and if everybody kept it up maybe the generals would get bored and go home. Not very likely, though; there are too many people in the rear clamoring for dead bodies and they are going to kick ass until they get them. I must be getting jaded. . . .

Baawooom! The mind-numbing explosion reverberates inside my skull. Rain patters on my unprotected head and tightly curled body. . . . Rain? . . . No. Not rain . . . dirt. It's raining dirt. Need my helmet. Where's my helmet? Can't feel it anywhere. Open your eyes, dummy. Frig a helmet, where's my gun? Oh, shit! No gun. It's vanished. Calm down. Nobody's firing at you. That's right. No one's shooting. All right, look around again. You have time. Let's see— explosion behind me there. I'm here. The gun must be in the same line. Crawl over there. Explosion must have knocked me this way—I probably jumped pretty good, too. That must've been it. Ah, my helmet! And there, a bipod leg sticking up behind that log. Thank God. I hope it still works.

"Is anyone hurt?" The question comes to me as a whisper, faint, hollow, distant.

No answer.

The question echos in my mind. Hurt? I hurt all over. No, I can't be hurt. I just crawled twenty-five feet. But many times there's no pain at first. I check my back and legs. Everything seems normal. Forget about that, concentrate on the jungle. What's that? One of ours? Yeah, that's Chandler crawling slowly, checking the ground before him. I'll bet that guy has traveled more miles on his belly than anyone else in the company. There's Norris moving up beside him. They exchange some words before the sergeant goes on, walking in a crouch, stopping, looking, moving on. He passes in front of me, to my left, disappearing behind some bushes fifty feet away. "Chandler. Over here."

After a minute the sergeant reappears, his eyes searching our scattered line of men. "It was a booby trap, Captain. You'd better call a medivac; that guy is still alive."

An almost audible sigh of relief passes through the men within the sound of the sergeant's voice. A booby trap means no firefight, not here, not now. Again it is not me who is mutilated. Again, the luck holds. Maybe tomorrow it will be my turn, but not here, not now.

Two men with bayonets search for trees of small diameter for stretcher poles. Three other men donate their shirts for the sling on which the wounded man will ride. Four men carry the stretcher into the bush. The man they bring out is missing his right leg. His left leg is wrapped in bloody gauze. I hope we get him to the medivac before he regains consciousness. On the other hand, it won't be much of a loss if he never makes it to the chopper. If we gave him a choice, I'll bet he'd opt for a bullet in the head. I think I would. But we aren't going to give him a choice. We are going to hustle this fresh cripple through the jungle to the nearest clearing where we can deliver him up to the sky. And if he doesn't bleed to death or die of shock, he'll live long enough to decide for himself if he's willing to go through the rest of his life without the benefit of a leg or two and God knows what else.

We fast walk and jog through unfamiliar jungle, heading for a spot on a map. But there is nothing here to guide us; the view is the same in every direction. Go by the sun, the watch, the compass, dead reckoning, and luck. Fifteen minutes into the journey our casualty begins to moan. Chandler hits him with another shot of morphine. He is not going to let this guy wake up.

Another fifteen minutes pass before we see the bright

B-52

reflection of light on an expanse of ground ahead. We break into a cratered clearing of the type made by a B-52 dumping its load. Forming a perimeter around our landing zone, we lie behind our weapons waiting for the chopper. A smoke grenade is on the ground. The Huey medivac beats the air over the treetops, dives into the clearing, and is away again, starting another one of us on his long journey home.

I lie in a crater staring into the jungle, listening to the silence left behind by the chopper. Slowly the sounds of the jungle return and we must go. Everything that lives in this tangle of vines and brush and trees knows where we are. We are the intruders, the ones who do not belong. The jungle stares back at me with unseen eyes that know my every move. Maybe that medivac is the only way out of here.

It is late by the time we return to the NDP. The tour of our new surroundings took longer than anticipated. Franklin, Boston, and I come together at our bunker. We pile our gear on the hot sandbags of the bunker roof and slump in the dirt. Even for men in good shape humping the boonies is a strain. Franklin's black face is etched with fatigue. It will take another patrol or two before he becomes accustomed to the long walks, the heavy loads, and the heat. It is already clear that he is going to be a good man, one we can depend on when things get bad.

Ten minutes later we are sitting in the same place, collecting the energy to clean and put away our equipment, when a voice breaks into our quiet space.

"You men get off your asses and start improving that bunker of yours. The first and third platoons already have the trench between their bunkers started. You're lagging way behind, and you won't get a chance to catch up tomorrow because you're going out again. Let's get with it, gentlemen."

The irritating, smug voice admonishing us belongs to the first platoon's Lieutenant Lassen, an ROTC graduate with one month in-country. I am tempted to point out that of course the first and third platoons are ahead of us with their bunker work. They remained in camp while we were humping through the bush. But even he must be aware of the inequity. This is the same idiot who blew his ambush into the NDP, killing two of our own men. He seems to have recovered nicely from his embarrassment.

However, Franklin is in no mood for smug idiots. He

jumps to his feet, eyes blazing, fists clenched, neck muscles bulging, sputtering, "You . . . you . . ."

This is great. Franklin is going to break this GI killer into small pieces, but no—wait—not here. "You bet, Lieutenant. We'll get right on it. First this trench over here," I say, pointing to a section of ground away from the still sputtering Franklin, "then that one, and I thought we'd put a three-foot wall right along here. I see your guys have done some nice work over on the east side there."

The lieutenant is easily led away. He did not miss the look on Franklin's face and he is probably grateful for an excuse to exit without confrontation. I wish this fool would restrict himself to hassling the men in his own platoon and leave our platoon alone.

When I get back to our bunker Boston is still trying to stifle his laughter. "Franklin, you stupid shit. You hit that man and you are going to be spending the next several months in the Long Binh Jail, and believe me, old LBJ is not a nice place to visit. Look, don't mess with that little prick. Just ignore him. If you want to get him don't fuck around, just blow him away the next time the company is in a firefight. Shit, man, I'll even help you. Killing that bastard will save the lives of a lot of good men."

"What are you talking about? That's crazy. I couldn't kill another GI."

"Why not? Killing GIs doesn't seem to bother Lassen any."

"Maybe not, but it would bother me," replies Franklin, sitting back down on the bunker. "Did you know the guy that stepped on the booby trap today?"

"Yeah, I knew him. That's what's really bothering you, isn't it? I saw your face when they brought Stubner out on the stretcher. You looked like you were going to lose your lunch."

"I did. Just thinking about that guy makes me sick. One minute he is walking along, a whole, healthy person, the next minute he is ripped to shreds. It could happen to me just as easily. Whole one minute, a cripple the next, with no warning and nothing I can do about it."

"It's not quite that simple. I mean, it can happen that way, but Stubner got it because he was lazy. He was supposed to be walking flank, right? Well, what the hell was he doing walking thirty feet from Shook? He should have been at least one hundred feet out. He was walking where he was because he didn't want to go through or around the outside of that thicket. He chose the natural path along our sides, which was the easiest route. That's why Charlie put a mine there. Why do you think we spend so much time walking through rice paddies and stumbling through the jungle instead of walking on the dikes and paths?"

"Maybe you're right, but it doesn't make me feel any better."

"Hey man, this here's a war. You're going to see a lot of dead bodies before your tour is over. And the worst part of it is, a lot of them are going to be your friends. You just have to learn to accept it or you'll go crazy." Boston leans back and laughs. "Of course, if you stay in the field for a year you'll go crazy anyway."

The next morning we leave the NDP early, heading east. This is a company-sized operation, minus the second platoon, which is staying behind to safeguard our incomplete camp. The canopied jungle is monotonously consistent during the morning, but by noon we have descended into a land containing a few rice paddies and open areas of high grass. We stop for lunch on a piece of high ground where the battle with the ants for our right to sit without being eaten will be less severe. During our meal a shot rings out from within our midst, bringing Norris on the run. Jesse walks out of the brush holding up a bamboo viper. "Hey, look what I got."

Boston gives a little laugh. "That has got to be the first time that dude has fired his weapon since he got in this country."

"I wish he had picked another time to start," I complain. "I don't care much for the noise."

Lieutenant Lassen, Jesse, and Sergeant Norris become involved in a quiet but intense conversation. Apparently Lassen and Norris do not care much for the noise, either.

Franklin wants to know, "Why did you say that about this being the first time Jesse has fired his weapon?"

"Because as far as I know, it's true. Jesse and those three black dudes he hangs out with are hiders. They rely on the rest of their platoon to keep Charlie off their backs. You see, they don't believe in this war. They feel that because the white man back home has treated them like shit they don't have any obligation to fight the white government's war.

Jesse says he doesn't want to kill a bunch of Vietnamese he hasn't got anything against. The only people he wants to kill are the rednecks back in Louisiana. If a lot of gray meat gets wasted over here, so much the better as far as he's concerned."

"Oh, that's brilliant," I say. "The middle of a firefight is no place for a political debate. The only way we're going to get out of here alive is if we all look after each other."

"Yeah, that's the way it is, all right, but Jesse and his buddies are as prejudiced as they make them. Besides, those dudes are so stoned most of the time I'd just as soon they didn't shoot at anything. There's no telling who they might hit."

"Hey, man, what is this shit? I don't know Jesse, but I haven't noticed any discrimination out here."

"Well, Franklin, there isn't much of it in the field, but—well, you're a brother—go over and talk to him sometime. You'll get a belly full of hate in a hurry."

Lunch is cut short due to the rifle shot. We move through an expanse of jungle, still heading east. After an hour the company is brought to a halt on the verge of a series of old paddies spread along the inside of a bend in the river. A dike running along our side of the river keeps most of the water out of the abandoned fields. The exposed paddies, the natural ford provided by the shallowness and width of the river, and the four-foot-high bank on the opposite side combine to give me a feeling of wariness. This is the first open area we have come across in over two hours. If I were the enemy, I would place my ambush behind that little rise on the far bank. Maybe I am getting jumpy. We pass a multitude of good ambush sites on every patrol without incident. There is no good reason to believe this particular crossing will be any different.

Our platoon has been walking point, so we are dispatched to reconnoiter the far side of the river. Norris leads the first squad across the old paddies at a run. When we reach the protection of the four-foot-high dike, Norris grabs my arm. "Follow me," he commands, leading me along the dike to a place where a paddy dike intersects with the main dike at the edge of the river.

"Set your gun up here and give us cover if we get hit."

With my helmet I dig a little hollow in the top of the dike in which to set the gun. Now only the top of my helmet will be exposed in case something happens. I check to make sure Franklin is close by. He has moved into a position next to me. Our eyes meet. He nods and quickly looks away. Is he embarrassed by his fear, or is it something he sees in my eyes that he is avoiding?

The second squad runs across the paddies to join us behind the dike at the river's edge. I train the gun on the top of the opposing bank, ready to fire at the first glimpse of movement. Norris waves the second squad forward into the water. They fan out into a fifty-foot line, their progress slowed to a walk in the knee-deep water.

I wonder if I should've linked a box of ammo to my hundred-round belt? Maybe, but if I need to move, it would be in the way. Quit worrying. It's too late, anyway.

This stinks. Those guys in the water are going to be in real trouble if we get hit. Can't they move any faster? Halfway across. Just fifty more feet. Maybe they are going to make . . .

There is a slight movement of the brush on the lip of the bank as shots ring out a split second before I can return their fire. The first squad hammers the far bank with a heavy barrage. I strafe a seventy-foot section of the bank, trying to maintain an accurate enough aim to make the VC keep their heads down yet keep the steady stream of fire high enough not to hit the men in the water.

I let up on the trigger for a moment so that I can get a clear look at what is going on. The men in the river are running in every direction, their feet sending showers of water into the air. Explosions erupt behind me. I can no longer see anyone on the far bank, but they must still be there. I resume firing until my gun clicks empty. Jerking the gun from its notch, I roll and scramble thirty feet further down the dike. Flipping open the lid of the gun, I look up to yell for Franklin when a can of ammo hits the dirt in front of my knee. Black hands open the box and hand me the end of the ammunition belt to slap down on the gun tray. I fire short bursts at the top of the bank, even though I feel fairly certain Charlie is already fading back into the jungle.

The last of the squad scrambles out of the water up the far bank. The river is empty again, except for the solitary figure lazily floating facedown around the bend.

I lie back against the dike, my body shaking almost imperceptibly. Two minutes. The entire skirmish could not have lasted more than two minutes. I fold my arms tightly against my chest, trying to stop shaking. Jesus, I hate this. I glance at Franklin, who is staring at the ground between his feet. I slap him on the back. "Good work, Franklin. Damn good work."

He keeps studying the ground for a minute before he speaks to his boots in a quiet, despondent voice. "I don't think I am going to make it through a year of this. Maybe I'm just not as brave as you guys, I don't know, but . . . well, I don't seem to know what to do and . . . Ah, shit, I was scared, man."

"Is that what you're worried about? For Christ's sake, Franklin, you're supposed to be scared. Every time someone tries to kill you, you go right ahead and get as scared as you want. Just don't forget to do what you have to do to make Charlie stop trying to kill you."

"You don't understand. Once the shooting started I didn't stick my head over the top of this here dike until it was almost all over. I just laid cozy against this dirt pile and lobbed M-79 rounds into the jungle.

"So what? You think you would have been any more effective sticking your head up where it could get blown off? You knew the distance and direction of the target. You did the right thing, stop worrying about it."

I get up and walk back to the intersection of the two dikes where I am closer to the rest of the squad. I stick my feet in a two-foot hole at the base of the dike, waiting for the word to move on. After a while Franklin sits down beside me. Some guys have gone downstream to fish our casualty out of the river. We will probably wait here for a chopper to take the body.

"Why did you move?" asks Franklin.

I look up at him in surprise.

"Why did you move from here down the dike when you ran out of ammo?"

"They knew where I was. I didn't want to get shot either."

We wade across the river to join the rest of our platoon setting up a perimeter for the medivac chopper. There is always the chance the VC will try for the chopper. I understand that the man who shoots down a helicopter receives an automatic promotion.

It takes the medivac twenty minutes to get here and set down in one of the dry rice paddies. We place the dead man gently on the floor. A friend turns away with tears in his eyes. The helicopter thrashes its way into the air, taking another one of us home. We will all get there sooner or later.

The sky darkens with rain clouds as we move through the jungle in a long single line. If we get hit here I'll go for that tree; now that dip on the left or that log on the right. I wonder if I'll ever walk anywhere again without looking for cover?

The company stops for dinner as the rain begins to fall. Its multitude of miniature bombardments obliterates all other sound, its high-speed watery lines obscure every view. Big drops coming close together, washing the land, turning the rivers a muddy brown, carrying some small part of everything in this jungle to the Saigon River, into the vast delta region, and eventually to its final rest in the South China Sea.

It will be an eternity before the Army sets me free. A time beyond imagining. There is no other time than now, no other place than here. The land across the sea is only a cruel trick of a fading imagination. This place, this war, is all there is. The only thing left is to go on living and to try to help my friends do the same.

When darkness is not yet full, we walk on in closed ranks. We move to the north at right angles to our previous line of march. Slowly, carefully, we move closer to our night ambush position. After several minutes, the line stops. The rainstorm lifts. The mosquitoes descend. Again I remind myself not to slap the mosquitoes. They are having an orgy on my freshly rinsed, repellent-free body. Mosquitoes are easy to hate, but the hate is only a distraction, revenge fruitless.

The line moves again through the darkness. Only a few minutes' walk this time before we are filed off into our positions for the night's ambush. I set up the gun next to a tree, put out my claymore, and lie on my back to begin the slow process of resoaking myself with mosquito repellent.

The ambush site is raked with machine-gun fire. I roll on my stomach to have a look, already knowing I'm not going to see anything. The fire is coming in three feet over our heads. Maybe I'll be able to see the muzzle flashes. Automatic rifles join the machine gun. Thank God I have a tree to hide behind this time. I can't see any flashes. On our north side lies an open area but to our east, where the source of the fire lies, there is foliage and the faint outline of trees. How could anyone know we're here? They sound like they're at least two-hundred meters away. They must've heard us—I know they can't see us.

The heavy, slow thump, thump, thump of an M-50 machine gun sends armor-piercing rounds screaming overhead. Our adversaries' possession of this weapon tells me many things. First of all, my tree will offer no protection from this heavy gun. Also, I doubt that the people shooting at us are VC. An insurgence unit does not usually sneak around at night with a gun that takes two men to carry just so they can shoot through trees. Shooting a pigeon with a cannon is strictly the style of the United States. Nobody but Americans would use M-50s, fighter bombers, and destroyers in a war where friends and foes are separated by feet. But even U.S. troops rarely carry M-50s to the field. This must be an ARVN outpost shooting up free American ammunition to discourage Charlie from venturing too near, or to let him know where the outpost is so that he can avoid it.

Behind me, someone is sliding on his belly through the mud, going from man to man along the line of the ambush. My boot is tapped. I slide back to lie next to Sandy.

"You will have the third watch tonight. Every fourth man will be awake as usual."

"Right. Who do you suppose is shooting at us, the ARVNs?"

"That's what the CO thinks. They are trying to raise them on the radio now. Our orders are not to fire unless Norris does, and for God's sake make sure the man you wake up doesn't sit up—he'll get his head blown off."

"Yeah, their fire does seem to be getting a little closer to the ground, doesn't it?"

"About two feet, I'd say. Just stay flat and you should be all right. Somebody will wake you if it gets any lower."

"Yeah, thanks a lot. Sweet dreams to you, too."

"What?"

"Never mind." Does he really expect me to sleep with these bullets whistling overhead? I wrap myself in my poncho liner and lie on my back, toying with the idea of putting my helmet on a stick to determine the true elevation of the fire. After a while I reject the idea. It would be inconsiderate to cause my helmet to be launched into the night with a disconcerting metallic clang. I could check the level of bullet holes in the tree behind me. No, I might lose a hand in that investigation. Well, I guess I'll just lie here all night and daydream about something nice, like sailing the South Pacific. Ah yes, my boat heeling to the wind as it passes through an opening in the reef, the surf pounding on the coral as I rise to a swell and shoot through the gap into a pristine lagoon, the water so clear I can see the beautiful array of tropical fish sixty feet below my keel. . . .

I start at the touch of a hand on my shoulder. My lagoon is lost in the darkness. I freeze. There is something I must remember. An imperative to recall before I move. Something firmly planted in my subconscious. Ah, yes, to sit up is death. There are bullets flying close overhead. A hand offers me a watch with a luminous dial. Midnight. The M-50 is silent, but an M-60 and an M-16 seem to be playing a song: *da, da, da, dit, dit, dit, da, da, da, dit, dit, dit.* It is hard to believe those idiots are still at it. I was having such a nice dream, they have a lot of gall waking me up to listen to this shit. A sliver of moon reflects light through a layer of scattered clouds. A dozen motionless forms are visible to my left. Two or three should be awake, but I cannot tell which are on guard in this light. They all seem completely at peace, lying there in the mud with death passing at supersonic speed two feet above their bodies.

Behind the line of men there is a small building consisting of three walls and some semblance of a roof. Even here the officers manage to find living quarters superior to ours.

Slowly my watch passes. The firing stops a few hours before dawn. We collect our gear and move out of the area on our knees. There are several offers from the troops to walk over to the ARVN outpost and thump some heads, but our offers go unheeded. We set off in the direction we came, careful to select a somewhat different route.

At noon we stop beside a huge area bombed clear of life. In the center of this devastation there is an island of trees some hundred meters square. While finishing my canned lunch I ponder the vagaries of war that created this odd sight when my thoughts are shattered by a continuous series of massive explosions that makes the earth tremble. I grab my gun thinking to run somewhere away from the explosions which are larger than anything I have heard before. Even the trees quake from the thundering blasts that come one upon the other. But where is it coming from and where is it landing?

"Boston, what the fuck is going on?"

Boston looks at my confusion and fright and laughs. "Look over there." He points to the island of trees that are now dancing and disintegrating. Some B-52 pilot is dumping his load."

Fifty to one hundred explosions rip the forested enclave. No soldier would choose to hide in those trees where his entry and departure could be so easily observed. If there is anyone in those woods we will see him running across the barren land. But no one emerges and I am sure no one will.

Did someone order the completion of this perfect square of annihilation? What possibly valid reason could there be for a B-52 strike on a lonely stand of trees?

It is late afternoon by the time we trudge through the new wire around our NDP. After a night on ambush and two days of patrol we usually shuffle off in our own directions to clean ourselves and our weapons, get something to eat, or just rest. But today the captain calls us into a formation. There is no stateside foolishness about coming to attention and dressing right. We merely stand in lines with our equipment, waiting for the officers to check or say whatever it is they have in mind. Today the platoon leaders are asking each machine gunner how many rounds he fired during yesterday's firefight. Next, they check what the gunners told them against the number of cans of machine gun ammo carried back to the NDP. Even though I was the only one who fired more than one hundred rounds, we now have eight less cans of ammo than when we left. The five men responsible for the shortage are quickly identified. Lieutenant Lassen unleashes a flurry of anger at the three culprits from his platoon that are causing him embarrassment in front of the company. Two of the violators are Jesse's "this ain't my war" buddies who reply to Lassen's accusations with quick lies and denials that seem to be putting Lassen in a state of uncertainty, even though their guilt is obvious by their empty hands. Lassen backs off from the force and unity of the two brothers to launch into his third offender, a slow-witted white guy from North Carolina.

"There is nothing as low as a man who won't carry his weight in combat, a man so lacking in respect for himself and his country that he doesn't even deserve to be called a man. No sir, a thing like that should be shot on the spot."

Lassen's degradation of the North Carolinian has its effect. His face reddens, his fists clench. He is being publicly disgraced while Jesse's friends are skating free.

"I want to know where you dumped that ammo. I want to know why you dumped it. I want to know how much of our ammunition you have given to the Vietcong, and I want to know right now," screams Lassen, his face no more than a foot from the Carolinian's.

The Carolinian responds with anger. "Why the hell should I carry ammo when those two never do? This is only the second time I've thrown it away—those two have been doing it for months, or at least as long as you have been here. After a while I said fuck it, if they don't have to carry ammo, neither do I."

Lassen must realize this confession is not helping his image. He returns to the attack. "When did you dump your two cans of ammunition?"

"During the first break yesterday, same as them."

Lassen glares at his men as he passes before them. Suddenly, he walks back two rows and comes to a stop in front of Franklin. "And when did you dump yours?"

"Now wait a minute," I break in. "He—"

"When I want to hear from you I'll let you know," retorts Lassen. "Now, soldier, I asked you a question."

Franklin gives off a faint smile. "A few minutes after the firefight I buried it in a crater because it was empty." Franklin is as cool and calm as he can be.

"You're a liar," screams Lassen.

That does it.

"Goddamnit, Lieutenant," I yell, leaving my place in line to confront him. "If you didn't have your head up your ass"—when I get next to him I keep walking slowly forward forcing him to back away—"if you had been paying attention to what has been going on—"

"Stop right there soldier!"

"—you would know that—"

"One more step and I'll see you in the stockade."

I stop. "—he is telling you the truth."

Suddenly Norris is standing between us, his hard eyes glaring at me.

"Back up," he says with quiet force.

For an instant I consider ignoring him, then with an "Ah, shit" I return to my place.

"You shouldn't have done that," whispers Franklin.

"If that son of a bitch ever gets the idea he's our platoon leader we're in big trouble. Besides, LBJ would be an improvement over this place. I hear that nobody has died there in weeks."

Boston pokes me in the back. "If that little turd messes with you, I'll waste him. I swear it."

He has no need to swear by his statement, I believe him. And his attitude is far from unique. What worries me is that his way of thinking is beginning to make sense. We are in Vietnam with orders from our nation to kill the opponents of a blatantly corrupt, inhuman dictatorship. While there may be no moral justification for this action, political views become irrelevant to us the moment someone starts trying to kill us. At that point, if we wish to continue living, we have no choice but to do our best to kill them. Our justification is survival.

People like Lassen are also killing us. Although he has not yet committed enough deadly errors to deserve being wasted, when he does, the justification for eliminating him will be the same as it is for protecting ourselves against our other enemies.

After a short conference between the captain and the platoon leaders the formation is dismissed. Franklin is not among the men sent to the CO's tent for disciplinary measures and so far, neither am I.

We spend the rest of the day digging. We complete our bunker and enlarge our cave to hold four people in some semblance of comfort. In the afternoon, Boston rounds up his dope-smoking buddies for a smoke-in, in what is becoming known as "the den." They slide down the tunnel, cover the entrance with sandbag material, and get stoned in the cool darkness, watching the glowing red tip of the joint pass from man to man.

Having gotten myself in enough trouble for one day, I spend the afternoon digging a trench. The work helps me endure the constant itch of jungle rot and keeps uncomfortable thoughts at bay. Maybe I should have been a farmer, spending my summers walking the fields with a shovel over my shoulder, checking how far the water has seeped down the furrows, changing the canvas dams. I could ride on the tractor crossing the fields, running the disks for summer fallow, spreading fertilizer or seeding, with nobody to tell me where to go or what to do.

President Johnson's people say they have the wisdom and the knowledge to know what is best. And the people who are older and wiser than I gave them the power to decide who deserves respect and who deserves to die. But it is becoming increasingly clear that the majority of our parents, our government, and our military leaders are less capable of determining the correct path than I am, despite my inexperience and lack of years. There is no doubt that my faith in my country and in all forms of authority is crumbling. This trench digging is not working.

Leaning on my shovel I see Norris emerge from the CO's tent. He scans the compound until his eyes rest on me. Concentrating on the red dust at his feet he closes the distance between us with his usual quick gait. It looks as if I am about to find out what the penalty is for demonstrating a lack of respect for an officer I do not respect.

"Shook, you are going out with first platoon on ambush."

"What?" I can't believe this.

"Get your stuff together, you're leaving in fifteen minutes."

"What's this all about?"

Norris gives me a smirk that for him passes as a smile. "It's not what you think. Their gunner left for R and R this afternoon. Lassen requested a replacement and you're it."

"Whatever you say, boss." I'd like to ask him if this is his idea. More than that, I wonder what this crafty devil thinks I am going to do bunked down with Lassen all night. He is gone before I decide how to approach the subject—not that I was likely to get an answer.

We leave the NDP at 1600. He was right. It is not what I thought. Lassen is not with us. It is a squad-sized ambush of only ten men. Jesse and one of his followers are with us, but we are without the services of his other two friends who like to leave their machine-gun ammo in the bushes. One of the guys carrying my ammo is in front of me and the other two are behind me. Something has happened; things are not usually so well organized.

We walk for only an hour before we stop to wait for the setting of the sun. I make a point to stay away from Jesse. This is not the place for a stupid hassle. I keep to myself through the bouts of bitching and bickering that pass between the men. When Jesse lights up a joint and hands it to his buddy, the Spec 4 who is the squad leader tells him to put it out. Jesse fingers his M-16 and tells him to fuck off. I sure hope we don't run into Charlie tonight.

At dusk we move a few hundred yards further west. When the sunlight fades completely we set up our ambush at the edge of one of the trails the company passed on patrol a few days earlier. We are on the inside of a bend, our claymores set up along the north–south portion of the path. Jesse and friend have been placed on my left, no more than twenty feet from the east–west section of trail that curves along the flank of our line. We are vulnerable from the left with all our mines set to our front.

This is ridiculous. We have a squad leader who doesn't know how to set an ambush, who doesn't have control of his men, and if the shit hits the fan, I'll find out what else he doesn't know. I'm tempted to get up and walk to the other end of the line so that if we get hit from the trail along the left I'll be shooting over the squad's head instead of them shooting over mine. Worst of all, I'm lying next to two guys who are stoned and will probably not stay awake for their watch. It's going to be a long, sleepless night.

Sometime around midnight I hear hushed voices to our left rear. A moment later the bizarre sound of giggling drifts through the moonlight-speckled jungle. At first I think the aberrant sound is a result of some fantasy unreeling in Jesse's mind, but then I realize it is coming from some place deeper in the woods. The giggling is gay, almost feminine. I reach out and wake the men on either side of me.

My gun is pointed 160 degrees away from the source of the giggles. It will make too much noise to move it to train on the people coming up the path from our left rear. I must wait until we are ready to fire. Again the eerie sound of stifled laughter drifts through the night. This is crazy. Are we being mocked? Is this some kind of perverse trick? The girlish tittering is near but not closing. The hushed singsong voices rise and fall, but do not move.

I wait, poised to swing the gun, staring through the trees and brush at the spot that is the source of the mocking sounds. I see nothing but tree trunks and leaves and shadows. There . . . a glow, a faint red ember.

I hear Jesse whisper to his friend, "Grass. Shoot them in the legs so we don't mess up their stash."

Shut up, you idiot, they could hear you. But he is right about the marijuana, I smell it, too.

The sounds come closer. Yes, they are coming . . . there . . . two men. Two M-16s blaze in the darkness, their magazines expended before I can lift my gun and find a target. There is a metallic rattle as men yank out expended clips and slap home new ones. My night vision is destroyed by the muzzle flashes and tracers. I cannot see the two men who went down. We wait, straining to hear. Gurgling noises come from the path. The rattle of death. The air is charged with tension and fear.

Jesse crawls toward the trail. He raises to his knees and fires two more bursts. "Hey, fool, I told you to shoot them in the legs. Man, these dudes are a mess."

"They dead?"

"They are now!"

"Get your gear. Let's get out of here."

I defuse my claymore and roll up the wire. On my way back I see Jesse displaying a bag of grass for his buddy. Jesse either has more guts than I gave him credit for or he is a lot crazier than I thought.

We move back toward the NDP, pushing through the undergrowth, feeling our way over the ground. Someone stumbles and curses to himself. It is difficult to tell if we are going in the right direction. With only the moon to direct us, we put distance between ourselves and the noise and death on the path. After a while we stop and set up in a semicircle with our backs to what we hope is the NDP.

Lying on my back, looking up at the spots of moonlight shining through the openings in the canopy of leaves overhead, I think about the story I heard of the lions attracted to the sound of gunfire. It is said they come to the scene of a battle to scavenge an easy meal. It sounds gruesome but I guess it doesn't make any difference if your body is consumed by a lion or by the birds and ants or by your own microbes. Death is an event I had never witnessed before I came here. Now it's more commonplace than Saturday afternoon football.

I wonder how I'm going to deal with a wife who color coordinates her pot holders and salt and pepper shakers with the vinyl on the kitchen floor.

A week passes with the same mind-numbing routine: daylight patrols, night ambushes, dirt, sweat, bugs, C rations, boredom. Lassen succeeded in getting his platoon lost twice during the week. After a day of trying to lead, cajole, and trick the lieutenant from his errant course, the one capable squad leader in the platoon was so embarrassed and frustrated that he later burst into the CO's tent to plead for a transfer to anywhere.

After a delay of almost three months, Sandy is now officially a sergeant. The always amazing Sergeant Norris produced a case of beer and a block of ice for the celebration. This is the first beer we have seen since the brawl in Di An.

Rumor has it that Norris is going to leave soon for some kind of additional training to become an officer. His replacement has not arrived yet, as threatened, but he is sure to show up soon. Our Kit Carsons have not arrived yet either, thank God. We did get a dog, however. A nasty German shepherd who drags his provider around behind him on a rope. As far as I can tell, the only thing the dog is good for is making sure his trainer is not disturbed during his many naps. No matter how many vicious snarls and lunges the dog makes at us, his trainer feigns undisturbed sleep. The dog is scheduled to take his human and depart tomorrow. This is unfortunate, as we have just learned to cohabitate with the grumpy pair. When the dog or his man are needed, we approach them with a pocket full of rocks and an M-16. We stop just beyond the reach of the dog's tether to lock and load the rifle. This is done for the benefit of the man, who is as surly as the dog but much easier to control. He will know there is an M-16 pointed in his direction, even with his eyes closed. With the rifle on the dog, in case he should accidentally get loose, we throw rocks at the trainer until we have his complete attention and cooperation.

A new mess sergeant and attendant crew have moved into the platoon tent. Several of us with nothing more interesting to do, collect in the back of the tent to watch the four cooks set up their field kitchen. They work quietly with downcast eyes, talking to each other in low voices only when necessary. They avoid looking at us as if our eyes might cause them some kind of damage. I remember the vacant, haunting eyes of the men of this company the first time I saw them sitting in the dust in Di An. It was like looking into the eyes of a wolf without the glint of wild intensity. Those men's eyes, while still observant of their surroundings, were dead and emotionless. I, too, avoided them.

The cooks set up two tables end to end, placing their stoves in a row down the length of the tables. Two five-gallon pots are filled with water and set over a flame to heat while the cooks bring in their personal gear. Canvas cots are unfolded, duffel bags unburdened of extra clothing, paperback books, cans of bug bomb, pillows, and a large civilian, battery-operated radio. The radio is placed in the far corner of the tent, the volume turned up no louder than the voice of its quiet owner. One of the guys squatting in the dirt behind me stands up to say, "Hey, turn that sucker up."

All four cooks stop what they are doing. They look at us and then at each other before one of them silently walks over to the radio to turn the volume up. I do not understand why, but those cooks are afraid of us. The silence that returns is interrupted only by the soft beat of rock and roll coming from the corner of the tent. At the end of the song a voice from some distant base camp wants to know, "Have you taken your malaria pill this week?" A conspiratorial grin passes between us. It is our belief that the malaria pills mask the symptoms but do not prevent or cure the disease. If we religiously take the pills we can continue fighting Johnson's war right through several malaria attacks, then deal with the disease when we return to the United States. If we do not take the pills we might get to spend a couple of days a month shivering in a comfy hospital bed attended by round-eyed nurses. A few men take the pills regularly, many more never take them, but the majority of men take them the same way they take their religion—and presumably with the same results—one every once in a while just in case.

The cooks continue the entertainment, their audience scrutinizing every move, appraising every possession. Like true showmen they unfold the item of greatest luxury last. At first the purpose of the T-shaped metal rods being fastened to each end of the cots is a mystery, but when fine mesh netting is unpacked and draped over the rods, the use of the contraptions becomes clear. The area under the net is sprayed with an insecticide from an aerosol can. I knew such things existed but this is the first time I have actually seen mosquito netting used in Vietnam. Imagine, a whole night without giving blood in exchange for little itchy bumps.

"Go to Tokyo, the land of enchantment, for your R and R," suggests the voice on the radio. Tokyo does not seem to me like the kind of place a soldier would want to rest and recuperate. We had a war there within memory of its residents. I want to go someplace where the people don't hate me, someplace where life has value and killing is a bizarre event. Someday I must search for such a place.

We stay in the tent until dusk when the cooks unwrap their *pièce de résistance*—steaks frozen in dry ice. The sight of this magnificent feast brings an end to our quiet vigil. Most of us openly praise our good fortune as we gather around the boxes of frozen meat, but as always there are some who claim such a bounty is only given before or after some planned disaster. They warn that tomorrow we will pay dearly for this feast. I must admit that the sudden appearance of cooks and steak is a bad sign, but I refuse to let my apprehension dull the succulence of my meal.

I go to sleep with a satisfied stomach and the smell of marijuana wafting through the air.

In the morning, the company leaves the security of its circle of denuded earth. Men file through the jungle knowing no more than ever as to why or where.

By late afternoon the patrol shows no sign of turning back, and from this it is known that the night will be spent in ambush.

The night is filled with the roar of battle, the darkness shattered with brilliant flashes of light: tracers of red and green, explosions of blinding yellow, the harsh lazy white of drifting parachute flares. The barrage rages over my motionless form, my body trembling in tune with the quaking earth. I cannot control my shaking any more than I can control the fire that passes through the air or the constant explosions of mortar shells. I am no more than an autumn leaf in an October storm due to return my chemicals to the earth for use by a more reasonable form of life.

A Willie and Joe cartoon I read years ago runs through my mind. A ludicrous fixation. A groove stripped in the record of my memory. The words keep repeating themselves over and over, as if they are trying to drown out the much louder voice that keeps promising me eternal rest. Focus on the words. Don't listen to that other voice. Don't get snared in the slimy gore of the forbidden valley of eternal horror from which there is no return.

An obscure childhood memory. A drawing of two grubby GIs hugging the war-ravaged earth, the air above their heads filled with pencil-line streaks of lead. The caption has Joe yelling, "Get down, Willie," and Willie yelling back, "I can't get no lower, Joe, me buttons is in the way."

A bean field. Not a bad place to hide an ambush, but a lousy place to get ambushed. If I let all the air out of my lungs and stay real flat . . . no good. These four-inch bean furrows are enough to protect the front half of me, but what good is the front half without the back?

Come on, God, deliver me the fuck out of here. It's too bad I don't believe in you. You could make a hell of a deal with me right now. How about when I was a kid? I went to church a bunch when I was a kid. Does that count? Not if he doesn't exist. Oh, well, sure—but how about just giving me a little three-inch increase in this furrow? I would almost feel like I had something to hide behind. Is that too much to ask? How about a gopher to dig the ground beneath me? We could pile the excavated dirt along my left side. I never had a pet gopher before. He could ride around in my pocket. I'd be glad to give him a ride. You never know when a gopher might come in handy. I wonder if he would eat C rations?

Gophers?!

People are going to start dying here soon. As soon as they find us. None of us will make it out of here.

I can't take this much longer. Why haven't they seen us yet? Rows of ten-inch-high bean plants aren't exactly a jungle. Those damn flares. It looks like high noon out here. It's a good thing they're making so much noise, it almost covers the sound of my teeth chattering. I feel like a metal duck at the county fair, with the whole town having a grand time trying to knock me over and win a prize.

I wish that bastard with the bullhorn would get laryngitis. He's only trying to draw our fire, but he's driving me nuts with that "GI, you die," stuff. The satanic joy of his shrill voice amplifies into a hollow, unearthly screech that pierces through the sounds of rifles and exploding shells to reverberate inside my head, ricocheting across my skull causing psychic damage with each pass. "GI, you die. GI, you die. GI, you die."

I lie rigidly fixed to the ground, fighting with every ounce of will to survive by doing absolutely nothing. If I could switch off my mind maybe this nightmare would go away. Who is this maniac who shrieks at us like a possessed hyena, making me wish for his death above all things? The temptation to fire blindly at our tormentor is nearly overpowering but that's exactly what they want. All it takes is one man a little more terrified than the rest of us, one nervous finger.

I've never known an NVA unit to waste so much ammo. They're blowing up the countryside as if they were Americans. Maybe they've been caught with far more munitions stored in the nearby village than they can possibly carry and have decided to use it on us rather than risk losing it. Whatever, they're wallowing in an orgy of power while we cringe and pray.

The words spoken by our interpreter two weeks ago keep coming back to me: "Beaucoup VC in village, beaucoup VC." How come no one asked him if he was talking about ten VC or twenty VC—or was it more like three hundred VC? Not that it matters now. He was talking about VC, and most of these guys are NVA. Some civil war this is. We are on one side and everybody else is either passive or on the other side.

I've got to do something. Anything. If I could just move. At least let me die trying. Lying here in fear with my face in the dirt is such an inglorious way to end.

"Nightingale to Fire Fox One. Nightingale to Fire Fox One. What the hell is going on down there?"

Jesus . . . what's that? Talking! There should be no talking. No talking, no moving.

"Nightingale, this is Fire Fox One. We are pinned down in a bean field. NVA. Estimate battalion strength." The calm voice of Captain Wilkins comes from three feet behind me. He is talking to Major Barlow on the radio. I suppose being quiet is not very important anymore, considering all the noise Charlie is making.

"I am in the air now, One. Will arrive at your coordinates in five. Are you returning fire? Over."

"Negative. Enemy in cover on north flank. Our position exposed. No chance of surviving engagement. I repeat, no chance of surviving engagement. Immediate air support imperative."

"I don't want to hear that shit, Captain. You have a company of infantry at your disposal—use them. Engage enemy at once."

"Negative, Nightingale. Engagement is suicide. Our position is untenable."

"Then launch an attack. Blow your claymores and attack behind the barrage. I want an all-out effort here. Under no circumstances are you to allow those gooks to escape. Under no circumstance! Do you read me, Captain?"

"Loud and clear. Fire Fox One, out."

Engage? He can't be serious. Of course he's serious. I'll bet he wouldn't say that if he were down here. He doesn't even know our situation. Doesn't know, doesn't care. Why don't you land that chopper just once, you prick, and take your chances with the rest of us?

"Body count crazed bastard," Wilkins snarls to his RTO. "Get battalion HQ on the phone. Find out when that air support is going to get here."

If the NVA and our position were reversed . . . If we could fire from the protection of the woods down into the bean fields . . . Shit, we will be firing into the backs of our own men if we charge from here. Even our claymores are pointing the wrong way. They are lined up along the path leading from the woods in anticipation of the enemy leaving the village by that trail.

If, if, if. If we all get up and run full speed, firing everything we have, we'll all be dead before we get halfway to the trees. We can't do it. It's crazy. The only reason we are alive is that they think we're still in the field to our right rear where we set up at dusk. The nearest cover is some two hundred feet to our left. If we slide on our bellies, some of us

McDonnell F-4C "Phantom"

might get out that way, if they haven't circled to the west yet. But we can't try the left unless everyone does. If one man's movement were detected it would bring death to the whole company. Those jets had better get here soon.

"Captain, Captain!"

"Go."

"The air base says Barlow has put a hold on the air strike until he can evaluate the situation."

"Damn! Give me that thing. This is Fire Fox One. I need air support and I need it now or you're going to have one hundred and two dead GIs on your hands."

"Fire Fox One, this is Bravo Hotel Two Three. Roger your request. Scrambling now. Out."

We'll never last until they get here. Never. How long does it take a Phantom jet pilot to get from his seat in the standby hut to the end of the runway in his supersonic rocket ship? How long will it take him to get from Bien Hoa Air Force Base to our location and then find the speck on the ground that is us?

"Fire Fox One, this is Nightingale. Come in Fire Fox One."

"Captain, it's the major again," reports Wilkins's RTO.

After a short pause the reply comes. "Respond, but when he asks for me tell him you can't reach me at the moment."

"Nightingale, this is Fire Fox One, over."

"Wilkins, you countermanded my orders. I'll have your butt for this. You are going to have those jets flying up your backside. I'm nearing your position now and I want to see your assault within thirty seconds or there's going to be a court-martial. Acknowledge. Over."

"Roger, Nightingale."

"Good work, Chaffey. Now call the platoons and make sure those vertical strobe lights are at the forward corners of our position."

I am glad that the CO set up so close behind me. The radio is a welcome distraction. For the first time I will know what is going on. It gives my mind something to focus on, something to cling to.

"Fire Fox One, where the hell's my frontal assault? You cream puffs, get off your bellies down there and kick some NVA ass. You copy me, Wilkins? Wilkins!"

"Nightingale, this is Fire Fox One, over."

"Shit. Put Wilkins on."

"Sorry, sir. I haven't been able to find him since before your last transmission."

"Bullshit, soldier. You put your captain on this radio right now, and that's an order."

"Wilco, Nightingale."

"Sorry about the heat, Chaffey," apologizes the captain. "You just keep stalling him and maybe we'll all get out of this yet."

"No sweat, sir. Getting yelled at is better than getting dead."

"Come in, Fire Fox One. Put Wilkins on. Now!"

"Fire Fox One, you had better answer this goddamned call right goddamned now!"

"Go ahead, Nightingale."

"Damn it, what's your name, soldier?"

"Spec 4 Chaffey, sir."

"You stay on this line, Chaffey. Is that clear? Now, why haven't you attacked yet? Over."

"I don't know, sir. I think the captain is coordinating with the third and fourth platoons now, sir."

"It is vital that we take full advantage of this opportunity. A chance like this isn't likely to come our way again. A whole battalion of NVA. Just think of it. I want those men on line, Chaffey. Let's show those gook bastards what we're made of. Come on, men. Pour it to them. Attack! Attack! Attack!"

Chaffey doesn't answer right away; when he does his voice sounds small and lonely. "I don't think anyone will follow me, sir."

"Jesus H. Christ, boy. Where the hell is Wilkins?"

"He should be back any second now, sir."

"Well, you can tell that man that his military career is . . ."

The radio is drowned out by a series of explosions within one hundred feet of our besieged ambush. The NVA have switched targets. They finally have the right bean field.

The volume and size of the concussions that rattle the earth increase substantially. My body and mind are consumed by the continuous thunder. Brilliant flashes of light strike through my closed eyelids. Squeezing the handgrip of the machine gun with my right hand to keep my arm from shaking, I pull the gun closer to me while checking the ammo belt with my left hand. There is no point in hiding much longer. This is it.

The beautiful, terrifying scream of a jet pulling out of a dive reaches through the mass of noise to lift my spirit in exhilaration. I realize that the latest bombardments are the explosions of rockets fired from the Phantoms, as one after another streak overhead, firing their load of terror into the trees. If the pilots continue to hit their target instead of us, we may yet be saved. But it is only a reprieve. What will happen in a minute or two when the last rocket is fired?

The jets are gone as suddenly as they arrived. Alien technology streaking over primitive jungle. Silence rushes in to fill the void. What now? Do we attack? Do we retreat, or do we lie here forever?

Tension mounts in the stillness as hundreds of men lie on their bellies, waiting. Waiting for whatever will happen to them next.

In the distance the faint drone of a propeller-driven plane works its way into my consciousness. It is not the sound of a single-engine spotter plane, nor is it the sound of a helicopter—which reminds me, where is our mighty major now? Did the jets frighten him away? Did his martini pitcher run dry? Maybe he went back to Di An for a pee and a quick snack. A man of his rank and exalted ambition is entitled to his creature comforts. After all, he may be our next Westmoreland or Johnson, and deserves the same respect.

The drone of propellers draws nearer. I hear voices in the tree line, the moans and complaints of wounded and dying men. Still we do not move but lie in dread, as our enemies now do. We fear their position and numbers. They fear the power we command in the skies.

Slowly turning my head to look for the approaching aircraft, I see a glowing scarlet line materialize in the black sky behind me. The streak of red light descends from the heavens, pointing a wavy flaming finger to the source of turmoil at the jungle's edge. The deadly line flashes overhead and splatters into the jungle before we hear the familiar deep belch of the Minigun. It's Puff, the magic dragon. Sixty thousand rounds a minute rip into the trees, creating terror and chaos in the jungle. Gone is their orgy of power, gone the bullhorn's promise of death. They cannot fight these machines that live in the sky. Faint noises drift in from our normally silent enemy. Surely now they will break off this engagement to live and fight another day.

But we remain like rocks in the field. The radio is gone or is silent. No orders pass along the line. No flares are fired to penetrate the dark. No noises are heard except those that cannot be separated from imagination.

The hours of the night pass, as they always must. My eyes grow heavy, my limbs relaxed. Lying here has been more tiring than I thought. As sleep creeps in, I remember what they said about the steaks. I hope I never see the day when the Army offers me another.

At dawn Delta Company lifts its collective belly off the ground. We cautiously cross the 150 yards of open field to the tree line occupied by the enemy the night before. With the entire company on line we sweep the woods clear up to the edge of the village. To my delight and Barlow's horror there is not one body to be found. True, gallons of blood, ripped clothing, expended cartridges, field dressings, and military paraphernalia of all kinds litter the ground. We even compile a considerable stack of munitions no doubt lost or discarded in the darkness during the panic caused by the air strikes. But of the many men who died here and the many more now lying somewhere in agony and despair, there is a conspicuous absence.

Discounting the damage to our egos and Captain Wilkins's military career, the operation was an outstanding success—perhaps not by some military standards, but certainly by my own—for we passed this night of motionless desperation without the loss of a single man.

One hundred two pairs of red-rimmed, bloodshot eyes stare indifferently at the very old and the very young who are all that remain of the population of the village. The ancient, bandy-legged men and the bent old women move slowly between the thatched huts doing the same early morning chores in the same way they have been done for hundreds of years. Here, there are no hot corrugated metal roofs or walls, no tin-can cups or pots. The industrial junk of advanced civilization has not yet reached this remote hamlet.

Wide-eyed children peek at us from the edges of huts and the shadows of doorways. Their eyes betray the fear they hold for the huge, brutal foreigners who are the subject of so many horror stories. We, the mongers of death, the napalmers, the burners of villages, the indiscriminate destroyers of all forms of life were not exterminated in the night—as reason would dictate—but instead appear before them with the rising of the sun.

In the faces of the old there is defiance and resignation. No words pass between us as we brush by them to poke in the ashes of cooking fires, look beneath woven floor mats and empty containers, sift through rice, and search the animal pens. Nothing is found until one old woman's refusal to move from her fire is overcome by a solid push from a booted foot. Beneath the glowing embers and six inches of dirt and ash we find the entrance to their tunnels. The woman is sent down first in case of booby traps, but the tunnels are empty.

Without words of warning or threats of vengeance we leave the old Vietnamese with hate in their eyes and walk back into the jungle. This time we killed their sons, next time it could be anyone. In a few days, the young men will return to their village, and in the weeks and months to come we will again try to kill each other. It is the way things are, and the way things will remain until the Americans leave this region or all the people in the village are dead.

Back at the NDP I look into the mess tent vaguely hoping for something warm or fresh to eat. The cooks lie on their cots. The stoves are cold and empty. I pick up a box of C rations on my way to my bunker only to decide that the effort of opening a can is greater than my desire for its contents. I crawl into the bunker and slide down the short, curved tunnel leading to the cool dampness of the cave. If I stay here for the next four or five hours I should miss the sandbag-filling detail that is as omnipresent as the mosquito.

I lie on my back staring up at the convoluted ceiling. Some of the light reflecting off the shadowed bunker walls finds its way into the tunnel and rebounds around the bend to cast a faint light across the cavern. My view of the inverted valleys and peaks above me is hazy but my imagination has no trouble filling the blanks. The coolness of the earth seeps through my sweat-soaked shirt, sending a pleasant shiver down my back. The sound of slow breathing fills the silence.

The diaphragm expands, the chest rises, the air flows in, the diaphragm contracts, the chest falls, the warm, oxygen-depleted air flows out between the lips in a cone-shaped stream, creating eddies at the edge of its flow as it pushes through the molecules floating above my head. With the breath expelled there comes a pause, a waiting, a time of no breathing before the buoyant molecules are again sucked toward the openings in my face, thus producing a pull on the other gas molecules in the cave, setting them in motion, drawing them toward me, streaming down from above, arching from the sides, swirling in confusion in the corners. You can get hung up over breathing used molecules and adjust your intake trying to capture the fresh, sweet-tasting oxygen-rich air, but after a few breaths the air is so stirred up that everything is mixed. You might as well lie back down and be content with used air.

At first you hardly notice it, but soon it is so dominant you wonder how you could have concentrated on anything else. Your head expands with its beating, your body throbs to its pulse. It oozes through its tubes, coursing at a rush to ease and slow to a trickle before the next rush pushes through. Eight beats a breath, ten beats a breath. A doctor counting fifty-eight beats a minute said it was odd, a bit low, but as doctors like to keep their mystery close, he declined to say more. Was it good, was it bad, did it mean I could fly?

Questions, questions, always questions, but rarely an answer. When I first came to this country there was a certainty in my mind that no matter what they said or what happened I would live through my year and return to my home and my girl. Now that has changed. Now I am home, and I shall be here forever until they kill me. My old self, along with my old life, is buried. There is a different me now that has not been here long enough for me to know. I look the same, maybe thinner, tanner, but I am not the same. I only pretend to be.

There is another change, at least I think it is a change. I do not dream about familiar things anymore. The people in my dreams are strangers, all the places unknown. I do not mean that I have no friends in my dreams; I mean that these are people I have never met, as the places are places I have never been to.

I do not know what this means—if anything—but I believe it has to do with my mind trying to control what is happening around it. It creates a new environment of its own making in which it controls every contingency. This enables it to ensure nothing traumatic or unexpected will take place. It is the mind's reaction to the reality it cannot control. Or can it? I find the convoluted dips and rises above me become tropical islands or forested mountains as easily with my eyes open as with them closed.

The breath goes in and out, the heart beats its steady rhythm. My mind is captured inside a dwindling 190-pound mass of panting, throbbing cells that carry on their normal functions with or without this part that thinks and loves and hates and wonders.

"Hey, Shook, are you down there?"

Franklin's voice penetrates my dreams and brings me back to the other reality.

"Yeah. What is it?"

"You have guard duty in ten minutes."

I look up the tunnel at the darkness. Another day has passed. I must have slept for several hours. "Thanks, Franklin. I'll be right up."

The NDP is quiet. Exhausted men asleep in barren bunkers. The great escape. Peace without pleasure. A hollow emptiness—the aftermath of battle. I pull an extra hour of guard for the pleasure of being alone.

Walking from my post I run into Boston squatting on his heels and pulling on a pipe load of grass. He is gazing into the east in deep contemplation or stoned oblivion, I cannot tell which in the dark. I sit on my heels at his side. It is a good night, quiet and peaceful with just enough breeze to keep the mosquitoes from congregating.

"You know, John, if you stare into the night jungle long enough you can see everything your mind can imagine."

"I know. And a couple of hits of dope doesn't dampen the effect any, either."

He chuckles softly and contemplates the east again, absorbed in his private fantasies.

"Do you really think they ever send anybody home?" he asks.

"What?"

"Have you ever seen anyone get on a freedom bird heading back to the world? I've been here for seven months now and I've known a lot of guys who have put in their year and left the company, but I have never heard from anyone who actually made it to the States, have you?"

"No, I can't say that I have."

"If you think about it, it doesn't make any sense for the Army to let us go. Why should they? They own us body and soul. They can extend our tour for the duration of the war anytime they are in the mood. Why should they go through the expense and hassle of drafting and training new guys to replace the experienced men already here? Sure, they need to replace the wounded and dead, but why should they replace us while we are still healthy?"

"Oh, man. Don't say things like that."

"I'm serious. What has the Army ever done for you? Why should they let us go before our usefulness has expired? They don't drive a tank for a year and then return it to the manufacturer to have a new one shipped out in pieces. Well, maybe that's a bad example. The Army might do something like that. There are a lot of people making a pile of money selling equipment to the military, but there's not much profit in sending over new bodies, so what's the point?

"The whole establishment has sunk into the slime, or maybe it was always there and I just now noticed."

Boston sticks his head behind a pile of sandbags to cover the relighting of his pipe. We are quiet for a while as Boston holds a big hit of smoke in his lungs and I settle cross-legged in the dirt. I still cannot squat on my haunches like the locals for very long before my knees hurt and my legs go to sleep.

He lets the smoke-laden air out in a rush. "Why do you think we are fighting this war, anyway?"

"Oh hell, I don't know. Money, I guess. All the power in the U.S. is based on money with the government in there backing the interests of the big money boys and placating the populace. How much money has been spent on this war, fifty billion? One hundred billion? Something like that. Fortunes are being made and spent blowing up this jungle.

"Then there are the goodies over here: the cinnamon and the rice and the marijuana and the opium and the big oil reserve that is supposed to be off the south coast. There is enough potential wealth in this country to keep a lot of greedy men sending other people's sons out to fight for them."

"Why, you cynic. And here I thought we were fighting to keep the commies off the California beaches."

He lies back on his elbows, sucking on his empty pipe. "Did you dig the way the South Vietnamese celebrated Ho Chi Minh's birthday last May? That fucker is a national hero on both sides of the DMZ. Most of these people don't know shit about communism or democracy. They just want to be left alone."

"Yeah, and if the South Vietnamese supported their government at all we would know the location of every VC and NVA soldier in the country. As it is, most of the people in the villages are more sympathetic toward the VC than they are toward the bunch of crooks that run this country. How can Diem keep screwing over the people on his side and still expect them to fight for him?"

"That's an easy one. Have you ever seen the ARVNs fight?"

"No."

"That's because they don't. The only time they get off their butts is to get out of the way when the enemy is coming through. What the hell. Why should they fight? This here's the most fucked-up program I ever hope to be associated with. We are flunkies to the corrupt and the greedy. This is certainly not the kind of war I can get enthusiastic about dying in."

"Right on. It's too bad it's such a long walk home."

I stretch out on my back, taking in the panorama of stars. "You know, I never thought I'd wind up over here. I'm legally blind in one eye, and was exempt until they went and changed the rules when I wasn't looking."

Boston lifts himself up on one elbow. "Really? Which eye can't you see out of?"

"The left one. But I can see out of it a little if I close my right eye. It's just that everything is so blurry and far away that my brain rejects the signal coming in from the left eye when I use my right one. It's a good thing, too, or I would have real spaced-out double vision."

"I can't believe you're in the field with only one good eye."

"Listen, the Army's getting so desperate for replacements they're sending guys to the field who are blind without their glasses. As long as one eye is correctable to twenty-twenty you're legitimate cannon fodder."

"Fuck that. I'll bet if you played it right you could get transferred the hell out of here—and with your education . . . what the hell was it?"

"Medical microbiology."

"Right. I'll bet you could get a job in a hospital. Really. Have you put in for a transfer yet?"

"Jesus, Boston. That dope has addled your brain. I know of a guy who is a nuclear physicist. They made him a sniper.

You know as well as I do that nobody gets transferred out of the field."

"True, except for physical defects, and you have a physical defect. Jesus Christ, Shook, you could get out of this death trap. I'm serious, man. This is great. Tomorrow morning you tell Phillips you want a request for transfer, form 1049."

He's really excited about this. Slipping a friend into a rear echelon job must be the next best thing to getting there himself. But the whole idea's ridiculous. I know I don't qualify for a transfer. "Ah hell, man, I know you mean well but it's a waste of time."

"No. No it isn't. This is the best thing that has happened in months. You have to do it. Tell me you'll do it."

"Okay, Okay. I'll do it. What can I lose?"

"Great! You have made my night."

"Glad to have been of service."

We lay on our backs pondering the infinite space above us. Do I dare allow myself to hope? No. He is living in a dream world. He has found hope in a fantasy. Well, I'll apply, anyway. I told him I would. It'll take months for the big green paper machine to crank out a rejection. By then, well, anything could happen.

"That glowing globule of gas will be along to recook our brains in a couple of hours. I'm going to grab some Zs." With that he rolls on his side and says no more.

I consider going back to our bunker where it will be cool for an extra hour in the morning, but I would probably disturb Franklin. After all, the dirt there is much the same as the dirt here, and this dirt is a lot closer.

In those first minutes after sunrise when the temperature rapidly rises through the seventies and eighties, I discover a disadvantage to sleeping in the middle of the NDP that I did not consider the night before. It comes in the form of lieutenants whose military sensitivities are offended by the sight of soldiers sleeping in plain view without even a semblance of an effort to sleep in tidy rows. I should have known better. Not at all proper. There comes a tapping, a rapping, a thumping upon my boot.

"Get up, you lazy oaf. There is work to be done and you've fallen way behind."

Well, he is right of course. How could I disagree? I've been lying on my backside ever since I got back from lying around in that bean field. "Yes, sir," I say. "Right away," says I, promptly rolling onto my other side.

"You too. Up and at 'em, scum bag." Lassen kicks Boston's feet, but no life shows there. "Get up, you lazy turd."

"Get fucked, you faggot," yells Boston, popping up to a sitting position.

Oh, shit. I don't want to hear the rest of this. Propping one eye open to secure my bearings, I crawl from Lassen's rising flood of abusive verbiage. A torrent of threats, combined with a well-polished stock of standard military insults, rises and blossoms in the early morning air. His voice elevates in its pitch with each increase in volume until the high, hysterical voice becomes the focal point of dozens of sleep-filled eyes sunken beneath brows furrowed by offended ears. The signs are clear. No more sleep for me this day.

"Come on, mule, let's dig us some dirt."

Boston's voice. Boston's boots. Then who is Lassen yelling at? I look back over the path I have crawled. Fifty yards away Lassen is standing alone, gesturing wildly, screaming at the void.

"Ain't that a sight?"

"Somebody ought to put that sorry son of a bitch out of his misery."

Slowly it dawns on the lieutenant what a ridiculous spectacle he is making of himself. The ranting fades in volume and pitch until it is reduced to a low, incoherent mumbling. I look up at Boston's shit-eating grin. "Aren't you a little worried he is going to hang your ass for telling him to get fucked, not to mention the part about being a faggot?"

"Hell, no. There's a rule in this man's army that says you can't be held responsible for your actions when you first wake up. I like to take advantage of that rule whenever the opportunity arises." Boston is thoroughly pleased with himself. "Well, my friend, we'd better fill some sandbags."

I stop. Suddenly alert. Catapulted from a cranial quagmire. Listen. . . . Ah, it's just a bird scratching through dry leaves. Where have I been? Look at that sun. It's almost noon. I've been in dreamland all morning. Hum, I don't remember any dreams, or thoughts. Just . . . nothing.

We have been walking through this jungle every day for the past six days. Today is number seven. Eight if you include the bean field. It all runs together. These days are very much the same. The nights alike. The jungle doesn't change. The bugs, the heat, the weariness—all the same.

It has been a hard, but quiet week. The usual sniper fire. Nothing serious. The same old drudgery. Oh, yeah. There was one bright spot. Four or five days ago.

The company was patrolling the area east of the village. We were lying in some long grass taking a break. A chopper passed overhead, banked, turned, and began a return run. Our pompous, homicidal overlord was making another courageous sojourn over his domain. This was his first gala appearance since the bean field. The troops resent the man. He was too blatant in his fervored efforts to trade our lives for the silver leaves of a lieutenant colonel.

One of Jesse's boys expressed his feelings by taking a shot at the major as his chopper made the return pass. Unfortunately, he missed the major but not the chopper. Getting shot at pissed Barlow off so much he had the chopper set down right there in the grass, giving us all our first view of his royal ass in the bush. No matter how much I hate the man I have to admit it took balls to walk among us like that. Then again, it would fit in better with what I know about him to chalk his actions up to blatant stupidity. He walked down the line asking each one of us who shot at his helicopter. Naturally, no one had the faintest idea. Well, he was determined to get to the bottom of this, but once he started asking questions and getting mostly stony glares in reply, I think he began to get the notion that taking a shot at him was a very popular idea. Anyway, after a few minutes he stomped back to his chopper and flew away. I half-expected a raspberry cheer, but such frivolity was out of place. Instead, a silent look, a finger salute, and a resolve to make a better effort the next time.

In the meantime, the major extracts his revenge. He sends us on patrol every day, ambush every night. At first I felt tough, mean, resentful. Now I'm just tired. Lately the only reason we go back to our NDP is to pick up supplies. Sometimes when they extend our patrol a day or two they drop supplies from a chopper. Sometimes we just get thin. I don't like the drops. Charlie can see that parachute from miles away.

All four platoons are looking for those three companies of NVA. Whichever platoon finds them is going to get squashed.

Trolling the jungle. Twenty-two pieces of bait. Negative vibes. Don't think about it.

So many trees. No need to look for cover. And Charlie. If he's hidden here, we won't see him until he's ready. If we're very quiet we might hear him. There's that chance. We must rely on another sense. The sense of presence. It lingers, to some degree, in all of us.

What is this? Everyone is down. Point has something. Norris edges forward. Checks it out. Slow minutes pass. A signal forward. Cautiously we enter a small clearing.

"Relax. These dudes have already been processed."

What?

The men cross the open space to climb an ancient four-foot dike. They stand in groups, looking down; some turn and walk away. I join a group. Seven or eight fighting holes are strung out along the top of the dike. Each position holds a body or two. Dead gooks. Perhaps a dozen. The one below me stares up at me with empty sockets. His eyes are gone, as well as his lips, his ears, and his nose. But most of his skin remains. Leathery stuff, parchment dry, stretched taut over an empty skull. A pith helmet still rests on his head. A bullet hole through the helmet halfway down from the crown. An ammunition belt slung across his boney shoulders. Black pajamas. Sandals. A rifle leans against the far side of the hole, rusting. Unbelievable. How long has he been here? Two, three weeks? A month? I cannot judge these things. No one has visited these dead men since their executioner. An air strike? Couldn't find this spot again, or didn't try?

Where the hell are we, anyway?

Norris gently lifts the helmet from the dead man's head. He wipes the band. Tries it on. Too small. He adjusts the headband. Tries again. A satisfied rap with the fingers. Good fit. He takes the sandals, the ammunition, the rifle, too. He checks the other holes. Everybody ready? Good, let's go. Time for lunch.

A can of pork and beans, a small tin of caraway cheese, and crackers. Off we go. West, then north, then west again. Two days out from the NDP. When are we turning back? Don't ask. Don't think about it. It's all the same.

Twenty-two men walk up the shallow ravine. We fill our canteens in the small stream, then walk to its source: a swampy pocket between hills. We push our way through a thicket of bamboo, moving in an open loop that brings us out, heading in the same direction we came. Up to a grassy knoll on top of one of the small hills. A clear view of our path below. Norris is a clever man. Not only are we overlooking the shallow ravine, we can see our entrance and exit through the bamboo as well. We will hold up here until dark. Eat some chow. Get some rest.

If there were normal decent evenings in Vietnam, they would come now. That remembered time when the day wanes and cools. Here, there is only hot light and hot dark, with a slow cooling of the dark. Some clouds drift by, casting shadows.

Someone is staring at me. I turn to meet the eyes. Boston. A beckoning hand. Insistent. Damn. I cradle the gun in my arms and low crawl to the edge of the hill. He points a finger down the ravine. One gook, head bent to the ground. No hat, black pajamas, no gun. Following our track. He reaches the edge of the marshy thicket, stalls, looks back. We follow his gaze. A second gook starts up the ravine. Then a third. No weapons. The first man waits until his comrades are close, then disappears into the thicket. Two and three follow. Their progress is easily traced by the swaying of the bamboo. We check back down the ravine. Empty. The ripples of the bamboo have stopped at the top of the loop.

"I'll take the left. You take the right," whispers Boston.

"Check."

"Hold it. I didn't see any weapons, did you?" It's Norris. I thought he was still back studying his map.

Boston looks up in disbelief. "So fucking what? They were dogging us."

"Cool it. I'll decide." Norris addresses the thicket in Vietnamese. The wavering bushes and voices below us go still. Norris stands, fires a burst into the air. The bushes and voices come alive with a clatter. Chattering nervously, the three men emerge from the thicket with arms raised. Norris volleys questions down the hill. A multitude of answers return. The interview ends with a curt "Didi mau." The sergeant offers no explanation.

"I'm telling you, man, we're going to regret that. We should've wasted those suckers," says Boston.

Seems like he's right to me, but then I can't see how it matters much. One way or the other, the enemy will soon know we are here.

It'll be dark in an hour or two. We can't stay here. Slip

back into the web gear. Descend the far side of the hill. Jump over a long-neglected ditch. A sign of existence long ago in some hamlet down below. Into the thickest jungle we can find. Deep into its hidden folds. A deadly game of hide and seek. We stop to wait, to hide. There is the feel of other men, but weak, not near. Norris goes alone to look around.

The sky turns gray, the light diffused. We must choose an ambush site before dark. The men's restlessness grows each minute the sergeant fails to return. He is late, but we must wait or lose each other in the dark.

A sound. Men with guns stare hard to recognize the man who holds the knowledge and the map.

Closely following the back before us, we work through the tangled growth, struggling to maintain a silence on a ground we cannot see. Abruptly, we are in the open, the air a lighter shade of black. In time we stop. No word is spoken. I feel a tap and follow the form turning away. The hand points at the ground then swings up to make a wiping motion from side to side: my field of fire. I settle in.

Men come to set cans of ammo at my feet, as if they are gifts of homage to the gun. I stack them three on the bottom, two on top, bullets pointing out. A small wall. Prop the helmet against the wall. Head behind the helmet. Body aligned. Same old stuff. Familiar routine. Small comfort there.

We set the watches: one hour on, two off. The ground is dry, not many bugs. The sweat stops. Weariness leads me quickly to sleep.

No dreams remembered, but the explosion felt. The mind knows. Too far away. No concern. Comes another. Closer. The blast of sound. The trembling earth. Through closed eyes the mind perceives the coming of first light. The body wakes but does not move. Senses alert. How far? How soon? How serious? The first mortar landed about one and a half football fields away. The second, on a line to our ambush, was about one football field out. The next one should land fifty yards in front of me.

Listen to the silence of the troops. They lie in frozen discipline. Some on either side of me. A line of men behind. Somewhere to the front are eyes that search for us. Up there on the left, perhaps. Looking for the movement that will betray us. Or maybe they have us already and are merely adjusting fire.

The third arrives with a shattering roar. I turn my head

to see. The plume of dirt filling the air looks fifty yards away to me. An inward smile of satisfaction. The calculation right. The next one should land here in our midst. Well centered. Dead.

Men fidget. Legs crouch. Fingers tense. Eyes scan. Minds race. Feet twitch. Three feet behind my boots is an ancient ditch two feet in width and full to the top with slime-encrusted water. I ooze to the lip of the ditch. Right toe in. Right fingers touch slick green. Why do I wait? The sound will be too late a warning. Yet I wait. Wait my death on the lip of safety. The repugnance of slime, the revulsion to snakes greater than the fear of death? I don't believe it will come when reason dictates it must? Yet I linger. The seconds expand into the stretch of time that makes up eternity. I am committed. I shall not go in. The proper time is passed. It worries me, this nonchalance with death. The less I care the closer draws eternal rest. I must find a change or drown in apathy.

Although we wait, it does not come. We leave the place in wonder. We slip into the jungle, avoiding open ground. We do not seek the mortar tube nor request an aerial view. I do not understand, but it was never required that I do.

We slip through the jungle for several hours before we stop to eat. The food supply is low. We share what remains. In the middle of a can of turkey loaf, a wild thought descends. What if the men we didn't shoot returned the favor in kind? Could they have walked the mortars in, then stopped to let us know: didi mau, GI; we can kill you anytime.

Late the next morning the platoon breaks out of the jungle into the circular clearing surrounding the NDP. The ragged clothes, the rivulets of sweat through the dirt of expressionless faces, the steady stride: the look of men who could walk another hundred miles or fall in a heap of exhaustion in another hundred feet. We drop our gear as we pass our separate bunkers, drawn like vultures to the mess tent where a savory smell rises from a steaming cauldron. Hungry stomachs rumble with desire. Eyes peer greedily into the pot only to be turned away. Apparently word of our platoon's arrival reached the cooks too late in their preparations. Being refused the ready food seems a cruel blow despite its being dealt without malice. Maybe I could beg for leftovers or lick the sauce from discarded paper plates. No, no, no. Running one's tongue over coarse, dry paper ranks with scraping fingernails across blackboards. I will gather my dignity about me—there is plenty of discarded dignity around—sit up here on a sandbag, smoke a cigarette, and be very cool and stoic. Damn cigarettes make me want to puke. I think I will crawl into the cave and transport my mind to someplace where the nights are cool, the women horny, and the beer runs free. A place where colors other than green and brown exist.

I awake in darkness to the smells of mold and rot, the feel of clamminess, the itch of crotch and chest. My clothes and body are in an advanced state of decay. With several helmetfuls of water and a towel used only once, I clean away the week's grime. Since the supply of clean clothes came and went two days ago, I rinse out the clothes I just took off. There are fourteen holes in my pants alone. I put them on dripping wet. They will dry in time.

Since the hour is not late a few members of the platoon are still awake. I roam, looking for some way to amuse myself. I find Boston in the mess tent, playing a game of cards. He certainly has a lot of energy considering where we have been.

"Hey, Shook. Come over here. Have you put in for that transfer yet?"

"Transfer? Oh yeah, that transfer. No."

"Shit, man." He throws down his cards in disgust. "You said you would. In fact, you promised. I thought your word was good."

"It is, it is. Take it easy. I haven't had a chance. I'll do it the first thing tomorrow."

"Tomorrow. What's the matter with right now?"

"What's this transfer shit?" chimes in another card player. "You think you're going someplace?"

"I doubt it, but it's worth a try."

"You're crazy. Nobody gets transferred out of the field. I know. I tried."

"Shut up, Spoons," Boston says, getting up and walking toward me. "Well? What are you waiting for?"

"What's the rush? Norris is probably asleep."

"Like hell he is. He was just here a minute ago. You stay put. I'll go find him." Boston strides from the tent—motivated. Is he trying to prove a point or is he trying to save a friend? Before I can come to any conclusion, Boston is back with Norris in tow. Norris and I sit down together on the dirt floor out of hearing range of the others. I make my pitch to the sergeant. To my surprise, he listens with interest. I finish my spiel with, "I would be more useful as a medical microbiologist than I am as a one-eyed machine gunner."

"Makes sense to me. I'll take it up with the captain in the morning."

"Thanks a lot, Sarge." Things have gone haywire. This isn't the way the Army works. The sergeant is supposed to say, "Tough shit, scum bag," and stomp off. Do I dare hope? Dumb question. Of course I hope. Cautious exultation is more like it, but don't get too excited yet. So far all I have is the absence of a no. My new lease on life still requires a yes from the captain and someone at battalion HQ willing to ignore the no-transfers-out-of-the-field-unless-you-are-physically-disabled rule.

The next morning, I am absentmindedly running a cleaning patch through the machine gun barrel when an uneasiness descends. I turn to find the captain gazing over my shoulder.

"Good morning," he says with a smile.

"Morning, Captain," I reply, getting to my feet.

"Sergeant Norris and I have been talking over your situation."

Judgment day is at hand. My voice betrays my nervousness. "Yes, sir?"

"I have decided to find a position for you in the rear where your education can be put to good use. Until we can find out what positions are available, and get hold of your medical records, I want you to stay in the NDP."

"Yes, sir!" Fantastic.

"We will keep you informed of any developments."

"Thank you, sir." Stupendous! No more patrols. No more ambushes. I've been saved. Hallelujah! Shhh. Do not make a scene. Do not attract any attention. Do not do anything to mess this up.

By midmorning the platoon is ready to return to the jungle. A surge of guilt washes over me as I watch Franklin hoist my machine gun to his shoulder. Although they have told me how glad they are that I am getting out of the field, I still feel like I am betraying them. I will no longer be there to help out, to share the danger, to increase the odds. I would gladly go with them one more time, if I knew it were just one more time, or one more week. Yes, I would gladly go, but I will not. By arbitrary decision, I may be the one to make it out of here, the one to be spared.

I stand alone in the wake of their going like a new but useless third shoe. I roam the bunkers of the third platoon eager for a friendly face to dispel loneliness. I end up sitting cross-legged in the shade of a poncho shelter playing cards with three other despondent souls. We play poker and hearts for MPC. They say the military script has value, but it is worthless here. These paper dimes and quarters with the feel of Monopoly money about them will not make a woman materialize or bring a beer to this alcohol-free plot of jungle. We have no use for this odd money except to trade it back and forth over cards. Still, when I walk away with twenty dollars of their money I feel guilty. It took someone three days of pulling ambushes, walking patrols, and filling sandbags to earn this money. I promise myself not to win again. I have enough good fortune without taking more.

The next day I spend working on the bunker. I enlarge the cavern, put another layer of sandbags overhead, improve the entryway, and dig a sump hole to kick grenades into.

Shortly after noon the platoon returns. They tell me of swimming three streams over their heads, of leeches, and of losing helmets. They seem glad that one of us is getting out of the field, if a little envious that it is not he. Already there is a change between us. I cease to be one of them. I hover on the edges. I am becoming one of the host of other people not really on their side. We who have been willing to risk our lives for one another feel awkward now. My life may have been spared but how many of them will make it through their year without mutilation to body and mind?

At 0900 orders come over the radio from battalion HQ. I am to report to the aid station in Di An. I say my farewells as I jam letters and writing material into a side pocket, roll my shaving kit in my poncho liner, grab my AK-47, throw a bandolier of ammunition over my shoulder, put on my helmet, and hustle to the chopper pad. By 0920 the circle of barren earth cut from the jungle fades from view. Miniature people shuffle through the dust of their island sanctuary amid an ocean of quiet hostility.

When we touch down in the 1st Division's base camp I head straight for the aid station. No fooling around. A bored clerk tells me to come back at 1300. I wander for three hours

AK-47

fighting off the urge to drown my nervousness in a gallon of frothy brew. At exactly 1300 I return to the aid station where I am assigned a chair in the corner. At 1340 a buck sergeant saunters in to confer with the clerk. On his way back out he tells me to get in his jeep. We hurtle down powdery roads with a rooster tail of dust billowing behind. We come to a halt at the guardhouse protecting the main gate where I had entered so long ago. Sober MPs glance at our pass and wave us through.

Outside the post the road is wide and graveled. The air streaming past the open jeep cools the body to the presweat level, producing a feeling of clean freedom. As we reach the outskirts of the town of Di An where the road becomes asphalt, we pass an old mama-san squatting in her front yard attending to a small child. I shove a round into the chamber of the AK. The sergeant looks at his passenger for the first time.

"Where did you get the Russian rifle?"

That's a stupid question, but there's no point in riling him. "The usual place."

"It looks like it's in good condition."

Three young women work a garden plot with hoes. Children play on the dirt strip between the houses and the road. An old woman does a fast shuffle in rhythm to the oscillating wicker baskets hanging from the ends of the pole balanced on her shoulder. People pass on bicycles and lounge in doorways. I cannot keep track of them all. "Yeah, the action is smooth. No rust pits." I will concentrate on the ones to our front and ignore those to our sides and back, although it makes me uneasy not knowing what is going on behind me.

"I'll give you a hundred bucks for it."

What is this shit? A soldier doesn't sell his weapon. A lot of good a hundred dollars will do me in a firefight. Stay cool. "Maybe. When I get a 16 to replace it."

We manage to streak through town without hitting a single chicken, dog, child, or wobbly bicycle. We roar past rice paddies, orchards of every kind, patches of virgin jungle, and the inevitable collection of thatch and tin huts.

"Where are we going?"

"Long Binh." He says the name the same way people say L.A. or New York, as if the name itself carries a meaning.

"Why?"

"Why? To get your eyes checked." There is a silent "you dumb hick" on the end of the sentence.

The jeep comes to a stop in front of a long, white, wooden building. Inside the building a guy dressed in white informs us that the doctor we came to see will be out for the rest of the day. I apply some gentle pressure that results in a referral to another doctor in another building. We pull to a stop beside a second long, white building exactly like the first.

"You wait in the jeep," the sergeant orders as he starts up the steps.

"I'd better come . . ."

"You just stay put, Private." He is irritated.

In five minutes he bounds back down the stairs with a piece of paper clutched in his hand. "There," he says, folding the paper and placing it in his shirt pocket. "That's all taken care of."

"What's all taken care of?"

"Your eye examination. All done."

"Pretty neat trick examining my eyes without me."

"Well the doc couldn't examine you, anyway. You see, I forgot to bring your medical records."

"Oh sure, that makes sense." This sergeant is much too pleased with himself. "Well? How did I do?"

"Oh, just fine. The doc certified you as combat qualified."

What went on in that building? Did a doctor really falsify my eye examination, or was it some clerk or aide not adverse to forgery?

Whether the sergeant coerced someone else's aide or did the deed himself, I ought to shoot the bastard somewhere outside of town and tell the MPs an old mama-san did it because he refused to pay after he screwed her daughter.

During the return trip to the aid station I brood over my escort's effort to speed my return to the field. Is he carrying out this fraud merely to expedite his day, or is there a baser reason? His smug satisfaction suggests a vengeance fulfilled. Have I become the brunt of the animosity between the rear echelon personnel and the field troops? The effects of that quiet rivalry are everywhere. A field unit making one of its infrequent overnight visits to base camp has much the same effect on the camp personnel as the Hell's Angels have on the locals at a neighborhood tavern. In retaliation for the real and implied physical threats, some of the people posted in the rear make sure items sent to the field are the worst available. The rancid milk and butter that always accompanies our few prepared meals did not get that way on their short trip from the base camp. They were rancid when they were selected for our consumption, along with the moldy bread and the rubbery meat. Supply sergeants can sell material slated for a field unit on the black market, then send reject material recorded as destroyed in its place. The weapons wagon plays its part by selling the weapons we give them for repair. I never did get my .45 back. The clerks chip in by delaying or putting the lowest priority on field promotions and skimming extra R and Rs for themselves and their friends. I am sure that most rear echelon personnel are not corrupt or vindictive, but orders and supplies go through enough hands that they generally get slighted somewhere along the line before they reach the field.

I do not understand the rules and intricacy of this new game. If I gave the sergeant my AK maybe he would change the falsified eye examination records in my favor. My rifle in exchange for a release from the field would be a mighty bargain, but my foolish pride disallows this tack. I'll be damned if I'll barter for my life with this treacherous bastard.

The clerk at the aid station tells me to return to the field in the morning. In the meantime, I am to report to my battalion area for night duty. I ask to see the paper that returned with us from Long Binh. He wants to know why.

"Because my eyes were never examined, that's why. Because that paper is a phony."

"How do you know it's a phony if you haven't seen it?"

"That's easily settled. Let's have a look, then we'll both know."

"Sorry, can't do that. These records are confidential."

"Do you think it's really necessary to keep the results of my own nonexistent eye examination from me?"

"Nonexistent? What do you mean nonexistent? The results are right here."

"But nobody looked at my eyes. They didn't even look at my records because the sergeant forgot them." I am trying to keep my voice low and calm so as not to attract the buck sergeant's attention, but my volume is beginning to increase in proportion to my frustration.

"Look," retorts the clerk, "you were brought in to have

your medical records updated. They have been updated.
Now you go back to the field."

"What's the problem here?" demands the buck sergeant,
joining the clerk behind his desk.

"I want to see what phony bullshit you wrote on that
paper and I am not leaving until I do."

The sergeant explodes into a long series of threats and
verbal abuses. A staff sergeant is drawn from the rear of the
office by the angry voice of his underling. He demands to
know the reason for this outburst. I explain my case as clearly
as I can between interruptions by the buck sergeant. The
staff sergeant does not like my attitude. How dare I question
the integrity of my superiors? I try to placate him with
respectful words and reason. No, I am not trying to cause
trouble. Yes, I am aware of the rules of military courtesy, but
they do not alter the fact that his sergeant submitted a false
document. The staff sergeant works himself into a rage, his
verbal abuses more polished, his threats more believable. I
demand justice. They demand a respect that requires that I
admit that no injustice has been done. The yelling, the frustration, the absurdity of the argument raises a rare anger in
me.

"Obedience is given. Respect is earned. He deserves no
one's respect," I charge. That did it. They are both yelling at
me. There is no hope of reasoning with them now, but I will
not back down. I am in the right. I demand to see their CO. I
am pushing the limit, but what can they do? They have
already assigned me to the worst possible fate.

"You want to see the CO?" leers the staff sergeant.
"Okay, I'll get the CO. You're making a big mistake, troop."
He knocks and enters a room at the back of the office.

"You're going to get yours now, smart ass," jeers the
buck sergeant. I should have shot him. It would have been a
lot easier.

A first lieutenant winds his way through the disorganized
array of desks and filing cabinets. He stops to glower at me,
clearly irritated by this trivial interruption. He makes his
position clear from the start. He does not want to hear a word
from me. He is not interested in my case, only in my gross
insubordination. He promises a court-martial, the stockade,
and an extended tour in the field. I listen in silence. I believe
he is serious. Military justice at work. My last hope is destroyed, only my anger remains. I must do something before

he finishes his tirade and gets to the "take him away" part. At the end of a sentence, while he is sucking in air for the next volley, I snap up my rifle, do an about face, and march out the door, not sure what I will do if they try to stop me. Perhaps they notice that the clip is inserted in the rifle. I am sure they are convinced that all grunts are crazy. Maybe they will leave me alone. I take the shortest route out of the area, resisting the urge to run. Avoiding the roads, I walk toward the center of the base camp, changing directions now and then to lose any eyes that might be following me.

After half a mile of ducking between buildings, tents, and outhouses, I pass a small, nearly deserted EM club. I double back. This looks like a good place to get out of the open for awhile. Two men sit at a table playing cards. The bartender perches on a stool trying to read a paperback in the dim light. Behind him the wall is completely covered with *Playboy* centerfolds. A feast of desire to the eyes of the starving. How the hell can a randy lad drink his beer with all that sumptuous temptation staring him in the face? I order a beer and sit facing away from the montage. I cannot stand to look at what I cannot have.

The beer is a cool stream of delicious bubbles running down my throat. The urge to have several more is undeniable, but midway through the second a deeper need wins out. I am too keyed up to sit here any longer. I have to move. If the MPs are looking for me the EM club will be one of the first places they look. Back in the glaring sun, I drift aimlessly until I calm down enough to realize that there is not much point in hiding. The aid station has my name. If the MPs are looking for me they will eventually find me. As soon as I report to my battalion area or rejoin my company they will know where to pick me up.

I drift down one unfamiliar road after another unable to decide on any course, my anger slowly dissolving into a feeling of helpless depression.

A jeep pulls to a stop beside me. "Do you want a lift?"

I stare dumbly at the three men in the jeep. Grunts by the looks of their boots and gear.

"You're heading out the gate, aren't you?" they ask, confused by my silence.

I pull my mind from its wallow and glance down the road. Sure enough, I am on the road to the main gate. "Why, yes. Thanks." I answer on impulse, eager to be with my own kind, among friends for a time.

As I settle into the back of the jeep they ask another disturbing question. "Where are you headed?"

"Long Binh," I answer immediately, not knowing any other destination that would sound legitimate at this late hour of the afternoon.

"You barely have enough time to make it before they close the gate," the driver says, checking his watch. "We're heading north out of Di An. We'll let you off on the outskirts of town so the MPs won't pick you up. You won't have any trouble hitching a ride to Long Binh from there."

"Great. That'll be fine." That's right, the town of Di An is off-limits, and the bases close their gates at dusk. Where the hell am I going, anyway? There's no answer to that. I don't know any place to go. I can always sleep in the bush. Wish I hadn't left my poncho liner at the aid station. I wish I had eaten today. Oh, well, it doesn't matter. Nothing matters except this sweat-drying blast of air and this feeling of release.

When the jeep stops, I jump out, looking forward to whatever lies ahead. I feel alive for the first time in weeks. Looking up and down the road, trying to decide which direction to take, I resolve to go with the first ride offered.

The sweat has scarcely resumed its course down the sides of my chest before a deuce and a half comes roaring down the asphalt. I stick out my arm, thumb pointing to the sky. With a double-clutched downshift, a squeal of brakes, and a belch of smoke, the truck lumbers by, shuddering to a stop fifty feet beyond. A curly blond head pokes out of the passenger's side window. "Jump in the back. We gotta roll." The truck is moving again before I reach the tailgate. A hand grabs a hold under my arm, helping me in. I roll over the gate to the floor. The hand is there again, asking to be shaken.

"Welcome aboard. My name's Roy."

"Howdy, Roy. I'm John." Shaking the hand I notice the worn, faded, recently cleaned fatigues, the dusty boots with only the faintest trace of the original black dye lingering—a distinguishing point of pride among field troops. His dirt is fresh and thin without the repellent oil and old sweat base. Like me, he has been near a bucket of water sometime in the last twenty-four hours. Glancing at his face I notice the distracting flaws on either side of his smiling mustache. Pinned to his collar like warning signs are two black metal chevrons.

"*Sergeant* Roy, I see." Grunts below the rank of staff sergeant rarely wear their rank in the field.

"Yeah. Tacky, huh? This is the third time I've worn them. They help, you know, when you're in the rear."

Two new guys made conspicuous by their shiny black boots, their dark olive fatigues, and their pale faces sit close behind the cab as if seeking its protection. They just nod when I say hi, not willing to be distracted from the important business of staying alive. They probably heard about the VC ambushing supply trucks, about the road mines. They look like they are going to be ready when it happens—ready to do God knows what.

"Where you headed?" Roy is feeling good, about as good as I am.

"Oh hell, I don't know. Where's this truck bound for?"

"Long Binh. They're in a hustle to get there before curfew. Me, I'm not in such a hurry. I figure to have me some fun before I check in. Say, why don't you come with me?"

Just like that. I've known you for two minutes; come with me and be my friend. He certainly is loose and friendly for a sergeant. He can't be a lifer. He's probably just another draftee who has survived the field long enough to become a sergeant. Well, I'm already in trouble. I can't see how a little more trouble can make much difference. "What do you have in mind?"

"First of all, we've got to get ourselves some beer. I've got a powerful thirst."

"I'm for that."

"Then we're going to get ourselves some women. I haven't been properly laid in months. If I don't get some soon I'm going to explode into a million shimmering pieces of frustrated desire."

"I hear ya."

"Great. You'll come then?"

"Why not? I sure as hell don't have anything better to do."

"All right. When this mother slows down for the turn into Long Binh we'll just ease over the back and step off. And keep that AK where they can't see it from the gate. The MPs will nab you if they see you carrying it."

"I've already been through that gate twice today. They never said anything."

"Yeah? Well, you never know, but it's illegal to carry one of those in the rear. Anyway, they will nab us for curfew violation if we don't get a ride right away."

There's a lot I don't know about life in the rear. Roy seems to know his way around. Perhaps I can learn from him, although this plan of his doesn't appear to be very well thought out. Oh well, I'm in it now.

We have turned onto a four-lane highway running parallel to the fence protecting the east side of Long Binh. Ugly concrete and sandbag bunkers protrude from the low, barren, dirt hills facing the rush hour traffic. Military trucks and jeeps, ancient Citroens and dilapidated Renaults vie for space with Vespa scooters, Honda motorbikes, and three-wheeled Lambrettas with their motor scooter engines and their canopied, miniature, pickup beds suspended between the rear wheels.

"Get ready. Hey, you guys, tell the driver thanks. We've got some business to attend to down the road."

We perch on the tailgate, ready to jump, but the truck does not slow down enough. The driver waits until the last second to jam on the brakes, taking the corner hard. We jump as the truck swings for its turn, raising our arms for a ride as soon as we regain our balance. I look over my shoulder at the gate. We are directly in front of the damn guard station, in clear view of the MPs.

Roy taps my arm, "Come on."

We jog up the road to a Lambretta that has pulled onto the shoulder. There are four Vietnamese and five chickens in the back of the strange little vehicle. There is not enough room for the bodies of two cumbersome Americans. The driver yells something in his high, rapid-fire, singsong language that seems to mean "Hurry up . . . get in" and who knows what else.

Undaunted by the crowd, Roy squeezes onto a side bench, creating a list to port. Through the flurry of flapping chicken wings he smiles at his neighbors. The old motor scooter engine whines and rattles in increasing rhythm to its pings. The gears struggle to mesh into first. Not wanting to be left behind I sit on the last few inches of floor, my legs dangling over the back, slightly lifted to keep them off the pavement. The grinding gears finally mesh, sending the

Lambretta lurching in the first of a series of forward and aft
rocking motions. Our weight nearly brings the front wheel off
the ground during the backward oscillations. The driver yells
over the engine noise, slapping the front of the carriage. Roy
and I slide forward between boney knees and excited chickens. The adjusted weight returns traction to the front wheel
and steering ability to the driver. Roy wedges himself next to
the cab, his knees drawn tight to his chest, a big smile on his
face. He pulls a pack of Winstons from his shirt, offering
them around. The Vietnamese take one each and stash them
carefully beneath their clothes.

We do not go far before Roy lets the driver know that
the crossroads up ahead is where he wants to stop. We offer
to pay for the ride. The driver refuses, "GI number one. No
money. GIs number one, okay?" He displays his bad teeth
with a smile and waves as he pulls away.

What is this? Goodwill between Americans and Vietnamese? I didn't know such a thing existed. We shout good
words after the departing Lambretta that are drowned in the
straining rattle of the underpowered engine.

We jog down a road heading east off the highway until
we are well out of view of the thoroughfare. Roy digs into the
back of his cigarette pack, carefully extracting a smoke with
both ends twisted closed. He runs it under his nose, inhaling
its fragrance like a connoisseur of fine cigars. "My last one.
We had better smoke it in case the MPs come by before we
reach the village."

Standing in the open on the edge of the gravel road we
pass the joint back and forth, sucking up the evidence. My
first dope in Vietnam. Not at all the safe, close gathering of
friends I had envisioned this time would bring. The potent
smoke begins to lighten my head before the joint has dwindled to a roach. Roy is working on the last remains when an
empty Lambretta rattles to a stop before us.

"You go village?"

"Right on. Ah, yes, we go village."

"Village number ten. Two GIs die in village. Boo coo
MP."

Yes, but he will take us there. For two dollars he will
take us. That is too much for so short a trip. Not too much.
The danger to him. The price of gas. They barter in pigeon
English and Vietnamese with words that sound French sprinkled here and there. I do not understand most of the words

but the meaning comes through, and I understand that if we do not get under cover soon we will spend the next several nights in the stockade. I give Roy a push. "Fuck the money, let's go."

Clattering down the road in the beat-up three-wheel machine, I begin to doubt that the possible pleasures of this village could be worth the risks. I suggest to Roy that we go to the post he described on the far side of the village so that I can fill my empty stomach, get plenty of beer to drink, and have a safe place to sleep.

"No way. If we go on that post we won't be able to get off again until morning. I'm not going to waste a night in the rear with a bunch of sorry GIs. We can get something to eat in the village, and anything else we need as well. Don't sweat it, man; we're going to have a good time."

"Okay, if you say so." What have I got to lose? All we have to worry about is MPs who want to put us in cages, VC that want to put us in our graves, parasites in our food, and venereal disease if we get lucky.

"By the way, this village is strictly off-limits. When we hit the street don't hang around in the open."

At the entrance of the village the road wishbones around an island of two-story, brick buildings with white plaster facing. Across the roads from this island of permanent structures are two solid walls of peasant hooches. Thatch and tin-sheet roofs intermesh to form a canopy over a maze of walls.

Our driver veers sharply to the left, urging us to didi mau even before we come to a stop. For a moment, as the Lambretta speeds away, we are left in peace to gaze at the village through the shimmering, fuzzy-edged haze of our marijuana high. Fifteen feet off the clean line of the dusty road curving out of view is a continuous wall of bamboo, tin, wooden planks, thatch, cardboard, and cloth. Individual dwellings can be loosely distinguished by a general consistency of building material over a ten- to twenty-foot section. Every few feet the wall is breached with openings for windows and doorways covered with bamboo or cloth to keep out dust, heat, and curious eyes.

Then the quiet chaos of the street alters as awareness of our presence radiates into the village. Children abandon their games in the dirt and materialize from behind the ragged wall to race to our sides. We are surrounded by shrill, urging voices and hands that beckon, pull, and push. Disagreements between factions flare and die as we are swept along the current. The main force of the adolescent stream deposits me before a sheath of coarse, brown cloth covering the doorway in a dusty bamboo wall. Here, I resist the current still buffeting my backside. I do not wish to pass beyond the brown curtain. I do not trust what lies within. A hand of many years grasps the drape, pulling it aside to reveal the peering eyes and weathered face of a mama-san of indeterminate age. The head bows slightly, an arm beckons me forward into her dusky lair. Not a chance, baby. Uh-uh, not me. Roy swirls by grabbing my arm as he passes. "Get off the damn street."

In the dim light of the hooch mama-san directs quiet, meaningless words at my face while the bedlam outside fades and dissipates. The composed, miniature woman before me could not be more than four foot eight or weigh more than eighty pounds. Her skin is leathery and deeply lined, but because most Vietnamese women begin to show the signs of age when they reach their late twenties and are old at thirty-five, I can only bracket this woman's age at somewhere between forty and sixty. Despite her venerable age and small frame, her manner indicates that here she holds the power.

I nod to her unintelligible words in agreement. Surely she must be right. The corners of her mouth stretch into the beginning of a smile. She turns and walks away, padding the hard earth floor with her sandaled feet. She leaves the room through another curtained door opening onto what appears to be a courtyard.

I stand in embarrassed stillness not knowing what to expect or do with my awkward largeness in this small, fragile space. As my eyes adjust to the dull light, the details of the room come into view. There are bamboo stringers an inch above my head. Free-standing cloth screens separate the box frame bed before me from a small living area with woven grass mats on the floor. A second bed is situated in an alcove on my left. A curtain is pulled across the alcove, revealing only the head of the bed and the shy, curious eyes of a small girl. I smile at her. She giggles and lowers her eyes, understanding far more than I.

It is not long before mama-san returns with two girls in her wake. The girls' eyes flit curiously between me and Roy, chattering their appraisal of fate's draw, teasing and laughing with one another, excited but reserved, like high-school girls at a dance. While the lady of the house confers with Roy on the relationship between pleasure and money, one of the girls tries a few phrases of broken English on me. She introduces herself as Kim and offers me a seat on the bed. With her hands resting gently on my leg, she manages to make pleasant small talk in a unique form of English. The nearness of this fragile, attractive young woman, and the imminent threat of intimacy, are unsettlingly alien to my life of dealing in death. Her people and my people are killing each other. Here I am contemplating cohabitation with the enemy, or at least coupling with the enemy. I must be paranoid. She does not look like the enemy. She does not even wear the usual props of her profession. She wears no makeup, no perfume, no plunging neckline or skirt split to midthigh, yet her femininity and sexuality could not be more apparent. Her smile, her small, delicate, even features, her clear, smooth skin, her pert breasts under the simple white blouse combine to permeate me with an urgent thrill of desire. Her smile deepens and her eyes shine with a devilish gleam as she observes my growing interest.

"How does fifteen dollars for the night sound?" Roy's voice retrieves me from the edge of my sexual mire.

The night? Fifteen dollars? Wait a minute. I never really agreed to this. What I agreed to was drinking some beer. This just sort of happened. The result of curiosity. After all, I was literally pushed into this place.

"I'm going to get a couple of packs of dope and some beer. Should I tell mama-san to get you the same?"

"Uh—sure, might as well." I'm not ready for this. I would like to take some time, think it over, settle it in my mind. What about my promise to my girl back home? Yeah, home—that distant unreal place on the edge of memory. I look into the young Oriental face before me and try to picture that other face with its Swedish features. I know it is in there somewhere with its blurred edges and unfocused face, but I am unable to conjure it into view just now. Neither can I make any connection between the two worlds. How could that girl from my old life have any relevance to this girl with her hand on my thigh asking me if I like her?

"Sorry. What did you say?" I have never been with a prostitute. What is happening to my resolve?

"Where you go, GI? You no like me?"

"Oh . . . yes, I like you boo coo." What the hell am I

procrastinating for? There is no way I am going to let this opportunity slip through my sweaty paws.

"Okay, you give money now."

"Money, right. Fifteen dollar."

"You take off, okay?" she asks, tapping my boot with her foot on her way to the back door.

I have extracted my fragrant feet from my jungle boots and am almost out of my shirt when mama-san, Kim, and one of the street urchins run into the room.

"MPs. MPs. Come quick."

I grab my helmet and rifle while the girl scoops up my boots and socks. Roy and his girl tumble from their bed, a mass of flailing bare limbs clutching for clothes to add to the bundles in their arms. In their panicked nakedness they look so unlike the composed couple that retired behind the alcove curtain a minute ago that I burst out laughing. Roy's girl, her bare behind parked on the dirt floor, a wad of clothes pressed to her bare chest, stares at me icily, then begins to laugh as well. Roy, who is trying to cover his erection, is not amused. He throws his clothes to the floor, then calmly plucks his pants from the pile. With an effort at dignity, he stuffs his legs and then his manhood into his pants. Kim hustles us out the back door muttering to herself about the dinky dau GIs.

We cross a communal courtyard created by the unbroken mass of surrounding hooches. The girls lead us through a gate that opens with a hidden latch. We crouch inside a small, fenced enclosure with wooden pallets on the floor, and a faucet at the end of a five-foot-high section of galvanized pipe. We are in an open-air shower. At the far end of the shower enclosure the girls are feverishly working a piece of wire between two boards. A release is tripped. A two foot by two foot hatch door falls from what appeared to be a solid wall. Behind the opening is a space seven feet long, four feet high, and just wide enough for the two single mattresses on the floor. All four of us pile into the little room, replacing the door behind us.

When the MP alarm was first given, directly after Roy and I parted with our money, I half suspected that this was a phony raid to cover mama-san's get away. Now with the girls at our sides I feel more secure, my innate mistrust of these people temporarily at rest.

Although the sun is setting, the crowded little room is stifling hot. Our bodies are soon slick with sweat. Roy's girl has climbed into the hideaway wearing only a blouse. She now exchanges the blouse for bra and panties while Kim strips down to the same level to keep her outer clothes from becoming soiled with sweat. Having two lithesome, shapely female bodies wiggle around beside me is more temptation than I can endure. I suggest screwing while we wait. Roy is game but the girls beg off, claiming we would make noises the MPs might hear. I promise not to utter a pleasurable word, but my pleadings are interrupted by the sound of water splashing on the wooden pallet of the shower floor. The girls put a finger to their lips in the universal sign, "shhh."

We listen through the splashing water for the sound of heavy boots on hard-packed earth. All, that is, except Roy. His full attention is focused on the crack where the wire fits through the wall to trip the release on the trap door. I assume he is acting as our lookout until a quiet series of oohs and aahs betrays his real interest. His girl forces him from ogling the form beneath the spray of water to take over the lookout spot herself.

No sooner do I hear the heavy steps I have been listening for when my ears are assaulted by a fiery torrent of Vietnamese from the girl in the shower. A few muffled, apologetic English words are offered in reply, but the blast of Vietnamese spews forth unabated.

The angry ruse continues for some time after it would seem to be necessary or useful. I think she is enjoying this excuse to vent her pent-up anger toward the meddling, intimidating military police. When at last her store of insults are all hurtled into the air, she turns off the stream of splashing water, dries herself, and departs with a slam of the gate.

We wait another ten minutes in the increasing darkness until the all-clear signal is rapped upon our door. Darkness, if nothing else, has brought a halt to the MPs' search. The girl who delivered the all-clear signal tells us through Kim's translation that one of the boys from a rival house informed the MPs of our presence. The dauntless, bantam-weight head of this house has gone to negotiate with her troublesome neighbor. The girls feel confident that she will put this treacherous act to rights.

Roy and his girl crawl from the saunalike atmosphere of our hidden room, their mass replaced by a rush of fresh night air. I lie on my back breathing the cooling breeze, feeling its pleasant tingle on my bare, sweat-covered chest. Kim asks

me something in her tongue; I pull her gently toward me in
reply. There is no reason to further delay indulging in the
pleasures of this delectable girl who has proven to be my ally.
For an instant her face hovers over mine, a distant, question-
ing look in her eyes. I cup her face in my hands, guiding her
lips to mine. We exchange a long kiss that tastes of salty
moisture. Slowly the body that I crave melts to the contours
of mine. My hands glide down the length of her back, lingering on the firm roundness of her buttocks, savoring the
creamy texture of her thighs. The feel of her courses through
my fingertips, filling me with a desperate hunger. She pulls
away to release beautifully formed breasts from their halter.
In the dim light I can still see the question in the large brown
eyes, but there is an intensity now, the distance gone. She
rolls on her back to slide silk panties down shapely legs,
revealing vaginal lips naturally void of hair. Our bodies join
in the steamy room, sliding smoothly over each other, lubri-
cated by the increasing slick of wetness between us. I revel in
the intercourse—no ecstasy is finer.

From the stories I have heard from other men I expect
her to lie perfectly still, urging me to hurry. To my intense
pleasure and amazement, she acts more like a lover than a
whore. She seems to enjoy herself almost as much as I—either
that or she has great skill and enthusiasm for her trade.

Afterward, she sits me on a stool in the starlit shower
enclosure, dousing me with water from a bucket warmed by
the day's sun. She rubs me with soap-lathered hands, thoroughly washing every inch of my body. A loving mother
never washed her child with more attention. I rinse myself
under the spray of cold water from the stand pipe while she
attends to the cleanliness of her own body.

After drying ourselves and dressing, she leads me by the
hand back to the hooch. She serves my bowl of rice and fish
sauce, and attends to my other needs, with quiet dignity, not
at all the silly teenager I first met. She knows she performs
her functions well and the pride she takes from her ability to
give pleasure is clearly displayed.

With my second bowl of rice and my second, surprisingly good Vietnamese beer, I relax. I am confident this girl
and all the people connected with this house will concern
themselves with my safety, at least for this one night. Still, it
feels odd hiding from Americans, being protected by Vietnamese. It is getting hard to tell who is on which side.

The girls retire to eat their dinner in another part of this maze of hooches. Roy relights the last half of one of his joints and gives me a rambling account of his ten months in the field. Like most grunts his stories concentrate on the amusing, on the capers of his friends. He avoids any mention of the Army and talks of firefights only as time references; just before the bridge ambush, three days after the big attack on the NDP. Between anecdotes he keeps saying, "If I have to stay in the field one more month I'm going to go out of my mind. I just can't do it anymore. I mean it. I'm going crazy."

I do not doubt him. After about nine months in the field, when the jungle rot and ringworm have turned patches on your skin black with decay, when almost everyone you met when you first joined your company is gone, when you have experienced enough death that you think you can take even your latest, best friend's death in stride—then you begin to realize that all your bases for stability are gone, and if you receive one more shock when your guard is down you are going to start screaming and you will never be able to stop.

During a moody pause we have carelessly let slip into depression, Roy's girl walks into the room. Roy jerks himself loose from his black mood, lets off a "hey hey hey, she has returned," swoops the girl off the floor, throws her on the bed, and slaps the curtain closed.

I lay back on my bed wondering what my future holds, but the sounds coming from behind Roy's curtain make serious thought impossible. I hear Kim enter from the back of the hooch. I am surprised at how pleased I am to see her. She stands silently at the foot of the bed looking at me. I cannot read the meaning held in her clear, expressionless face. After several seconds she arranges the screens for privacy. Without a word passing between us, she takes off her clothes and lies down beside me.

We caress each other in the shadowy lights of the bedside candle, savoring each curve, dip, and swell of the other's form. Our coupling quickly builds to a peak of excitement where it is carefully sustained, floating in a state of ecstasy, each movement sucking out a gasp of unsurpassable pleasure. She feels so good I'd give my soul to go on like this forever.

Afterward she washes me in a pan of warm water, then retires to attend to her own needs. I struggle up to procure another beer, and again become aware of my traveling companion.

"I needn't ask if you are glad we came." He sits on the edge of the bed, leaning back against the wall, the picture of relaxed contentment.

"No, you needn't ask."

He lights a joint. We pass it back and forth without conversation, taking in big hits of smoke, gazing at the dark walls with unfocused eyes.

Soon sitting up is just too much effort. Lying back on the bed, I make sure the Kalashnikov rifle is securely wedged between the head of the bed and the wall. With this act a vague sense of uneasiness creeps into my mind. I am lying ten feet from the cloth-covered door leading to the street. Anyone could walk in and do what they wished once Roy and I go to sleep. I ponder possible solutions to this problem as my heavy eyelids close. We could take turns standing watch, or tie a trip wire across the door with two cans attached so they would rattle together if disturbed, or tie our rifles to our wrists with a shoestring, or . . .

I wake to feel Kim's hand pressed against my cheek, my mind lifting gently from a pleasant dream. I have not slept this soundly in a long, long time.

"Sun come. You go now. Maybe MP come?"

I prop myself up, looking for Roy. He is sitting on the edge of his bed lacing his boot top over a marijuana-filled pack of Marlboros. I follow his example, making sure my pants are bloused to hang down over my boot tops to cover the bulges. When we have made the asked-for promises to return, a boy is sent outside to signal the driver mama-san has arranged to pick us up.

Roy passes the joint to me for the sixth time. In the distance a gigantic, glowing, red ball floats slowly up from behind the jungle. My body vibrates to the rhythm of the Lambretta's tires. Cars blur as they whiz past in the opposite lane. The air we are rushing past is deliciously cool. Last night's memories cling to me in happiness. I haven't felt this good at the beginning of a day since I was a small boy, and even that is probably a trick of time.

The Lambretta stops at a crossroad to let us off. Within minutes we are climbing into the back of an ARVN truck to join the three Vietnamese enlisted men already seated there. After polite nods all around, we are told that this truck is heading to their base camp on the outskirts of Saigon. Roy inquires about the availability of beer at their camp at this early hour of the morning.

"No beer until 1100, except in teahouse," they tell us, "Teahouse always open, but beer expensive. Teahouse expensive."

"This place is right on the post," I ask, "with girls and everything?"

"Yes, on the post."

"What a great setup. Nothing like some ladies of the evening to keep the troops content. I must suggest a similar arrangement on U.S. posts the next time I see Westmoreland," I quip.

"Westmoreland?" retorts Roy in disbelief. "Westmoreland isn't the commander in Vietnam anymore."

"He's not?" I ask, feeling that I've missed something important. "What happened to him?"

"He was replaced by Creighton Abrams a couple of months ago."

"No shit? Nobody told me." I can't imagine why it matters, but I like to know which group of fools has my life in its feckless hands. .

"Hey, fuck this army stuff."

"Oh, right. Sorry."

We tell the ARVNs that we will buy the beer if they will show us where this teahouse is. They giggle and exchange knowing looks—dinky dau GIs want to get drunk before breakfast—but, okay, they will show us. A few hours in the teahouse would cost them a week's wages. How can they say no?

The thatch-roofed bar we walk into is deserted except for a middle-aged Vietnamese woman lavishing her attention on a teenaged stud perched on a stool behind the bar. They reluctantly divert their mutual attention to the less-interesting task of attending to these customers with the bad taste to call at this ridiculous hour. We order two rounds of beer to fill the time while mama-san shuffles off to wake some of the girls.

Our laughter echoes through the empty bar in answer to Roy's string of dirty jokes. Our beer supply is drained and replaced again before two sleepy girls plop down beside Roy and me with a disturbing lack of enthusiasm. By the time a third and fourth girl have been pried from their beds and prodded to our table, three more rounds have passed, leaving our guides on the edge of serious drunkenness. The tea the girls are drinking, at fifty cents a shot, is doing nothing to improve their gloomy countenances. The two latest additions to our table are further miffed by the demeaning assignment of attending to peasant enlisted men whose lack of funds usually excludes them from this place. The battle of egos between the drunken men and the offended women comes to a head when the most handsome of the Vietnamese men declines to buy his girl a second tea, suggesting a reduction in the twelve-dollar fee for sex instead. The insulted girl flies into a rage. The target of her anger is too proud and drunk to shy away. He stands his ground, countering her rage with demeaning retorts. The anger spreads until all the Vietnamese are yelling at one another with growing vehemence.

"Well, Roy, I'd have to be drunker or hornier to go to bed with any of these women. What do you think?"

"I think I just lost whatever interest I was working up. Let's get out of here."

We ease through the angry fog of words, retrieve our rifles from behind the bar, and sail out the door.

We catch a ride with the first truck heading out the gate. With the back of the truck to ourselves, we each light up a Marlboro joint to quell any suspicions that might be raised by passing one joint back and forth. My head begins to reel from the effects of the potent grass added to the alcohol high that has yet to reach its full impact. To calm my spinning mind I concentrate on the travelogue of picturesque tropical countryside flicking by on its 360-degree screen. The announcer's voice is muffled, drowned in the roar of the wind against my eardrums. At first I struggle to comprehend the theme of the film, but I am soon content to sit back and enjoy the cinematography.

The whirling in my head leaves without notice. My face smiles. Part of me knows this is ridiculous; the rest of me agrees and thinks it's funny as hell. Roy interrupts my travelogue by launching into a weird story that only occasionally makes sense. The more I listen and pretend to understand, the more confused I become. The trouble is, he always starts laughing at the beginning of the funny parts and is in uncontrollable stitches, barely able to gasp incoherent words, before he gets to the punchline. He makes such a hysterical fool of himself and enjoys it so completely that I can't help joining the contagious laughter.

We are clutching the laugh pains in our sides when Roy interrupts a guffaw to make an astute observation. "Man, this is great stuff"—which is closely followed by a brilliant suggestion—"let's have another one."

After careful deliberation I deliver my concurring opinion, "Yep, great stuff"—and agree with his projection for future action—"ah, okay."

Toward the end of a series of smoke-filled breaths Roy catapults from his seat, looking hard at the sun then down at the countryside and back at the sun.

"Where the hell are we?"

"Don't ask me. Somewhere in sunny, fun-filled Vietnam."

"Well, shit! We're going the wrong way."

"You're absolutely right. The world is that way," I say, pointing down the road stretching behind us.

He ignores me, intent on pounding on the canvas-covered cab.

"Dung lai. Dung lai."

The driver brings his truck to a halt. We pile over the tailgate to land in a heap of uncontrollable laughter at the edge of the road.

"Shhh. Shhh. Come on, man, we've got to get our act together. Nobody is going to pick up a couple of lunatics lying on the side of the road," I manage to squeeze out between bursts of laughter, not moving from the comfortable position on my back.

"They'll stop for us. They'll think we're wounded," chuckles Roy, staggering to his feet only to fall into a ditch a few feet away.

I prop myself up on an elbow to try to locate my errant friend. Hollow snickers issue from beneath a pair of legs lapping over the edge of the ditch.

"Man, you're a wreck."

"Wrecked, wasted. Call a medic," he yells.

I struggle to my feet to help extricate him from the ditch. Standing over him, I offer my hand. He latches onto it and gives a mighty tug that sends me into the ditch on top of him, resulting in another bout of uncontrollable laughter reverberating down the ditch.

"Quiet. I hear a jeep."

We scramble out of the ditch, raising our arms to the approaching ride, desperately trying to stifle our giggles.

"Oh, shit. There's an officer in that jeep. Act straight."

"Straight it is, Sarge."

The jeep stops before us.

"Fine day, isn't it, sir?" I greet the captain in the passenger's seat, grinning like an idiot.

"What the hell are you guys doing out here?"

"Lost, sir." I answer, climbing into the back of the jeep despite the lack of invitation. If he looks at my uncontrollably beaming face for another second he will know that I am stoned.

"We thought this was the road to Duc Phen, sir," adds Roy, giving me a look of exasperation.

"Duc Phen? Where the hell is that?" asks the sergeant behind the wheel, eyeing me suspiciously.

"Twenty-five miles northwest of Saigon," I answer immediately, relieved that he does not know where Duc Phen is, because neither do I. "Where are you headed?"

"Bien Hoa."

"Well, I think we had better go back to Long Binh and try again," I say, noticing that Roy is clutching the spare tire, his body jerking in spasms of silent mirth. I think he knows where Duc Phen is, if it's anywhere at all.

I am thankful the noise from the jeep and the roar of passing air discourages further conversation.

A series of rides delivers us to a second teahouse near a metropolis that is probably Saigon. The cavernous main room with its fifteen-foot ceiling and long-screened, glassless windows bathe a checkered tile floor with harsh daylight, driving out any vestige of the intimate security found in the dark close spaces of a comfortable bar. Roy and I cross an expanse of floor large enough for forty couples to swap sweat simultaneously, and slide into one of the paint- and vinyl-covered plywood booths that line the walls. Like a stadium before a game, the room is stripped bare for action, void of decor. What drab, mercenary mind would dare make a cathouse this cold and barren? There are places to sit, booze from the bar, and women who appear and disappear at random. The necessities. Two ARVN NCOs and a young Vietnamese dressed in civilian clothes huddle close to their women, conversing in hushed tones as if to preserve the tomblike atmosphere.

Roy and I work restlessly at our beer while the two pros at our sides sip their tea and chat indifferently between themselves. The girls are pleasant enough to look at, but they are hard and bored and uninviting. This mortuary of debauchery drags our rarefied high into the mind-numbing pit of reality. When the girls start clamoring for another tea we drain our beers and head for the door.

Back in the glaring sun, people and machines bustle across the blurry-edged tunnel of my vision. Anesthetized by the energy flowing around me I stand immobile, waiting for some of the cast-off power to seep into my pores. Instead, the low modulations of a listless voice casually vibrates its message: "I have to be in Long Binh before twelve."

The words crumble the last remains of my party mood. I had pushed all thoughts of the aid station from my mind. Now I must face reality. We make our way north in silence, trying to focus muddled minds on the immediate future. If I return to Di An now, whatever disciplinary action the brass might take should be minimal. On the other hand, why should I sacrifice my sanity and my body to this meaningless display of military bravado? Desertion seems the most reasonable course of action, but try as I might, I cannot think of any viable way for a nearly broke acting corporal to flee the country. The idea of walking away from this war and this army does not trouble my sense of honor. They are both amoral, corrupt, foul institutions deserving no respect or dedication. But the desertion of my company and my country would haunt me. I would be a fugitive in my own home, wondering if one of those stark faces I see when I close my eyes would go on living, if one less leg would be severed, if one mind would be preserved to return home to heal, if I had remained where I was supposed to be.

Across from the gate to Long Binh, the truck stops to make the left-hand turn across the flow of traffic. I say a quick farewell to Roy as I slip over the tailgate, eager to put distance between myself and the MPs in the guardhouse on the opposite side. In less than a minute I am in the back of another truck, heading north. I challenge my drugged mind to make a decision about my destination, but by the time we pass the Di An cutoff that decision remains unmade. I have the truck stop, feeling that I should decide something before going on.

I stumble into the brush to escape the highway traffic, automatically checking the ground before me for booby traps. I could go to Saigon and engage in black marketeering. With care I should be able to avoid being picked up for the months it would take to accumulate the necessary money to hire a

plane to Cambodia or Thailand—if there are any nonmilitary
aircraft in this bloody country, and if there is a place where
we could land without getting arrested. And then what?

I reach the road to Di An and follow it toward the town.
I could just wander around Vietnam for a while. It feels good
to be free. Of course, I would start going hungry tomorrow
when my money ran out. In fact, I have no need to wait until
tomorrow; I am hungry now. One meal yesterday, none
today. I wish I had the five hundred dollars I sent to the bank
in California. With that kind of money I could set myself up
in some kind of lucrative, shady business.

My train of thought is broken by a jeep stopping beside
me. A Vietnamese major addresses me in his language. His
words are meaningless to me. He tries again. I assume he is
offering me a ride. I thank him but decline. Looking offended
he issues some sharper words that include bac bac and VC.
No, I say, no ride, thanks anyway. He assumes that pissed off
superior-officer look. For a moment there is an awkward
silence, then he jams his finger toward the northeast, "Di
An?"

"Yes," I agree, that is the direction of Di An. He nods,
points at me, then at the back of the jeep. I give up and
climb to my appointed spot. I have again made a decision by
default. Facing it, I suppose it is the only decision I can live
with—at least for now. Maybe when I get crazier and know
more I will take a shot at freedom, but not yet.

I trudge through the powdery, roadside dust of the base
camp, dreading reporting to battalion, dreading even more
the prospect of running into the personnel at the aid station
where I am heading to pick up my poncho liner and shaving
kit. The shaving kit I can do without, but the poncho liner is
the one luxury item I own and I would like to hang onto it. If
it is still outside the aid station door I will attempt to retrieve
it. After all, one man in jungle fatigues and helmet looks
much the same as any other from a distance.

From the corner of an adjacent building I can see my
goods propped against the outside wall just the way I left
them. I adjust the strap of the AK over my shoulder, obscur-
ing the stock as much as possible with my back and arm.
Walking as casually as my altered equilibrium will allow, I
head for the left side of the aid station door where I cannot be
seen from within. Scooping my belongings off the ground, I
skirt the side of the building, cross an open patch of ground,

and shield myself from view between two barracks. That was easy, now all I have to do is deal with whoever is waiting for me at battalion.

The battalion is spread over three separate areas. The first cluster of four buildings is designated for the occasional overnight use of the four field companies. Moving east along the southern perimeter of the base camp is a larger area for new personnel and field troops pausing in transit. Further east is a much larger area containing the offices, the mess hall, and the barracks where the rear echelon personnel are stationed.

As I walk into the field company's rear area I realize I don't know where I'm supposed to report. I'll act dumb and play it by ear. I won't have to fake the dumb part. My brain feels like a useless lump of mush. This is the first time in my life that I've produced a hangover before lunch. I glance through all four of the bleak buildings. The place is as deserted as a ghost town. I'm tempted to stay here, out of harm's way, a lone form haunting the shadows of the Army. However, the longer I delay the more trouble I bring down on myself. I cross the road to the east.

My anxiety is somewhat relieved when I see a loose formation of new men gathered outside the orderly room. I'll just blend into the back of the formation and pretend that I belong there. Five steps short of the last row of men, a voice booms from the front of the formation, "Name?"

I look over the rows of new camouflaged helmet covers to meet the eyes of the well-muscled, surprisingly young E-7 in charge.

"Shook," I answer, hoping the name elicits no special response.

"Where the hell have you been?"

Uh-oh. Half the heads in the formation swivel to get a look at this deviant soldier. Very unmilitary of them. I seem to be blending poorly. Let me see, where have I been? That question covers a lot of territory.

"I've been to the aid station." That's a nice safe answer until I can determine how much he knows.

"That was yesterday. Where have you been since then?" He's getting testy. I'd better come up with something believable.

"After the people at the aid station finished not doing what they were supposed to do, I returned to my company's rear area. But nobody was there so I, ah, went to the EM club and got drunk and, ah, woke up a little while ago in one of those bunkers and came looking for somebody to report to. Is this the right place?" I think that hits the correct balance of ignorance and stupidity.

The sergeant grumbles at his clipboard. Even if he does believe my story he can still get me for not reporting for duty last night and this morning.

"Shook, you see that truck over there?"

"Yes, Sergeant."

"It is leaving for the heliport in two minutes. Get on it and return to your company."

"Yes, Sergeant," I answer, trotting away. Thank heavens the easiest thing to do with a malcontent is to let someone else worry about him. It is a good thing I did not get here two minutes later. If I had missed this truck the sergeant would have done something to me for sure. What am I saying? Whatever he would have done would have been better than returning to the field.

Jogging to the truck makes me aware of the two packs of marijuana in my boots. Maybe things worked out for the best after all.

Back at Delta's NDP I am disappointed to learn my platoon is on patrol. I was looking forward to a reunion, even though I have only been away for thirty hours. Well, I guess it doesn't matter. The guys and I will be seeing plenty of each other over the next several months.

I find the XO talking to a sergeant in front of the HQ bunker. I explain what did and did not happen with my eye examination. He listens with apparent interest, then tells me he will get back to me.

I am engrossed in the effort of reading a moldy western by the fading light of day when the XO stops by to tell me I will be accompanying him to the rear in the morning. He offers no further information and I resist asking, not wanting in any way to disrupt a good thing.

The next day the first available flight does not reach Di An until the early afternoon. I have not learned any more from the XO except that he is still working on a reassignment for me and he wants me to stay in the rear until my reassignment orders come through. Perhaps there is hope.

I consider it unwise to face the E-7 at battalion alone after ruffling him yesterday. I decide it will be best to announce my return at evening formation where he will not have as much time to concentrate on my case. I head for the EM club to celebrate what I hope will be my permanent retirement from the field.

Handing the bartender a paper dime in exchange for a cool beer, I look over the scattering of drinkers in the nearly empty bar. Against the far wall, with his back to me, I spot a vaguely familiar head of thinning hair bent over a pad of paper. As I get closer he looks more and more like Allen Gillis without glasses. I walk over and say hi. He looks up at me from far away until recognition lights up his face with a big smile.

"Shook, you sorry son of a bitch. How are you? Still in one piece, I see. Sit down."

"You look different without your glasses. Did you find a miracle cure for myopia out there in the dark reaches of the jungle?"

"Hell, no. I found a cure for being in the field when the shit is getting heavy."

"Are you trying to tell me that you're in here shirking your duty to God, country, and Graves Registration?"

"That about covers it. Things are getting hairy out there. We got a lot of guys hurt. I had to get out of there for a while so I put the boot to my glasses."

We were on the outer edge of a different world when we last met. I have not seen Allen since we spent our first two weeks in-country together. He is an unlikely combat soldier with eyes that cannot see anything beyond twenty feet without glasses. Back in the world he was an art teacher with a well-developed sensitivity toward all living things. He was drafted from a cozy job at a college on the edge of the Rocky Mountains. He loved it there with the coeds and the cabins in the forest. Some people do not make good killers. Allen is one of those people.

He is going to be in the rear for a few days while his new glasses are being made, so we both have something to celebrate. The beer comes around and goes down, lubricating the kind of intense conversation neither one of us has had for weeks. Eighteen empty cans litter the table before we slosh to the battalion in time to make the evening formation.

Sergeant Schultz, the E-7 in charge of the new men and the transient field troops, recognizes me immediately.

"Shook, I told you to rejoin your company. What the hell are you doing back here?"

"Just following orders, Sergeant. I went back to the field. My XO told me to come back her and stay here until I am reassigned."

"That doesn't cut shit with me. I haven't got any orders on you."

"The lieutenant flew in with me this afternoon. He is still around here somewhere, you can check with him."

"We'll see about that. In the meantime report to the communications bunker. There is a prisoner there they want a field troop to guard."

I have to ask directions twice before locating the building referred to as the communications bunker. The actual bunker turns out to be located deep beneath the building, a concrete haven restricted for the use of the important people and their radiotelephones in the event of a serious attack.

"Somebody here send for a guard?"

"Over here," answers a lieutenant turning his attention from the panel of electronics before him. He looks me over, his eyes settling on my rifle. "What the hell are you doing with an AK?"

"I didn't think it would be appropriate to bring my M-60, sir."

"I hope you have the ammunition to go with it."

"Certainly . . . sir."

"Good. That little jerk over there is your prisoner. If he tries to escape, shoot him. I'm tired of sending people to look for him."

The man in custody is not a Vietnamese as I had assumed; instead, I am faced with a very gloomy GI. Pulling up a chair across from the nineteen-year-old criminal, I try to engage him in conversation to keep the excess of alcohol and my lack of food from putting me to sleep. He is not communicative but eventually I learn he has been awol for most of his first four months in-country. He is facing three Article 15s, a court-martial, and an extended tour of one year and eight months in Vietnam—not counting whatever time he draws in LBJ. It is a sobering revelation considering my own plans.

At 0200 I escort the prisoner to the outhouse at his request. Standing outside the latrine door, smelling the sweet fragrance of marijuana drifting through the fly screen, I realize what a mistake they made picking me for this duty. There is no way I am going to shoot this guy. I can easily outrun him, but if he took off I am not sure I would give chase. There he is standing in the doorway offering me a toke—this guy is never going to make it. I take him back inside where he promptly asks the lieutenant if he can lie down. The lieutenant obligingly handcuffs him to a metal cot.

I sit in a chair at the foot of the bed waiting for the great escape to arrive. Macabre newsreels flash through closed eyes, depriving the mind of its rest. Battle scenes filled with fear and frustration alternate with scenes of rioters screaming at their rulers. The rulers stand staunchly erect under an impressive weight of rare jewels, elevated before the mob in impregnable glass cases, sparkling eyes focused upon some distant point, smiling lips pulled back to reveal sharpened, blood-drenched fangs.

I awake at dawn thankful to find my prisoner asleep. A quiet half hour passes before my relief arrives. I head for the mess hall to placate a disgruntled stomach. The food at the battalion mess isn't actually good, but the milk isn't curdled, the butter isn't rancid, and the bread hasn't begun to mold. The eggs even come out of shells. The meal is a hungry grunt's delight.

Looking forward to a new life in the security and comfort of a large base camp, I join the morning formation ready to happily perform whatever rotten detail Sergeant Schultz has dredged up. He doesn't keep me in suspense. I am the first item on his morning's agenda.

"Shook, get on that truck. You're going back to the field."

"What?" I wasn't prepared for this.

"You hard of hearing this morning, Private?"

"But Sergeant, I was told to stay here."

"Now I'm telling you, until I get orders to the contrary, you're going back to the field."

"But Sergeant . . ."

"Get on that truck."

His tone makes it clear that further argument would be counterproductive. There must be something I can do. This can't be happening again. I feel like a piece of misaddressed mail.

The big Chinook eases down into the jungle clearing with nothing on board except me and the crew. Something is going on. The entire company is milling around piles of gear. I make my way through the confusion until I find Sandy.

"What's going on?"

"The company is moving to a new NDP. What are you doing back here?"

"That's what I would like to know. Where's Norris?"

"He was over by the ammo bunker a minute ago."

"Thanks."

Norris is in the bunker giving instructions concerning which crates will accompany the platoon to the new NDP. When he is finished he turns to face me.

"Shook, what the hell are you doing here?"

Jesus. The question of the week. "Sergeant Schultz ordered me back to the field. He said he didn't have any orders for me to stay in the rear."

"Orders? Well, shit. Stay put, I'll be right back."

I stand around for ten minutes feeling completely out of place waiting for my future to be decided while my buddies are busy packing their gear. Captain Wilkins approaches at a fast gait, his face radiating irritation. He is the last man on earth I want to aggravate. I go to meet him.

"I thought I left orders for you to stay in the rear until you were reassigned."

The realization that this is exactly the problem flashes through my mind. Out here orders are verbal and no one questions them. In the rear orders are delivered on pieces of paper. "Yes sir, you did. I informed the sergeant in charge that the XO told me to stay in the rear until I was reassigned, but he said he didn't have any such orders and demanded I return to the field. I am sorry to cause you a problem, sir, but the sergeant was most adamant."

Wilkins focuses his attention on the ground. I can almost see my life being chased around inside his skull. I stand very still. He looks up and smiles. There is hope in that smile.

"You tell that sergeant that I am a captain and he is a sergeant and I have ordered you to stay in the rear until you are reassigned. Now I know you won't disobey an order from your captain."

"No, sir, I certainly won't."

"You stay here tonight and fly into Di An with my XO in the morning. I don't want to see you out here again."

"You won't, sir—and thank you."

He grins and walks away. The relief I feel is mixed with sorrow. There goes a man who may have saved my life, and I will probably never see him again. God knows I am grateful, but he has no legitimate reason I know of to send me to the rear. I respect the captain for his determination to maintain his honor and integrity, while many of those around him seek only personal glory, but I fear his action on my behalf is the aftermath of the destruction of his career. Major Barlow does not need to bring Wilkins's disobedience in the bean field up for disciplinary action to permanently damage the captain's career. Bad fitness reports will do the job without exposing the criminally reckless nature of the major's orders.

I find Boston and Franklin in time to help carry their gear to the waiting chopper. We yell good-byes over the roar of the Chinook's twin jet engines. As they jog up the ramp to the cargo bay I cannot help wondering if this is the last time I will see them. If I knew they were going to be all right it would not bother me to be left behind. But their chances of finishing their tours unscathed are poor, and if I stay with them our chances would still be poor. I will have to settle for feeling sorry for them and for being grateful that unexplainable fortune is allowing me to escape. Besides, if Boston thought I purposely screwed up my chance to get out of the field he would never forgive me.

Four hours later the first load of men from the replacement company descends upon our jungle clearing. Delta's remaining platoon takes their place on board the big Chinook. Twin props blast the ground with gale-force winds as the cumbersome machine makes its way into the sky. I turn to watch the chopper fade into the distance, feeling an undefined significance in its parting; an altering in the course of lives.

The next day I fly in from our old NDP to stand once more in Sergeant Schultz's noon formation.

"Private Shook, I see you have returned to us again," says the sergeant. "Well, you're in luck. There is a supply truck leaving for Delta's new NDP this very afternoon. Get on it."

"Sorry, Sergeant, not this time," I answer in a calm voice, hoping to stir his curiosity rather than his wrath.

"Listen, Private, I don't want to hear no shit from you. You get your butt on that truck right fuckin' now."

"Can't do it, Sergeant. My captain told me to tell you that he is a captain and you are a sergeant, and he ordered me to stay in the rear until I was reassigned. I must obey my commanding officer regardless of what you say."

Schultz is speechless. He knows he should not bring himself into direct conflict with an officer, yet how can he endure this defiance of his authority in front of more than forty witnesses? He stands behind his podium, glaring in impotent fury. After a couple of minutes of awkward silence he regains control of himself and carries on with the other business at hand.

When he dismisses the formation he curtly orders me to come with him. I follow him around the side of the orderly room to the edge of a shallow hole.

"I want this hole six feet deep, six feet wide, and twenty feet long. Start digging."

Taking the shovel from his outstretched hand, I start to scoop dirt from what I presume is going to be a bunker similar to those adjacent to each of the barracks. Schultz stands above me with his arms folded across his chest, more than ready for me to show some sign of insolence. When I offer none, he returns to his office in the orderly room.

I dig into the soft ground at a measured pace I can easily maintain until dinnertime. Periodically I feel Schultz's eyes peering at me from the dim quiet of the orderly room. After I have exposed my back to the tanning effects of sun and soil for five hours, my overlord comes to inspect my work. He contemplates the hole, then me, then the hole again, not seeming to gain satisfaction from either view.

"Go to chow" is his only comment.

I spend the night on guard with two new guys. This is their first time on perimeter guard and their nervousness shows. While I demonstrate how to set out the claymores, they constantly glance up to scan the half-mile strip of barren land separating the base from the surrounding jungle, as if they expect a hoard of enemy soldiers to come slithering toward us at any moment. I do my best to assure them of the security of our position. I explain about the artillery, the mortars, and the armored vehicles behind us. I point out the fifty-foot towers with their radar and starlight scopes placed along the perimeter line between every seventh bunker. I tell them about the rows of wire before us, the mines, the trip flares, the fifty-gallon drums of foo gas. They are reasonably impressed, but not overly assured.

Sitting under the sloped tin roof of our sleeping shelter

we watch a sudden rainstorm pelt water into growing puddles and overflow into the bunker before us. The roof, thundering under the heavy drops, is just high enough in front to accommodate a man sitting upright. A slightly raised wooden floor protects us from the flood spreading across the ground. Sandbag walls, four rows high, offer some protection from the sides and rear, but in the event of an attack we must plunge into the water rapidly filling our bunker.

We arrange the watches into segments of one hour and twenty minutes each, so that each man is responsible for two relatively short turns at guard. I draw the first watch. For an hour the rain prevents me from seeing or hearing anything at a distance of more than twenty feet. Then it suddenly stops. A quiet lull ensues, as if all creation is straining to hear the vanished sound. A frog belches into the void. It sounds as good as ever so it lets loose a second croak, which is answered by a neighbor. Rubbing together its forewings a cricket chirps the all-clear signal to its kind, and they rejoice, filling the air with a brash symphony. I wake the next man, and roll into my poncho liner.

Perhaps I should not have assured my companions that they are as safe in Di An as they will ever be in Vietnam, or perhaps I should have mentioned that one can be shot for sleeping on guard in a combat zone. In the dawn's gray light I marvel at the peacefully sleeping forms beside me. Going to sleep on guard is not all right, not even to a fuck off like me. But perhaps I am overreacting. This is not the field. Nonetheless, I point out that while the protection in front of us will slow down an assault, it is no guarantee against a few men slipping through the wire and cutting our throats. Although they are respectfully quiet during my discourse, I do not believe their stateside mentalities have yet accepted that here the continuation of their lives cannot be taken for granted.

At the morning formation Sergeant Schultz radiates a vengeful glee as he informs me that I am henceforth permanently assigned to the shit-burning detail. Of all the rear echelon tasks the Army has yet devised, shit burning, as I learned in my early days at Long Binh, is at the top of their long list of rotten things to do. The latrines of Di An are essentially your basic, time-honored, two- to four-hole outhouses. The one major deviation from the standard is the lack of a hole beneath the structure. In the hole's stead squats a fifty-gallon oil drum cut down to a height of twenty inches. My duty lies with these drums.

Every morning after breakfast I lift the screened hatch in the back of an outhouse, drag the brim-full containers from their resting place, ease them down the six-inch lip of the concrete foundation with a splash of the nauseous contents, drag the weighty, oscillating wastes twenty feet, pour a liberal dose of diesel over the mess, add a dash of gasoline, and stand back to flip matches into the barrels. I then retreat as far as possible as odiferous black columns of smoke billow to pollute the air.

Once a week the barrels require emptying. The most difficult part of this task is finding a previously unused patch of earth within a reasonable distance of the outhouse. Each time I plunge my shovel into the ground, slimy evidence of previous burials appear. When I finally locate a plot of unfertilized earth, I dig a pit and dump the barrels, careful to prevent any upward thrusts of globular matter from touching my person. Flooding the area with diesel, I purify the whole disgusting mess in an inferno befitting a godly man's righteous wrath.

My first experience with this task at the placement center in Long Binh nearly brought up my lunch, but subsequent dealings with the lifeless forms from which this matter comes has steeled my sense of revulsion. If Sergeant Schultz is counting on this unpleasant chore to make me clamor for a return to the field he is woefully out of touch with reality. I cannot even manage to work up a healthy dislike for the man. As long as he concentrates his energies on an attempt to make my life miserable instead of procuring orders for my return to the field, I am content.

Besides, there is a good side to the fecal detail. No person of authority ventures anywhere near my work. They are content to supervise from afar. The pillars of smoke rising from the east, south, and west peripheries of the compound are ample proof of my diligence. Except for the once a week burial detail, my morning work is done by ten, leaving me ample time to wash up and disappear.

I head for the dilapidated movie house across the street from the main EM club. I climb into the projectionist's platform where I cannot be seen from below. Secure in my hideaway, I smoke a little grass and write despondent letters or watch birds scratch the dirt floor for scraps of food left by the men who come to watch the weekly movie. Shafts of sunlight stream through the multitude of cracks in the weathered wooden walls, illuminating vertical slabs of dust-filled air, splashing bright streaks across the wooden benches and up the torn bed sheet movie screen hanging from the far wall.

Here in the quiet of this rickety shell of a building there is peace and solitude and space to wonder. Somehow this safe, meaningless existence is more depressing than being in the field—not that I would trade depression for horror and misery and fear.

At 1100 the EM club opens. I wander over to tilt a beer or two, and by lunchtime I am blessing the luck that brought me here.

Life in the rear soon settles into a stagnant routine. I return from breakfast to join the line of men policing the four-acre compound. The sun emerges over the horizon to the crunch of paper and the clink of empty cans dropping into plastic sandbag receptacles. After the morning formation the new guys are sent to brigade school while I send odiferous smoke signals to heaven. After lunch and noon formation I work on the orderly room bunker until dinner. Every night I guard the perimeter and sleep five hours on the shelter floor. Twenty-six cents an hour, twenty-four hours a day, seven days a week.

After two weeks it is clear that my routine differs from that of the other men. The difference is in little things, like the hour or two they get off every afternoon, or a free evening every second or third night, or no duty on Sunday morning. But I cannot complain. I know a hundred men who would gladly take my place.

My complacency seems to mystify Sergeant Schultz. Is it curiosity that brings him daily to the excavation site to work at my side, or is it for the exercise, as he claims? For half an hour he sweats in the sun and engages me in conversations that can almost be termed congenial. He has also begun sending me assistants. One day I got an ancient, shriveled up, betel nut-stained, four-foot four-inch mama-san. Her job was to hold sandbags while I filled them with dirt, but she did far more than prop up sandbags. For five hours she lectured me on many and varied subjects in rapid, exuberant Vietnamese. Unfortunately, I could not understand more than twenty words of the entire monologue. I tried to talk her out of some of the betel nuts that I figured were the main contributing factor to her good humor, but she just laughed and told me I was a dinky dau GI.

Another day a matched pair of invalids was assigned to help me with the weekly shit memorial and cremation service. My helpers were from Bravo Company; they both had broken forearms and both injuries occurred on the same night. Neither wanted to talk about it. I suspected their broken arms had a lot in common with Allen's shattered glasses. The mere fact that they were assigned to help me indicated that somebody believed their injuries were not kosher. Then again, maybe the joke was on me; a man with one arm is not too swift with a shovel.

Although there is no indication that Sergeant Schultz intends to slacken my schedule, he now provides drinking water in the afternoon, and even pokes his head out of his office once in a while to tell me to take a break. His anger has cooled, but there is something else, something that motivates him to keep pushing me.

I soon learn that virtually all new men sleep on guard. The few times a buck sergeant was sent to inspect the perimeter he found only one or two men awake, and once, every man in our seven-bunker area was asleep. The sergeant reported the situation to his superiors, but to my surprise and disgust the local hierarchy decreed this was not an issue of importance. Well, if they didn't give a damn about the conduct of the men on guard I figure I might as well go along with the wisdom from above.

This is my eighteenth consecutive night on guard. I'm so bored I could scream. One of the new guys is bitching about being put on guard for the third night in a row. I can't stand it. I'm going for a beer.

The sergeant of the guard has already been by to make sure our positions are manned. If he sticks to his previous schedule he won't be back until after midnight, if at all. I tell the guys that I must return to the company area for an hour or two. Promising to bring them some goodies upon my return, I skirt the company area and head for the main EM club.

To my delight I find a familiar face at the crowded bar. One of the medics from Delta Company is in the rear for the night en route to Hawaii to meet his wife for R and R. Together we fantasize endless sexual encounters and tall drinks with ice and bikini-clad bodies on white sand beaches and showers and rolling in clean sheets and snorkeling among tropical fish and walking hand in hand with our ladies until I beg him to stop before he drives me crazy with impossible dreams.

To change the subject I ask him for news of the company, half afraid of what I might hear. Thankfully, there has only been one casualty since I left. A guy I knew only by sight was shot through the neck by ARVNs. He subsequently died because the medivac was forty-five minutes late reaching the patrol.

Th.e is a moment of silence as the medic stares at his hands, remembering again, as he will always remember, the death he tried so hard to prevent.

"How's the captain doing?" I ask, trying to change the topic to a lighter subject.

"He's gone."

"Gone? Where?"

"I don't know. We came in from ambush one morning and were greeted by a first lieutenant who told us he was our new CO."

"What happened to Wilkins?"

"No one's saying. If his tour was up, we would know. I mean, there's no reason to keep that secret. Some of the guys think Barlow got him."

"That bastard."

"Yeah, there are a lot of folks that would like to put an end to that maniac's life. Unfortunately, I think we missed our chance. He only has about a month left on his six-month tour. That chicken shit hasn't come near us since one of the boys put a hole in his chopper."

"Don't you have any good news?"

"Nope. The battalion has pulled back to take up a position four miles north of here. VC activity is picking up in the area. We haven't gotten much of it yet, but Alpha and Bravo have been getting mortared pretty heavily."

"Sounds like something is building up."

"That's the word, all right. Oh yeah, the XO is getting so short he won't go out to the field anymore, either. Two more weeks and he will be on the freedom bird to the world."

"Well, now that you've gotten me depressed and half drunk, I think I'll go back to the perimeter and see if anyone has missed me."

Wishing him a satisfying reunion with his wife, I head for the battalion EM club where for a small tip the bartender will violate regulations and give me unopened beer I can carry back to the guys on guard.

At the sleeping shelter I unload six beers and a can of shoestring potatoes from my pockets. The guys are delighted. We sit in the dark drinking and swapping stateside stories. A 105 artillery shell streaks overhead, seemingly so close you feel like you can almost jump up and touch it. After a short pause a dozen more shells scream overhead on their way to support some poor bastards lying on their bellies somewhere out there in the bush.

My first watch ends shortly after the last beer is drained. I roll into the back of the shelter, confident that I shall not be disturbed until morning.

Three days later, while washing real and imaginary traces of fecal material from my body, Sergeant Schultz unexpectedly walks into the outdoor shower. He demands to know what I am doing here, as if this mixture of soap and cool water has no right to be mingling on my person. I reply that if he had been burning shit all morning he would be taking this shower instead of me. I do not think it would have made any difference what I said. From now on I will have no more free time in the morning. My movie house sanctuary days are gone.

With a broom obtained from the supply room I begin sweeping the first of three barracks, as ordered. Pushing chunks of dried mud and cigarette butts across the floor, I am abruptly confronted with an abnormally clean area surrounding a lone bunk. I pause, wondering what kind of cleanliness nut belongs to this space when I suddenly realize I am staring at my own bed. This is not a case of cleanliness—it is the result of total disuse.

"Twenty-one fucking days and I haven't slept on it yet."

The four guys at the other end of the barracks look up from their card game to observe some nut with a broom talking to his bunk. I go back to my sweeping, feeling abused, bitter, and generally sorry for myself. Suspecting that this is exactly the reaction Schultz has been patiently striving for only makes me more bitter. I've got to get out of this place. With Captain Wilkins gone, I am going to be in a bind unless I get transferred before the XO ships out. Without the support of at least one of those two men my request is sure to be scuttled.

Shouldering open the back door, I give my collection of mud balls a hearty sweep into the sidewall of a tent. Now where the hell did that come from? It wasn't here yesterday. I walk around the side of the tent and stop short. At least thirty Vietnamese soldiers are busily erecting a second ten-man tent behind the first. I go back to the barracks to find out what the card players know about this miniature invasion.

"What are all those gooks doing in our backyard?"

One of the players looks at me with a knowing smile. "Those are our friendly allies. Last week they were shooting at us. This week they are learning how to point their rifles in the other direction."

"Chieu hois?"

"That's it. Each company is going to be blessed with eight of the little traitors."

"Boy, they are going to be relieved to hear that."

"Relieved? I wouldn't trust one of those—"

"They heard they were getting sixteen of them," I interrupt. "They will be pleased that things are only half as bad as they thought they were going to be."

After lunch I head for the battalion HQ area to check on my overdue reassignment orders. I begin asking questions. The answers are all the same. No one has ever heard of me or of my request. The clerks resent my intrusion into their world. Persistence eventually rewards me with a series of referrals that lead back to the desk of the clerk where I began. In exasperation the first clerk refers me to a Specialist 5th class who refers me to the CO who is out. The specialist informs me that his captain was due back forty-five minutes ago and is sure to show soon. Would I care to wait? Nice guy, this specialist. Reminds me of some executive's secretary. Smooth. Deceptive. His boss is probably in Bangkok. Well, this is the end of the line. I'll wait.

Half an hour passes. Schultz's noon formation has come and gone. The longer I sit here the more grief will greet me upon my return. I am going to find this truant captain.

I return to the mess hall. The dining area is empty, so I head for the next most logical place—the local officer's club. I stand outside the barracks that has been converted into a bar, staring at the officers only sign, wondering what kind of trouble I'm going to get into by entering this sanctuary. What the hell—many field officers don't wear any insignia. I'll just walk in and act like I belong. Inside, the place looks for all the world like a standard hick bar in Anyplace, U.S.A. Considering it is 1400, the club is surprisingly full. Men sit in captain's chairs huddled around cocktail tables or lean against the well-stocked bar. I ask one of the men watching the play on the pool table if he has seen the captain in charge of personnel. He points out the man I seek among a group of three in conversation along the bar. With some trepidation I introduce myself and give a brief account of my situation. He listens attentively while carefully steering me out of hearing of the major with whom he was drinking. Yes, he seems to recall such a request coming across his desk. He orders another drink. After some polite chitchat he admits shelving the request in favor of more important matters. I can appreciate that drinking takes precedence over paperwork, but suggest that after three weeks my request is properly aged and that perhaps we might now get together and hash something out. To my surprise, he is agreeable and instructs me to wait for him outside his office.

I wait. An hour passes before he drags himself away from the bar. At first he tries to convince me that my best move is to rejoin my company, as that is the only course of action that doesn't require any paperwork. I tell him my CO ordered me not to show up out there again. The captain mumbles and scratches and paints a bleak picture of the jobs that might be available to me. Finally, he concedes. If I can come back tomorrow he will have something definite for me.

ECHO COMPANY

Through high-powered binoculars I scan the vast barren strip between the base camp wire and the distant tree line for the twentieth time today. Only the cast of the shadows has changed. A scattering of half-dead bushes struggle for survival in a sea of parallel bulldozer ruts that radiate from the perimeter wire like waves upon an earthen sea.

The entire base has been put on alert, and for what? The most threatening force facing us is the legions of rats that thrive and multiply in the garbage dump to my far right. No VC is foolish enough to appear on this open swath of ground by day. The only reason I am going through this routine again is that by the time I return the field glasses to their place we will be five minutes closer to the end of another day.

My partner sits slumped in the observation chair, engrossed in an old copy of *Saga Magazine*. As I look at the downward-tilted head of carefully combed, oily black hair, I marvel again at his patience. Don and I have been in this eight-foot-square box on stilts since yesterday morning, yet he shows no signs of restlessness, no indication that this confinement is any less natural than breathing. I, on the other hand, am going crazy. To someone who had difficulty sitting in one spot for a single hour, it is staggering to consider that I have endured sitting and standing in this elevated box for thirty-six hours, with the frightening certainty that twelve more hours of the same looms before me.

With a sigh I resume my seat on the four-inch-thick floor

M-107

planks, knowing I will not regain interest in the paperback I have been reading, but determined to give it another try.

Ever since the captain in charge of personnel at battallion HQ reassigned me to Echo Company, I have spent most of my time in this tower guarding the perimeter. Overall, I am happy with the change. We are frequently given four hours off after an eighteen-hour shift and receive every third night off as well—except when there is an alert. This one started late last night with a mortar attack. The base receives a few incoming mortar rounds every week, but last night there were more than usual—at least this is what I was told. I have become so accustomed to the thundering roar of our own artillery that I slept through the mortar barrage, waking finally to the all-clear siren at 0200, just before my turn at watch. We were to be relieved this morning, but because some fool decided to call an alert we are stuck here until tomorrow.

Turning the page, I realize I have not comprehended a single word in the last several paragraphs. I drop the book, throw back the hatch door in the tower floor, and descend the fifty-foot ladder as fast as my legs will move. Jumping the last six feet to the ground, I sprint around the four telephone-post legs of the tower. Around and around I go, leaning hard to the inside to counter the centrifugal force. The edge of my boots dig into the ground, pushing up a bank around my circular course, improving the footing, enabling me to push harder, faster. Blood pulses through stagnant tissue, rejuvenating listless cells, washing away the dragging sense of uselessness permeating an otherwise healthy structure. I am still alive, you bastards—despite your best efforts to bore me to death—I am still alive. I make a running leap at the stairs, hands clutching the two-by-four steps, arms pulling, legs pumping, grab, release, grab, the steps blur by. At the top too soon, back down, the toes of boots touching steps, sliding to the next, faster, faster, hit the ground, and run free.

In time a welcome fatigue develops and I slow to a jog that disintegrates into a walk. Breathing heavily to repay the debt of oxygen owed to my muscle tissue, I contemplate the reaction of a chance observer to my spontaneous, maniacal exercise program. Checking the surrounding area en route a final circuit of the track, I am heartened that no one is rushing a straight-jacket to my location. Then I remember Don. He must think he has a Section 8 case for a partner. I look up to see him casually leaning against the four-foot tower house wall. After six months in the field with Bravo Company and three months of tower guard duty, he is as placid as if every idle hour of every idle day were that first relaxing hour after he comes home from work to settle into his easy chair with a cold brew at his side to relax and read a bit while the smells of cooking drift in from the kitchen.

"Are you finished now?" he hollers down.

I nod.

"You don't have any other peculiarities that I should know about, do you?"

I do not know what to say, so I just grin. When I catch my breath, I climb the ladder on shaky legs.

"How about giving me a little warning the next time you decide to go berserk? I thought the world was coming to an end for a minute there."

I apologize for startling him. He studies my face a minute, trying to gain insight from the cover.

"Do you partake of the local weed?"

"I have been known to partake occasionally."

"I recommend that you get into it with great regularity. It will save a lot of wear on my nerves and it might prevent you from breaking your fool neck. There is only so much sitting a person can stand. Without a bit of weed to ease the boredom, there is no way I could keep a sane mind to enjoy this cushy duty."

"So that's the secret to your calm outlook on life. Do all the guys on the towers smoke?"

"Only about half of them. We try to keep the two groups separated."

"You worried about getting turned in?"

"That's only part of it. The major reason is that we can't stand to work with them. After about twelve hours of duty they start getting on each other's nerves. Then they get to arguing like a couple primed for divorce. It makes me nervous to have armed men angry at me. Besides, none of the straight guys have been out in the field. They get their blood pressure up over nothing and ignore some of the important things. It's peaceful here. I don't need a bunch of scared, crazy kids screwing things up for me. I'm getting too short for that kind of shit.

"Look, I figure I can trust you, so I'm going to show you

where our stash is located. Just be careful who you open it in front of, and replace what you use when you get the chance."

He slips a fingernail under the head of one of the nails in the back wall and pulls it halfway out. Using the nail as a handle, he pivots a two-by-six into the room. Reaching into a space hollowed out of the sandbags that surround the outer wall, he extracts an M-16 ammo can. Inside the can is a pipe, some kitchen matches, two packs of cigarette papers, and about six ounces of marijuana. He rolls two joints and replaces the can. I count the number of boards from the top of the wall to the hole before swinging the two-by-six back in place. They have done a good job. It is an expertly crafted stash hole.

When you are confined to an eight-by-eight-foot space for long periods of time, something akin to a prisoner's mania for hiding places emerges. The radio that softly beats the latest rock and roll into our elevated room is a good example. The receiver is buried in the sandbags against the front wall. A concealed wire runs from our six-foot field radio antenna to the AM radio. Another wire goes through the wallboards into a speaker mounted inside a flashlight where the bulb and reflector are normally located. The radio is turned on by pushing a nail into a hole under the front counter.

Another, less secretive cache is located in the platform that elevates the observation chair to a height adequate to allow the occupant to see over the front wall. The top of the platform lifts off, providing a handy receptacle for books, magazines, writing materials, playing cards, and the checker game in case these need to be swept quickly from view.

The need for all this subterfuge is due to the harsh penalty extracted from those found in possession of any of the above items while on tower duty. The penalty for even the smallest violation is a court-martial. We have been repeatedly assured by our bevy of questionably superior officers that they will prosecute any violation of their rules to the fullest possible extent.

We of Tower 15 consider it essential to the maintenance of our sanity as well as our duty as common soldiers to shun these rules at every opportunity. This obligation must be upheld even if it means the occasional neglect of our objectives as lookouts. After all, we have never been seriously harassed by a VC ground attack, but we are constantly harassed by officers.

Browning .50 Cal. HMG

I pass the remains of a finger-burning joint back to Don, who places it on his wetted tongue and swallows.

"Never leave a roach lying around. This isn't the field. There is all manner of low life skatin' around in the rear that would just love to turn us in."

"Right. You roll 'em and I'll eat 'em."

I am beginning to enjoy the benefits of my mentor's wisdom. I drift into a world of calm that abounds with fascinating objects: the soft summer grain of the gray, weathered planks has been worn by rain and wind, receding below the harder, thinner grains of winter growth; the frayed, colored threads in the plastic webbing of the folding aluminum chair sparkle in sunlight; the slow-motion drift of puffy cumulus clouds. I settle in the observation chair that is our lone piece of furniture, watching the changing forms within the clouds: a winged horse distorts and fades, to emerge as an airplane that evolves into a dragon, and then slips into the image of a whale. For an hour I am entranced by the interplay of cloud forms and imagination until nature's back lighting dwindles and fades, turning the world into hazy shades of gray.

A third man joins us for the night shift. We arrange the watches into three-hour stints that will allow two of us six hours of uninterrupted sleep. One man will sleep behind the 50-caliber machine gun on a platform halfway down the tower, a second man will sleep on the planks of the tower house floor, while the third man operates the radar and starlight scope.

Leaning against the sandbags that protect the M-50 position, I fire up the last half of a joint in the hopes that it will make dreamland more interesting or my board bed softer. Behind me, the base is dark, the clubs and movie screens silent, in deference to the attack that will never come.

Morning arrives without a whisper of threat to the post. The yellow alert is canceled. We are relieved from our perch to engage in the Army's eternal hobby of burrowing into the ground. After forty-eight hours of enforced idleness, even the dirty, sweaty job of building bunkers is a welcome change.

The work continues into the afternoon when the sergeant of the guard comes to read off the names of the men assigned to the towers for the night. To my amazement, my name is not called. Foolishly I recheck the list with the sergeant; surely the omission of my name is an error. But there is no error. For the first time in twenty-seven days I am given an entire night off to wallow in the luxury of my previously unused bunk.

The next morning Don and I are back in the tower. Don wastes no time delving into his hidden stash of grass. I decline the offered joint, feeling it is somewhat decadent to be stoned so early in the day.

A dozen checker games, two letters, the last third of a novel, and ten stints with the binoculars pass the day. In the darkness I help Don convert his fourth joint into smoke, ash, and an altered sense of reality. Properly primed, I entertain myself with the big starlight scope secured to the top of a surveyor's tripod. Its power to gather the available light amazes me. When the moon is up the view through the scope is equal to that of binoculars in daylight. By the light of the stars alone I can detect an erect man at a distance of half a mile. The image that reaches the eye is an eerie green that varies in shade with the amount of reflected light.

Next I turn my attention to the mysteries of radar. Inside a blunt-nosed cylinder with a diameter of approximately eighteen inches and a length of twenty-four inches, huddles a clairvoyant collection of electronics that stimulate the needles in the panel dials to sway and jump in response to invisible elements in the air that are only of interest to, and perhaps the imagination of, the classified machine itself. As if this were not enough to capture the attention of the operator, there is, in addition, a set of headphones that transmit a jumble of static that ebbs and flows with the breeze. Using the two instruments in tandem produces an other-world atmosphere of ghostly green forms in a rutted, surrealistic landscape accompanied by the sound of spatial static and galactic winds. The radar is more often used for its unearthly utterances than it is for its questionable ability to detect enemy movement.

The four majors in charge of this section of the perimeter have the utmost faith in our technological toys. Although they have little understanding of the workings of these machines and less comprehension of their limitations, their ignorance in no way dampens their confidence. It is because of this confidence that the rest of the defensive line is allowed to slumber at their posts. The security of three thousand to seven thousand men is placed solely in the care of the men in the towers, men like Don and myself . . . pass the joint.

Either our captain or one of the majors assures himself of our alertness and capabilities at least once every other night. The captain walks the line once a week. His purpose is to make sure we are ready for the more frequent visits of his superiors. He checks our performance on the radar, our knowledge of the passwords, and our ability to call in accurate fire coordinates. He checks the landline telephone and the field phone. His attitude is friendly and businesslike. He does not come to gig us for some minor flaw in appearance but to make sure everything functions properly.

The majors, on the other hand, have an entirely different approach. They are spirited out to the perimeter in chauffeured jeeps. Once on the perimeter road they douse their headlights and command their drivers to sneak the jeep toward one of the towers. When they are within a hundred feet, they disembark (one major rolled from a moving jeep into the ditch to mask his approach) to cover the remaining ground in a commando-style rush. Through the binoculars we watch them hurry along the roadside ditch in a cautious crouch. They do not seem to realize that the ditch offers no visual screen from the fifty-foot tower or that crouching only makes them more visible from above.

After pausing a moment beneath the tower to collect their dignity or catch their breath, they begin stealing up the tower ladder. The game is for us to catch them before they reach the halfway point. Failing to do so is a court-martial offense. Waiting until the last moment before shattering their hopes of catching us napping, we throw back the hatch with a bang, jam an M-16 down the hole, and command them to halt. Once we startled a major so much that he slid all the way back to the ground. He must have been scratched and bruised, but being made of good stern Army stuff he regained his poise and reclimbed the ladder, never mentioning the mishap. After exchanging passwords, the major mounts the remaining stairs, tugs his shirt smooth over his torso, erects his military bearing, and barks out a crisp verbal inspection.

To be fair, there was one major who came around for a while who was not loud or brash or too proud to seek information. But for the rest, their ignorance of the functioning of Di An's primary line of defense is appalling. They convey the belief that as long as we are vigilant we can pick up any enemy's approach. Yet their test questions about the instruments make it clear that they know little about their operation. I doubt that they are aware that the radar is broken down fifty percent of the time, or that both the starlight scope and the radar are useless on the kind of rainy night the VC always choose to attack. This, coupled with the men being allowed to sleep through their late watches in the bunkers below, leaves the base without any effective guard on every stormy night.

Sometimes the majors are so puffed up, so removed from reality that it takes supreme effort to keep from laughing at their foolishness. Only by reminding ourselves of the absolute power they hold over us is it possible for us to put on the required facade of respect that keeps them satisfied. Naturally, these men never ask advice or leave an opening for comments. Nor do they give the impression that they would be in any way receptive to even carefully phrased criticism of the way they run their section of the base's security.

Ah, well, at least our majors and their defenses look formidable, and so far that has been enough.

I try again to concentrate my wandering thoughts on the static coming over the headphones. The sound I am striving to hear has been described as a slushy, crunchy noise, like the footsteps of men walking on wet gravel. I have been assured that on a windless, rainless night, it is possible to pick up this combination of sounds that is the radar's reaction to men on the move, but I have not been able to confirm this assurance. In the hope of becoming familiar with the sound as an aid in future identifications, I aim the radar at a man walking along a road on the base. What I hear is the throb of engines, ascending in pitch with acceleration, dropping in tone with gear changes to climb the scale again like an audible tacometer. The clear, unmistakable sounds of jeeps and generators overwhelm all other signals. Well, if the VC ever steal enough vehicles to launch an armored assault we will have no difficulty detecting their advance.

Giving the effort up, I swing the unit back to the front. Clouds move in, blocking the light from the stars. The wind pushing the clouds fills the headset with blasts of static. I am about to put an end to the assault on my eardrums when I hear a faint undercurrent of noise that was not there before. Focusing the radar on an area five hundred meters to our front, I detect a slushy, crunchy quality in the pervasive static, but I cannot identify anything that even vaguely resembles footsteps. I ask Don to have a listen. Tolerant of my curiosity he fits the earphones to his head. While he listens, I scan the area with binoculars and starlight scope, but there is not enough light for either to be effective.

After a minute, Don lifts the headset off. "I don't believe it, but it sounds like a couple of dozen men out there. We'd better call it in and get permission to fire a flare."

HQ informs us that our sighting is a brigade school practice ambush. We are commended for our alertness, being the only post so far to report the movement.

"Alertness, is it?" I say. "More like blind luck. A platoon is walking around just outside the last string of wire and it's a miracle we picked them up. It's such an inspiration being a part of a crack outfit like the U.S. Army."

It is now 2200. Our third man has not shown for the night shift. We should report him absent, but we would rather lose a little sleep than get whoever it is in trouble. Besides, we have all those new men protecting our front. The ears of a nervous man are far better than our instruments on a night like this.

Suddenly, a series of explosions shatter the night. I

tumble from the observation chair to join Don on the floor. M-16s fire on full automatic. The brigade school has blown its ambush. They don't do that for practice. Don grabs the binoculars while I use the starlight scope to try to locate the enemy.

"That won't do any good," says Don. "Call HQ. Give them a report."

He is right. The light given off by the tracers overloads the scope. My view is blank. I pick up the phone.

"Don, you spot anything?"

"No. Too dark. I don't even see any incoming."

"Do you think the brigade school just spoo—"

"Look out!"

We hit the floor again as a spray of bullets whine over, under, and around the tower.

"Incoming," Don announces with an uplifted finger.

"Is this place bulletproof?"

"So far."

"Excuse me, I have a call," I say, noticing I still have the phone in my hand. I give HQ a report and then risk a hand over the top of the wall to replace the handset. We sit side by side with our backs to the front wall, listening to the passing bullets, hoping one will not penetrate the combination of wood and sandbags, wondering if there is something we should be doing. We seem to be attracting most of the enemy's attention. Charlie must have been given the same indoctrination speech on our technological toys as our officers. It appears that Charlie is trying to convince us to keep our heads down while he makes his escape. I am convinced. No point in losing your head trying to halt the enemy's advance to the rear.

Don has laid the radar and starlight scope on the floor to prevent damage. The number of rounds passing through the space between the wall and the roof is not diminishing. Perhaps the enemy's advance is not too near the rear.

"If they don't stop this pretty soon I'm going to start getting nervous."

"Me too," answers Don as he pulls open the floor hatch to check for infiltrators. Abruptly he jerks his head back from the hole, letting the hatch close with a bang. "Damn! That was close."

"Well, don't be sticking your head out there for those nasty people to shoot at."

"I just wanted to make sure Charlie or one of our officers isn't sneaking up on us."

None of our mighty majors are going to come here with this going on. And none of the guys in the bunkers are firing, so an invasion must not be imminent.

"Why don't you stick your head up there for a look? You're supposed to be a lookout, you know."

"I can see just as well from here, thank you. I'll look again when they get either closer or further away. And what the hell are you doing to aid the cause?"

"Preserving troops and equipment—and rolling a joint."

"Aw, shit. This is no time to get stupid."

"Idle hands, you know. Just keeping busy. Strictly for later, you understand."

"Hey. Listen."

"They've stopped."

"You got a match?"

A day later Don and I sit in a jeep in the center of the town of Di An threatening a two-story brick building with a 106 artillery piece. Stick 'em up, building. There is no partic-

Jeep-Mounted 106 mm. recoilless

ular significance attached to this building. It just happens to be at the end of the street on which we are parked.

On our left, an open-air market is enjoying a brisk mid-morning business. Hundreds of voices intermingle in heated barter for the goods displayed under cloth awnings. Live chickens and butchered pigs, rice and vegetables of all kinds compete with black market PX goods such as laundry detergent, Coca-Cola, watches, and transistor radios exhibited at full volume.

Across the street on our right is the medical entourage we have been assigned to protect. An army doctor and two medics are giving free medical attention to a long line of Vietnamese peasants while a dozen ARVNs stroll back and forth in their capacity as interpreters and guards.

The 106 recoilless rifle is mounted in the back of our jeep, its ten-foot barrel aimed over the hood at chest level. While we threaten to blow a hole through the west side of town, Echo Company's other jeep-mounted 106 is casually trained on a small hooch to the east.

Don and I manage to slide a beehive round containing thousands of darts into the gun's chamber, and locate the elevation and traverse cranks. Don claims he can fire the piece, but he has had no previous experience and does not seem overly confident. I am unconcerned, however. If we are attacked, we will be killed long before we can bring the piece to bear on the target.

When an officer points at a jeep with an artillery piece on it and tells me to drive it to Di An, I do it. But now that I am here I cannot stop wondering what we are doing with artillery in the middle of a town. An artillery piece is not usually the weapon of choice for a street fight in close quarters. I guess I will have to chalk it up as another case of typical Army brilliance. Perhaps the crystallized brains of our leaders gave birth to the idea that if no one were here to practice our medical goodwill upon, the 106s could whip up some business in a hurry, thus teaching these ignorant peasants to accept a good thing when it is offered.

I just hope 106s are not on the VC shopping list this week. Parked here at the edge of the market they could easily get close enough to waste the entire medivac team before we knew what was happening.

Don distracts me from the uneasiness I always feel when in close proximity of hundreds of potential GI killers by filling me in on the latest news from the field. When the battalion assumed its new position four miles north of here it was greeted with three nights of mortar attacks. A buildup of enemy activity was predicted to follow but, in fact, the opposite occurred. For the next three weeks the entire sector was quiet. Then, as frequently happens when the tension of waiting for the unexpected to shatter the silence has built up enough to make the men edgy, the battalion begins shooting at its own people. Bravo Company shot one of its LP five times thinking he was a VC. Then Charlie Company had a firefight with themselves, wounding eight. Shortly afterwards, two more men were killed by friendly fire. The details of this last action are not available.

The battalion has now moved thirty miles further north, somewhere in the vicinity of my last stay in the field. Enemy contact has been heavy. As of yesterday, Charlie Company had suffered fifty casualties. Two days ago Alpha Company had four men killed and thirty wounded. He has not heard from Delta Company.

"Thanks, Don." Now I am depressed instead of uneasy.

For three hours the local population studiously ignores our presence while drugs are administered to the sick, and disinfectant and sutures repair a small part of the civilian damage inevitable when large amounts of explosive are used on small elusive targets in populated areas. Our mission is completed without a single disturbance. This peace is undoubtedly due to both pro- and antigovernment factions benefiting from our medical services. Each patient's identification card is checked, but an enterprising Vietcong can easily obtain an ID card from the corrupt officials he seeks to overthrow.

Having dispensed our allotment of goodwill for the day, we clamp the barrel of the 106 into its forward support and follow the medivac unit back to the base.

Because of an increase in the number of our men being sent to the field to operate starlight scopes and radar equipment in various companies' NDPs, our tower guard and 106 squad has been reduced to eight. More and more of my time is spent in this little room in the sky. This platform with its hidden treasures is my home, its plank floor my bed. It is quiet here and peaceful. The war seems far removed. I am lucky to be here, but I must find a way to deal with the boredom, the sameness of the days, before my impatience drives me to perform a foolish act I will later regret.

Last night six VC attempting to sneak through the wire on the west side of the base added a touch of excitement to our lives. One of the tower guards spotted them and sent out the alarm. Despite a heavy barrage laid down by the noncombatants manning the western perimeter, five of the VC escaped across the half mile of open ground to the shelter of the jungle. How all those clerks could have missed five open targets is a mystery, but with the help of the entangling coils of concertina wire they did manage to capture the helpless sixth man without injury to anyone involved.

As the predawn light eased into the base's POW camp, a routine head count revealed that the camp was one head short. Every tower guard on duty was dispatched to search his sector of the perimeter for signs of the escapee's route. Except for the area of last night's section, no clues were uncovered. It appears that the thwarted attempt by six VC to gain unauthorized entrance to the base was instead the exposure of the last leg of a successful prisoner rescue mission.

I wonder if all this passing of the enemy through our primary defenses suggests anything to the people in charge of those defenses? If it does, we will probably suffer an increase in boot polishing, not overlooking the unlikely possibility that they will consider this a serious problem, calling not only for gleaming boots, but for the addition of starch to the laundry as well.

Ah, but I need not worry about starched shorts, even if I wore them, for at least a week. It will take a few days for the base commander to assign blame, and another few days for the person of assigned blame to instruct the squadron of majors in charge of the various sections of the perimeter to enact corrective measures. And of course, it will take a few more days for the majors to settle the local share of blame among themselves and come up with an improved security plan to pass on to their captains to pass on to their lieutenants to pass on to their sergeants for final disposition by the men. So why worry? We could be overrun before then. Besides, after five consecutive nights in the tower, it is my turn to walk upon the earth, to pursue the pleasures of drink, and the company of someone with at least one new story to tell.

Gathered around one of the tables in the EM club are five men with various sections of their anatomy wrapped in fresh, white gauze. At the end of the beer can-littered table sits a sixth man with no obvious sign of a recent wound. I approach the table to inquire after his health.

"How are you, my friend?"

"Who is that?" he asks, squinting up in my direction.

"It's John. I see that you have lost your glasses again."

"So I have. Those slippery devils once again sought refuge beneath my boots in a time of stress."

"Well, good for them. But isn't your CO getting a bit suspicious?"

"He is indeed. My number is up. I shall have to develop a fresh ploy. And there is no time to waste. Look at my friends. They are a mess, and this is the best of the lot. There are little yellow people out there in the jungle trying to kill us. If they don't hurry up and put a hole in my body, my mind will crumble under the stress of false anticipation. I have got to get out of the field. I'm serious. We must think of something right away."

"He has been talking like that all afternoon," the guy with the bandaged head informs me.

"Don't worry about Allen," says the guy leaning against the wall because of a bullet crease in his right rear cheek and a wrap on his right calf. "It's far too late to save his mind."

"How about slamming a door on my trigger hand or breaking my arm?" suggests Allen.

"Shit man, that's dumb," says the guy with matching bandages on his forearms. "How you going to paint without your hands?"

"Good point. I need my hands. How about a leg then?"

"Yeah, a leg would be good," offers Scalp Wound Two. "We could get a baseball bat or a four-by-four, wrap it in a towel to protect the skin, lay your leg over a log or something, and smash that sucker good."

"This calls for more anesthetic," I say, heading for the bar.

By the time I return, the removal of toes and fingers by rifle fire has been suggested, and the art of dropping an ammo box on a bare foot draped over a doorsill is under discussion. The proper method of self-inflicted flesh wounds is brought up but soon discarded as too temporary a measure.

The course of the conversation takes a slight turn when the black guy with his left hand encased in gauze points out that there is no sense in breaking any of poor old Allen's

bones until the end of the week, as it will take at least that
long for him to be fitted with new eyeglasses and prodded
back to the field. There is unanimous agreement on this
point, but Allen is still not content. He says that he is afraid
all this well-intentioned talk will evaporate tomorrow when
everybody sobers up. This comment perpetrates an outburst
of rude noises from the gathering. They swear they have no
intention of sobering up tomorrow, or of forgetting Allen's
plight either, for that matter. Nevertheless, Allen says his
mind would rest easier if someone would promise now to
break his leg later.

After thorough consideration of the request, and another
trip to the bar, a decision is handed down by Scalp Wound
One.

"In five days we will check the level of enemy activity
around our NDP. If at that time the fighting is still heavy we
will draw straws to determine which one of us will inflict
Allen with the injury of his choice."

The announcement is met with a chorus of "here, here,"
with an occasional "right on" thrown in for balance. This
show of good fellowship seems to satisfy Allen, who is too
drunk to remember that his buddies are scheduled to return
to the field before him.

With Allen's trepidation temporarily relived, Scalp Wound
Two cries, "More beer for me aching head."

"More anesthetic for me aching ass," adds the man
slumped against the wall.

Without a word, the black deftly rips the beer can from
the grasp of matching forearms and pours the contents onto
the cigarette-ignited fire smoldering in the gauze wrapping of
his left hand.

And so we launch into some serious drinking, interrupted only by an occasional yelp of pain as one of the boys is
reminded in which part of his body the stitches lie.

Last night as I lay in my bunk in alcoholic slumber, a
major was creeping up a tower ladder. He passed the motionless form asleep upon the halfway platform. With care, he set
his foot silently upon the next rung, and then the next, slowly
rising toward the hatch in the tower house floor. Never
before had he achieved this height without a challenge. Never
before had his goal been so near.

Over the past weeks he had learned that it was not so

much the noise of his tread as it was the vibration sent up the ladder by his shifting weight that alerted the guards and thwarted his efforts. But he had learned, and now victory lay before him. With an upward thrust of his arm, he flung back the hatch in jubilation. After almost two months of effort he had succeeded in reaching the top unchallenged.

The man on watch, who had been leaning over the sidewall in search of the source of uneasiness that had come upon him, swung around to face the major as he emerged triumphantly through the floor. The man whose watch had ended the hour before pulled himself off the planks to make room for the major to walk around.

"Do you boys know what it's like to be an inmate in Long Binh Jail?"

"No, sir."

"Well, the three of you are going to find out all about it. You can count on it."

"But, sir—"

"No buts, soldier. I don't want to hear any of your sorry excuses. Save them for your court-martial."

The major did not care that the two men who were sleeping were supposed to be sleeping, nor did he care that the man on watch had the radar headphones on when this assault began. The major had clearly defined the rules and had pursued his game in earnest. He had not only passed the halfway point without being halted for the required password, he had gained the tower house itself. He had won fair and square; these men were going to fry.

As a result of the major's triumph over his men, I spent an hour this morning making a gate for the ladder. Using a rock as a hammer, I rearranged the structure of a discarded wooden pallet so that it fit over the face of the ladder, blocking access to the rungs. A rope attached to the gate enables us to raise and lower it from above. Although the gate can be circumvented, this can be accomplished only with a good deal of noise and effort. My handiwork is crude, but it will prevent visitors from arriving unannounced.

Shortly after the completion of the gate, Sanchez comes by to relieve us for lunch. We are surprised to see the likable little Puerto Rican, as he is one of the men arrested last night. He tells us that he and his partners were under guard all morning before our captain could convince the major that without the prisoners one of our two towers would not have the required number of personnel. Sanchez could hear the two officers arguing in the major's office. The major was confused and angered by the captain's attitude. The major expected expressions of awe and congratulation from his subordinate; what he got were expressions of disgust. The shouting ended with our captain proclaiming his intention to be a witness for the defense and departing the area in the ensuing silence.

"All this trouble—it is my fault," says Sanchez. "I on watch when major come. I know I break rule, not challenge major, but why my amigos in trouble? They do no wrong. This I do not understand. Also, I not understand how I can listen for enemy on radar and listen for major at same time. I have only two ear. What they want me to do?"

"Your problem," I say, "is confused priorities. You spent too much time looking for the enemy to your front, who is yet to bother you guys on Tower 14, and too little time looking for the enemy to your rear, who threatens you almost every night. That major hates our guts. I figure the only reason he is having you court-martialed instead of shot is that shooting his own troops would draw too much bad press."

"But the radar—it is my job."

"Your job is to protect yourself from your enemies. For now, at least, your greatest enemy is the U.S. Army."

"I am confused. This does not make sense."

"Sanchez, this is the Army, it is not supposed to make sense."

After lunch Sanchez walks despondently back to his tower, rigs a trip flare to the ladder, and sits in the open hatchway with an M-16 across his knees.

Nine days later, the eight men who stand watch in Towers 14 and 15 are summoned to the office of the senior of our four majors. As we are ushered into the presence of a stiffly erect figure standing inside a carefully ironed set of starched fatigues, it strikes me that the only authority representing our group is Buck Sergeant Harris. Since we are primarily a rear echelon company, we have more than our full complement of officers and NCOs, but none of the eight men below the rank of senior major and above the rank of Sergeant Harris are present. What happened to the chain of command? Majors should talk to captains—sergeants talk to the enlisted men. But not today. Today we are privileged to listen to an original rendering of military wisdom from its source.

The major begins his talk with a general appraisal of our performance, starting with words like incompetent and progressing to gutter descriptions of the low order of life arranged before him. The barrage of insults and degrading descriptions of us as individuals and as a unit becomes more vivid with the passing minutes: our personal behavior is criminal, our attitude is irreverent, our appearance atrocious; we are scum, fit only to wallow in the excrement of the stockade latrine.

The viperous tone of the speech is not what I expected. I wonder what we did to merit this scathing hail of abuse. I remember this man inspecting the tower a few times, but I do not recall anything unusual about the visits. After failing to come upon us undetected, he asked the usual curt questions and left.

What is the purpose of this meeting? I wish he would get to the point, if there is one. Thus far he has confined himself to demeaning generalities without making a single reference to a specific incident.

The major's oration rises in pitch with heightened emotion, bringing a fine rosy glow to his untanned cheeks. Just as he works himself up to an admirable fervor that any evangelist would be proud to emulate, he sputters and stalls, unable to vent a single fresh abuse. Mumbling used insults he wanders to his desk to shuffle absently through the neat stacks of paper on its surface as if he expects to find a complete and updated list of insults among the other forms. A stunned silence falls upon the room.

After a few moments he looks up from his desk, a calm, confident expression on the moist, white face. "From this day forward, two men will be awake in the towers at all times. From 2200 hours until 0700, the third man on duty will be permitted to sleep on the platform behind the M-50 machine gun. There will be no more slack time. When you are not on duty in the towers you will be put to work improving our defenses. We are going to tighten up this sissy outfit, gentlemen. We shall create an exemplary unit in which men will be proud to serve. Are there any questions?"

So that is what this is all about. This has been a shorter, more intense form of the old basic training ploy. First the men's egos are torn apart, then they are rebuilt on a base of new values.

But what is this bullshit about questions? He can't mean it. He must've gotten carried away. Officers only ask for questions in the movies. In the real Army they take it for granted that everyone is confused. At any rate, I can't pass up this rare opportunity.

"Sir, are you aware that with the schedule you have laid out, we will get only three hours of sleep a night? I doubt we can stay alert with so little sleep."

"How the hell do you come up with that?"

"Two men up and one down over nine hours, sir. That is a maximum of three hours of sleep per man."

For a moment the major glares at me in silence. "How would you like to go back to the field, smart ass?"

"I see your point, sir." I answer in my most respectful tone of voice. There are several other items I want to bring up, but it is clear that the one question has exhausted the major's patience.

"Do any of the rest of you want to return to the field?" He knows he has stumbled upon a real crowd quieter with this question. He surveys the gathering defiantly. We carefully study the floor.

"No one? I thought not. Well then, gentlemen, I trust we understand one another. You are dismissed."

Released from the oppressive presence of our leader, we waste no time gaining the building's exit. At the door, I ask Sergeant Harris, "What do you think of our commander's answer to the base's security problems?"

"Is that what you think that crazy asshole was talking about?"

"Yes, I think so."

"He could have fooled me."

Five days after our new schedule had been instituted, one of the majors found two of the tower guards in a bona fide state of slumber. The names of these men were added to the list of those awaiting court-martial.

The next morning Sergeant Harris informs me that he has seen my name on a roster of personnel due to be sent to the field. On good terms with the sergeant, I am granted permission to visit HQ to attempt to stay this potential disaster.

Through a clerk I know in personnel, I verify the sergeant's information. I have to act fast. I am scheduled to leave for the field in the morning. This gives me less than twenty-two hours to come up with a plan that will again delay that morning helicopter ride into the jungle.

Paperwork and incompetence are the Army's greatest weaknesses. Somewhere in the mountainous volumes of paper lies the solution to my problem. The correct form, properly signed, is needed to begin every action, but inaction should be easier to achieve. If I cannot remove my name from the field roster, perhaps I can submit a form that indicates my disposition is in another direction. What I need are orders sending me to a new location. It is not necessary for the papers to be complete, but they will need at least one legitimate signature.

Ever since we were put on a twenty-one-hour workday our captain has been in poorly concealed conflict with his conglomeration of superiors. Now that five of his eight guards are up for court-martial, his frustration and discontent are obvious.

When I arrive at the captain's office I am told that he just left for a 1030 meeting and is not expected back until noon. It is now 1015. In the hope of catching him before the meeting, I run back to HQ. I check the communications bunker and the paymaster's office. On my way to records I see him leaving the personnel office.

After supplying him with a cursory account of my situation, I ask if he knows of any units that would accept my application for transfer.

"No problem," he answers with a smile. "I can have you transferred to my reconnaissance unit today if you like. I was just in the personnel office putting out a request for volunteers. I am surprised you haven't been contacted about joining us before. I'm sure I saw your name on the recommendation list a couple of weeks ago."

Oh, shit. This conversation is going in completely the wrong direction. I heard a rumor that I was to be reassigned to reconnaissance, but I thought it was only a rumor. I'm not surprised that his unit needs replacements; they keep going into the jungle in small groups and coming back in smaller groups. Does he think I'm crazy?

"Your offer is tempting, sir, but before I do anything . . . ah . . . like that, I would like to make an attempt at finding a job as a medical microbiologist where I could use my training and education."

"Oh, yes, I see. Well, in that case you should get over to the Long Binh Medical Center right away and find out if there is an opening in your field. If there is, I will take your name off the field roster and hold you here until a transfer can be worked out."

Just like that? Unbelievable. May the good fairy leave a pound of gold under your pillow tonight. I thank the captain at least once more than necessary and head for the west gate to hitch a ride to Long Binh.

I made the trip to Long Binh and back in just over three hours. I talked to a captain at one hospital and a major at another. Both facilities are in desperate need of lab technicians. Both officers said they would assist in every way they could to get me transferred. The trip had gone so smoothly it was a little hard to believe.

I return to my friendly personnel clerk and convince him to type up the forms. Going through my records he discovers that I am still assigned to Delta Company, which explains why I was almost returned there. I have already informed Echo Company's captain that there is a job waiting for me at Long Binh Medical Center, so I have no need to worry about being sent to the field tomorrow, but I am beginning to get the feeling that this transfer is not going to go as smoothly as I had hoped. When my friend the clerk tells me my request must clear my company, then the battalion, then the division, and then be accepted by Long Binh Medical Center, I become even less optimistic. The battalion and the division are notorious for hanging onto their personnel.

Whatever happens, it will take a few weeks for the paperwork to make the rounds. In the meantime I will stay in Echo Company. My plan has succeeded far better than I thought possible this morning. I may not end up at the medical center, but I will be in a nice, dry, bug-free tower tomorrow.

It has been a drab day, more typical of Oregon than Vietnam. The drizzle began last night and has persisted. It is not a heavy mist or a light rain—it is authentic drizzle. I have seen enough of them to know.

Back home, the drizzles arrive in the fall and stay until spring with dismally few interruptions by sun or snow. When the gray drabs penetrated my resolve to ignore them, I went for long walks in the woods, gaining solace from those who thrive there: the Douglas fir, the Noble fir, the spruce, and the hemlock. Or I played football in the mud, or visited my girl and made love under the blankets where the gloom could not reach.

But I am not back home; I am alone in a tower. The drizzle, the boredom, the lack of sleep, and six days of continuous duty have finally dinted Don's calm countenance. Twenty minutes ago he stood up, announced he needed a beer more than he needed to stay out of jail, and left.

Night has come again. In the distance there is a lightning storm. I have been watching it come closer and closer, the jagged streaks of electricity ripping through the black curtain of night, revealing for an instant the blinding power beyond.

In a convulsive flash I hurdle from the observation chair, collide with the far wall, and sink to the floor.

Stunned, I look along the wooden planks, over the toppled chair, and up the wall. What the hell happened? My entire body tingles the way an arm does when it is reviving from being asleep.

A flash of brilliant light fills the room. Lightning? But I would be dead if I was struck by lightning. I crawl shakily to the aluminum-frame chair. In the dim light I examine the tubing for burn marks. I find none.

Crouching on the floor, I stare blankly at the four-foot sidewall, waiting for an answer to reveal itself. A crackling roar behind me strobes the wall into relief, leaving behind a clear image of the field radio imprinted upon my mind. Of course. When I sit in the observation chair, that phone is only an inch or two from my left shoulder. The lightning must have hit the antenna on the roof, traveled down the wires to the phone, and arched through the air to my shoulder. I pick up the phone. Dead. A quick examination reveals that the wires leading to the antenna are burned through. The wires acted as a fuse, greatly reducing the electrical charge transferred from the lightning bolt to me—thank God.

In the wake of the electrical storm, a steadily rising wind gathers force from its source in the South China Sea. By the time Don returns from his unauthorized jaunt to the EM club with our night guard in tow, the tower is humming like a tuning fork, plucked by the friction of the passing air. The right front corner of the roof begins to clatter and bang as nails loosen their hold in the wooden rafter.

With the carrying strap from an ammo can, we resecure the rafter to its beam. The strap should hold for several hours before the constantly chattering timbers chafe it through, but the roof is already working loose in several other places. The prospect of losing our cover is not a major concern. It is the vibration and sway of the tower itself that worries me.

With flashlight in hand I climb a short distance down the ladder to inspect the underpinnings of the tower house. The floor is spiked to four four-by-ten beams that are in turn bolted to the four telephone-post legs of the tower. So far, the big spikes and bolts are holding up well against the battering wind and the strain from the swaying legs. Switching off the flashlight, I cling to the ladder, feeling the exhilaration of the storm.

Then I hear it.

Far beneath the sounds of the groaning tower, the howling wind, and the clattering metal roof, is the muted roar of a stormy sea. But it is not the continuous intermingling of thundering waves that produces this sound, it is a wall of rain sweeping through the jungle. Captivated by the ominous sound I linger on my perch, listening. At the last moment I push through the hatch door to be struck by a torrent of water slashing through the open sides of the tower house. In seconds, we and everything around us is streaming with water.

The roar overhead is deafening. The sound of thousands of marble-sized water bombs impacting on a sheet of corrugated tin suspended over a partially enclosed space produces a considerable racket. The air beneath the tin is thick with energy, sound waves, and water. I envision the rain beating the roof nails back into place and the wind ripping them out again in a fast, shuddering rhythm. Like cattle in a field, we stand with our backs to the storm, waiting.

After an hour or more I feel the hatch door bump against the back of my legs. A camouflaged helmet emerges through the hole followed closely by a billowing poncho, slick, shiny, and streaming with water. The face of Sergeant Harris tilts toward the disintegrating roof. He shouts soundless words. For a moment he stares at the huddled forms around him, then he moves to the field radio and picks up the handset. I tap his shoulder to draw his attention to the frayed wire ends in my hand. He nods and tries the landline phone. His lips move to words yelled into the mouthpiece. After a while he shrugs and replaces the handset.

In pantomine he points to an ammo box, a rifle, a poncho liner, then at the three of us and at the ground. The message is clear. We grab our gear and follow him down the ladder.

On the ground, where a shouted voice can again be heard, the sergeant instructs us to stand the rest of our watch in the bunker dug into the earth a few meters to the east of the tower. The bunker does not have the usual sleeping shelter attached, so we are obliged to pass the night in the black confines of the four-by-six-foot bunker.

We dam and divert a rivulet of water trickling down the entrance to add its volume to the foot-deep pool of water covering the bunker floor. There is nothing we can do to stop the water seeping through the sidewalls of the hole. With our gear cradled in our arms we stand in the quiet of this wet, lightless hole contemplating the unseen water covering our boots. The sound of an ammo box splashing into the water is followed by a sigh and "Well, lads, I think we best find something to keep our collective asses out of this lake."

A half hour of scrounging through old bunkers and empty barracks rewards us with a four-foot board and two crates. Hauling our booty back to the bunker, we erect a bench with the hope that the rain will stop before the slowly rising pool reaches our perch. Wrapping wet poncho liners over our sodden clothes, we light up a joint and prepare our minds for a long, damp, sleepless night.

By morning the storm has passed. The sun breaks through the dissipating clouds to bake the water-covered earth, sending wavering mists of steam into the vapor-laden air. At lunch I collar Sergeant Harris and talk him into giving me the night off. It is my twenty-fourth birthday.

To celebrate the passing of another milestone on my long journey toward becoming a very old man, some friends and I suck up a couple of joints and slip into the fantasy unfolding on the torn bed sheet hanging against the dilapidated movie house wall.

After the show my companions head for their bunks to rest from the sleepless, stormy night and the other nights of little sleep that had come before. I cross the road to the EM club alone, determined to place a memorable event in this passing slot of time. Digging in the bottom of my pockets for damp little wads of military currency, I place my current fortune upon the bar. Two dollars and thirty cents. More than enough. I order six beers, load them on a tray, and wander between the tables looking for a familiar face.

"Hey, man, you lost?" comes a voice at my elbow.

I recognize the speaker as one of Allen's friends from Alpha Company whom I had met briefly a week or two ago.

"I'm not lost, I just don't know where I am going. Here," I say, unloading my tray, "special table-side service, today only."

"Ah, manna from heaven." He introduces me to his two friends. "So, what have you been up to since we last met?"

"Not much. Too little beer and too much boredom. But tonight's my birthday, and I'm not in the mood to let it pass with a mere whimper."

"A birthday. All right."

"What are you doing buying us beer on your birthday, John? It *is* John, isn't it? Yes, well, you'll not be buying any more beer this night, I can tell you."

"Right on. It's party time. Let's do it up right. A good celebration is just what we need."

As the night progresses the festive atmosphere increases, as does the number of people at our table. By the time the club closes I have poured more free booze into my stomach than I had previously considered possible for that sadly abused organ to hold or retain. As we stagger through the dirt in search of our beds, boisterously slaughtering some sweet tune, our brotherhood dwindles until I find myself being bid good night outside a vaguely familiar door. If this is my barracks, then my bunk is the first one on the left, fifteen feet beyond this door. I open the door, take aim on my target, and launch myself forward. Rebounding off a wall, I collide with the upper half of a double bunk and collapse in a sprawl on the lower bed. The bunk immediately begins to spin in a counterclockwise direction. I press a foot to the floor and slap a hand against the wall in an effort to hold it steady. The vortex slows, but will not stop. A sea of nausea engulfs me. I recoil from the bed, and lurch through the vortex to the door, passing cleanly through on the first rebound off some unidentified object.

Outside, on my knees, I try to eject the evil within me. It wallows in renewed contentment, sloshing and gurgling from the security of its inner cavern. Determined, I shove a sandy finger down my throat, then two and three without success. I never did have any luck with self-induced vomiting. My stomach is its own master, delivering up its hoard only when unsolicited.

I cannot go to bed and I cannot throw up; there is only one solution to this dilemma. I must walk until I am sober enough to lie down in peace. With a good many detoured steps left and right to maintain balance, I begin the difficult journey along the quiet dirt road running past the barracks toward the perimeter. By the fourth or fifth return trip I am able to proceed with no more than the normal stagger, despite the alcohol still working its way through my system.

After an hour I long for sleep and return to my bunk for a second try. The moment I am horizontal the whirling begins and no amount of determination or utterances of heartfelt oaths can stay its course.

Wearily, I return to the road. Back and forth, back and forth, I travel the dark road to sobriety. Watching moonlight sparkle off the mud puddles along my route, I think of other times and old friends and opportunities let pass. Alone and tired I begin to sing "Happy Birthday" to myself in a slow, melancholy rhythm.

Time hobbles by. I grow impatient with my progress. I try to jog but stumble and fall and try again and fall again and rise again in anger. Slowly I start, with a shuffling walk, shoving the boots hard into earth, working the arms, picking up the rhythm. By the tenth passing of the barracks I am jogging; by the twentieth, with concentration, I jog without swaying. The jog works into the long, even strides of a run. A barrier is reached and broken, the blood courses freely, the air flows in and out without effort. Around and around the cinder track I go, getting in shape, preparing for the meet, pushing until the legs burn, and keep pushing until they threaten to buckle with exhaustion and then push more until I am sure the next stride will put me on my face; then walk, careful of wobbly knees, back to the bed to collapse in a sweat-soaked heap and to let blackness suck me into its folds of oblivion.

One week after submitting my request for transfer to Long Binh Medical Center, I am summoned to the battalion personnel office. The news awaiting me is likely to be unwelcome. There is no way a low-priority item like my transfer could have received the attention of four august officers and their bevy of attendants in the brief span of a week. My request must have been ambushed somewhere along its treacherous route.

Sitting in the chair at the side of his desk, I glance over the Form 1049 my friend the clerk has given me to sign. The form is identical to the one we sent to the field a week ago.

"Why are we doing this again?" I ask. "What happened to last week's 1049?"

He reaches two fingers into the waste basket and gingerly retrieves a wrinkled, mud-covered piece of paper.

"I am sorry. I sent it out to Delta Company without your signature. It sat there until your executive officer noticed it lying in the mud and brought it back here."

"So we start again."

"I'm afraid so."

I sign the paper and watch as it is placed in a pile with its fellow forms to again begin its grand adventure through the maze of Army bureaucracy. Alone, this thin plane of reformed tree fibers must overcome staggering incompetence, rise above rampant apathy, and skirt potential nays from officers unwilling to see their empire dwindle by even a single man.

As I leave, I silently wish my slim emissary luck, but we both know the odds are heavily weighed against us.

THE POPULAR FORCES

Shortly after noon the following day a jeep pulls up to the bottom of the tower. From the driver's seat Sergeant Harris hollers, "Shook, grab your gear and get down here."

With my helmet, my poncho liner, an M-16, and a bandolier of ammunition clutched in my arms I pile into the passenger's seat. The jeep bumps and jolts back onto the dirt road, heading for the perimeter gate.

"What's up? Where are we going?"

"To the ARVN compound," Harris answers as he breaks for the MPs at the gate. "It's not bad duty," he offers, "no Army bullshit out there."

He is quiet while we pass through a throng of kids and chickens on the outskirts of the town of Di An, then turn north onto Highway 13. He drives fast on the theory that the faster he goes the harder it is for the guy trying to shoot him. The theory has some merit if the advantage is not canceled by getting into a wreck.

Slowing for the congestion at Lai Khe, Harris addresses me again. "I guess I'd better fill you in. Up until a few weeks ago this place we're going to got overrun once a month . . . every month. Each time the VC hit the compound the ARVNs stationed there ran for their lives and got their butts shot up in the process. The VC walked into the abandoned compound, picked up whatever weapons, ammunition, and food they could find, blew the bridge, and walked back into the jungle. In the morning the ARVNs would return to the

263

compound, the Army Corps of Engineers would rebuild the
bridge, and life would go on as usual until the next month
when it all happened over again."

Somewhere between Lai Khe and An Loc we turn left
onto a single-lane road heading northwest. On both sides of
the lane large tracts of waist-high grass extend undisturbed to
their palm-forest borders. No animals graze in the long grass,
no crops grow in the abandoned fields. The untended land
stands in testimony to the Saigon government's ability to
collect farm products for taxes and farmers for soldiers, and to
the VC's ability to collect what remained.

"A few miles up the road from the bridge, at the end of
the road, is an ARVN compound. The colonel up there is
pissed off because half the time he can't get his men and
supplies across the river, and our brass is pissed off because
they have to keep rebuilding the same damn bridge. So they
sent us up here as forward observers to try to put a stop to
the recurring cycle. The three guys from our unit are supposed to locate Charlie with the starlight scope and radar,
and the three guys from the other battalion are supposed to
call their company, which has a fire support base one and a
half miles to the southwest, and blow him away. By the way,
these guys at the compound aren't actually ARVNs."

"No?"

"No. They are the hamlet's militia. You ever heard of the
Popular Forces?"

"No, I haven't."

"Well, that's who we'll be working with—twenty-four of
them. And listen, if we do get hit don't expect much help
from the PFs."

We enter a quiet hamlet of some thirty traditional bamboo and thatch huts clustered in the shade of a grove of palm
trees on the inside bend of the river. On the far side of the
hamlet a single-lane steel truss bridge spans a fifty-foot-wide
section of the river. Harris brings the jeep to a stop in front of
the bunker guarding the northern end of the bridge. At the
foot of the bridge, huddled on the edge of the river, is a
compound so small and compact that a thrown beer can could
easily traverse its length. Two twenty-foot planks span a
six-foot dry moat that separates the bunker from the compound. The compound is enclosed by a three-foot-high wall of
sandbags. Eleven above-ground bunkers extend inward off
the wall. A mortar pit and ammunition bunker have been

placed in the center of the remaining space, leaving enough room between the various sandbag structures for about forty people to stand or squat on the hard-packed earth.

After a few hours of getting acquainted with my new post and its people, it is apparent that someone has overlooked the possibility that the Americans and Vietnamese in this outpost might have a need to talk to one another. Not one of the six GIs speaks more than a few words of Vietnamese, and only one of the PFs, Le, is even slightly more proficient in English.

In the middle of an afternoon poker game, the buck sergeant in charge of the compound appears at the door of our hooch with his corporal in tow. We respectfully interrupt the game to give him our attention. His speech is short and crisp—loud enough to be easily heard at four times the distance separating us. When he leaves I ask Harris, "What was that all about?"

Harris shrugs. "How the hell should I know? Deal the cards."

At the northwest corner of the compound is a bunker higher than the others. Its flat top provides a view of the surrounding grass and brush for a quarter mile or more until interrupted by either hills or trees. In the center of the bunker roof a low sandbag wall has been built for a lookout position. A four-foot-square sheet of corrugated metal supported on two-by-four legs provides protection from the sun and rain. It is also a good place to catch the faint, late afternoon breeze and watch the evening procession of wives and children being brought into the protection of the compound for the night. .

Le, who occupies the adjacent bunker, is the only PF whose wife lives full time in this outpost. A year ago Le was transferred here from his home in a nearby village because there were no longer enough men in this hamlet to make up the two squads of PFs guarding the bridge. Six months ago he met a girl whose husband and family had been killed. He wanted a woman and the extra allotment he would receive for having a wife. She wanted food and a place to live.

Lan is a pretty girl of eighteen with clear skin and intelligent, smiling eyes. But best of all, she can carry on a conversation in halting English. Lan had the rare opportunity to spend two years in the Vietnamese equivalent of high school. Her haughty education is a sore point with Le, but unlike the PF sergeant, apparently too proud to seek the aid of a woman to interpret his words, Le does not hesitate to make use of her talent.

Over the past four days the lookout bunker has become an evening gathering spot. Some of the GIs come for the breeze, some for the view, some come to learn about the people and their language, and we all come to be close to Lan. Although our individual time in-country ranges from three to nine months, this is the first opportunity any of us has had to talk with a Vietnamese.

Eager for information, we pepper Lan with questions. She defers some of our questions to Le, answers others herself, or directs them to one of the PFs who occasionally stop by. The Vietnamese are very careful what they say about the Saigon government, but they are much more candid about the war. They do not understand what is going on any better than we do, and they have almost no feeling for the ideological differences between communism and democracy. In fact, they do not seem to deal with the problem on this level at all. Their concerns are for their family, their land, their hamlet. Forms of government do not seem to concern them. It is as if they are merely waiting for life to return to its proper order.

From Le we learn that a PF's salary is about half the pittance the ARVNs receive. He was drafted into the PFs three years ago. He was a private then, as now, and is likely to remain one until the end of the war when his service obligation is over. Despite his acquisition of an attractive, educated woman, Le is still a dissatisfied man. He wants more from life than to be an impoverished soldier waiting in this pile of sandbags for an early death.

Our transcultural communication requires a good deal of patient persistence, charades, sound effects, interpretations, and the drawing of pictures on the ground. But the common effort and the exchange of information has drawn us all closer together.

I look down at Lan squatting beside a small cooking fire, stirring a pot of rice that will soon be dinner for eight. Phil is on one knee beside her, adding a can of beef to the pot. They are chatting and joking with each other, trying to decide which of the other ration cans scattered about them will best enhance their culinary effort. I glance over at Le, wondering if Phil's interest in Lan is as obvious to him as it is to me. He is watching the preoccupied couple at their task by the fire, but his stoic face reveals nothing.

We finish dinner, watch the sun go down, and then retire to our hooch to smoke an evening joint and play some cards by candlelight. Two hours into the game Phil slips into the hooch glistening with sweat and excitement.

"Man, that was great. You wouldn't believe where I've just been."

"Okay, so where have you been to get yourself worked up into such a lather?"

"You guys have to promise not to tell anyone. She said if any of the Vietnamese found out she wouldn't do it anymore, so you got to promise."

"If it's such a big secret why are you telling us?"

"She said it was okay to tell you guys, but not anybody else."

"So we won't tell anybody else. Now, what the hell are you talking about?"

"I just screwed Lan. Man, is she fantastic. I think she liked it as much as I did."

"You're shitting me. You screwed Lan, Le's—"

"Shhh. Keep your voice down, for Christ's sake."

"All that blood running into your prick must have short-circuited your brain. Le is going to cancel your number when he finds out."

"No, he isn't. Le is the one who suggested it in the first place."

"You mean Le is pimping his own wife?"

"Well, I've been talking to them and I'm not sure they are married, but yeah, he is."

"I don't believe it. I flatass don't believe it, and I don't like it, either. It sounds like trouble to me."

"If you don't believe me, go over there with six bucks or a case of C rations and find out for yourself."

"You mean Lan will screw for a case of Cs?"

"Why not? Six dollars is twice the going rate for a 'short time' and a case of Cs is worth more than that on the black market."

"All right! That's like getting it for free. We must have almost thirty cases of Cs and more coming in every day."

"Wait a minute, you guys. I think we should cool this

thing, at least for tonight. You sure you understood Le right? His English ain't so good, ya know."

"I'm sure. They were both right there. There wasn't any doubt about it."

"Well, I still think we should cool it."

"Yeah, me too. This could get out of hand in a hurry."

"That's okay by me, but I'm telling you she is waiting over there for one of you guys to show up right now."

Phil's excitement infects us all with a mixture of curiosity and lust, but eventually we all agree to suppress our desires until we can appraise the situation in the harsh light of day.

At least I thought we had all agreed. As I settle in for the night on a sandbag roof, I see Art wander over to Le's bunker and disappear in the shadows. A little later I notice him leaving our hooch with a case of C rations in his hands. As Art and his gift reenter the darkness of Lan's doorway, Le emerges from the same darkness to sit in solitary vigil atop the lookout bunker.

So Phil's story is true, I muse, shifting my position, trying to find a more comfortable alignment of bumps and valleys on the gently sloping roof. Getting it on with Lan is a tantalizing idea, but to do it with her man fifteen feet away just doesn't fit with human nature. It's too much like a chaperoned love-in with the neighbor's daughter.

It has been a week now since the stockpile of C-ration cases began shifting from our hooch to Le's bunker. Lan's desire to veil her prostitution from the other Vietnamese in the camp has restricted her time of business to the one to two hours between the camp's bedtime and the time when Le's desire for sleep exceeds his desire for money—long enough for two customers.

Lan's second night in business brought her the same two eager lads as the night before. The third night brought her Sergeant Harris, and with him came change. Nightly he entered the dark folds of Lan's bunker and immersed himself in an orgy of physical delight that showed no signs of letting up. He dominated her time, and our food supply dwindled at an ever-increasing rate.

When Phil attempted to arrange for Lan's favors he found her willing, if she could find the time, and if he would meet the new price of fifteen dollars or two cases of C rations. Fifteen dollars was outrageous. He would not pay it and neither would the rest of us, but Lan stood her ground. She had all the customers she needed in the good sergeant. She and Le were making more than twice Le's monthly salary every night.

In a community where a man is separated from his neighbor by the width of a sandbag, it is impossible to keep anything secret long. Everyone knew what Lan was doing, who she was doing it with, and the current fee for getting it done. The Vietnamese were suffering, not so much from moral indignation, as from an acute sense of "they are getting rich and we are getting nothing."

We were grumbling because Harris was monopolizing the only woman available to us, as well as rapidly and recklessly spending our mutually held resources.

Even Le was becoming disenchanted with his business bonanza. With each passing day he seemed to become more withdrawn. He spoke to his countrymen only when necessary, treated his woman with disdain, and talked to us grudgingly. I think the pressure from his fellow PFs and a good dose of jealousy were the major contributing factors to his dour mood.

Another situation arose at this time that made the consequences of fooling around with Lan pale by comparison. A woman from the hamlet who took refuge in the compound at night began watching me. When I looked back at her, she smiled and turned away. She is an attractive girl about my age, tall by local standards, with the slightly darker skin of a Cambodian.

The watching and smiling continued for two days before I attempted to speak to her. An errand took her past my seat on the edge of the mortar pit. I greeted her in my best garbled Vietnamese. She stifled a giggle, produced yet another smile, stared at me a moment, said something incomprehensible, and walked on, leaving me mystified, frustrated, and intrigued.

I practiced my Vietnamese, worked up a few phrases, strung them together, and tried them out on her at the next opportunity. She seemed delighted by my efforts and delivered in return a somewhat lengthy address of her own. She must have assumed I knew much more of her language than I did, for although I caught a word here and there, the overall meaning of what she said completely escaped me. Again she left me in a state of confusion.

While sitting there trying to force some meaning from the echo of her words, I glanced up to meet the penetrating eyes of the PF corporal. He stood across the compound, arms folded across his chest, an undeniable scowl etched upon his weathered face. Before that moment I had not bothered to connect the girl with anyone else. There had only been me and her and my imagination. Now the corporal was in the picture—the corporal and the girl together—and I was outside the frame looking on.

The next evening the corporal came up to me and without preamble asked if I liked his woman. Neither his face nor his voice revealed any emotion. His question was so unexpected that my mind was still fumbling for an answer when he spoke again. Pointing at his wife he said, "Number one mama-san, yes?"

She glanced up at the gesture, then turned away. Was he baiting me or proposing a business deal? I remembered the look on his face the preceding night, visualized a man with a knife in the dark, and told him he had a good woman, all his, not for me. That night and for the next two nights he asked his question again and always I answered the same. The more he asked the more sure I was of the correctness of my answer. I avoided all further contact with his wife. After three days he asked no more and I began to hope the issue was forgotten.

I warned the other guys to stay away from the corporal's woman because, if I was reading him correctly, he was an unreasonably jealous man. To the best of my knowledge they heeded my advice and avoided the girl, so it came as a shock when a week later the corporal burst into our hooch with a hand grenade in each outstretched arm.

There were five of us in the hooch at the time. We took one glance at him and froze. He began to speak with the force of commitment, his voice a low-threatening menace rising slowly into an emotional fever that sent quivering spasms through his body. One of the tense forms beside me whispered, "What the fuck is he doing?"

There was no answer.

My mind focused on the danger in his voice, my eyes on the greater danger in his hands. "There aren't any pins in those grenades," I said in a slow, soft voice, not sure that the others heard me amid the torrent of Vietnamese. To my surprise his aggression was not directed solely at me—but at all of us.

While my ears struggled to understand the foreign words, my eyes scrutinized the hands, and my body tensed to move the instant the hands released the firing levers. Would there be time to remove the corporal from the doorway and find cover before the grenades exploded? I saw three choices. I could try to grab the hands enfolding the grenades to prevent the spoons from being released, then overpower the corporal and hope that if I missed and he released one of the grenades someone would be able to retrieve it and throw it clear in the inevitable rush for the door. Or I could knock him unconscious with a right to the jaw, run like hell, and pray the other guys could get out and behind cover in time. Or I could sit very still and hope he did not open his hands.

Suddenly I realized I could understand parts of his speech, not so much by recognition of the words as by a combination of what I knew of him and the overall meaning of his speech—it was not hard to guess his meaning. I interpreted, "He says if we take her away from him . . . touch her . . . he will kill us."

At the sound of my voice he stopped talking and stared at me, waiting. What could I say except that none of us would touch his woman? Over and over I repeated the promise, backed up by four other voices with uniform sincerity. His hands dropped to his sides. Silence smothered the tiny room. The corporal looked at each of us, then turned and walked away. A moment later two explosions reverberated from the river behind our hooch.

Phil snatched a rifle and slammed home a magazine. "I'm going to kill that son of a bitch."

We blocked his exit. A heated discussion erupted. In the end Sergeant Harris and Phil, loaded weapons in hand, set out to find the sergeant in charge of the PFs.

The ARVN lieutenant slows the jeep as we approach the entrance to Long Binh. An MP steps out of the guardhouse to wave us through without question. With the confidence born of familiarity, the lieutenant threads his way through the tanks, trucks, jeeps, and soldiers in constant motion over the miles of roads on the big sprawling base camp. At the main PX, I purchase three cases of beer for the boys back at the compound while Greg (who was sent out last week to replace

Sergeant Harris) gets a tape deck for the lieutenant with the money the lieutenant has given him.

Our next stop is a battalion mess where our escort chats amiably with four mess sergeants in the rear of the kitchen. Our ARVN supply officer gives one of the cooks a small parcel containing a white satin negligee for his girlfriend. A second cook is assured that his Montagnard crossbow will be delivered on our next visit. Greg and I look on in silence as the customary social pleasantries are satisfied before the E-7 in charge here announces he has been saving a special gift for his ARVN friends. Three cases of frozen steaks are brought from the freezer and proudly displayed before the lieutenant. The lieutenant is appropriately appreciative, assuring the sergeants that his colonel will be very pleased with the gift. I wonder if the Vietnamese, accustomed to a diet of rice flavored with small pieces of fish, chicken, or the occasional strip of pork, have any taste for the blatant hunk of flesh that is a steak? No matter, three cases of meat is a valuable gift regardless of taste.

The mess sergeants enthusiastically load the steaks, and various other crates and tins of food, into the trailer we are hauling behind our jeep. Securing a tarp over his bounty, the lieutenant thanks the sergeants for their generosity and drives to the next battalion mess to top off the load.

When I first encountered this exchange of trinkets for substantial quantities of food, I was concerned that the lieutenant might be involving me in a black market operation. However, I soon learned that if there was something shady about these food-gathering trips there was nothing secretive or conspiratorial about the way they were carried out. The ARVN first lieutenant was openly received by the mess sergeants and the officers of every battalion mess we visited. Furthermore, the food in the trailer was indeed delivered to the ARVN encampment down the road from our PF compound. I have no way of knowing what happened to the food after it reached the colonel, except for a six-man serving of tasty fried rice mixed with shrimp, ham, eggs, and greens brought to us after each trip.

I stopped worrying about my tacit complicity in corruption on the morning the lieutenant introduced me to an army captain who drove us to an officer's club to be introduced to his major. The major greeted us enthusiastically and ordered his captain to keep Greg and me supplied with beer while we waited outside the club for our adopted lieutenant.

After an hour we were returned to the mess where the last of the crates of food, tables, chairs, and other unidentifiable objects were being loaded into our trailer and a two-and-a-half-ton truck the lieutenant had brought along for this special trip. As we were preparing to leave, a five-gallon tub of ice cream, packed in dry ice, was handed to the lieutenant with the wish that his colonel have a pleasant birthday party.

Whatever the reason for the eagerness with which the colonel was bestowed with gifts, the openness of the giving and the major's involvement were enough of an official sanction for me. Maybe this giveaway was all done in the name of goodwill between allies, or maybe it was another drop in the ocean of corruption. I really did not care.

On our way out of the Long Binh gate I ask, "Lieutenant, why do you take us along on these trips? I mean, we don't do anything. We don't load the trailer or really talk to anyone. Occasionally I do a little interpreting when someone doesn't understand your brand of English, but mostly we just seem to be along for the ride."

"I find it most helpful to have American soldiers in jeep when I go onto American post," he answers. "Besides, you number one liaison man for me. I like you come with me every time." He looks at me with a faint smile. "Next time I have surprise for you. We go Saigon. I have very special girl for you. You like, yes?"

"Uh . . . sure. Sounds great. I'll look forward to it." That is another thing I do not understand. As a first lieutenant he makes less than thirty dollars a month, yet three times a week he takes two GIs from the PF compound on these supply trips and buys them beer, lunch, and women. This food must be making money for someone, and some of this money must be filtering its way back to the lieutenant, who in turn gives it to beer peddlers, shopkeepers, and clean whores. Why, we are a microeconomic system stimulating free enterprise through food grants from Uncle Sam. But that is all conjecture. I do not understand most of what goes on in this country, nor am I meant to. I am merely along for the ride, and right now this ride is heading for that sweet little whorehouse on the outskirts of Lai Khe.

I do not volunteer for these trips because of the free beer or the free food. I volunteer because of the jeep ride through the country, the sweat-drying wind, the view—and the free women. Yes, mostly for the free women.

The lieutenant turns off the side street and stops in front of a large iron gate set in a thick, twelve-foot-high concrete wall surrounding the forecourt of what was once a substantial building. A boy materializes to open the gate. The shell of the building and its brick courtyard now serve as a lowly parking lot secure from vandals and the vigilance of the MPs.

On the opposite side of the street a young girl admits us into a ten-by-fifty-foot concrete hallway. It is barren except for a table and four chairs standing against a wall. A middle-aged mama-san hurries from the far end of the hall to greet the lieutenant like an old and revered friend. Three bottles of ice-cold Vietnamese beer are automatically brought to the table as we are seated. In the corner an elderly woman sits on a bamboo mat with a baby at her side. Her hands and eyes are occupied with the sewing in her lap, her quiet voice drifting across the room in a constant flow of words directed at no one.

Two women enter the hall and squeal with delight as they recognize their visitors. They rush to sit in our laps, hugging and tickling us amid bursts of giggles and sultry crooning. At twenty-three and twenty-four these women are already developing the more matronly figures of older women, but their friendliness and enthusiasm compensate for their somewhat softer, fuller figures.

Unlike many of their professional sisters, these women are in no hurry to complete the business at hand. We sit at the table enjoying each other's company and the taste of the local beer. Although the women are equally attractive, Greg and I always end up with the same partner. It is not that I have any complaints with the lady on my lap, but it does seem as if they have chosen us rather than the other way around.

After a second beer the girls lead us out of the hall into an expansive walled garden gone half wild with inattention. We enter a bamboo hut built in a shady corner of the enclosure. The small room contains two double beds separated by six feet of floor space. Draperies hang across the side of each bed to provide visual privacy.

"You stay long time, make boo coo love," implores my partner as she unlaces my boots. While I work free of the rest of my clothes, she sheds her blouse and pants to reveal a slightly plump form with a skin like cream. "We love long, long time. Make fine baby for me," she continues, sliding her body over mine.

I find this desire by a near stranger to have my child a bit unsettling, yet it is difficult to deny any request made by a woman who is in the process of giving me such exquisite pleasure. Still, I cannot resist asking, "Why do you want my baby? You know I won't be here to help you take care of it."

"Baby not for you. Baby for me. I want you for papa-san."

I can't deny the possibility that she may become pregnant by one of our encounters. The idea both disturbs and intrigues me. I don't like the thought of leaving offspring scattered around without my knowledge and attention. On the other hand, if I stay in this country, having six or seven children and their mothers to visit periodically has a certain appeal . . . oh, that feels good. Perhaps this baby routine is just a standard come on and . . . oh my, I can't think about it now.

Our lovemaking ends far short of a long, long time, but my partner isn't annoyed. She informs me that we'll try again as soon as I have rested. Perhaps, perhaps not. I'll let the thought percolate awhile. I lie on my back in a languid haze while a cool, damp cloth bathes my skin from head to toe. Ah, this is the life.

The women's conversation floats with laughter across the room. They are comparing the sexuality of the bodies beneath their washcloths. They seem to be getting a great deal of enjoyment out of the exchange.

Greg's partner steps from behind their curtain to join her friend rinsing off in a pail of water. She catches me watching her and pirouettes her sweat-sheened body. "You like?" she asks with a taunting smile.

"Very nice," I answer, returning my guilty gaze back to the ceiling before jealousy is aroused.

My lady lays her freshly cleaned body next to mine, talking idly to me in a lazy, contented voice. She is a nice person, I decide: comfortable to be with, lighthearted, and full of fun. Her fingers make little circles on my thigh, her touch gentle and undemanding. Soon the feel of her and the soft voice rejuvenate my interest. Abruptly the voice stops, then laughs in satisfaction. She chats to her friend across the room as she titillates and gives pleasure. They are comparing notes again. Airy, singsong conversation and laughter accompany us through three changes of position. Returning to her original place on top of me, she suddenly kisses me, disengages herself, and bounds through the curtain. A second later the curtain parts again as Greg's girl jumps on my bed in a bubble of girlish giggles. I am joined with this new delight of feminine curves and soft, delectable nakedness with hardly a pause in motion.

So this is what the girls were brewing with all that chitchat. Judging by the mischievous grin beaming from the face of my new partner it would appear that I am not alone in finding pleasure in the change.

At the height of my excitement the women change partners once again, and swiftly bring the extravaganza to a climax. She is ecstatic—not, I fear, from orgasm but from triumph. "Ahheee!" she exclaims. "Make boo coo love. Make number one baby-san. Very happy."

I lie spent, smiling faintly back at her. There is no pretended love here, just recreational sex at its jolliest, a sharing of wholehearted lust. I have a tender feeling for this woman, and with it comes a feeling of sadness for I do not see much happiness in the future of these professional givers of pleasure. I pray she has no child of mine; I doubt that it will ever know me. Then again, which of us can wring a guarantee of satisfaction from the future?

Freshly cleaned and flowing in an aura of contentment, Greg and I reenter the hall to be met by the knowing smile of the patient lieutenant.

We head the jeep north on Highway 13. With a relaxed hold on the loaded M-16 leaning against my left knee, I settle back in the passenger's seat to enjoy the verdant country scenes rolling by. The spindly trunks of coconut palms precariously support their crown of fronds high above the lush tangle of lesser trees. Waist-high grass grows undisturbed from one tree line to the next; the big shiny leaves of banana trees cast their shade on village huts or around the border of the occasional family crop waiting in rows for the sun and water to bring them life. Men escape the afternoon heat in shadowy shops, relaxing over cups of tea or bowls of steaming vegetables.

It is peaceful, as if nothing here has ever felt the ravages of war. It is hard to believe part of this route is known as "thunder road" because of the frequency with which convoys are ambushed. Although it always makes me edgy to travel through country that is home to so many VC, we are relatively safe; our enemies are not likely to waste their precious mines and men on a single jeep. It is the certainty that they can destroy us whenever they choose that sustains my uneasiness.

We stop for a late lunch at a village cafe. A thatched-roof veranda shades a brick, wood-burning stove with a large steaming pot built into its top. Chopped greens are placed in a wire-mesh basket and lowered into the pot of hot broth where slices of pork are already brewing. The proprietor hurries to greet us with a polite bow. The dozen-odd customers lower their voices and look away from the three armed soldiers walking past them to a table where two of us can sit with our backs to the wall. The lieutenant orders beer and soup for three.

While we wait for our soup I ask the lieutenant if he was involved in the ARVN action that took place six hundred yards west of the PF compound yesterday afternoon. A firefight had taken place in our backyard and I was hoping the lieutenant could tell us what happened.

The ARVNs were from his unit, he answers, but he was not with them. These days he goes out in the field only when his colonel takes the entire unit on patrol. It was not always this way, he explains. He had fought with the Koreans and the Americans when he was an NCO. For two years he was attached to the U.S. forces fighting here and received a silver and two bronze stars for his efforts.

I had often wondered how an officer of apparent quality could reach his late forties without advancing beyond lieutenant. It appears that he made something of a hero of himself as a sergeant and has been rewarded with a commission and a cushy job. I suspected there was a proud core beneath his overt politeness and passivity.

"Yesterday," he continues, "we catch VC that mortar your compound. We kill two, wound three to take captive. Find many mortars and rifles."

"That is good news," I say. "Tell your men that we appreciate their work."

We had taken mortar fire from that location a week ago, but the fire was so poorly aimed that the only thing that really worried us was the reaction of the PFs. With the notable exception of Mouc, their machine gunner, the first whistle of an incoming round sent every PF scurrying for

40 mm. M-79 Grenade Launcher

his bunker where he stayed long after the last explosion erupted one hundred feet north of our enclosure. At first Mouc ran for his bunker with the rest, leaving six GIs looking at deserted positions in disgust. Not even their bellicose sergeant had the courage to show his face. We were trying to figure out how we were going to bring fire to bear on a mortar position beyond the range of our M-79 grenade launcher when Mouc returned with his gun. Unfortunately, rifle fire was no help to us either as the enemy mortar crew was firing from a hole.

What we needed was a mortar tube of our own.

Mouc does not understand a word of English, but when I pointed to the mortar pit in the center of the compound and then simulated a round arcing skyward from the pit, he quickly grasped my meaning. He ran to his corporal's bunker to retrieve an old 60-millimeter mortar and a crate of shells. Art, who is a member of his company's mortar section, took charge of the mortar while Mouc went back to look for the stand that holds the tube and contains the adjustment for windage and elevation. Art examined the inside of the tube by the feeble light of his Zippo. After peering down the bore for some time he stood up and threw the tube in the dirt.

"That thing hasn't been cleaned or oiled for months, maybe years. It's so damn rusty it's more likely to explode than launch a round."

A shell exploded two hundred feet short of our position. Mouc returned with the base plate, indicating that he was unable to find the other missing parts. For a moment he stood there while Art raved about the PF's cowardice and incompetence, then Mouc picked up the mortar tube, knocked the dirt out on the base plate, fitted the tube to the plate, and indicated he would support and aim the tube with his hands while one of us dropped in a round. Art would not have it. He stuck his finger down the mouth of the tube and displayed his dirty finger for Mouc while pantomiming an exploding tube. Mouc was unconvinced, but the rest of us decided that since it was extremely unlikely that we could hit our target, there was not much point in risking death in an attempt to launch a round.

All this time Murphy was trying to raise his company on the radio. It was vital that we launch some kind of retaliation, otherwise Charlie could take all the time he needed to zero in on our position. A single round landing inside our cracker-box compound would do considerable damage.

A shell exploded, closer this time, but still short and a little to the south.

Murphy's company RTO kept telling us to "wait one." Maybe he thought we were just calling in our nightly status report, or maybe he was occupied with more urgent calls. We switched over to the frequency used by one of their patrols on ambush. Turning up the gain we heard a whispering voice say that a VC patrol was entering their ambush zone. We waited a few seconds, then switched back to our frequency and demanded that someone from the mortar unit get on the line. There had to be more than one person in the HQ bunker.

"Roger, wait one," came the reply.

If we did not receive assurances of mortar support within the next minute we would have no option but to go after the enemy ourselves. Murphy and Art would stay behind to operate the radio and direct the company's fire—if and when it came.

This left the four of us hurriedly putting on boots and

collecting the necessary gear in preparation for the crawl through the grass outside the wire. We had to get close enough to be sure of a total kill. I did not want any VC coming after me out there. They knew this ground—its holes and tunnels and trails—we did not.

Our minute had passed.

The second man in our patrol was crossing the plank spanning the moat when an explosion erupted 100 feet north of the compound. They had our range, now all they needed to do was adjust 120 feet to the right. I was glad I was leaving. As I pushed myself off my belly to move on, I glanced back to see Mouc standing alone behind his machine gun—one brave man out of twenty-four.

We had decided to swim the river rather than expose ourselves while crossing the bridge. The four of us were good enough swimmers to make the crossing despite the weight of our arms. What worried us were the PF bunkers on either side of the bridge. The men in those bunkers did not know our plans and would probably fire on us if they saw or heard any movement below. We could not go further upstream because it was mined, and detouring around the bend downstream would take too long.

I quietly slipped into the river, trusting that the PFs were too scared to venture looking through their firing slits. As the water reached my chest a mortar round exploded several hundred meters away, too far away for even the ineffective VC mortar crew. I stopped where I was, feeling some safety in the protective waters. If the last mortar was one of ours, a closely grouped volley would soon follow.

Greg was frozen in a crouch at the river's edge. The head of our third man was just visible at the top of the bunk, with the fourth man still out of sight in the grass. We waited for the explosions that would relieve us of the dreaded task of going after Charlie in the dark.

Finally they came—five explosions followed by five more, followed by a silence that stretched on and on. With a cautious eye on the bridge bunkers, we returned to our hooch to work out which half-empty beer belonged to whom.

Three bowls of soup are placed on the table before us. As I pick the porcelain spoon up, the Army's vivid description of the long list of pains we would endure if we ate the local food passes through my mind. Carefully stirring the steamy brew I wonder what bacterial mayhem waits in these greens, what amoebas lurk in the yonder broth, what slender nematodes lie in wait among the cells of previous pig.

The lieutenant notices my hesitation. "Good soup here," he assures me.

What the hell, I'll probably get shot long before these microbeasties bring me down. I dip up a portion of broth. Could it have been poisoned? I glance over at Greg. but he's still gazing into his soup as if expecting a revelation—or a worm. I swallow.

"Mmm, very tasty," I offer encouragingly. No point in dying alone.

Greg gives off a rude sigh before digging in with the enthusiasm of a man going to visit his girl's parents for the first time.

"Not bad," he admits.

Once past the first spoonful, I finish the meal with relish on the theory that one swallow is enough to do me in so the rest is superfluous. I accept a second bowl under the protection of the same theory.

After lunch the lieutenant drives us and our three cases of beer back to the compound. There are still three hours of daylight to fritter away before the drinking, smoking, card-playing evening can begin.

I'm restless. I feel like going for a walk, but of course that's out of the question. The road isn't safe. The hamlet isn't safe. We don't venture beyond our island of sandbags except to go for a swim. That's what I'll do, go for a dip in the river. Swimming is our only form of exercise and I enjoy the feel of the cool, flowing water. Unlike the warm, murky, leech-ridden water of lower elevations, the river here is clear and the current is strong enough to keep the water free of leeches.

Greg and I stash our shorts in the iron framework of the bridge and dive into the river. The water wraps me in a cocoon of silence as I slide through its weightless world. The momentum of the dive gradually erodes until my speed over the bottom matches that of the river. Slowly rising through the sun-filtered water, I bob to the surface to begin a hard, steady crawl against the current.

I swim on and on, keeping pace with the mainstream. The bush with the broken limb continues to appear directly opposite me on the bank. When I begin to tire I will swim back to the bridge in the calmer water along the shore.

After a while I notice Greg drifting close to the bank, doing a relaxed breaststroke to slow his downstream movement. We never swim above the bridge because of the barbed wire and mines implanted there to protect the compound, and we never allow ourselves to be swept around the bend one hundred meters below the bridge where we would be beyond the sight of help. It would be interesting, though, to see what is around the corner. I roll on my back to study the sharp southernly curve in the river below. There might be a nice little beach on the inside of that curve. . . .

A bullet spits into the water behind me at the same moment the crack of a carbine retorts from the southern riverbank upstream. I dive for the bottom, not daring to look back at the gunman. Nine feet down, the water presses in like a premature grave. Twenty feet ahead, Greg's shadowy form expands and contracts in slow motion as he frog-kicks for the protection of the bend.

Two bullets enter the water three feet to my left front. I veer to the right, hoping the feeble breath I took before going under will last until I round the sweeping curve somewhere ahead.

Damn! I'm not going to make it. I need air! Pushing out the last strokes, I allow myself to float toward the surface, the back of my neck tingling at the thought of taking a bullet at the base of my skull.

A thin ray of bubbles streaks through the water directly before me. I freeze in midstroke, mesmerized by the stream of bubbles rapidly decelerating in speed until I can see the movement of their leading edge. The delicate, shimmering bubbles rise in wavering lines to the surface where I cannot go.

Lungs screaming for air penetrate my clotted mind. A gravel bar passes beneath me. Praying I am around the bend, I expel all the air in my lungs while taking three desperate strokes up and toward the shore.

I burst to the surface, mouth gasping for air, eyes straining to see through the water streaming down my face. A quick 360-degree scan tells me I am fifteen feet beyond the bend. No one waits for us on the shore with a gun in his hands. Greg lies in the shallows ten feet away, his head erect, gulping air while his saucer eyes dart over the grass and bush upstream—a mirror image of myself. I start laughing, uncontrollably.

Startled by the sound, his head snaps towards me, his attention riveted. Slowly the tension melts from his face, then a smile appears. A second later he, too, is laughing. Seeing his reaction makes me laugh all the harder because he is laughing at the same joke I am—only there's no joke.

"What the hell are you laughing at?" he asks in a strained whisper. "Someone's trying to kill us."

"I know, I know," I croak, desperately trying to get the ridiculous laughter under control.

"Have you lost your fucking mind? We've got to get out of here. That guy could be coming down this bank any second."

"I know. Calm down." My mind is perfectly clear despite the aberrant sounds issuing from my chest.

Rising from the water we run in a crouch across the pebbled beach to the shelter of a palm tree. The physical action combines with a massive dose of willpower to reduce my laughter to a silent chuckle.

In exasperation Greg whispers, "Will you straighten up?"

"I'm trying, I'm trying."

To our front, a stand of palm trees extends for a hundred meters before being interrupted by the first of the irregularly spaced huts of the hamlet. The ground beneath the trees has been pecked clean of vegetation by the local chickens. There is not a soul in sight; no one to be seen in the foliage along the river, no one in the hamlet.

"This is getting to be a recurring nightmare, you know what I mean? No, of course you don't. People keep shooting at me when I don't have any way to defend myself."

"Can we talk about this later?"

"Talk about defenseless. Look at us. Stark-ass naked, hiding behind a damn tree trunk that's skinnier than we are, waiting for some stranger to put a bullet in us. It's crazy, man. This whole fucking thing is crazy."

"Yeah, yeah, it's crazy, all right. Now would you please shut up before you get us killed?"

"Okay, sure. You're right. But listen, how are we going to get back to the compound? We're going to have to go right by the spot where that dude was shooting from."

"I don't know, but I know we have to move. Let's go."

"Great plan, Greg. Just great." But he's already behind

the next palm. I realize I can't rely on him for a plan. He is moving because that's what his instinct is telling him to do. I'm the planner. I can always dream up a plan or two. Why can't I think of one now? Maybe it's because I never imagined I'd be running around naked in a combat area. It's just not the kind of thing that ever came up before.

With nerves jangling we slip silently through the palm grove. Easing through a scattering of chickens, we reach the back wall of a hut without raising a squawk of alarm. I scan our surroundings again for signs of the enemy or a hint of what to do next. Nothing is revealed. I arch my eyebrows at Greg—now what? He shrugs his shoulders in reply.

Without really thinking about it, I decide to go through the hut instead of around it—some vague feeling about being less visible. I step through the doorway.

An old man works with strips of bamboo in his lap. An old woman bends over an infant on the bed. A young woman with her back to me attends to some chore on the hard-packed dirt floor while talking to a child of three or four at her side.

Greg and I are well inside the hut before our presence is detected by the child. Staring fixedly at me, he reaches out blindly with his left hand to tug at his mother's clothing. The three adult Vietnamese turn in unison to gape at the nude Americans who have inexplicably appeared in their home. For two long seconds the silence and immobility is complete. Cautiously moving my left index finger to my lips, I signal for continued silence, hoping to waylay any latent urges to laugh or scream. They remain transfixed.

I cross the room to scrutinize the area to the front of the hut, confident our hosts will remain motionless. Few civilians have had more experience with nervous soldiers. They know that their best interests will be served by doing nothing until we are gone. There is no one to be seen outside. It seems unnatural, but then I have never been here before. Maybe they are keeping a low profile because of the rifle shots.

I signal for Greg to follow and run for the sidewall of the next hut. Silently agreeing to avoid making any further obscene house calls, we race for the next hut at the edge of the road. Breaking the silence for the first time, I ask, "So what do we do now? Streak down the road for the bridge?"

"What else?"

"I don't like it."

"We have a choice?"

"Several, but they would take hours with no guarantee of being any safer."

"Well, this is it then. You ready?"

Hunched over, we run for the road, turn north on the oiled surface, and straighten into a full sprint. With arms pumping, privates swinging, and white bums flashing in the sun, I am fully aware of the spectacle we are presenting to the locals—hardly the image of the cool, sophisticated warrior. I would laugh myself, if I could spare the air, if the man trying to kill us would evaporate.

The bridge appears in my jarring vision. We break from our straight-line course into a zigzag, cross the bridge, fly over the moat, and land panting in the sanctuary of our sandbag home.

Now in possession of boots, pants, rifles, and a hate born of fear, Greg and I begin to question everyone we can lay our hands on. Who fired those shots? Why didn't anyone come to our aid, or at least investigate the reason for a rifle being fired within a hundred yards of the compound?

Now that I have time to think, I begin to piece the incident together. The rifle was a carbine, a weapon of last choice to the guerrilla, but one common to the PFs. The shots were fired from an area near the bridge, an area between the compound and the hamlet. It would be the most risky position possible for a VC to choose. The only escape routes were to sneak through the hamlet, swim the river, or cross the road next to the compound. I think it unlikely that our assailant was a VC. Why would Charlie risk coming into our midst in broad daylight to shoot haphazardly at two swimmers?

Incredibly, all the people we questioned either did not hear the gunfire or did not think anything about it. No one has the slightest idea who the shooter might have been, and since the only damage was to our nerves, no one but Greg and I is more than mildly concerned over such a common situation as a near miss.

Still, I have a hunch. I believe that the man we are looking for is none other than our own PF corporal. A man who previously threatened us with hand grenades, a man who could quickly take refuge in his hut in the hamlet, a man who, along with his rifle, is not now in the compound.

Nevertheless, it could have been a VC with friends in

the hamlet to hide him. That possibility will keep the corporal alive—at least for the time being.

Today we are picking up a load of food from a battalion mess in Di An. The ARVN lieutenant presents the mess sergeant with a flimsy stone-bladed hatchet. The sergeant in his turn places four hundred pounds of food in our trailer. The exchange strikes me as an appropriate reversal of the powerful, sophisticated invaders bartering the socks off the ignorant natives. The transaction is smooth and simple; everyone is satisfied.

At my request we make our next stop at my battalion headquarters. My friend, the clerk, tells me my request for transfer has been approved by the company and the battalion and is currently on hold at division. I ask for his estimation of the chances of the Form 1049 passing division. The answer comes back: fair to poor. The ugly prospect of returning to Delta Company looms before me once again.

All this past week the lieutenant has been encouraging me to let him talk to my first sergeant about extending my tour with the PFs. The lieutenant knows in a few days I will have been at the compound a month and am therefore due for reassignment. Up until now I have been putting him off, hoping my transfer would come through. Now I give him my consent, even though I do not believe a mere ARVN first lieutenant will have much influence with the demigod who is Echo Company's first sergeant. Still, I have underestimated the unassuming lieutenant before. Since I feel certain my current duty is the high point of my army life, I would gladly welcome an indefinite extension of same.

While the lieutenant dispatches his self-imposed diplomatic duty in the orderly room, I go in search of a clean set of clothes and my first shower in over three weeks. The water from the wing tank splashes cold on my head and shoulders, offering temporary relief from life in a tropical steam bath. Toweling off, I study the shadow of my former self. Few of the thirty-five pounds I lost humping the bush with Delta Company have been regained. If the part of me that vanished somewhere in the jungle was fat I would not mind its absence. But I have never been fat, and to lose all that hard-gained muscle and revert to the skinny kid of middle high-school years is disheartening.

I wonder if Julie would recognize me? Oh, I am sure she

would recognize the thinner version of my outward form, but what about the rest of me? My God! She still thinks the guy she said good-bye to is going to come back and marry her. I cannot marry anyone. It is out of the question. How can I deal with the emotional quagmire of a woman, the easy tears over little things, the constant need to be reassured of the depth of my love? How can I share her concern for style, the shape and tint of her hair, the pains taken with makeup? How can I participate in the frantic drive for acceptance and success that will be expected of me?

Something has happened here to love, to tender emotions. They have been disallowed, invalidated by violent death. I still cherish kindness, and I can risk my life to try to save someone else's, but because I must always be prepared for their screams of terror when they see their own shredded flesh, I cannot love or even care beyond the commitment to casual friendship. Although I know an emotional block is essential to the maintenance of my sanity, I did not ask for it, or bring it on myself willingly. It came on its own and I do not know when or if it will go away.

No, there will be no wedding, for I cannot take care of another's emotions or offer them mine. Poor Julie, patiently waiting for me to come back and take her to the altar. It is not going to happen. I must tell her to stop waiting. Yes, I must tell her, and soon.

The first sergeant and the lieutenant sit on folding chairs outside the NCO barracks talking quietly. Their conversation appears amiable. I did not know the first sergeant had any amiability in him. He looks different, too. Ah, yes. It is because I have never seen him outside before.

As I approach the sergeant looks up, squinting against the sun. "Are you Shook?"

"Yes, Sergeant."

"First sergeant," he snaps.

"Yes, First Sergeant." Let's not piss the man off.

"The lieutenant here has been telling me good things about you. He has asked me to extend your stay with the Popular Forces so that you can continue to work with him. Is this agreeable with you?"

"I would be glad to be of whatever service I can to the lieutenant, First Sergeant."

"Good, then it's settled." The sergeant studies the creases on the back of his black hands for a moment before continuing. "We are going to be pulling out of that location soon, anyway." Then to the lieutenant, "You have probably heard about the NVA buildup along the major infiltration routes in Cambodia."

The lieutenant nods his head in affirmation.

"Our company has been asked to send three FO units up there, so I can't promise your man here will be with you much longer."

Cambodia! Shit! I don't want to go to Cambodia. I'm stationed too damn close to that place already and don't want to get an inch closer.

Instead of pleading with the first sergeant that I am far too valuable a person to use as a border spook the way I would like him to, my buddy the lieutenant takes the news gracefully, thanking the sergeant for his cooperation and understanding.

Well, shit! Bad news always seems to dribble out of someone's mouth just in time to cancel the good news.

Forty-five minutes later we are in Saigon looking up at the lieutenant's three-story concrete house with its small shuttered windows facing the street. Inside there are high ceilings, white walls, tiled floors, and sparse furnishings. I am seated at the end of a long table in the dining room while the lieutenant gathers his family together for lunch. I wait quietly in the cleanliness and perfect order of the lieutenant's home, thinking how much more at ease I would be if we could have this meal served to us outside in the dirt.

Descending from above, a procession of children come to sit and stare at the foreigner in their home. I am introduced to six boys, three girls, and one wife. For a moment I wonder why the majority of this troop is not in school, being of that age, until I realize today must be a Saturday or Sunday. Lunch is quiet, reserved, and uncomfortable. Afterward, the family vanishes as quickly as they appeared.

Ten minutes later the lieutenant and I are drinking beer in the neighborhood whorehouse, waiting for my special treat to arrive. The lieutenant seems to be looking forward to her appearance as much as I am. I hope his taste in women is similar to mine.

A beer and a half pass before a spry girl dressed in a traditional ao-dais hurries through the double-doored entrance and sets an unwavering course for the rear of the building. The lieutenant nudges me, nodding his head at the receding figure. "That's her," he says with excitement in his eyes. I failed to get a good enough look at her to get excited myself, but I make the expected sounds of appreciation nonetheless.

A young boy leads me down a long hall with evenly spaced louvered doors along its left side. He ushers me into a small room containing the inevitable bed and a wicker chair. The screened and shuttered windows in the far wall open onto a narrow courtyard that extends the length of the row of bedrooms. Everything is clean and bright. I sit on the edge of the bed to wait.

The door is flung open to admit my gift, now wrapped in a robe of silk.

"Why you not undressed?" she demands, walking past me to drop her robe on the chair and flop naked on the bed.

Because sitting alone in a strange place without my clothes on makes me feel uncomfortably vulnerable, is my unspoken answer.

She lies on her back, legs together, arms at her sides, eyes on the ceiling—ignoring me. She is young, about sixteen, which is considered the prime age for women in this country. And she is prime. Her face and body are the perfection of dreams.

With yet a button to be loosened, I study the frozen form on the bed, so like a stunning painting in which the artist has fumbled his attempt to create the warmth of life. But there is more here than stoic detachment. Hate, or deep resentment, exudes from this classic oriental nude.

Hoping to break through the icy chill I ask, "Well, my distant beauty, how are you today?"

She shifts her gaze from the ceiling to my face and then back to the ceiling. "Hurry up, Joe, you wasting time."

Enough. Aloof loathing is not the tune of titillation. I stand to leave, then pause for a last look at the resplendent form below me. What a pity the mind and the body do not match. Her head turns on the pillow to look at me.

"What's the matter, Joe? You no like me? You want another girl?"

"No," I answer.

Addressing the ceiling she says, "Make up your mind."

She must hate being a whore, or perhaps she hates GIs, or perhaps she is so well insulated in her beauty that she has never been prompted to consider that there is more to being a prostitute than lying on her back. Should I offer her some kind of explanation, or just walk out? Oh, damn. What am I going to tell my friend out there with the gleam of anticipation in his eyes? What about the time, money, and effort he has put into this meeting? Walking out will be an insult to his sense of taste—a loss of face. Maybe I could persuade this girl to continue her imitation of a fresh corpse for fifteen or twenty minutes longer. That is a reasonable solution for everyone involved, but it will not work. As soon as I tell this teen queen that I no longer wish to rent her luscious body, her pride will require her to flounce out of the room in a huff—again a matter of face. Besides, Vietnamese women are notorious gossips. If I am right in suspecting that this is one of the lieutenant's regular haunts, then he will eventually discover the subterfuge.

Is there no easy way out of this? With sarcasm instead of hope, I ask, "I don't suppose there is any chance you could fake a little enthusiasm?"

"What you say?"

"Enthusiasm. Never mind. Something you know nothing about." What the hell. You go to a whore, you can't expect to be loved. I undress with serious doubts about my ability to properly conclude this transaction. Even if I am so blessed, I am willing to bet a month in Nam that she doesn't move a muscle in response.

Afterward a flush of embarrassment comes over me as I walk back to the table where the lieutenant and a girl are talking. I feel like I just masturbated in public. Although I finally did manage to fantasize my way into a whimper of a climax, she not only lay motionless but turned her head to the side and stared at the wall. Made me feel like a mating slug. It was awful. Probably put me off sex for at least a week, not to mention the possible permanent psychological damage done to my libido.

A single concrete beam begins to span the river in a graceful arch before abruptly ending in midair twenty feet beyond its foundation on the riverbank. The fractured beam is all that remains of the bridge the French erected here years before. The severed arch gives you the feeling that it is a not-so-ancient ruin, hinting at a millennium of strife. Certainly hundreds, if not thousands, of men have died here in their struggle to defend or capture this crossing. Perhaps if I knew its history back to the Chinese invasions of the third

century A.D., I could glean a sense of honor from its defense—
or perhaps of the futility of wasted lives.

Propping a helmet full of river water against the base of
the arch I lather my whiskers in the reflection of a new metal
hand mirror. I was in the PX buying some stationery to
replace the C-ration box tops I had been using as makeshift
postcards when I came across the durable mirror. Having no
need to look at my face to locate it for shaving, the only
excuse I had for making the purchase was a bit of vanity
regarding my first-ever mustache.

An appraisal of the upper lip hair leaves me undecided
as to whether the new growth is an improvement or not. Of
course, it is difficult to make a clear comparison since the
before-mustache view is not available. But there is a simple
solution to this problem—I'll shave half of it off.

Hum, I still can't decide. Looks like a toss-up to me. I'll
leave it half and half awhile, maybe get a second opinion. I
rinse out my helmet and walk up the bank to the compound.
Holy shit—a major. What the hell is he doing way out here?
Up until this moment the Army has left us blissfully alone. As
I approach the group of men gathered outside our hooch, the
sound of years of military wisdom whiffs through the vaporous air.

". . . and clean up this mess." A pointing finger con-
demns a dozen empty cans in our trash box. "I won't have
flies and rats spreading disease because you men are too lazy
to bury your garbage."

"We bury it every evening, sir."

"What's that?"

"We'll take care of it right away, sir."

"You bet your ass you will."

If he finds the beer and dope stashed away none too
carefully in our hooch we are all going to get busted. Considering my olive-drab, boxer-shorts uniform, and my half-and-
half mustache, I feel this is definitely the time for a tactical
retreat. I think I'll just ease back down the bank and jump in
the river. Drat, too late. His lieutenant has spotted me.

With a final visual sweep of the area, the two officers
start back toward their jeep and driver waiting at the side of
the road. I square up perpendicular to their line of travel,
hairy side outermost.

"Morning, sirs." I give them a smart salute even though

such an act is frowned upon by field officers—might get them shot by an observant VC.

The major glowers at my tan skin and green skivvies. "Why in blazes are all you men out of uniform? Being in the boondocks doesn't excuse this kind of sloppiness. You're still in the United States Army and I expect you to look like soldiers."

"Yes, sir," I say as he moves around to my nonmustache side.

"Those men couldn't even tell me who was in charge here. Perhaps you can enlighten me?"

He's got me there. We have never bothered to figure out who has the most time in grade. We have been running a democracy here, but I can't tell him that. "That would be the senior specialist fourth class, sir."

"Since you men are functioning without the benefit of an NCO, your statement is blatantly obvious. What I want to know is the name of the man in charge."

Benefit of an NCO? Not likely. But I'd better steer clear of that topic. "Frankly, sir, I don't know who is in charge, but I don't think it's me."

"You don't think so? What is your rank?"

"Probably a PFC, sir."

"Probably? Are you trying to tell me you don't know your own rank? What company are you from?"

"You're not going to like this, sir, but I'm not sure of that either."

"This is outrageous. Explain yourself."

"Well, sir, I was in Delta Company—not your Delta Company, sir, the other battalion's Delta Company—then I was transferred to Echo Company, but it turns out that I may still be assigned to Delta Company, unless that has been changed, and of course by now I could have been reassigned to the Long Binh Medical Center, but the last I heard division HQ hasn't decided on that one yet." Why am I doing this? Well, no sense stopping halfway. "So you see, sir, if I am with Delta Company I am an acting corporal, if I am with Echo Company I am a PFC, but if I am with the LBHC I am automatically a Spec 4. Honest, sir, it's not my fault."

Silence fills the space between us. Maybe he thinks I'm crazy. That would help. I wonder why he hasn't mentioned my mustache. Surely he's noticed it. I'm still standing at attention with my eyes straight ahead so I can't see his face, thank heavens. Nothing's happening. There, he's moving. His lieutenant passes in front of me. They're leaving.

When I ask the guys how much trouble we are in, they assure me the only items that concerned the major were the ration cans and our lack of military attire. They had spotted the officers soon enough to put our hooch in respectable order.

"Did he say anything about the local VC population or the PF's refusal to fight?" I ask.

"Ah, he didn't say anything about that stuff."

"No, and he didn't want to hear nothing from us, either."

"Maybe we'd better make another report on that squad of VC that passes by here every evening before some rank finds out about them and begins to wonder what we have been doing out here," I suggest.

"No way, man. You want to start a war, go someplace else and start it. If we hit those VC, they'll get their buddies and come back here and wipe us off the map. The only reason they haven't turned us into a greasy spot so far is that we haven't hassled them. We have our own little island of peace here, let's keep it that way."

"I agree, but things have changed. If I read your major correctly, he is going to send us a sergeant to make sure we keep our shirts on. If the guy they send is even half awake he is going to wonder why we have VC walking by here in plain view. We can report them tonight after they have disappeared into the brush on the outskirts of the hamlet. That way it will be too late for your company to blast the neighborhood into a pile of rubble and we will have covered ourselves. What do you think?"

"Makes sense to me."

"Okay, as long as we keep Sergeant Bolinski from lofting any mortars in our direction. That fool doesn't know a windage from an elevation."

At dusk our local contingent of VC appear right on schedule, as they have every night for the past two weeks. They come from the northwest, pass six hundred yards south of us, and vanish in the darkness as they approach the area at the far end of our hamlet. At first they were cautious; now they make no attempt to conceal their movements. For a half mile of their track they are in plain view, walking single file down the same path they always take.

Tonight there are nine of them. Sometimes there are

one or two less, sometimes a few more. We report their movement to Bravo Company's NDP as we did once before, and as before, since there is no immediately available target, the matter is dropped.

Having done our duty, we tune in the armed forces FM station on our civilian radio and lay back to enjoy a quiet evening with the Bee Gees singing, "I just got to get a message to you," in the background.

At 2200 we call in our status report and prepare to turn in when one of the guys from Bravo Company picks up a transmission between his captain and a lieutenant who has just blo⸝n his ambush at a half dozen passing VC.

Captain: "Tiger Delta, this is Papa Tiger. What is your estimated enemy kill? Over."

Lieutenant: "Enemy kill—zero. I told you, they were too far away."

Captain: "You missed all of them?"

Lieutenant: "We have probably hit on one, possibly two. All escaped into the tree line."

Captain: "Damn it, Lieutenant. I want those Victor Charlies. Go after them. And don't come back empty-handed."

Lieutenant: "Go after them, sir? Now? In the dark?"

Captain: "Affirmative, Tiger Delta. Right now. Dispatch a squad and make it clear that you want results."

Lieutenant: "Sir, if we go crashing through the jungle after Charlie the only bodies we are going to find will be our own."

Captain: "I am not interested in your opinion, Lieutenant. You will do as you are told. Pursue and eliminate the enemy, immediately. Those are your orders."

"Will you listen to that shit?" I say. "Nobody in his right mind goes trudging after Charlie in the dark. The only way that squad is going to find Charlie now is by walking into his fire."

"That's our captain for you. No duty is too perilous for his men, no duty safe enough for himself. You know that man hasn't been seen outside his bunker in more than three weeks. He's been hiding out ever since one of the boys took a shot at him during our last company-sized operation. The damn fool got so excited at the sight of our exalted leader out in the bush that he blew the only good shot any of us are likely to get for a while."

"You see, Old Captain Fearless can't decide if he is more

frightened of the VC, his own men, or being passed over again for advancement. If he could just get promoted it would solve all his problems. He would never have to go into the field again except to fly high overhead in his helicopter. Then he could concentrate on killing off his other two enemies in safety."

"It sounds like your captain is going to grow up to be just like a major I know."

"I'd like to think that our brand of leader is unique, but I have heard enough stories from other units to know better." Turner pauses to shake his head and contemplate the mess. "You know, Old Fearless has been with us four months now and as long as I've known him he has walked at the very end of the company, surrounded by four of his most trusted cadre, pushing us into one dangerously stupid situation after another."

"It was a good company before Fearless got his greedy mitts on it. The sad fact is that, despite all his gung-ho chasing after Charlie, we are now killing fewer Cong while our own casualities have almost doubled. That is why some of the guys are determined to frag the bastard before it's too late. Most of the company, including myself, are too chicken-shit to actually kill the turd, but we'd swear on a stack of bibles that Charlie Cong committed the act once the deed was done."

"Still, it's not all bad. We have a couple of officers who know their stuff. Like Lieutenant Carlson, who you just heard on the radio. I'm willing to bet he doesn't send anyone after those gooks."

"How can he do that?" I ask. "He has been given a direct order to pursue."

"Easy. He can send some men out to sit behind a tree for an hour, then tell Fearless their search was unsuccessful. Or better yet, report that they found two bodies for the CO to add to his tally. That will keep everyone happy as long as Fearless is smart enough not to demand proof."

Ten minutes after their last transmission the captain calls the lieutenant for a report. The lieutenant replies that his men are just about ready to set out. The captain is furious at the delay, aware that now he has lost all hope of catching the VC. Nevertheless, he orders the men to set out at once and stay out until they have found what they were sent to find.

We decide not to stay up to listen for further developments.

In the morning, orders come over the radio to prepare to abandon the compound. Transportation is scheduled to pick us up in the early afternoon. The Army has apparently advanced its timetable for our redeployment.

The news is disappointing. We were hoping to enjoy another week or two one step removed from the mutilating grasp of our superiors. While packing our gear we start a list of the goods stolen from us during the past three weeks. When we are finished the total comes to 280 dollars plus thirteen miscellaneous items of varying worth. No wonder the PFs are always smiling at us. Despite their thievery, their apparent sympathies with the VC, and their unwillingness to aid in their defense, we hold very little animosity toward the PFs. Most of them are pacificists doing their best to live through yet another struggle for power in their country. Everything considered, I can find little fault in their behavior.

We give Mouc a case of C rations and split two of the remaining three cases among the rest of the Vietnamese enlisted men. We have been well supplied with M-16 ammo, and with nothing else to fill the day, we decide to reduce the weight of one of the boxes.

With two beer cans thrown in the river eighty meters upstream, we begin a contest to see who can keep their can in the air the greatest proportion of time. I am surprised at the accuracy displayed by five out of the six of us. Putting a round through a can in the water sends it leaping into the air. The instant it lands back in the river another round pushes the can into the water, which reacts to propel it skyward again.

The gunfire disturbs the locals, but it makes us feel a little better, even though we know this display of marksmanship is of little merit in a conflict where we rarely see our enemy.

Shortly after lunch Sergeant Harris brings his jeep to a stop at the edge of the road. He shakes his head knowingly at the group of men laden with boxes coming to greet him.

"Belay that, gentlemen. You're not going anywhere." Ignoring our questions he languidly unbends his large frame from around the steering wheel and leans into the back of the jeep to retrieve a case of Budweiser. "Grab that block of ice, will you?" he asks the man nearest him. "The rest of you might as well cart them C rations in."

Settled on a canvas cot outside our hooch, we wait for Harris to work himself around to telling us the news. He methodically rolls a can of beer on the ice, which melts a depression into the block and supplies a film of ice water that clings to the outer surface of the spinning can.

"Looks like you boys are going to be here awhile yet."

"How long do you figure a while is going to be?"

"There is little profit in trying to outguess the Army. Even if you chance upon the correct date today, you will be wrong again by tomorrow. However, if you want my current estimate, I'd place your remaining time here at a minimum of one week, a maximum of two." He slowly cracks the tab on the cold beer to relieve the built-up pressure, losing only a fraction of the contents to the parched earth. "At any rate, I thought I'd better replace some of the supplies I had so much fun spending when I was last here. Unfortunately, I see that John is the only one left out of our original group that I can pay my debt to. Well, no matter."

He looks over the piles of sandbags baking in the sun. "Is Lan still around?"

"Still around, but not here at the moment," I answer, suspecting he has just revealed the main reason for his visit. "She has been spending more of her days away from the compound lately. I think you spoiled her for normal men offering normal prices."

My words cause a shadow of disappointment to cross his light brown, freckled face. He cools and drinks a second beer. Apparently the thought of tumbling a local lass has not lost its appeal. Before he leaves, he asks me for directions to a house of pleasure along his route.

An hour and a half before sunset a helicopter swoops out of the sky to squat on the piece of road opposite the compound. A stout staff sergeant emerges from the blind side of the chopper, jogging awkwardly with his head bent beneath the blades. Once clear of the universal fear of decapitation, he slows his muscled and fatty frame to a fast walk.

"There is a man who has been successfully avoiding the remarkable trimming effects of viewing the splendor of this country on foot," I comment to Turner. "One of yours?"

"That, my friend, is trouble," replies Spec 4 Turner. "I am afraid we are about to experience the benefits of operating under an NCO. Before you walks the mighty destroyer of all things outside the target area—our own beloved Mortar Sergeant Bolinski."

Bolinski is all bristle and business. He asks for a rundown on the enemy activity we have observed. We begin reluctantly, but his enthusiasm soon induces us to release a complete and accurate account of the VC that pass every evening to our south as well as the sightings we have made now and then on the hill to our north. He is pleased with our report, accepting of our nearly complete uniforms, unconcerned with our neatly repacked hooch, and delighted at the offer of a cold beer.

He checks our communications with his company and gives his mortar crews the coordinates for preselected targets along the VC trail we have marked on his map board.

I am confused by the sergeant's apparent competence. He is doing his job correctly instead of ignoring it in favor of haranguing us about haircuts and dust on our helmets. I suppose my expectations have been jaded lately by too much contact with rear echelon officers. Still, his own men do not trust him and that is not at all the same as a run-of-the-mill dislike for a reasonably competent superior who also happens to be a jerk. It is the difference between deadly incompetence and gleeful harassment.

The day drops into moonless night. The VC have failed to make their customary appearance on the trail at dusk.

Disquietude prowls the compound. Men shift their rifles from shoulder to hand and peer into the blackness.

Sergeant Bolinski's disappointment leads to doubts and sharp questions concerning the accuracy of our report. He is becoming irritating, but there is another reason for our uneasiness. The failure of the VC to follow their established pattern lends strong support to our suspicion of complicity between the VC and at least one of our PFs. Someone in the compound had an hour and a half to learn of the sergeant's intentions and warn the VC.

Our sanctuary now contains one man determined to start a battle before he leaves, and at least one other man capable of killing us in our sleep.

Bolinski is getting into the beer a bit more than is good for him. Normally I would not mind if he drank himself into oblivion, but not tonight, not while he is giving me orders. Turner, Greg, and I conspire to remove the temptation.

One at a time we wander over to the beer supply, pick up one of the nineteen remaining cans in the second case, and drift into the darkness to plant the brew beneath one of the thousands of sandbags around us. As long as we are careful not to be seen too frequently near the vanishing supply we should be able to convince him that the beer is being consumed in a normal, if somewhat rapid, manner.

We allow Bolinski to finish his beer and have one more before he returns to find an empty carton. Our problem now is that we will never relocate all our beer and we have an inebriated sergeant on our hands who thinks we are the greedy drunks.

Bolinski's grumblings are cut off by a call from Greg, who is standing watch with the starlight scope. "Sergeant, there are four or five men on the hill, just to the west of that old abandoned house."

Bolinski climbs on the bunker roof to have a look for himself. Taking hold of the eyepiece to steady himself, he inadvertently swivels the scope up and to the right on its tripod base. He curses in frustration at the sight of the unfocused hilltop. "Where is the focus on this damn thing?"

"You shouldn't need to focus it. Just bring it down to the middle of the hill and you will have it," advised Greg.

"Jesus, don't you think I can tell when something is out of focus? I know how to use this thing. Just answer my question."

Greg steps back, clearly hoping to disengage from any further contact with this man.

"It's right here, Sarge," I interject, not caring how long it takes him to relocate the target.

As Bolinski repeatedly goes through the full range of focus while radically changing the position of the scope, I begin to understand why his men have skeptical opinions of his competence. A starlight scope is hardly more difficult to use than binoculars.

After a few minutes Bolinski decides the scope is defective and orders me to attempt repairs. Vaguely hoping our neighborhood opponents have had the good sense to disperse by now, I point the scope at the abandoned house and bring it into focus. A short distance to the left of the building, a group of men are gathered around a faint light not visible to the naked eye.

"There you are, Sergeant. If you don't mind my saying

so, I think Mouc's machine gun and a couple of M-16s would be more effective on that target than mortars."

"I do mind. Go tell Turner to call up the company. And tell him to get that radio out here."

Turner's soft voice comes out of the darkness behind us. "Mortar crews standing by, Sergeant."

"Tell them to give me one round two hundred fifty meters due north of our position," orders Bolinski.

Turner hesitates, then places the radio on the bunker and slowly slumps to his knees to study the map under the light of a red-lensed flashlight. Watching him for a moment it becomes clear that he is merely stalling to give himself time to figure a way to circumvent his sergeant's latest folly.

We have had ample opportunity to study the house on the hill over the past weeks and know its distance to be close to five hundred meters. Furthermore, a single badly placed shot will cause the target to scatter. The VC are not likely to oblige us by sitting still while the mortar crews adjust their tubes and fire for effect. If the target was much closer, or our position uncertain, a shot for location would make sense. But in this situation, if we do not hit the target with the first volley, we might as well give up the effort.

Irritated by the delay, Bolinski jumps down from the bunker roof. "What the hell is the holdup here?"

"Calling in the coordinates now, Sergeant," answers Turner, apparently coming to a decision.

"Give them to me," demands Bolinski suspiciously. Turner recites the numbers as he picks up the radio's handset. "Hold it a minute," says Bolinski. "Let me see that map."

"I know my business, Sergeant. The numbers are correct," insists Turner, withholding the map.

Bolinski snatches the map from his man's hand. After a moment of silent figuring he looks up to sneer at his underling. "So, you know your business, do you, you impudent fool. You have figured two hundred fifty meters wide."

"Sergeant, that house is five hundred meters from here, not two hundred and fifty. Your shot will land exactly halfway between us and the target," answers Turner.

"I didn't ask for your opinion, Specialist," growls the sergeant. "You call in exactly what I tell you and nothing else."

Turner makes the call. Standing next to the three-foot

perimeter wall, the sergeant looks down with contempt at the six enlisted men cautiously taking cover.

A round whistles in from the southwest to explode on the flat, halfway between our position and the target.

"Right, two hundred fifty. Fire for effect," calls out Bolinski.

"What?" cries Turner in disbelief. "Sergeant, you mean *left* two hundred fifty."

"You insolent son of a bitch. You question my orders one more time and I'll see you court-martialed."

"You're going to blow us all to hell, you stupid bastard," explodes Turner. "Right two hundred fifty will put six rounds down our throats."

"Shut up. I'm warning you for the last time. Call in my shot right now or I'll do it myself and hang your ass for disobeying orders under fire."

"You goddamned fool. You want to commit suicide—go right ahead and welcome to it." Turner throws the handset to the ground and turns away.

In the ensuing moment of stunned silence I attempt to interject some quiet reason. "It really should be left two hundred fifty, Sergeant. If you think of yourself back with your mortars, that hill would be to your left and—"

"Shut up," snaps Bolinski. "You'll stay the fuck out of this if you know what's good for you." He retrieves the handset from the ground, then looks up to glare at the men slipping back into the darkness. "I'll deal with all of you when this is over," he rails.

We take refuge in the near-side bridge bunker. The two Vietnamese guards there are in a state of agitation because of the angry words that have passed between the Americans. I attempt to explain to them what is about to happen, urging them to warn their comrades cowering in their bunkers. The two PFs understand my words all too well. They adamantly refuse to venture outside.

Because we are still only about eighty feet from ground zero, Turner, Greg, one of the PFs, and I decide to move to the bunker on the far side of the bridge. Once there, we sit down to wait for Bolinski's bombs to arrive.

Perhaps he has had a chance to cool off and realize his mistake. Maybe our exodus has convinced him to interject a measure of conservatism into the plan he has clung to so tenaciously. For some reason, I cannot believe that Bolinski is actually going to blow himself up.

A chorus of shrill whistles, descending in pitch, sends the Vietnamese to the floor in terror. A series of explosions rock the earth, closely followed by three secondary explosions as mines on the perimeter explode from the force of the impact.

Either the mortar unit had the good sense to look up our coordinates and refrain from dropping shells on us, or Bolinski had reduced his request somewhat, because the nearest mortar crater is thirty feet north of the compound wall. No one cares to ask the sergeant, who has withdrawn from our company, why he is not dead.

In the morning a chopper arrives to relieve us of the benefits of operating under an NCO.

Two days pass without any word or indication of Bolinski's much-promised retribution. It is still too early to discount his threats, but our hope that he will be too embarrassed by his own bungling to bring the incident before his superiors appears to be well founded.

Since our mortar attack upon ourselves in no way threatened the Vietcong, there has been no counteraction on their part. The gaping holes in the inner two rows of perimeter wire have been repaired and the shredded sandbags in the encircling wall replaced. The uneasy coexistence between enemies has returned to the verdant flat at the base of the foothills.

In the afternoon an ARVN Ranger sergeant leads his five-man reconnaissance team into the PF compound for an overnight rest from their four-day patrol. These same men have been stopping here every third or fourth evening for the past two and a half weeks. They are quiet, capable, proud men. Men who can be counted upon not to cringe in a hole to await providence. Their calm confidence and physical strength stand in stark contrast to the cowed demeanor of the PFs. It did not take us long to recognize that in these Rangers we had allies that we could depend on, and an easy friendship soon grew between us.

One of their members, a short, pleasant corporal by the name of Kum, had some command of English. Using two languages and pantomime we struck up a conversation in which I learned that he had been fighting in this war for four years, an occupation that threatened to continue basically unchanged for untold years into the future. I quailed at the thought of it. Yet his years of dealing with death had left no mark upon his boyish face, nor had they dampened his ready humor. This inconsistency led me straight to distrust until I noticed that when he thought he was alone and unobserved his face went blank and his eyes took on that familiar haunting, unfocused glaze of the weary veteran. The instant someone made contact with him, the dour mask would vanish, to be replaced by the boyish eager look that begged you to poke fun or tell a joke so that it could smile and laugh again.

Kum loves to gamble. Lacking the necessary Vietnamese cards to play the games he knew, I taught him blackjack with my Hoyle deck. We played for pennies until his losses reached the dollar mark, then he began to double and redouble his bets in an effort to gain the upper hand. Somehow the finer points of the game elude him, and although he is just as surprised and amused when he loses as when he wins, there is no denying that he is a rotten gambler.

At the current time he is thirty-five dollars down, twenty of which is yet unpaid. Now, thirty-five dollars is a considerable sum for a Vietnamese corporal to squander and I have been doing my best to encourage him to forego payment, but he is a man of pride who cannot ignore a debt.

As soon as he dumps his gear, Kum searches me out to slap two thousand piasters in my hand with a smile. My protests are to no avail, but my will is not to be denied so easily. I shall return his money in the only way he will accept. A bond has grown between us over the past weeks, and I shall make use of that and anything else that comes to hand to lead him down my path of friendly deception.

"Now that I have all your money, what shall we play for? Maybe you have nice sister, yes?"

"Sister married, you no like. I play, but not for money. Kum empty."

"Oh no. We play for big money. Fifty pia. Your credit is good with me."

"Fifty pia! No can do. Credit didi mau."

"Listen, my friend. I have been in touch with the card fairy. She tells me that today Kum very lucky, win big money."

He eyes me with a suspicious smile. "Smoke in head make GI dinky dau, have fairies in eyeballs."

Eventually I cajole him into playing for money. With

him dealing, it should be easy for me to lose nearly every hand. Not wanting to be too obvious about throwing the game, I plan to stand pat on the occasional twelve or thirteen and hit everything else until I have gone bust or reached the infrequent twenty or twenty-one.

I am a reasonably competent gambler, and although I have always suspected fate of being a tad stingy when dealing out my share of the luck, and despite my habit of soaking my game in beer, I generally manage to struggle to the up side of even by the game's end. Before this game began it had never occurred to me that losing at poker could be a challenge.

As Kum deals the cards with increasing reluctance, lady luck continues to unleash a maddening display of bad timing by squandering my next five years' allowance of superb cards on this single game. I have not been able to lose more than one or two hands with each passing of the deck. Finally Kum lays down the cards, unwilling to go on. Despite my best efforts, I have plunged him seventeen dollars further into debt.

In desperation I suggest we go for double or nothing on a cut of the cards. He declines. "What we gamble for? You want my boots, too?"

"No, not your boots," I say looking down his five-foot two-inch frame to his extra small jungle boots. "Not even my baby brother could fit into those. Let's play for your shirt—I am in need of a handkerchief."

It takes maximum effort on my part to tease, insult, and cajole him into wagering his debt of seventeen dollars on a single card. To assure that he wins, I plot to eliminate luck's fickle nature from the game. Distracting him with talk of his comrades, I slip a deuce to the bottom of the deck when he turns to identify one of his mates for me. I shuffle without disturbing the bottom card, then cut the deck. Picking up the bottom portion of the deck I squeeze their width in the palm of my hand so that when they are placed on top of the unaltered cards, the two and all the cards above it have a slight upward curve down their center. With the deck neatly stacked I can easily feel the separation with my fingertips. It is a shabby trick no true cardsharp would consider using, but if your opponent is not expecting devious behavior, it can be effective.

Kum turns over a five to beat my two of spades. The win encourages him to play again for the same stakes. I cut the deck twice, leaving my two near the bottom. This time Kum tries his luck first. He shows an eight. Tickling the ends of the deck, I locate the hint of a gap. With a silent sigh of relief I expose the two of spades once again. Kum's delight at winning thirty-four dollars outweighs his suspicions of the reappearing two.

Picking the same card three times in a row would be too much for anyone to accept, so I mix the cards until a four appears on the bottom of the deck. Repeating the maneuver with the four, I succeed in losing again. With all but one dollar of Kum's money returned, I retire. From now on I will stick to playing for pennies.

The stimulation of the game over, I begin to slide into lassitude, my overheated brain beyond original thought. Waves of liquid heat shimmer off the glaring white and faded green sandbags. Those few men who are active move through the thick air at a pace carefully measured to produce minimum exertion.

A series of angry, staccato shouts rip through the languid atmosphere, jolting men into activity. Twenty-four PFs scramble to don helmets, boots, rifles, and bandoliers.

Alarmed, I scan the surrounding bush, but the only threat I can find is the fired-up PF sergeant whose voice set this activity into motion. For the first time in the five weeks I have been here the PFs are putting on the airs of an armed force, if an extremely uneasy and uncertain one. Their quick, nervous conversations and agitated movements are checked by the intimidating bark of orders from the sergeant as he lines the men into two files.

This unprecedented call to arms seems to be as much a surprise to the PFs as it is to me. Since Vietnamese spoken at its normal rapid rate is still just a blur of sound in my ear, I am unable to gather any meaning from the sergeant's speech to his assembled troops. I turn to Kum for an interpretation.

"They go to bac bac VC," he explains.

"Them? Kill VC? No way," I counter.

"Yes. Ambush VC on trail. Orders from their captain."

When I ask if the Rangers are going as well, he says no. They do not work with the PFs. They cannot trust them to fight, and if they did fight, whose side would they be on?

Our curiosity piqued, we move to the bunker roofs to watch the drama to our south unfold. Leaving six men behind to guard the bridge, the platoon dips out of sight behind the berm on the far side of the river. A few minutes later we pick them up again in the binoculars. They are making good use of the available cover; if we did not know where to look for them they would be extremely difficult to spot. Approximately seven hundred meters to our south–southwest the eighteen men set up their ambush at the edge of the trail. I check my watch. The squad of VC is due in forty minutes.

To pass the time we exchange opinions and wagers on whether or not the local enemy intelligence will be able to react fast enough to save their squad from the deadly trap waiting for them. Except for the night that Bolinski was here, the VC have rigidly maintained their routine, as if flaunting their confidence in their organization. We, too, have confidence in their organization and its network of supporters—our bets are running heavily against the VC putting in an appearance tonight.

Ten minutes past their accustomed time, with the last light of day quickly fading, eleven men materialize on the path to the northwest, moving in a steady single file toward the ambush site. Four hundred meters separate the two groups, then three hundred, two hundred, one hundred. The column of VC comes to a stop. A minute later they begin moving again—only now they are heading southwest, away from the trail. We follow their movement for one hundred meters before they turn east again and disappear into the brush and darkness. We have been betrayed again.

With the starlight scope and radar we stand vigil for half an hour more but are unable to detect movement from either group. With no way to contact the men lying in ambush, the onlookers disperse in dejected silence, leaving me with the instruments and two Rangers to stand the first hour's watch.

An hour later there is nothing new to report to the relief watch. The dim light spilling through the doorway of our hooch, the muffled voices of two cultures, and the laughter that needs no translation draws me forward. But at the edge of the light, the contrast between my dour mood and the festive atmosphere within makes me hesitate.

Not ready to put aside my bleak feelings, I stand on the edge waiting for something to nudge me one way or the other. It has long been clear that most of the people who live around here are not on the same side as the U.S. military. In fact, no two identifiable groups seem to be on the same side. Even the underlings and overlords within each group are at

each other's throats. Add to this tonight's further evidence of
traitors in our midst to fuel our already well-developed feelings of futility and waste—why are these men acting like it's
party time?

The air at the entrance to the hooch is heavily laden with
the smell of marijuana. A few yards beyond, the nearly empty
compound is masked in darkness, and whisper quiet. What
profit is there in sitting in some solitary corner to brood? The
road of moody dejection and despair is a dead end. Perhaps it
is better to follow Kum's example—start smiling and soon a
recent friend will feel obliged to justify that smile.

I step into the candle glow, check that my rifle hanging
from its nail beside the doorway is ready for instant use, and
take a seat on an upended crate. Slanted eyes and round
squint in turn against acrid smoke rising from the ember glow
of local weed. Smoky tendrils and lightened minds buoyed on
dreams drift and disperse to places as far away as they are
varied, places where the scope of imagination is the
only limitation.

A continuum of stories and ribald jokes interrupts the
card game until it dissolves unnoticed on the ammo-crate
table. Kum's two-way translations stall midline in fits of giggles. The laughter echoing through our tiny shack keeps time
with the dancing human shadows the single candle casts upon
the walls and bends in copied animation across the ceiling.

From here we can go anywhere; don't you see my dream?
I will paint my picture in your mind of freedom and friendship and wide ocean beaches and beautiful, willing women.

Changing with the hours, stoned men stand with private
dreams, peering at pale green, ghostly scenes through the
eyepiece of the starlight scope. Their senses and their instruments tell them all is quiet—an observation of little meaning.
Men slump in corners to ease the fantasy flow, or wander off
to lose themselves in the changing patterns of passing clouds.
Kum and two of his mates sit shoulder to shoulder on the
lower half of a cot, bubbling with childlike amusement at my
incomprehensible wit and foolishness.

My throat is dry from smoke and talk, my belly tight
from laughter. A mud slide of woven dreams oozes across my
skull to cause my weighty head to seek the gentle rhythm of
a hammock. Stretching out below the changing patterns in my
mind, I tune in the oscillating song that is the native's tongue.
Within the song there is a story about an old man who

could not get his water buffalo to work the fields. Although the old man coaxed, and threatened, and finally beat the buffalo's thick hide with a stick, the water buffalo would not pull the plow. For seven days the buffalo stayed in the shade, ate the tender spring grass, and ignored the farmer's urgings. The old man became very worried. How could he plant the crops to feed his family without the help of his buffalo?

Finally the farmer asked his young grandson if he would try to get the stubborn old bull to plow. The old man knew the boy was friendly with the buffalo. Sometimes the big animal would even let the boy ride down to the river on his broad back. Perhaps the boy knew of some way to cure the buffalo of its laziness, thought the farmer. It would not hurt to try.

The boy approached the buffalo cheerfully, stroking the strong neck as he talked softly into the animal's ear. Suddenly the buffalo reared his head and trotted to the plow idle in the field, stamping his feet to let it be known how impatient he was to begin turning the soil.

The old man, watching from his hut, was amazed at what he had seen. He hurried to his grandson's side to ask what he had said to make the buffalo so eager to go to work.

"I told him that he need not worry about working anymore, that he should stay in the shade and eat grass all day long so that he would become soft and very fat," explained the boy.

"I don't understand," said the grandfather. "How could telling him that make him want to go to work?"

"Because then I told him that, as everyone knows, the season for planting is quickly passing," the boy went on, "so this year we will all relax in the shade and eat buffalo meat."

I join the three Vietnamese in their enjoyment of the simple tale. As the laughter dies out I notice that Kum is giving me an inquisitive look.

"What you laugh at, GI?" he asks. "You no understand what we say?"

"Sure I do," I counter, retelling part of the story to prove my claim. In the retelling, the incongruity of what just transpired dawns on me. I cannot understand Vietnamese, no more than a few dozen words. And yet I had grasped the meaning of the tale without fully comprehending most of the words. How is that possible?

A burst of automatic rifle fire rips through the hooch

inches above my elevated perch. I tumble from the hammock to the floor as the room plunges into darkness. The man hurling himself from the adjacent cot lands on top of me, crawling and kicking for the door. Although the three-foot wall of sandbags encircling the hooch offers us some protection, there is a claustrophobic scramble to grab weapons and get out. Buffeted by passing feet and legs, I struggle to my hands and knees only to have a boot tread on my right hand in the last of the blind congestion at the door.

Knowing exactly where my rifle hangs I reach out for it but grasp only air and wooden wall, then hit the floor again as more small arms fire pours into the compound. The M-16s return the fire as the first of our men reach the perimeter wall.

Cold dread runs down my spine as I expose my back to the now continuous incoming to grope along the wall until my fingers loop over the empty nail. It's gone. Some asshole has taken my rifle. This can't be happening, not again.

With an edge of panic seeping into my self-control I hurriedly run a hand across the east wall, finding nothing but bare wood where moments ago a bevy of weapons hung. A mixture of fear and hate boils through my nervous system. Damn it, I won't go through another firefight defenseless. I'll find the guilty bastard and strangle him with my bare hands.

I crawl to the nearest bunker and peek over the top. The firing in both directions is heavier now. There is yelling on the bridge, hysterical Vietnamese yelling. The sound of utter panic sifts thinly among the heavier roars of weaponry. It is a black night, a void of vision punctuated by muzzle flashes and the crisscrossing streaks of tracers. The little deadly lights are enough to tell me that the VC are on the far side of the bridge between us and the hamlet. The PFs must have been ambushed crossing the bridge and are now pinned down in the cross fire.

The end is not imminent. There is yet time. The fear of things unknown ebbs with this new shred of knowledge, clearing the mind. Perhaps the man who has my rifle did leave his weapon in the hooch. I'm useless out here empty-handed, I should go back and look more carefully.

The cigarette lighter casts a flickering, shadowy glow upon the walls. The bare wood punctured with rusting nails supports a single helmet and nothing more. I don the helmet for its psychological support and lie on the ground where I can think for a second without worrying about getting shot.

Scouring the compound for the missing weapon is out of the question until things quiet down. I could stay here until the firing stops or we get overrun. No I couldn't. I can't endure doing nothing. I'm no fatalist. There must be something in here I can use as a weapon. What about a machete? No, I can't remember seeing one in here. Hand grenades. That's it. Somewhere among the crates at the back of the hooch there's a box of them. With the aid of the lighter I quickly locate the grenades and a box of M-16 shells as well. Stuffing my numerous pockets with both kinds of ordnance makes me feel slightly more at ease . At least I can fill empty magazines or throw grenades if Charlie has rounded up enough folks to have a run at us.

I crawl across the compound on my belly until I come up against the east wall, then work my way south along the line of sandbags. The first person I come upon is a GI firing carefully aimed single shots at the spots of light one hundred meters away.

I touch his shoulder. He spins to face the unexpected presence, bringing his rifle around with him. My position inside the arc of his swinging rifle prevents him from completing the arc. Turner curses me royally as he slumps back in recognition. Scared him some, I reckon.

"Is that your 16?" I yell.

"What?" he yells back. It is difficult to hear over the nerve-jangling noise, or maybe he is having trouble believing he heard my question correctly.

"That 16. Is it yours?"

"What the fuck—who cares? I just grabbed one."

"I care. Someone took mine and left me with nothing."

He looks at me hard as if he is trying to decide if it is safe to ignore me.

"Where was your rifle when this shit started?" I press.

"Hanging in the hooch."

"Well, it's not there now." Turner's reaction makes me realize that whoever took my rifle probably has not even considered the jeopardy he has placed me in. When I find the culprit and he is forced to face the choice of being defenseless or exposing himself to fire to retrieve his own weapon, he will understand the jeopardy well enough.

I stuff a handful of M-16 shells into Turner's pocket

before crawling on toward the river and the next man. A huddled form against the protecting line of sandbags turns to exchange magazines as I approach. The Ranger glances in my direction before returning his attention to the muzzle flashes across the river. This man was not in the hooch when the first shots were fired. I move on.

After a few yards I come to the gap in the perimeter wall that is the entrance to the compound. I pause, straining to penetrate the darkness beyond or to distinguish a human sound below the staccato roar of fire. A whiff of muted noise, as uncertain as imagination, reaches my ears. I take a hand grenade from my side pocket, finger the pin, and crouch to wait.

People are firing from the bridge. Stupid PFs, that's no place to make a stand—no cover.

I wonder if anyone has informed Bravo Company of this action, as per our standing orders? Christ, I hope not, not with Bolinski. . . .

A body dives through the entrance, landing in a hard sprawl six feet away. He lies motionless, the details of his form engulfed in darkness. Is he ours or theirs? Should I break his neck or leave him alone? He is wearing jungle boots, that much I can tell. If he is a VC he would probably have come in firing, and not alone. The boots move in a low-crawl shuffle and disappear.

I move quickly across the exposed entrance, then pause again to listen. I'm not sure, but there seem to be people in the moat. Two grenades dropped into that ditch would waste them all. No, I'd better not. If there are people down there they are hiding, not fighting, a phenomenon peculiar to the PFs. I crawl on, resuming my search.

The lump on the side of the wall is so still I am not sure the form is human until I am almost close enough to touch it. The bottom of the GI's helmet is held level with the lip of the wall, a stubby M-79 clutched firmly to his chest. There is no movement in the kneeling outline of the figure frozen beneath the shattering noise and deadly little lights.

Remembering Turner's startled greeting, I prudently decide not to disrupt this man's fixation on whatever devils are tormenting him. I begin to skirt around the man when suddenly some sixth sense alerts him to my presence. He swings around in a blur. I catch a glimpse of the butt of his grenade launcher coming at my face as I duck. The stock of his

weapon slams into the side of my helmet. My outflung hand
catches his upper arm as the momentum of his attack carries
him toward me. I wrench the arm downward, pulling him
with me as I roll to the ground, yelling for him to stop. He
trips his knee against my back, losing balance as he topples
over me, providing the time I need to pin his arms to his
sides. He lies without struggle beside me, trembling in my
hold.

"Sorry," he says in an unsteady voice.

Yeah, I know, nervous instinct. I release him and crawl
back to the protection of the wall. When I am sure of my
balance again, I grope for the helmet and grenade dislodged
during the brief tumble. After making sure the pin is still
secure in the grenade, I lean against the sandbags and allow
myself to feel the dejection that has come to replace the
anger and fear. My friends are more of a danger to me than
my enemies. I think I'll abandon the search for my rifle until
this is over.

The sound of incoming begins to fade. A few seconds
later the streaks of red tracers are heading south. It takes five
minutes more for the PFs in the far-side bridge bunker to
bring their fear of the menacing shadows around them under
control and allow the night to regain its silence.

When I return to the hooch I find my rifle hanging from
its nail with only its hot barrel to testify to its absence. No
one will admit taking it, so I vent my feelings on the subject
to my barely tolerant fellows and let the matter drop.

A head count reveals there are six men missing from the
ambush party. It is believed that two of the men have been
shot and left on the bridge, while one or two more have
probably taken refuge in the bunker on the other side of the
river; the remainder are either in the river or have slipped
off somewhere in the confusion. The PF sergeant makes
the incredible decision to delay any rescue mission until
morning.

How is it that these men have become so demoralized,
so cowardly, that they will not even risk a confrontation with
darkness to prevent their closest comrades from bleeding to
death alone in the dark while their neighbors and brothers
fighting for the NLF are consistently willing to subject themselves to great risk to recover their own dead and wounded?

*   *   *

In the morning the six Rangers leave the compound to resume their jungle patrol. As always, I am sorry to see them go. Their company and their rifles will be missed.

Four of the six missing PFs sheepishly return to the compound in time to help carry the two dead men on the bridge to the burial ground at the edge of the hamlet. Because the tropical climate makes prompt disposal of bodies a necessity, preparations are hurriedly made for the ceremony to take place in the early afternoon. With all but three of the PFs at the funeral, the compound takes on the hushed, forlorn atmosphere of the house of the departed.

I had hoped that the ARVN lieutenant would stop by today to remove me from this air of gloom, but his jeep does not haul into view until late evening when his personal driver arrives with a plastic bag of fried rice and vegetables. The driver asks if it would be convenient for me to accompany his lieutenant to Di An and Long Binh in the morning. I assure him that I will be ready and waiting.

As the rice is portioned into the six empty C-ration cans we use for plates, the PFs file quietly back into camp. They present a sorrowful scene with their listless gait and their hung heads. The absence of their usual chatter and noisy card games, the lack of children playing in the dirt and women serving the day's last bowl of rice adds to the air of despondency. Another blow has registered on a broken people, broken except for one.

Mouc marches to his bunker in silence like all the others. But unlike the others he reappears with a machine gun in one hand and a can of ammo in the other. He places the gun on the south wall, hooks up the belt of ammunition, and draws a bead on the VC trail. He seems to be intent on launching a one-man reprisal.

Mouc's actions draw three of us to his side simultaneously. When questioned he shrugs us off with anger, resentful of any intrusion upon his unsupported vendetta. It takes us a few minutes to calm him enough to convince him that our intention is not to stop him, but merely to find out what he plans to do and why.

"These men sit and wait to be butchered like the village chickens. Mouc is no chicken. Mouc kill many VC before he die and no chicken-man stop me. No one stop me," he proclaims, glaring at each of us in turn.

Amply convinced that Mouc will not be swayed from his

plan, we call the Americans together for a council. The opinions of the men are equally divided. One group claims our purpose here is to observe enemy activity and assist in the defense of the compound by calling in supporting fire. They say it is not our function to instigate offensive action. But their main concern is that if we do succeed in killing some of the local VC, the result will surely be a subsequent attack by a much larger force than the seven of us can hope to repel.

The second group counters that while these points are well founded, they are now irrelevant. Whatever unofficial truce existed between the VC and the compound dissolved with last night's action. Since the VC already have provocation to eliminate us, and since Mouc is going to start a fight regardless of what we do. it would be better to help him cripple the local squad of VC than to let him make a weak, one-man strike that will allow the VC to launch another counterattack tonight, or add their numbers to a larger assault at a later time. Besides, Mouc has supported us; there is a matter of loyalty here that we cannot ignore.

The exchange of views helps clear the air but changes only one man's stand. Greg, recognizing that he will be involved with or without his permission, volunteers to act as spotter. We spread out along the south wall, taking up supported prone positions on the bunker roofs.

As we wait through the appointed time and beyond, with Greg switching to the starlight scope as the darkness becomes full, it becomes apparent that our time and our arguments have been wasted. Half an hour later with still no sign of the elusive VC, we call off the vigil, retiring with relief to the hooch.

The two men who declined to join us in Mouc's aborted attack are waiting to corrupt us upon our return. Six joints lie ready upon the table. Two mischievous grins crease the faces of those I suspect of conspiring to divert us from further plans of violence. A minimum of effort is required for our corruption. All the grass is soon ignited and the smoke not absorbed by lungs swirls in a haze in the closed-off room.

Not satisfied in achieving the blithering babbles, some fool rolls two more of the potent cigarettes, and to prove that there are no fools bigger than ourselves, we smoke them.

Mouc bursts upon our bended minds with some prattle about VC on the hill. We receive the commonplace news with indifference. Who wants to shoot at VC when we can have a good time instead? In the midst of explaining to Mouc that we are too fucked up and otherwise disinclined to mess with any VC tonight, it comes to my attention that he is not anywhere in sight. I lift the corner of the poncho covering the doorway to see where the lad has gone. One look makes it blatantly clear to me that there is nothing but dark out there. I drop the flap before the image of a stocky little dude carrying a big gun reaches my mind. Confused, I stumble outside for another look. Yep, he is at it again. Give 'em hell, Mouc. I blunder my way back through the poncho flap to give the boys the news.

"Guess what? Mouc is about to break up the gook's evening hillside social hour."

"Let's hear it for Mouc the Gook Killer."

"Get some, Mouc."

"You dummy. Mouc is a gook."

"Don't bother me with semantics, my man, it all fits with the rhythm of the times."

"Tell Mouc to waste all them gooks with the first burst, will you? We got enough holes in the roof already."

"Hey, wait a minute. Any second now Mouc is going to blast that hill. Mr. Cong up there, he going to shoot back. This hooch ain't got no protection from fire coming off that hill."

"Oh, shit."

The collective realization of the vulnerability of our position causes the mass transport of six GIs from the smoke-clouded room to Mouc's side. Mouc is crouched behind his machine gun, peering through the sights at some unseen distant object. The only reason he has not already commenced firing is that he is having difficulty relocating the target when he moves from the starlight scope back to his gun.

We try to talk him out of stirring up trouble by pleading diminished capacity, sensitive ears, and a predilection for peaceful evenings. Mouc is decidedly uninterested in our case, but does consent to hold his fire while we prepare for the consequences. Since we have already been over the pros and cons of this situation, we are spared the need to make an attempt at logic now. We take up arms: four for the attack, two for the defense.

Turner calls Bravo Company to inform them of our intended action and to make sure they have the coordinates of the target in case someone there gets an itch for destruction. While Turner is busy with the radio, I peek through the preset scope for a look at the opposition. If it was not for the faint, steady light in the middle of the circle of five squatting men it would be difficult to distinguish them from the brush and small trees on this moonless night. The scene is the same as it was a week ago. The same men in the same place with the same light. Maybe it is an illusion, a cardboard imitation of reality.

Checking the rest of the area like a good scout, I scan to the west, then back to the east. Starlight reflects off the concrete walls of the old, abandoned house—a glowing shrine standing against a shadowy background alive with the play of demons. . . . Try to keep your mind on what—what was that? A flicker of movement to the east of the house. Inside that clump of bushes. Probably just a bird. A bird in the bush is better than a bird in the hand. No, that's not right, unless you're an environmentalist instead of—there it is again. An arm extended in gesture—now gone—but there—a head, perhaps. Suddenly, as if my eyes just came into focus, I see the silhouette of the heads and shoulders of four men among the twigs.

"Hey, Shook. This isn't the drive-in movie, you know." The men are waiting, impatient to begin, to get on with it, to be done, to sleep. "Are you going to direct our fire or what?"

"Right. Fire the M-79 at maximum range. When the grenade explodes, one M-16 and the machine gun open up on the target fifty meters west of the house. The second M-16 will fire independently at the target east of the house. Mouc, remember to fire in ten-round bursts so the scope will have a chance to clear from the overload of the light from the muzzle flashes. Okay? Fire the 79 when ready." Boy, that sounded pretty official to me, almost like I knew what I was doing, like this was the real thing.

A hollow pop emits from the grenade launcher. A flash of light appears on the hill one hundred feet short of the target. The scope glares at the burst of fire, blank white, then clears to the sight of gracefully arching tracers distorted into slow motion by the powerful lens.

Standing on the bunker roof behind the starlight's tripod, I yell corrections to the men below me.

"79, up thirty meters. Machine gun, left ten, up twenty. Rifle, up fifteen."

The circle of men take our second burst hugging the ground, their light extinguished.

"79, they are beyond your range. Rifle and gun, up five."

The VC are on their feet, scrambling for cover.

"Go right, they are heading for the back of the house."

Streaks of light blaze down the hill toward the compound, but they are wild shots fired on the run. I am hit with a feeling of exhilaration and relief. The incoming fire verifies that our targets are indeed VC and not some venturesome innocents risking their lives by violating the sundown curfew.

As Mouc swings his fire to the right, the flashes from his weapon interfere far less with my view of the action. The paths of our tracers are now crossed by more accurate fire originating from the three glassless windows and the open wooden door along the front wall of the house.

The light show coming to me through the eyepiece has a fascinating surrealistic quality, as if I had suddenly been plucked from my armchair and inserted into a TV episode of *Combat*. I am bestowed with the power of wizards. My vision can pierce the veil of night, my eyes perceive speeding spheres of lead. Even my voice has the power to command a hail of fury. Yeah, tho' I walk through the valley of death, I shall fear no evil, for I am the evilest mother fucker in the valley. The dudes who thought up that line must have been stoned, too.

I'm definitely beginning to enjoy the excitement as I guide our fire closer and closer to the windows, my body swaying to the right or left with the passing streaks of tracers.

"Up one, Mouc. Ring the bell. Rifle Two, you're on the roof." A round I didn't see whines overhead. "Rifle One, you're on target. Down one, Mouc. That's it. On target. On target."

Bullets spray through the windows, splinters fly from the old wooden door. Five hundred meters in the dark and right on target. Yes, sir, that's impressive, impressive indeed. We have them pinned down, there isn't an incoming tracer in sight. Of course, only every third to ninth round is a tracer. . . .

My God! What am I doing?

I jump from the roof to huddle in the lee of the bunker, consumed by thoughts of what might have been. You fool. Damned idiot. Standing up there like a lunatic, daring Charlie to shoot you. Thought you could duck bullets, didn't you?

M-42 "Duster"

Lord, save me from any more drug-induced heroics. Heroics nothing. Blatant stupidity, clear and simple.

Four heavy shells erupt in quick succession against the base of the hill.

"What the hell was that?" asks a voice in the dark. "That damned Bolinski isn't after us again, is he?"

The men have broken off their small arms fire in deference to this new development. Four more shells slam into the hill. One of the men abstaining from this action has been monitoring the radio. "It's coming from a First Cavalry vehicle," he reports. "They want us to direct their fire."

"Who asked for their help? Tell them this is a private party."

"I don't think they are going to take orders from me. As long as they are going to blow things up, we might as well have them put a scare into Charlie."

With a few minor adjustments, the 1st Cavalry is soon decimating the trees and brush around the old house with a high rate of efficiency. On the sixth volley the flashes of light spewing from twin cannons become visible as the dark hulk of their machine lumbers up a rise a mile to our southwest. With a deep-throated diesel rumble the duster vomits fire and destruction like the roaring dragons of legend, licking the night with their flames.

No matter that the bombardment left the old house, its target, untouched. No matter that the VC most likely left the area with the first of the forty explosions. No matter that the local folks were probably shaken right down to their sandaled feet. It was an impressive demonstration of raw power. Personally, I thought it was a wonderful fireworks display, and almost in time for Christmas too.

The rays from the oversized orange ball creeping up the horizon signal the end of four hours of deep sleep. Shifting my hips to a more comfortable position on the bunker roof, I prop myself on an elbow to search the countryside for the feel of eyes looking back at me.

A woman crawls out the entrance of her sandbag cave, then stands and stretches out the stiffness caused by sleeping with just a bamboo mat between her body and the hard-packed earth. She moves through her morning chores with quiet practice, leaving the morning's silence undisturbed. She does not venture outside the five-foot circle that is her allotted space, or lift her eyes to check the weather, or scan the horizon for danger, or notice me watching her. Her life, for now at least, is contained in the comfortably familiar routine of preparing the morning rice.

I shift my attention to the house standing in solitary vigil upon the hill, expecting it to reflect some of the violence that was focused there a few hours before. From this distance, only the eye familiar with the view can detect the latest shallow pits ripped from the earth, attesting that the night did not pass in quiet dreams. The house itself reveals no hint of change.

I wonder if we will be sent there to search for fly-swarmed bodies bloating in the sun? Seeking escape from that unpleasant thought, I head for the river to prepare myself for the trip to Di An.

I am ready and waiting to be gone from this place two

hours before the lieutenant and his quiet assistant arrive. As we pass through the peaceful morning air, I inform the lieutenant of my desire to stop by battalion HQ sometime during the day. He responds by making the cluster of barrackslike offices our first stop.

I enter the personnel office with little hope or concern for the disposition of my transfer request, convinced that whatever the news, my life will continue basically unchanged. Five minutes later I am back outside, fully aware of the folly of my convictions. In a bit of a daze, I walk around to the driver's side of the jeep to say good-bye to my Vietnamese friend.

"Lieutenant, I want to thank you for everything you have done for me. All the—ah—gifts and tours of your country. I really appreciate them."

"It ends now?" he asks. "What happened?"

"All the Americans have been recalled from the Popular Forces compound. We are being reassigned."

"You go to Cambodian border now as we hear before, yes?"

"That's right."

"John, it is my pleasure to work with you. I know you will do well wherever you go. Come and see me if you can. I tell wife you always welcome."

"Thank you. And good luck to you, sir."

Wishing I could find more fitting words to express my feelings, we shake hands in silent farewell. Watching them drive out of my life as so many others have done before, I consider his parting comment about doing well wherever I go. Others have said it before and it never fails to bother me. I get by, I muddle through, but I never do well. Why do people say that to me? I can never decide if I should be ashamed of my lack of achievement or galled at their presumptuousness. What the hell, it is probably offered as a general parting remark, like wishing someone luck.

Being told to prepare for transfer to the border tonight was not the only news I received in the personnel office. My transfer request has been turned down with an addendum reconfirming my combat status. To cap off the round of ill tidings, personnel informed me that I have not been reassigned to Echo Company as I was led to believe. Instead, I have been ordered to report to Delta Company's XO when he returns from the field in the morning.

Naturally, the order to meet with the XO early tomorrow does not jive with the order to leave here tonight, but I am beyond worrying about such inconsistencies. In a way, the conflicting directives give me a choice. I can refuse to go the Cambodian border tonight, because doing so would not allow me to comply with my XO's orders. Or, I can make sure I am sent out tonight so that I will not be available to go back to the field with Delta.

Ah, but what is the point? Whatever action I take will only delay Delta's disposition of my case for a day or two. Besides, how can I—being of reasonably sound mind—actively choose either of these totally unattractive fates?

As I wade through the reddish brown dust on my way to Echo Company's area, I admit to myself that the real problem is that I don't have the energy to try to outfox the Army again. I must be getting worn down. I just don't care about much of anything anymore. Sure, it's nice to get high in good company, and it's nice to get laid now and then, but everything else is just passing time.

Opening the door to the barracks I am stopped by the sight beyond. Where bunks once stood on an expanse of concrete, there is now a hallway running the length of the building. The used lumber walls are broken at regular intervals with doors that open into partitioned rooms. After a quick glance back outside to make sure I have the correct building, I push open the first door on the left to see if I still belong here.

The eight-by-ten cubicle with a white silk cargo parachute ceiling contains the familiar, if seldom used, bunk bed in the corner. A stranger is bent over my old bed sorting through a mess of gear spread out on the mattress.

"Hello." I greet his back. "It looks like I've been moved. I don't have any use for a bed, but perhaps you could tell me where I could leave my gear for a while?"

"Hey, you must be John," says the stranger with a friendly smile, "my mysterious roommate for the past few months. It's nice to finally meet you in the flesh. You just get in?"

"Yes, for the day, anyway."

"Oh? You must be part of one of the three-man teams they were sending out tonight."

"Were?"

"That's right. When we got off the chopper this morning

and reported to the orderly room . . . did you know we had a new CO? He just got in yesterday. Anyway, he said the operation has been delayed again. We won't be going out for a few days at least."

His smile fades at some shift in thought as he turns to pass his hand aimlessly over the little piles of personal possessions. "Still your bunk. I'll move this . . ." His voice trails off.

"No need," I assure him.

He swiftly dips into his locker to come up with a bottle of Johnny Walker Red. Holding the unopened bottle before him, he asks no one in particular, "Didn't this used to be a bottle of Ballantine?"

"I confess. I drank your Ballantine and replaced it with that. I hope you don't mind."

"Not at all," he says, turning back to me. He seems relieved. "That's what it's for. Lord knows I don't have much, but feel free to use whatever there is. The only reason I ask is that . . . well, I'm not too sure about things these days. I'm glad I remembered that, anyway."

Shaking his head slowly he places the bottle back in his locker, then takes it out again. "Here, better have some. All three of us are perishable."

I am about to break the seal on the cap when Sergeant Harris's head appears around the edge of the door.

"Ah, Shook. You made it back. And into the booze before lunch, I see. Don't you guys get too fucked up, and don't go wandering off. The first team is going out at 1800."

"Wait a minute. The CO just told me we were cancelled," objects my roommate.

"What? When was this?"

"A little over an hour ago."

"Oh, well then, I've got the latest update. You're going."

"Damn. Come back when you have some good news, will you?"

Harris leaves without comment. I pour warm scotch down my throat.

After lunch the three teams that have been brought in from the field are called into formation and told that the operation is officially off. However, we are cautioned to stand by in case there are further developments. To ensure that we stay sober and together we are relegated to the sandbag-filling detail for the rest of the afternoon.

Four hours later Harris arrives to call a halt to the work

and to inform us that the operation is on again. We are scheduled for departure at 1900.

In the mess hall for dinner I am hailed by my old friend Allen Gillis. He attracts the attention of half the mess by yelling slanderous quips at me while I wait in line to fill my tray. It amazes me that Allen does not get thrown out for his raucous behavior long before I get the chance to join him and confirm that he is even more drunk and desperate than the last time I saw him. Trying to get him to simmer down is as useless as pissing on a pyromaniac. He is purposely inviting trouble—any kind of trouble that will delay his return to the field in the morning.

Allen is not a fighter. It is hard for me to imagine him hitting anyone, even in anger. But he is asking for a fight now with each snide remark, almost begging for it, not so that he can vent his frustration with his fists, but for the hope of a broken arm or skull that will put his body where no one will shoot at it and that will give his mind a chance to deal with a lifetime's accumulation of treasured values that have been trashed like the bodies that rotate through his life.

Gone are love and honor and decency and respect. Gone are faith in country and God and the inherent goodness of mankind. Come to fill the void is the single new high tenet: kill or be killed. Yet one value remains. The value of friendship and he clings to it tenaciously, gripping it physically with hands and arms.

Allen Gillis is in serious trouble. The kind of trouble that evolves when all the visions of flowered meadows are replaced with scenes of torn flesh. Allen's struggle to maintain a working level of sanity breeds in his friends both a revulsion at his display of the weakness and the fear that they have succeeded in repressing in themselves and an empathy that manifests itself in a desire to protect the emotional morass that, with one more shock, could be theirs.

Allen is at the stage where screaming and breaking things is desired, but he must know that once control is lost he may not be able to get it back. Instead, he talks incessantly, his body jerking with nervous energy. He giggles and yells, dumps a shaker of salt on my dinner, turns over plates of food to squish the contents into the table and makes rivers of milk and coffee through the goo, spreading and patting it all with a spoon. When he starts using his spoon to launch the gruel at passing diners, I grab him by the back of the shirt and hustle him outside. He may think that getting thrown into one of the metal crates they use for jail cells here will protect his body and mind, but I am not so sure.

At Allen's insistence we head for the half-barracks that contains the battalion EM club. The presence of beer seems to have a calming influence on my old friend. His behavior becomes less erratic, his disjointed speech more rational. Despite the taboo on mentioning anything connected with the military, the names of the recent dead and wounded men of Alpha Company manage to slip into his conversation.

After half an hour it is clear that Allen's company has taken a beating. A portion of his company is in the rear to regroup and collect discharged patients. Allen does his best to avoid talking about the fighting he has seen, so I cannot ask him about it, and I am out of time for listening. I must get back to Echo Company. Putting down his pleas to stay where we are until we are dragged away, I help him stagger back to the barracks behind mine where his unit took up residence this afternoon.

After leaving Allen in the care of his comrades, I spend some time making sure my equipment is in order. As darkness approaches, I begin to wish I knew more about the impending mission. Trucks do not usually travel the roads after dark, so we must be flying to our destination, although making a helicopter drop in the dark is unusual as well.

It is time to go, yet we have not been issued rations or ammo or given any instructions. The Army sure has a penchant for keeping its men as ignorant as possible for as long as possible. This waiting is making me nervous. It is already past 1900. I tell one of the staff sergeants where I can be found, then head for Alpha's barracks.

Two small pools of candlelight radiate through smoke-laden air to cast a murky sundown haze upon the thirty men sitting or lying on half as many cots. The white of freshly bandaged heads and hands and arms and chests casts a ghoulish reflection on the high-energy revelry taking place in the near end of the room. Beyond the partiers the cots are filled with men trying to sleep off their exhaustion or pain, while others sprawl dead drunk on the concrete floor.

The dozen or more men still in the mood to celebrate their fleeting safety are making the most of this rare opportunity to have a party. The talk is rapid, filled with energy and forced lightness. I have been here before. In a way the whole thing is a put on, keeping the talk fast and light, acting like you're loving it even if you have to fake it. You can't let yourself get mean drunk with bitterness. You need to keep a positive thrust in the atmosphere and stay close together so you can keep an eye on each other. You need to stay away from people that don't know the field, people that might get you thinking about the real enemy, because when you are drunk and emotionally charged there's only a short distance between thinking about the real enemy and wanting to do something about them. But the real enemy is hard to find and you can't just walk up and kill them, you need clear and recent provocation. For once you have attacked the real enemy there is no road back; you have brought your life to a dead end.

So you keep it light and you don't let anyone slip into a sullen silence. You keep everything going full speed until one by one you all go numb with alcohol and dope.

I find Allen maintaining a nearly upright position in the midst of the group so immersed in conversation that everything beyond it has ceased to exist. When I make my presence known, Allen grabs my shirt to haul me down beside him. There is a suspension in the cascade of words around us as Allen abuses my good name and person with friendly jibes. Then sweat-glistened faces loom from the indistinct distance to offer hands with names attached before fading back into the haze. Some of these people I have met before, but the light is poor, and their bandages are not where I remember them, so I have difficulty attaching any history to the faces.

The conversations resume as beer and dope are pressed upon me, heedless of my proclaimed intention to stay fairly straight for the coming night. The shirtless man across from me with the white foot powder spread over the big patch of blackened jungle rot on his chest describes our last drunk together with great detail and amusement while at the same time another man asks me to remember a second but equally amusing caper we shared while a third man with his arm draped around my shoulder tells me in confidence about a million-dollar wound apparently connected with his bandaged left hand. My attention is so fractured that it is no attention at all. I resort to smiling and nodding in agreement to I don't know what.

Shortly, Allen's head comes to rest on my shoulder, then

slips down onto the cot. He is immediately resurrected and prodded into a conversation to keep him awake.

On my left Chicago continues his dialogue in hushed conspiratorial tones. His need to share his elation over getting out of the field through the miraculous good fortune of having his little finger carried away by a bullet is strong, but there also seems to be a need to keep some part of the event secret. This conflict, coupled with an advanced state of inebriation, is being further confused by the guy on the other side of Allen who is telling me about his R and R.

"What is a pinky compared with a life?"

"I never dreamed a girl like that would want to have anything to do with a sorry dogface like me."

"Eight months of humping, busting my balls for nothing, you know?"

"I thought I was in heaven, man."

"You reach a point . . . too much crazy stuff . . . you have to save what you can."

"I mean, the very first night in Sidney, I'm sitting there having a cold one, grooving on civilization, and this girl comes over and asks me to dance."

"Nobody is going to do it for you. We owe it to ourselves, right? The time comes, you have to step in and direct your own fate."

"I take one look at all that beautiful blonde hair and that pair of gorgeous legs sticking out the bottom of a miniskirt so short it barely covers her panties—well, I don't need to be asked twice, you know?"

"You have to take responsibility for your own life."

"No sooner do we get back to her place and she wants it right there on the kitchen table."

"These people got us doing this stuff we would never normally do."

"I don't know what that girl has against beds . . . I mean, we got it on against the wall, in the chair, in the shower, on the floor . . . every damn place except the bed."

"They say it's right, but after a while you know they're full of shit. It's all a con. They are just using you . . . you're a tool to their end . . . they don't give a shit . . . you're just dog meat."

"That girl had a hunger, I can tell you."

"I'm sorry. I have to apologize for this."

"She screwed this poor boy's ass ragged."

"Forgive me. I shouldn't be laying out this heavy shit, but you know what I'm talking about."

"I'll tell you, when I got back I had one big pain in my primary member that wouldn't go away."

"God, I don't know why they are doing it . . . power . . . a thousand different personal greeds, and they won't stop on their own."

"After about a week I got myself choppered in to see the doc."

"They'll keep this shit going until someone forces them to stop. They don't care about death as long as it's not their own."

"Well, it wasn't the clap like I feared. The doc said it was just a case of gross overindulgence."

"A pile of bodies over here. A pile of money over there. Well, I took this body out of the pile."

I light a fresh cigarette off the butt of the last. Allen struggles to his feet, stands swaying for a moment, then tilts off toward the door.

"Where are you going?"

"Fuck you. I got to pee . . . or puke . . . or something."

"Somebody go with him."

Allen and his guide veer unsteadily around the man sitting cross-legged on the floor in the aisle between the cots. The man on the floor continues to rock, singing and muttering to himself quietly as he has been doing since before I came in. He is a pendulum of constant motion with a voice for his own entertainment.

"Is that guy all right?" I ask Chicago.

"Who, Hap? He and I are the only all-right people in this room. We don't have to go back to the field in the morning."

Chicago beams with pleasure at the thought.

"Hap is a great guy but he is a little out of it tonight. Too many drugs, huh, Hap?" Chicago says in a voice loud enough for the rocking form to hear.

Hap interrupts his swaying and humming to look up into the air as if expecting to find the source of the voice suspended from the rafters.

"No way. Need more drugs. Who's got a Darvon?"

"Sorry, my friend. You ate them all," comes a sober voice from just outside the conversation circle.

"Come on, guys. My head . . . it's going to explode . . . brains leak onto floor . . . crawl away like worms," slurs Hap. "All you wounded dudes . . . must be one pain pill to spare."

"You took them all, Hap. Don't you remember?" placates the sober voice as it moves closer to Hap's side. "You already took a week's worth, remember? Your bottle is empty, see?"

"Scrambled eggs. Can't remember, Lieutenant," answers Hap.

"I'm not surprised," comments the lieutenant.

"I've had this fucking headache for a week, I remember that. Pills don't work. Give me something to make it stop: dope, booze—anything," pleads Hap.

"Give this man a joint," orders the lieutenant.

Chicago places a joint between Hap's unsteady fingers. But Hap's general shakiness and his inclination to exhale when he should inhale combine with Chicago's slowly weaving match-hand to make ignition of the joint a difficult feat. With determination, a dozen matches, and endless admonishments for the other guy to hold still, the joint finally begins to glow near the tip.

When Chicago returns to his place in the circle he explains, "We have to keep an eye on our bro, there. He will take anything he can get his hands on. He must have swallowed twenty Darvons before we could stop him. I'm amazed that he hasn't passed out yet."

I look at the bandage covering the back of the head that has resumed its rocking motion, the joint burning forgotten between his fingers. "What happened to him?"

"Fragments at the base of the skull. He just got out of the hospital today. They took out most of the metal in his head, but decided to leave three of the pieces in because they are too close to the spinal column. The doctors were afraid they would paralyze him or something, so they just left them three pieces alone. I think that is why he gets headaches all the time."

"Well, shit, they aren't just going to leave him like that? They're going to send him home for further treatment, aren't they?" I ask, picturing Hap getting paralyzed by an accidental jolt to the back of the head.

Chicago lets loose a roar of sardonic laughter. "Oh, man, that's rich. Just because the medicine men don't want to mess with him anymore doesn't mean the Army is through with him." He pauses to wipe the sweat off his forehead with the back of his bandaged hand. "Get real, man! You know the only way any of us grunts are leaving this place is crippled or dead," he says in a flash of bitterness.

"Hey! You flipped out? You know better than anybody not to bring that kind of downer talk in here," interjects the man with his chest wrapped in gauze. "Come on, lighten up. It's party time."

Embarrassed by the depth of his transgression, Chicago jumps to his feet to apologize to his friends, berating himself for spreading bad vibes among the only people who matter anymore, his people, who deserve better from him. He busies himself by passing out a fresh round of beer with smiles and back slaps as the conversations again begin to pick up.

But I cannot shake Chicago's comment from my mind: the only way any of us grunts are leaving this place is crippled or dead. After a few months in the bush I began to suspect that no one still able to fight would be allowed to leave. After a few more months, the suspicion took on the form of reality. We had been dropped into an alien world that quickly changed us from what we had been into what we needed to be to survive. The primitive jungle life and the killing have become a permanent part of us—the whole of us. There is nothing else left except old, distorted memories. We who have been made here shall never leave.

I have begun to have dreams about the future, and the future is always the same. No matter what I do, no matter where I run, I am always and forever in Nam saying, "But I have already done this, my tour is over," and the Army always says, "Just one more year . . . just one more year . . . just one more year."

My thoughts are interrupted by someone calling my name. Greg is standing in the doorway trying to distinguish faces in the smokey candlelight.

"Over here, Greg."

"Where the hell have you been? We've been looking all over for you."

"Don't sweat it. I told the staff sergeant where I was going. Come over here and meet the guys."

"I can't. I've got to get back. Jesus, we were supposed to be the first ones to leave, but when we couldn't find you they sent out one of the other teams. Since then, the second team has been sent out as well. We're the only ones left." He pauses, his eyes passing over the silent faces around him. "Maybe you'd better stay here awhile longer. Harris is really pissed. I'll go talk to him."

"Thank you, my man. I'll wait right here. I'm not going anywhere."

Where could I go?

EPILOGUE

I did not go to the Cambodian border that night, nor did I return to my field company in the morning. Instead, my XO sent me to Delta's awards and decoration section, where I was to remain until that elusive transfer could be arranged.

With two other men, I began work on a long list of overdue citations. Since most of the men due awards had finished their tour of duty months ago, we were concerned that if their medals were not sent out soon they would not be sent out at all.

It became immediately apparent that my rate of production was going to be less than copious. My fingers kept getting stuck in the spaces between the keys and straying to letters not intended. Although I spoke the truth when I told the lieutenant that I knew how to type, I did not say that I could do so with either speed or accuracy, and there the requirement for accuracy was absolute. We were allowed no errors, no corrections, no blots upon the paper of any kind. There was also the problem of my sustained ignorance regarding the proper combining of letters that make up recognizable words. I could not spell or recognize a misspelled word when it lay before me.

When at last I produced a perfect page (the first one took ten hours) it was shipped to a major who inevitably felt it his duty to change a word or two. After a marathon struggle to retype the no longer perfect page, it was returned to the major, who usually decided there was another word that needed changing after all. A third typing brought the paper back to the major. If he felt no further impulse for change, he passed the citation on to his colonel, who seemed to justify his existence by changing the major's changes. Retyped yet again, the paper returned to the major, who on spiteful days would alter the colonel's alterations, and around it went.

One day a lieutenant hurried into the office declaring, "My major has decided it is time he got himself a Silver Star. Who is going to write it up for me?"

Following the pointing fingers of my senior partners, the major's aide pushed the neat stack of papers on the corner of my desk into a bent cornered pile to make a clearing for his rump. "There is a posthaste, top priority demand on this. The major is going home next week and he means to have his medal in hand before he leaves the country. It is now 1800. All the administration offices are shut down for the day, so I can give you until 0900 tomorrow to get this citation ready to go."

"Yes, sir. Just let me look through my lists here to see what information I have on him, and make sure the proper authorizations are in order."

"Belay that shit. You won't find his name on any of your lists. This is a major, not one of your enlisted men. You new at this, or just stupid?"

"Been here almost a week now, sir."

"Another grunt evading his field duty, eh?"

"That's about the size of it, sir."

"Well, I haven't got time to educate you. You just worry about writing it up. The major will take care of the authorizations. I am going to be carrying it through channels myself so there won't be any delays. Now let's see. . . . I guess our best bet would be that action that took place outside of that little village southwest of An Loc. There was a good body count on that one, and he did fly in close to the fighting.

"You know the routine: with flagrant disregard for his personal safety he led the attack against an enemy of over-whelming strength, displaying the crucial leadership necessary to rally his men to snatch victory from the dark abyss of defeat. No, that last bit won't do."

"Under extremely difficult circumstances he provided the decisive decisions crucial in turning the tide of battle," I offered. "In keeping with the highest standards of military conduct, his exemplary display of excellence reflects the utmost honor on his service, his country, and himself."

"Yeah, that's the kind of thing we want. I need two pages, single spaced. I have to go. . . ."

"Wait a minute, sir. You're not giving me much to go on here. Haven't you got anything more concrete? A few details I can hang this stuff on?"

"The man flew out to watch an air strike and flew home again. What do you want from me?"

A few days later I was sent to Long Binh to guard the colonels and generals stationed at the U.S. Army Headquarters for Vietnam. They wanted men with a minimum of six months' combat experience and clean records to guard the sidewalks outside their offices by day and the bunkers outside their mobile homes by night.

Marching back and forth over a sunny section of concrete in starch-stiffened fatigues and spit-polished boots for six uninterrupted hours at a stretch was a vast improvement in my life, but boring as hell. After a few weeks on the job, many of the men started taking drugs to stretch their patience. The worst offenders were a batch of airborne troops who had spent nine to eleven months chasing NVA units around the jungle before volunteering to extend their tour in Vietnam in exchange for an early discharge and reassigment to the rear.

One airborne trooper I hung out with was sent to the rear after a bullet missed his upper lip by half an inch, smashed through the center section of his radiotelephone handset, and passed through the palm of his hand, thus ending his attempt to call an air strike on the U-shaped ambush killing his unit. When I knew him, he had developed a liking for going into a connex with four to six guys, closing the door, and smoking grass until the oxygen had been replaced with a thick cloud of marijuana smoke. He also had a habit of keeping a club at the head of his bed for the purpose of taking a sudden swing at anyone who woke him to go on a detail when he had the legitimate right to be sleeping after an all-night guard tour. It was not the only way to get some sleep after night duty, but except for taking the morning bus to Saigon to sleep with the whores, it was one of the few.

Then there was the night he got drunk and jumped off the roof of a two-story barracks to demonstrate his landing technique. He must have been good because he did not kill himself.

Another man I became acquainted with lost the entire month of February as a result of an extended "black-widow" high (a local drug that came in a big black pill—exact contents unknown). He was out there guarding the generals every day with the rest of us, but he claimed not to remember anything from the end of January until he woke up in March. The memory gap scared him back to the semistraight world of marijuana and beer, but after a few weeks he decided there was nothing worth remembering and went back to the pills.

One night he was assigned the duty of guarding the first-floor main entrance to the four-story Army HQ building. His post was in a foyer in the middle of a darkened hallway that gave access to rows of deserted offices. He took a black widow to ease the monotony, then took another to ease the monotony of taking one. Two hours later his tedium vanished. Steam rose from the cracks between the tiles on the highly polished floor. Jungle creepers sprouted from the ceiling and burst into growth like a time-lapse horror movie, steadily expanding and intertwining. Bright red and orange spiders spun their webs in the corners. Deadly snakes slithered along overhead vines and dropped to the floor, their eyes fixed on their terrified prey, their tongues flicking out to taste his fear. The snakes backed him against a wall, hissing and staring and oozing ever closer until he was forced to take refuge on a six-by-twelve-inch ledge bolted into the wall to hold the telephone.

The phone in his lap reminded him of the help he could summon from the sergeant of the guard. But that would bring with it trouble far more real than the hallucinations. In a frantic search for sanctuary in another direction, his wandering eyes settled on the double glass doors of the entry. Waiting until a tenuous path cleared on the snake-littered floor, he made a rush for the doors. Bursting into the heavy night air he came to a shuddering stop. A body length before him reared a terrible beast. A hot, angry roar blasted over huge fangs as it slashed at him with razor claws. Heedless of the snakes at his feet he sprinted back to his narrow perch and screamed his terror into the telephone.

He waited and trembled and clutched himself until at last he saw the guard's jeep appear outside the entrance. With a flood of relief he ran for the street, but as soon as he passed through the doors the jeep disappeared. In confusion his eyes darted to left and right and then up just in time to throw himself to the concrete as a giant eagle dove at him with claws extended.

Ten minutes later the sergeant of the guard brought his jeep to a stop outside the building and honked his horn. The hysterical call he received had been a blur of gibberish. The caller had not identified himself or his post, but the sergeant knew his men and had no trouble conjecturing its source. He honked again impatiently, but still there was no response. Finally he walked up the steps and through the door to find his man perched three feet above the floor with his knees clenched tight to his chest, his large round eyes staring in disbelief at this latest apparition.

After three months with the generals, a half dozen of us were shipped to Zian to add some combat experience to a school for NCOs who were being trained to work with the ARVNs. Life at the ARVN school was quiet and easy, almost like a stateside unit. All we had to put up with was an alcoholic sergeant and a bit of discrimination against field troops.

During my last month in-country I finally got my seven-day leave and my R and R. I took the latter in Australia where I was enchanted by a beautiful girl named Anna.

Even when my year of duty finally dwindled to a day and a wake up, I did not believe, or dare hope, that they would really set me free. On the morning of my final day, I woke up nervous. I treaded lightly through the morning, avoiding encounters and noise. I felt a fragile sense of good fortune hovering around me, and I feared it might dissolve at the slightest disturbance.

When at last I was sent to out-processing with all my gear, I began to allow a leery touch of hope. Still, it was not until the plane lifted from the ground with a rousing cheer from its passengers that I began to believe there could be life after Vietnam.

When we landed in Oakland, half the personnel there were on Independence Day leave. It took our group three days to be processed out of the Army. We were fed twice during those days, and if we slept at all it was on a bench or the concrete floor, but there were no complaints.

At 2400 on July 4 I left the Army with American money

in the pockets of new dress greens. I took a taxi to the San Francisco airport, stuffed my new uniform into the rest room garbage can, and changed into the clothes I wore when the Army and I first met. I could not get a flight to Portland to see Julie until morning, so I called my folks to see if they would make the hour's drive to fetch me. I let the phone ring until someone answered. It was my new stepbrother. He told me that the folks were out sailing somewhere off Santa Cruz and that he no longer had a driver's license, but what the hell, he would come anyway.

One of the guys I met during out-processing could not get a flight home for many hours yet, so I invited him along to my folks' house. Together we paced the airport, for the first time giving thought to what we might do with the rest of our lives. We came up with things like walking on the beach, drinking beer, listening to the stereo, looking up old friends, and in a month or two, when our money ran out, we would need to find a job.

My stepbrother arrived.

When we got to the house, my new friend pulled out some marijuana he had smuggled out of Vietnam in his Zippo cigarette lighter. I was amazed that anyone would risk extending their stay in the Army for such a small amount of grass, but I was glad enough to help him smoke it. After we had reacquainted ourselves with the miracles of the refrigerator, the electric range, and the flush toilet, we settled into soft chairs for beer, music, and conversation. Although it was 3:00 A.M. we were still too excited to sleep. It was like a lifetime of Christmas mornings when everything you had dreamed of lay before you.

Sometime before dawn, the yard light illuminated a girl in a flowing white gown dancing past the window. I bolted from the chair and flung open the door, sure that my eyes had betrayed me. There, across a patch of lawn, running lightly beneath a grove of oak trees, was the girl in white. She was looking up into the boughs, her arms extended, her running slowed to quick little steps from side to side. As I drew closer I could see that her gown was made for sleeping, her feet were bare, and her smooth face had not seen more than sixteen years.

When I asked her what she was doing, she replied, "I have lost my nets. Will you help me find them?"

"Your nets?"

"Yes. I cast them on the wind and they floated into the trees. Can you see them?"

Yes, I was home at last. Back in the real world.

GLOSSARY

AIT	advanced infantry training
AK-47	Russian-made Kalashnikov automatic rifle
ao-dais	type of female dress
ARVN	Army of the Republic of Vietnam
bac bac	to shoot
boo coo	very much (perversion of French *beaucoup*)
chieu hois	open arms (a U.S. program to encourage enemy surrender)
choi oi	exclamation of exasperation
chop chop	food
CO	commanding officer
connex	large metal shipping crate
didi mau	shortened form of the Vietnamese "didi mau lieu": to run quickly
dinky dau	to be crazy
DMZ	demilitarized zone
dung lai	stop
EM	enlisted men
E-7	Sergeant First Class
FO	forward observer
foo gas	mixture of explosives and napalm, usually set in a fifty-gallon drum
4-F	classification given those deemed unfit for military service
GI	government issue (usually in reference to American soldier)

HQ	headquarters
klick	kilometer
KP	kitchen police (usually in reference to a kitchen detail)
LBJ	Long Binh Jail
LP	listening post
mama-san	respectful term for an older Vietnamese lady
medivac	medical evacuation helicopter
MP	military police
MPC	military payment currency
NCO	noncommissioned officer
NDP	night defensive position
NLF	National Liberation Front
NVA	North Vietnamese Army
OCS	officer candidate school
OP	observation post
PF	Popular Forces
PFC	Private First Class
POW	prisoner of war
PX	post exchange (Army post store)
R and R	rest and relaxation
RPG	Russian-made, portable ground fire rocket
ROTC	Reserve Officers' Training Corps
RTO	radio telephone operator
slick	helicopter used for transporting troops
Spec 4	Specialist Fourth Class
TO	tactical officer
VC	Vietcong
XO	executive officer

ABOUT THE AUTHOR

Eleven months after receiving his degree in microbiology the author was drafted into the Army to serve as an infantryman in Vietnam. At the end of his tour of duty he returned to his job with the health department where he stayed for eight years before buying a sloop in San Francisco to sail to Hawaii. After cruising the islands for nine months, he flew to Alaska to visit his partner on their homestead, and then to Oregon to start a business designing and building homes.

An injury to his hand provided a year of free time to begin his first book, *One Soldier*. During the next two years his summers were spent working construction in Alaska, his winters writing in Nova Scotia. Having spent the summer of 1985 backpacking through the mountains of British Columbia and Yukon Territory, Mr. Shook is currently living with his wife on Cortes Island, B.C. where he is working on his second book.